St Petersburg

"All you've got to do is decide to go and the hardest part is over.

So go!"

TONY WHEELER, COFOUNDER – LONELY PLANET

D0107069

THIS EDITION WRITTEN AND RESEARCHED BY
**Tom Masters,
Simon Richmond**

Contents

Plan Your Trip 4

Explore St Petersburg 48

Understand St Petersburg 185

Survival Guide 225

St Petersburg Maps 254

(left) **Peterhof p160**
Peter's summer palace.

....

(above) **Kunstkamera
p134** Ceiling painting at
the city's first museum.

....

(right) **Winter Palace
p54** A statue inside the
baroque institution.

....

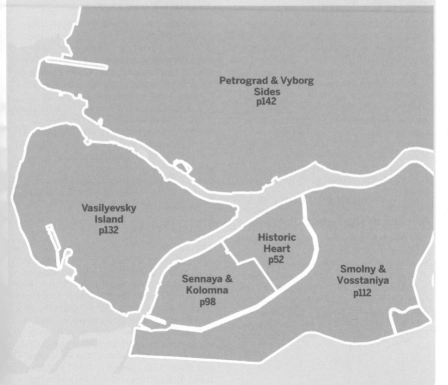

Petrograd & Vyborg
Sides
p142

Vasilyevsky
Island
p132

Historic
Heart
p52

Sennaya &
Kolomna
p98

Smolny &
Vosstaniya
p112

Welcome to St Petersburg

Once a desolate swamp, Russia's imperial capital is today a dazzling metropolis whose sheer grandeur never fails to amaze.

City of the Tsars

Built from nothing by westward-looking Peter the Great, St Petersburg was from its inception to be a display of imperial Russia's growing status in the world. Fine-tuned by Peter's successors, who employed a host of European architects to add fabulous palaces and cathedrals to the city's layout, St Petersburg grew to be the Romanovs' showcase capital and Russia's first great, modern citIt has retained this status despite the capital moving back to Moscow following the revolution. Despite all that history has thrown at it, St Petersburg still feels every bit the imperial capital, a city largely frozen in time.

Venice of the North

Whether you're cruising the elegant canals, crossing one of the city's 342 bridges or watching ships on the mighty Neva River at night, you're never far from water in St Petersburg. With the historic centre's canals lined by Italianate mansions and broken up by striking plazas adorned with baroque and neoclassical palaces, it's unsurprising that the city is often compared to Venice.

Artistic Powerhouse

St Petersburg is an almost unrivalled treasure trove of art and culture. You can spend days in the Hermitage, seeing everything from Egyptian mummies to Picassos, while the Russian Museum, spread over four sumptuous palaces, is perhaps the best collection of Russian art in the world. Add to this world-class ballet and opera at the Mariinsky Theatre, classical concerts at the Shostakovich Philharmonia and a slew of big-name music festivals over the summer months, and you won't be stuck for cultural nourishment. If contemporary art is more your thing, there's also the fantastic Erarta Museum, showcasing the best in modern Russian art, and a small but buzzing gallery scene.

White Nights

The city's White Nights are legendary: those long summer evenings when the northern sun barely dips below the horizon. Revelry begins in May, when spring finally comes to the city and parks are filled with flowering trees, and peaks in mid-June, when the sky doesn't get dark, festivals pack out concert halls and the entire city seems to be partying over the brief but glorious summer. But don't worry – even when the skies are grey and the ground covered in snow, St Petersburg's rich culture still dazzles and delights.

Why I Love St Petersburg

By Tom Masters, Author

There is something about St Petersburg that gets under your skin. Despite preferring Moscow when I first came to Russia almost two decades ago, St Petersburg lingered; its colours and incredible light stayed with me, its history haunted me. When I came to live in Russia in 2000, I didn't hesitate in choosing St Petersburg. Today what excites me about the city is the growing underground art and music scene, the hedonistic atmosphere and the sense that great things are once again happening here. The city has emerged from Moscow's shadow and will, I hope, show you a very different side to modern Russia.

For more about our authors, see p272.

Top: Ballet performance at the Mariinsky Theatre (p101)

St Petersburg's
Top 10

White Nights (p24)

1 The ultimate St Petersburg experience is in mid-June when the sun slumps towards the horizon but never fully sets, meaning that the nights are a wonderful whitish-grey. Petersburgers indulge themselves in all-night revelry, several festivals take place and the entire city enjoys an uncharacteristically relaxed atmosphere. It's the busiest time to visit the city, and most hotels are booked up weeks in advance, but there's nothing quite like it, so don't miss out – even if you come in May or July you'll be impressed by how late the sun stays out!

WHITE NIGHTS FESTIVAL CELEBRATIONS

Month by Month

The Hermitage (p54)

2 Perhaps the world's greatest museum, the Hermitage's vast collection is quite simply mind-boggling, with Egyptian mummies, more Rembrandts than the Louvre, and a collection of early-20th-century art unrivalled by almost any other. Plus your entry ticket allows you to walk around the fascinating apartments and dazzling staterooms of the Romanovs. Then there are still the other museum sites: the Winter Palace of Peter I, General Staff Building, Menshikov Palace, Imperial Porcelain factory and excellent Hermitage Storage Facility.

Historic Heart

PHOTOAGENCY INTERPRESS/GLOBAL LOOK / CORBIS ©

STUART COX / GETTY IMAGES ©

St Isaac's View (p78)

3 No other viewpoint of the historic centre beats the one from the stunning gold dome of St Isaac's Cathedral, which rises majestically over the uniformly sized Italianate palaces and mansions around the Admiralty. Well worth the climb up the 262 steps, a panorama of the city opens up to you – with fantastic views over the river, the Winter Palace and the *Bronze Horseman*. The cathedral's interior is also well worth seeing, with a wonderfully over-the-top iconostasis framed by columns of marble, malachite and lazurite. MARIINSKY PALACE FROM ST ISAAC'S CATHEDRAL

⊙ *Historic Heart*

Russian Museum (p70)

4 Even though the Hermitage is unrivalled as St Petersburg's most impressive museum, that shouldn't stop you from visiting this lesser-known treasure trove of Russian art, spread out over four stunning palaces in the centre of the city. The main building, the Mikhailovsky Palace, presents a fascinating collection of Russian art from medieval icons to 20th-century avant-garde masterpieces, while the Marble Palace houses a wing of the Ludwig Museum, and the Stroganov Palace has some of the most spectacular interiors in the city.

Historic Heart

Church on the Spilled Blood (p77)

5 The spellbinding Church on the Spilled Blood never fails to impress visitors. The church was built to commemorate the death of Tsar Alexander II, who, in an event that gave the church its unusual name, was attacked here by a terrorist group and later died of his injuries in 1881. Despite its grisly heritage, the glittering, multicoloured onion domes and intricate interior mosaics are quite simply stunning, and have to be seen to be believed.

Historic Heart

Tsarskoe Selo *(p165)*

6 Arguably the most beautiful of the tsarist palace areas that surround St Petersburg, Tsarskoe Selo (the 'tsar's village') at Pushkin is an idyllic place for a day trip. Arrive in good time to see the lavish interiors of the Catherine Palace, including the famous Amber Room, enjoy the gorgeous formal gardens and have a picnic lunch in the landscaped park where Catherine the Great so loved to walk. Nearby is the scenic estate and palace of Pavlovsk, also well worth a visit and a beautiful place to escape the crowds. CATHERINE PALACE

◉ *Day Trips from St Petersburg*

Mariinsky Ballet *(p109)*

7 What could be more Russian than seeing a ballet at the city's famous Mariinsky Theatre? Formerly known as the Kirov, where Soviet stars such as Nureyev and Baryshnikov danced, today the Mariinsky is one of the premier ballet troupes in the world. Tickets to see shows here are always sought-after, so book online before you travel to ensure you don't miss out during your stay. Even if ballet isn't your thing, the historic building is a sight in its own right, as is the next-door Mariinsky II, Russia's first new ballet and opera house since the revolution.

☆ *Sennaya & Kolomna*

6

Taking a Banya *(p44)*

8 For real cultural immersion, head to a St Petersburg *banya* (steam bath) and get the detox of a lifetime. In between basking in the infernal wet heat of the *parilka* (steam room), having your toxins removed through a sound birch-twig whipping and then plunging into ice-cold water, this is a great place to relax and chat with locals for whom the weekly *banya* is a semisacred rite.

☆ *Entertainment*

Cruise the Canals *(p30)*

9 St Petersburg is, quite simply, a city that is best appreciated from the water. Despite Peter's efforts to make the population use the canals for getting around the city, boat transport never quite caught on in the 'Venice of the North'. Even so, don't miss a canal or river trip so that you can drift down the charming canals, see some offbeat architectural gems and ride on the mighty Neva. While cruising the canals is only possible outside the winter months, if you're here when they're frozen over be sure to wander along their banks for a visual treat.

🏃 *Guided Tours*

Peter & Paul Fortress *(p144)*

10 The city's first major building is on little Zayachy Island, where Peter the Great first broke ground for St Petersburg. It's immediately recognisable from its extraordinary golden spire, visible all over the city centre at an incredible (for the 18th century) 122m high. A visit to this large complex is a must for history buffs: you'll see the tombs of the Romanovs, visit an excellent history museum and even be able to relax on a surprisingly decent beach with stellar Hermitage views! SS PETER & PAUL CATHEDRAL

👁 *Petrograd & Vyborg Sides*

What's New

General Staff Building

The Hermitage is in the process of making the most progressive change in its 250-year history – shifting its celebrated stash of Impressionist and post-Impressionist works from the main building to the newly modernised galleries of the General Staff Building to sit alongside a steadily growing collection of contemporary exhibits. (p68)

Mariinsky II

After more than a decade of construction, the Mariinsky Theatre's state-of-the-art new building finally opened in 2013. A superb new opera and ballet venue for the city, it's a must for any music lover, even if its thoroughly modern exterior hasn't exactly thrilled the city's preservationists. (p101)

Central Naval Museum

The new premises for St Petersburg's long-established Central Naval Museum brings the impressive collection of models to life with excellent lighting, plenty of space and interactive displays, all in a new location across from New Holland. (p103)

Anti-Cafes

St Petersburg's latest fad is pay-as-you-go cafes and 'creative spaces'; pay by the minute and enjoy coffee, snacks and access to everything from wi-fi to computer games and musical instruments. Some of these places are palaces of leisure and worth a visit just to see!

Fabergé Museum

This new museum, in a beautifully restored palace on the Fontanka, celebrates the zenith of Russian artistic craftsmanship from the time of Peter Carl Fabergé and his contemporaries. (p82)

Taiga

From having your whiskers clipped at a trendy barber to browsing the best of local fashion, this new haven for Piter's creative classes near the Hermitage is worth searching out. (p95)

Street Art Museum

The derelict remains of a still-functioning plastic laminate factory are the incredible canvas for this colourful explosion of creativity by top Russian and international street artists. (p154)

Museum of Soviet Arcade Machines

Have fun with nostalgic Russians at this fully interactive museum, filled with working arcade game machines manufactured in the USSR during the 1970s and '80s. (p85)

Kupetz Eliseevs

This restored Style Moderne stunner on Nevsky pr is a pleasure for the eyes *and* the stomach as you enjoy the quality groceries, edible delights and drinks on sale inside. (p96)

Oranienbaum

After years of renovation, the Great Palace at Prince Menshikov's former country estate overlooking the Gulf of Finland is open again and looking very impressive, with the gardens also restored to their former imperial glory. (p171)

For more recommendations and reviews, see **lonelyplanet. com/st-petersburg**

Need to Know

For more information, see Survival Guide (p225)

Currency
Rouble (R)

Language
Russian. Limited English is spoken by younger people. In this book Cyrillic script is provided for all points of interest (sights, restaurants, hotels etc) where there's no clear sign in English.

Visas
Nearly all visitors need a visa, which will require an invitation. Tourist visas are generally single entry and valid for up to 30 days.

Money
ATMs are widespread, and credit cards accepted in most good restaurants and shops.

Mobile Phones
Local SIM cards (giving internet data as well as calls) can be bought for as little as R200 and used in unlocked phones.

Time
St Petersburg uses Moscow time, which is GMT+3 year-round.

Tourist Information
St Petersburg Tourist Information Centre (Map p256; ☑812-310 2822; http://eng.ispb.info; Sadovaya ul 14/52; ⊙10am-7pm Mon-Fri, noon-6pm Sat; MGosti-ny Dvor) Maps, tours, information and advice for travellers.

Daily Costs

Budget under €50
➡ Dorm bed: €12
➡ Supermarket and business lunches for food
➡ Cheap theatre ticket: €15

Midrange €50–€200
➡ Double room: €60
➡ Two-course dinner with wine: €50
➡ Theatre ticket: €30

Top End over €200
➡ Four-star-hotel double room: €150
➡ Three-course dinner with wine: €100
➡ Best seats at the Mariinsky: €125

Advance Planning

Three months before Get working on your visa. Book hotel rooms for the White Nights.

One month before Book hotel rooms during the rest of the year, Mariinsky tickets during the summer months.

One week before Buy your Hermitage ticket online and print it out. Train tickets to Moscow are worth buying before you arrive for ease and choice.

A few days before Dinner reservations at very popular restaurants.

Useful Websites

➡ **Lonely Planet** (www.lonelyplanet.com/st-petersburg) Destination information, hotel bookings, traveller forum and more.

➡ **The St Petersburg Times** (www.sptimes.ru) News in English.

➡ **In Your Pocket St Petersburg** (www.inyourpocket.com/russia/st-petersburg) Excellent local guide.

➡ **Way to Russia** (www.waytorussia.net) Visas and other know-how.

WHEN TO GO

May to September is best, with the White Nights the peak. Winter is cold and dark, but beautiful. Go in early May and September to avoid the crowds.

°C/°F Temp
30/86—
20/68—
10/50—
0/32—
-10/14—
-20/-4—
-30/-22—
-40/-40—
-50/-58—
J F M A M J J A S O N D

Rainfall inches/mm
6/150
4/100
2/50
0

Arriving in St Petersburg

Pulkovo InternationalAirport
From St Petersburg's superb new airport, an official taxi to the centre should cost around R900, or you can take the bus to Moskovskaya metro station for R30, then take the metro from Moskovskaya (Line 2) all over the city for R28.

Moscow Station (Moskovsky vokzal) Easy connection to the nearby Pl Vosstaniya (Line 1) and Mayakovskaya (Line 3) metro stations.

Finland Station (Finlyandsky vokzal) Direct connection to the Pl Lenina (Line 1) metro station.

By Boat Taxis are easily caught at all cruise terminals in St Petersburg, but all are within walking distance of metro stations or have bus routes passing nearby them.

For much more on **arrival**, see p226.

Etiquette

➡ **Meeting People**
Handshakes are the standard form of greeting. Do not shake hands over thresholds though: according to Russian folklore this will lead to an argument down the line! Remove your shoes and coat when arriving in someone's home.

➡ **Presents** If you're visiting friends in their home it's courteous to bring a small present. Flowers are always popular, but do be sure to bring an odd number, as even numbers of flowers are given only at funerals.

➡ **Drinking** You'll be expected to drink a vodka shot in one go if you're a man, but women will not be judged too harshly if they sip. Once a bottle is finished, put it on the floor, not back on the table, as this is bad luck.

Sleeping

St Petersburg has seen an explosion of hotels in recent years and now everything from great hostels to international brands can be found. However, if you're travelling in summer (and particularly during the White Nights), book in advance. Hostels are now very plentiful in the city – standards can vary hugely between them, but the very best are superb. Minihotels are a local speciality – usually housed in old apartments with fewer than six guestrooms – and can be both charming and great value. Hotels in St Petersburg tend to be relatively expensive (eye-wateringly so in the four- and five-star categories); the best deals are often available on hotel websites.

Useful Websites

➡ **Lonely Planet** (www.lonelyplanet.com/russia/st-petersburg/hotels) Hotels and hostels.

➡ **HOFA** (www.hofa.ru) Homestays and apartments.

➡ **Intro by Irina** (www.introbyirina.com) Apartments.

For much more on **sleeping**, see p174.

GAY & LESBIAN TRAVELLERS

Despite a new Russian law outlawing the 'promotion' of homosexuality to minors, St Petersburg remains a perfectly safe place for gay and lesbian travellers. Hotels are normally problem-free about two men or women sharing rooms, and while discretion is the safest policy on the streets, there is a thriving gay scene that's worth exploring.

First Time St Petersburg

For more information, see Survival Guide (p225)

Checklist

➡ Make sure you've got your visa and have checked the entry and exit dates on it.

➡ Inform your bank if you plan to pay for things or take money out on cards in Russia.

➡ Be sure your travel insurance includes coverage in Russia.

➡ Book tickets online for the Mariinsky Theatre if you want to see a specific ballet or opera.

What to Pack

➡ European plug adaptor if you're travelling from outside Europe or from the UK.

➡ Anti-mosquito spray or tablets if you're travelling between May and September.

➡ Comfortable shoes – there's a lot of walking involved in St Petersburg.

➡ Clothing for all weather: temperatures can vary massively.

➡ Sunglasses for both the summer and (surprisingly bright) winter months.

Top Tips for Your Trip

➡ St Petersburg is a huge city, so don't try to bite off more than you can chew: stagger sightseeing and allow plenty of time to take it easy and watch the city go by.

➡ Get a metro smart card if you're going to be using the metro a lot. You'll save money and avoid queuing for tickets.

➡ Take advantage of deals such as the Hermitage's two-day ticket, which allows you access to all its sites over 48 hours, or the Russian Museum's four-palace ticket that does likewise.

➡ Look for cheap *biznes lanch* (business lunch) deals at restaurants, as these three-course set meals are often excellent value.

➡ Learning the Cyrillic alphabet repays the effort tenfold, and you'll be able to understand more than you would otherwise. Some basic phrases in Russian go a long way.

What to Wear

Clothing is very important to Russians, many of whom are surprised at how sloppily foreigners dress! Shoes are considered of particular importance, so it's a good idea to keep yours clean. That said, Russians remain quite casual and you'll rarely be expected to be in smart clothing outside the ballet and good restaurants.

Be Forewarned

➡ It's not unusual for foreigners to find Russians quite brusque and even unfriendly. Remember, this is a cultural thing, and try not to be offended by it. Russians take a while to warm up, but when they do they're exceptionally friendly.

➡ There is sadly an ongoing epidemic of racist attacks in St Petersburg. If you look very obviously non-Russian, it's a good idea to avoid the suburbs and to take taxis at night.

➡ Due to legislation criminalising the 'promotion of homosexuality' to minors, levels of homophobia are higher now than they have been for some time. Gay travellers are advised to remain discreet.

Money

ATMs are everywhere in St Petersburg, and generally accept all major credit and debit cards. You may save on fees by bringing cash in US dollars or euros with you and changing it at any bank or exchange office (обмен валют), where you'll often get a better rate than that offered by credit cards.

You can pay by debit and credit cards in most smarter restaurants and shops, but it's never a good idea to rely on being able to do so: always carry some cash.

For more information, see p233.

Taxes & Refunds

There is an 18% VAT rate in Russia, and while it's always included in goods and services, it is sometimes conveniently left off hotel rack rates, so do check before booking, as this could be a very nasty end to your stay.

There are no tax refunds available to travellers.

Tipping

➡ **Restaurants** Leaving 10% on the table is the norm when service has been good. Not necessary at very cheap places.

➡ **Bars** Not expected unless table service is provided. Then tip 10%.

➡ **Taxis** Not expected, but round up or add R50 for a long trip.

➡ **Hotels** R50 per bag.

Fountain at Peterhof (p160)

Street Names

We use the transliteration of Russian street names to help you when deciphering Cyrillic signs. The following abbreviations are used:

➡ bul – bulvar (бульвар; boulevard)

➡ nab – naberezhnaya (набережная; embankment)

➡ per – pereulok (переулок; lane or side street)

➡ pl – ploshchad (площадь; square)

➡ pr – prospekt (проспект; avenue)

➡ sh – shosse (шоссе; highway)

➡ ul – ulitsa (улица; street)

Staying Connected

Wi-fi is available for free all over the city. All hotels have free wi-fi available to guests, while most restaurants, bars and cafes have this as well.

Nearly all mobile phones can roam in Russia, though it is usually expensive. If you want mobile internet, buy a SIM card (SIM karta; about R200) from a phone shop for your unlocked handset.

Language

English is widely, if poorly, spoken. Younger people tend to speak the best English. You don't need to know any Russian to travel here, but learning the alphabet and some basic phrases will be a huge help. See p236 for more information.

Getting Around

For more information, see Transport (p226)

Metro

The fastest way to cover long distances, the metro has around 70 stations, costs a flat fare of R28 and works from approximately 5.45am to 12.45am each day.

Bus

Better for shorter distances in areas without good metro coverage. Can be slow going, but views are good.

Trolleybus

Trolleybuses are the slowest of the lot, although they're cheap and plentiful.

Marshrutka

The private sector's contribution, these fixed-route minibuses are fast and you can get on or off anywhere along their routes.

Tram

Largely obsolete and little used, trams are still useful in areas such as Kolomna and Vasilyevsky Island where there is little else available.

Key Phrases

How do I get to....?
Как мне добраться до...? (kak mnye dobrátsa do)

One ticket, please.
Один билет, пожалуйста (adín bilyét pazhálsta)

Can you tell me when to get off for....?
Подскажите, пожалуйста, когда мне надо выходить на...? (Vy podskázhitye kagdá mnye nada vykhodít na...)

Stop here please.
Остановитесь здесь, пожалуйста (astanavítyes zdyess pazhálsta)

Key Routes

Metro Line 1 Every station between Ploshchad Vosstaniya and Avtovo is worth getting out to look at.

Tram 6 Great for travelling between areas north of the river without going through the centre: connects Vasilyevsky Island with the Petrograd Side and the Vyborg Side.

Trolleybus 7 Goes from Smolny along Nevsky pr, over the river, along the Strelka and to the Petrograd Side.

How to Hail a Taxi

➡ Stand on practically any street and stick out your arm: you can be assured that sooner rather than later a car will stop for you.

➡ State your destination and a proposed price.

➡ A short ride in the city centre should be around R200, rising to R300 or R400 for longer ones.

➡ Official taxis are reliable and cheap; order them by phone.

TOP TIPS

➡ For ease of use, buy a smart card (R55) from a machine in any metro station and load it with prepaid journeys.

➡ Be aware that at interchange stations on the metro each station tends to have a different name.

➡ Even if you're staying near a metro station, it's worth checking local bus, tram and *marshrutka* routes as these can often be more useful.

➡ When entering a metro station, be sure you're using the entrance (вход) rather than the exit (выход).

Cycling

Despite local traffic being still in the learning stages about basic respect for cyclists, cycling is a great way to get around this huge and flat city.

➡ Many youth hostels and bike shops hire bikes for as little as R500 per day.

➡ If you're keen to do a lot of cycling, bring a helmet, bike lights and a good lock from home, as these are hard to come by.

➡ A bike-sharing system (www.velobike-spb.ru) was launched in St Petersburg in 2014. With 28 rental points around the city centre, online registration and weekly membership, it's an excellent option for visitors.

Travel Etiquette

➡ When on the metro escalators, stand on the right, and run on the left.

➡ Do be sure to hold the metro entrance door open if there's someone behind you.

➡ Inside the metro carriages, give up your seat to older or less able travellers when the metro is full.

➡ When getting on to a *marshrutka*, take a seat and then pass your fare to someone sitting between you and the driver, and they'll pass it along.

➡ If there's an empty seat on a bus and everyone else is standing, it's probably the conductor's seat, so don't take it.

Tickets & Passes

➡ Transport in St Petersburg is very cheap. Single metro tickets cost just R28, while you will save even more by buying rides in bulk on a smart card.

➡ *Marshrutka* costs vary: some charge flat fares, while others will charge you according to how far you want to go on their route. You always pay the driver directly.

➡ Trams, buses and trolleybuses all have conductors on board. They will come around the vehicle and sell you tickets, and can usually be recognised by the red sash they wear.

➡ There are no transport passes for mass transit in St Petersburg that are of use for short-term visitors.

For much more on **getting around**, see p228.

TRAVEL AT NIGHT

St Petersburg is a difficult city to travel around at night. Not only does all public transport shut down some time after midnight, meaning that taxis are your only option, but there's also the issue of the bridges over the Neva River rising nightly between April and November. This means that if you want to cross the river late at night you need to plan accordingly. See p229 for a list of bridge times.

Top Itineraries

Day One

Historic Heart (p52)

Begin your first day in St Petersburg by taking a stroll down Nevsky pr, the city's central avenue that connects the Hermitage to the Alexander Nevsky Monastery at the far end. Start at Ploshchad Vosstaniya, cross the lovely Fontanka, drop into the **Church on the Spilled Blood** and the **Kazan Cathedral** and end up at the dazzling ensemble of **Palace Square**, the **Winter Palace** and the **General Staff Building**. Wander along the embankment to the **Summer Garden** and then wander back along the Moyka River.

 Lunch Enjoy some rustic Russian dishes at Yat (p90).

Sennaya & Kolomna (p98)

Continue along the Moyka to **St Isaac's Cathedral**, visit the astonishingly elaborate interiors and then climb to the top of the dome for superb views of the city. Continue down the Moyka to the **Yusupov Palace** and the **Mariinsky Theatre**, ending up at the beautiful sky-blue **Nikolsky Cathedral**. Drop into **Entrée** for coffee and cake.

Dinner Book ahead for gorgeous Teplo (p106).

Historic Heart (p52)

If it's a weekend, head down to **Dumskaya ul** for a raucous time with locals who like to congregate here for drinking, dancing and general debauchery. For something a little more elegant, have a cocktail at the **Belmond Grand Hotel Europe**.

Day Two

Historic Heart (p52)

After a hearty breakfast, head to the **Hermitage** and get ready for a day of artistic exhilaration. Choose which parts of the collection you want to see, though leave some room for on-the-spot decision making – the exhibition is so enormous that you'll inevitably discover something new. As well as the art, don't miss the staterooms, and allow yourself plenty of rest stops to avoid exhaustion.

 Lunch Bring your own lunch or face the underwhelming Hermitage cafe.

Historic Heart (p52)

You may still want to spend a few hours in the museum and make the most of your day ticket. But if you leave and still have some energy, wander along before picking up a **sightseeing cruise** around the canals – the best way to sightsee without having to do any more walking!

Dinner Enjoy the multilevel eating at Biblioteka (p89).

Sennaya & Kolomna (p98)

If you've booked ahead, dress up to spend the evening watching a ballet from the classical repertoire of the **Mariinsky Theatre**. Even if you haven't booked, it's usually quite possible to do so last minute in one of the other theatres in town. For a post-Mariinsky drink, head to **Mayakovsky**.

Stroganov Palace (p79)

Day Three

Petrograd & Vyborg Sides (p142)

 Begin day three with a trip to the beautiful Petrograd Side. Start with a visit to the **Peter and Paul Fortress** to see where the city began, wander past the **mosque** and perhaps drop in to see either **Peter's Cabin** or the very interesting **Museum of Political History**. Wander down **Kamennoostrovsky pr** to take in the Style Moderne architecture.

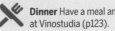 **Lunch** Enjoy a relaxed and stylish lunch at Mesto (p156).

Vasilyevsky Island (p132)

After lunch, walk across to Vasilyevsky Island and wander the historic ensemble around the **Strelka**. Visit the **Kunstkamera**, Peter the Great's personal cabinet of curiosities, and drop in to see the very interesting **Menshikov Palace** to see the oldest standing palace in the city. If you enjoy contemporary art, continue on to the excellent **Erarta Museum of Contemporary Art**, which is definitely worth the hassle of a *marshrutka* ride to get to.

Dinner Dine in understated Russian elegance at Restoran (p140).

Smolny & Vosstaniya (p112)

Head south to happening Vosstaniya to gallery-, bar- and gig-hop around **Ligovsky pr**. See some new artwork at **Loft Project ETAGI**, enjoy a drink in the sand and some table football at **Dyuni** or have a superlative cocktail at **Dead Poets Bar**.

Day Four

Day Trips from St Petersburg (p159)

Head out of the city early to spend the day in tsarist opulence. Go first to **Tsarskoe Selo** in order to visit the **Catherine Palace** and have a walk in the gardens. If you're still wanting more, **Pavlovsk** is a quick bus ride away and the park is even wilder and more beautiful.

Lunch Eat at White Rabbit (p166) in the town of Pushkin.

Historic Heart (p52)

Head back to the city in the afternoon and slot in the **Russian Museum**, the perfect complement to the Hermitage. This spectacular (and far more manageable) museum showcases seven centuries of Russian art from church icons to the avant-garde. Buy the full ticket and add on the **Stroganov Palace**, **Marble Palace** and **Mikhailovsky Castle** for some fabulous interiors too.

Dinner Have a meal and plenty of wine at Vinostudia (p123).

Smolny & Vosstaniya (p112)

Enjoy the bars around ul Rubinshteyna and the Fontanka – have a drink at **Terminal Bar**, **The Hat** or **Mishka**. For music, have a Soviet-era dance at **Petrovich**, or head to alternative favourite **Griboyedov** for a taste of what's cooking on the local music scene.

If You Like...

Art

Hermitage There's nowhere else quite like the Hermitage, perhaps the world's greatest art collection. (p54)

Russian Museum This fantastic survey of all Russian art is also essential, even if you know nothing about the subject before going. (p70)

Erarta Museum of Contemporary Art A stunning museum of modern Russian art on Vasilyevsky Island. (p135)

Loft Project ETAGI A popular complex of galleries and shops housed in an old bread factory on Ligovsky pr. (p120)

Rizzordi Art Foundation Check out this great temporary art space in the middle of nowhere. (p120)

Pushkinskaya 10 The one-time centre of the city's alternative scene has aged a little, but it's still worth a trip for art lovers. (p119)

Hermitage Storage Facility In case you came out of the Hermitage wanting more, this state-of-the-art space will definitely sate you. (p152)

Architecture

Winter Palace It's hard to beat this spectacular piece of baroque excess. (p79)

Church on the Spilled Blood See the multicoloured onion domes that have come to represent the city. (p77)

Peterhof The fountains and views of the palace from Water Ave are breathtaking. (p160)

Smolny Cathedral This soaring sky-blue Rastrelli masterpiece never fails to awe. (p116)

The *Bronze Horseman* statue (p81)

Singer Building Style Moderne at the heart of neoclassical Nevsky pr. (p96)

Chesme Church This unique, striated red and white church is well worth the trek out of the city centre. (p119)

House of Soviets An unbeatable example of Soviet architectural taste in southern St Petersburg. (p119)

Russian Literature

Bronze Horseman Brought to life in Pushkin's eponymous epic poem, the sculpture that inspired him is a must-see. (p81)

Site of Pushkin's Duel The scene of great tragedy for anyone who knows the work of Russia's national poet. (p153)

Dostoevsky Museum A wander around Dostoevsky's apartment is a fascinating insight into the writer. (p120)

Raskolnikov House See *Crime and Punishment* come to life in the seedy streets of Sennaya. (p102)

Nabokov Museum Visit the house immortalised by the *Lolita* author in his autobiography *Speak, Memory*. (p104)

Anna Akhmatova Museum This museum honours the most quintessential Leningrad poet and survivor of the Great Purge. (p118)

Alexandrinsky Theatre See the theatre where Chekhov's *Seagull* was first performed to terrible reviews. (p94)

Icons & Incense

Kazan Cathedral See the dramatic interior of this Orthodox stunner. (p79)

Sampsonievsky Cathedral One of the most impressive iconostases in St Petersburg. (p153)

Nikolsky Cathedral Perhaps the prettiest church in the city, this place is stunning both outside and in. (p104)

Church on the Spilled Blood Dazzling domes, incredible mosaics. (p77)

Alexander Nevsky Monastery One of Russia's most important religious centres. (p114)

Buddhist Temple Incense also burns at the world's most northerly *datsan*. (p153)

Soviet History

Finland Station (Finlyandsky vokzal) Where Lenin famously arrived to lead the October coup. (p153)

Cruiser Aurora The ship that fired a blank round to signal the start of the October Revolution. (p148)

Winter Palace Where the provisional government was arrested. (p79)

Smolny Institute The home of Soviet power, and still the seat of the city's governor today. (p116)

Kirov Museum Home of Sergei Kirov, Stalin's ill-fated man in Leningrad. (p148)

Monument to the Heroic Defenders of Leningrad The moving memorial to the 900-day Nazi blockade. (p119)

Parks & Gardens

Summer Garden The oldest park in St Petersburg has been newly redesigned and looks superb. (p80)

For more top St Petersburg spots, see the following:
→ Museums & Galleries (p34)
→ Eating (p36)
→ Drinking & Nightlife (p40)
→ Entertainment (p43)
→ Shopping (p46)

PLAN YOUR TRIP IF YOU LIKE...

Pavlovsk The best tsarist palace grounds to wander around. (p168)

Gatchina Wild and extremely beautiful, this is also a wonderful place for a ramble. (p170)

Mikhailovsky Gardens The most beautiful park in the centre of St Petersburg. (p82)

Botanical Gardens A fascinating botanical garden that's a real pleasure to walk around. (p148)

Russian Culture

Mariinsky Theatre There's nowhere like the Mariinsky for world-class ballet and opera. (p101)

Feel Yourself Russian Folkshow A surprisingly good Russian folk music and dance show. (p110)

Mechta Molokhovets Look no further if you want to experience the very best of Russian cuisine. (p122)

Russian Museum A one-stop shop for Russian art and culture. (p70)

Russian Vodka Museum An excellent look at the 'little water' that is so important to Russians. (p105)

Month by Month

January

Deep in the Russian winter, the days may be short and dark but the city often looks magical as snow continues to fall regularly.

✤ Orthodox Christmas

Russia celebrates Orthodox Christmas (Rozhdestvo) on 6 January. Exclusively a religious holiday, it is not widely celebrated, although services are held at churches and cathedrals around the city.

February

Intensely cold, with snow and ice everywhere still, February is a great time to see St Petersburg in full winter garb, as long as you don't mind the short days!

✤ Maslenitsa

Akin to Mardi Gras, this celebration kicks off Orthodox Lent and involves eating lots of bliny. Exact dates depend on the dates of Orthodox Easter, but it is usually in February or early March.

March

You can still expect snow on the ground, though in warmer years March can also see the beginning of the thaw.

✤ International Women's Day

Russia's favourite holiday – 8 March – was founded to honour the women's movement. These days, men buy champagne, flowers and chocolates for their better halves – and for all the women in their lives.

April

Finally the thaw comes, but you might prefer snow to the grey slush that can engulf the city in April! Orthodox Easter and the Mariinsky Ballet Festival brighten the scene, however.

✤ Easter

Easter Sunday kicks off with celebratory midnight services in which Orthodox churches are jam-packed. Afterwards, people eat special dome-shaped cakes known as *kulichy* and exchange beautifully painted wooden Easter eggs. As with Easter in the West, dates vary year to year, and Orthodox Easter is normally not on the same weekend as Easter elsewhere.

☆ Mariinsky Ballet Festival

The city's principal dance theatre hosts a week-long international festival, where the cream of Russian ballet dancers showcase their talents.

May

Spring is finally here, and with it a slew of holidays in the first two weeks of the month. Late May is a great time to come to St Petersburg before the summer crowds arrive.

✤ Victory Day

Celebrating the end of WWII, 9 May is a day of huge local importance, when residents remember the 900-day Nazi block-ade. Crowds assemble at Piskaryovskoe Cemetery to commemorate the victims, and a parade along Nevsky pr culminates in fireworks over the Neva River in the evening.

🎇 City Day

Mass celebrations are held throughout the city centre on 27 May, the city's official birthday, known as *dyen goroda* (city day). Brass bands, folk-dancing and mass drunkenness are the salient features of this perennial favourite, which marks Peter the Great's founding of the city in 1703.

June

This is St Petersburg's high season, and there's certainly no shortage of things to do, as the nights are white, spirits are high and the city has an almost surreal atmosphere.

☆ Festival of Festivals

St Petersburg's annual international film festival is held during the White Nights in late June. Co-sponsored by Lenfilm and hosted at cinemas around the city, the festival is a noncompetitive showcase of the best Russian and world cinema.

☆ Stars of White Nights Festival

From late May until mid-July, this annual festival showcases world premieres of opera and ballet. Performances are held around the city, especially at the Mariinsky Theatre. The festival culminates in a fabu-lous ball at Tsarskoe Selo (Pushkin), which draws the event to a close.

July & August

High summer is hot and bright – a great time to see the city in all its vividly painted, Italianate glory. There are few festivals in July and August, but with weather like this, who needs them?

🎇 Navy Day

On 25 July St Petersburg celebrates its thousands of naval officers and rich maritime history with a flotilla of boats on the Neva outside the Admiralty and a general party along the banks of the river – great if you like a man in uniform.

September & October

Two great months to visit – September is still usually warm and tourist numbers are dropping off, while October is cool, if not yet cold, with even fewer visitors.

☆ Early Music Festival

This musical festival aims to revive forgotten master-pieces from the Middle Ages, the Renaissance and the baroque era. The festival features a baroque op-era, as well as performanc-es by the Catherine the Great Orchestra. Musicians perform at various venues from mid-September until early October.

November

Winter is already here in November and you can expect to see the first snow on the ground, which gives the city a magical look.

🎇 Day of Reconciliation & Accord

The former October Revolution day – 7 November – is still an official holiday, although it is hardly acknowledged. It remains, however, a big day for flag-waving and protesting by old-school Communist Party members, especially in front of Gostiny Dvor.

December

Christmas isn't such a big deal in Russia (and it's in January anyway), but New Year's Eve is huge. St Petersburg is freezing, snowy and magical.

☆ Arts Square Winter Festival

Maestro Yury Temirkanov presides over this musical highlight, which takes place every year at the Shostakovich Philharmonia. For 10 days in late December and early January artists stage both classical and contemporary works, including symphonic music and opera.

🎇 New Year

Petersburgers see in the New Year (Novy God) by trading gifts, drinking champagne and listening to the Kremlin chimes on the radio or TV. A great time to see Russians at their merry best!

With Kids

With its focus on art, history and architecture, St Petersburg may not be an obvious place to bring children, but there are plenty of activities that they will love, especially in the summer months when the whole city is something of an outdoor playground.

Accessible Sights

Top museums for children include the Museum of Zoology (p136), with thousands of stuffed animals (including several mammoths) on display; the Museum of Railway Technology (p104), where you can see a range of trains and carriages; the ghoulish Kunstkamera (p134), which is not suitable for smaller kids; and the Artillery Museum (p148), which is great for any children who love tanks. Three fascinating old Soviet naval craft on Vasilyevsky Island can be great fun to explore: take a tour of the *Krasin* (p137), an Arctic icebreaker, or either the *People's Will* (p137) or the C-189 (p137), two Soviet subs now open to the public. Suitable for all ages is the terrific St Petersburg State Circus (p95) on the Fontanka, or the Leningradsky Zoo (p148) on the Petrograd Side.

The Great Outdoors

The Kirovsky Islands (p149), on the Petrograd Side, are an excellent place to get away with the kids. Amusement parks, boats and bikes for hire, and lots of open space make this a great option just a short journey from the centre of the city. Kids will love the fountains at Peterhof (p160), as well as the hydrofoil ride to get out there. Alexandrovsky Park (p148), on the Petrograd Side, is a great place for youngsters too, with the zoo, planetarium and plenty of other diversions among the trees. Another fun outdoor activity is taking a boat trip on the beautiful canals of the historic heart.

Child-Friendly Eating

There is no shortage of family-friendly restaurants with playrooms, children's menus and high chairs for toddlers. Some of our favourites include Yat (p90), Teplo (p106), Botanika (p121), Moskva (p122), Khochu Kharcho (p106), Sadko (p107), Zoom Café (p89), Koryushka (p156) and Stroganoff Steak House (p107).

For child-friendly snacks on the hoof, try ubiquitous blin outlet Teremok (Теремок), found all over the city, for cheap and delicious sweet or savoury pancakes.

Puppet Shows

Russia has a proud tradition of puppetry and St Petersburg boasts two renowned marionette theatres, both with large repertoires that will appeal to adults and children, and to non-Russian speakers and Russian speakers alike.

The excellent Bolshoy Puppet Theatre (p128) has been producing wonderfully innovative shows since its inception in the dark days of Stalinism, becoming a much-loved local institution. The theatre currently boasts 22 shows for children – including an excellent version of *The Little Prince*.

The Demmeni Marionette Theatre (p95) is also an excellent venue, with a large range of shows, including *Gulliver's Travels* and *Puppets and Clowns* (a lively hour-long circus-style show performed by puppets).

Do check with the theatres about which shows are suitable for children – both do literary and arty performances aimed solely at adults as well.

Money-Saving Tips

There's no getting around it: St Petersburg is no longer a cheap destination. Sadly, hotels and dining are expensive, as are admission prices to many essential sights, where you'll often be charged more than locals. Here are our tips for how to save when you can.

Discounts

If you're a student, get an ISIC card before you travel, as most places won't accept any other form of student card as evidence of your status. If you want to see a lot of the Hermitage, it's well worth booking the two-day ticket online, which is great value and allows you to visit the museum's other, lesser-known buildings at no extra charge. Senior citizens and children also sometimes get free entry, but will need to bring some proof of age with them, such as a passport.

Free Entry

You can visit the Hermitage (p54) for free on the first Thursday of each month. Yelagin Island (p152) is free on weekdays. Always free: Nabokov Museum (p104), Alexander Nevsky Monastery (p114), Grand Choral Synagogue (p103), Piskaryovskoe Cemetery (p153), Summer Garden (p80), Alexander Garden (p82), Cruiser Aurora (p148), Kazan Cathedral (p79), Sampsonievsky Cathedral (p153), Rizzordi Art Foundation (p120), Geological Museum (p138), Pushkinskaya 10 (p119), Loft Project ETAGI (p120), Red Banner Textile Factory (p147), Nikolsky Cathedral (p104), Mendeleev Museum (p136), Buddhist Temple (p153), Sigmund Freud Museum of Dreams (p149) and the Metro Museum (p138).

As well as these excellent museums and sights, there's a wealth of gorgeous parks that make great picnic spots. In central St Petersburg try the charming Mikhailovsky Gardens (p82), the wide open spaces of the Mars Field (p83), the overgrown beauty of the gardens at the Alexander Nevsky Monastery (p114) and the spacious and pleasant Tauride Palace gardens (p116) in Smolny – all free and perfect on a sunny day.

Money Saving

At museums try to get the Russian price wherever possible – if you have a local friend, go along with them and keep quiet at the ticket office. If you'll use the metro a lot, buy a magnetic card (R55) and buy trips in bulk to save money. Eat business lunches *(biznes lanch)* in restaurants, which are great value and very filling. Book in good time for the ballet to get the best choice of seats and not to be limited to the most expensive. The Russian Museum's four-palace ticket (R600) is superb value, as it allows you to visit not only the superlative Russian art collection in town, but also the Stroganov Palace, the Marble Palace and the Mikhailovsky Castle.

Cheap Frills

Try the excellent Museum of Decorative & Applied Arts (R100; p117), the Anna Akhmatova Museum (R80; p118), the Derzhavin House-Museum (R80; p121), the Kirov Museum (R120; p148), the Museum of Political History (R150; p147) and the Petersburg Avant-Garde Museum (R70; p149) – all excellent value for money. Another great-value thing to do is to take yourself on a tour of the city's most impressive metro stations, which will only set you back R28!

Visas

Russia's visa regime is the single biggest turn-off for potential visitors to St Petersburg. Nearly all visitors require a visa to enter Russia, and while it's certainly an annoyance that needs to be dealt with, it's not nearly as painful a procedure as many people imagine.

Visa-Free Travel

Those with Israeli, South Korean and many South American passports enjoy the positive luxury of 60- to 90-day visa-free travel, while those arriving by cruise ship and ferry in St Petersburg enjoy a 72-hour visa-free regime, though it comes on the (rather poorly enforced) condition that a tour is purchased through an officially recognised travel agency. This is a restrictive way to travel, but perfect if you just want to spend a few days in St Petersburg. Legislation is currently being considered by the Duma to allow a similar 72-hour visa-free regime for anyone arriving in Russia on a flight with a Russian airline.

Types of Visas

The primary types of visas are tourist visas (valid for a 30-day stay) or business visas (for 30- to 180-day stays). The specific requirements of Russian embassies in each country differ slightly, so check with the website of the embassy you're planning to apply through. Be aware that unless you live abroad, you won't usually be able to obtain a Russian visa anywhere but in your own country.

Generally for all visas you'll need to submit your passport, a photo, an invitation from either a hotel or a travel agency in Russia, a completed application form (downloadable from the embassy website) and, in most cases, a certificate of health insurance coverage.

Invitations

The most annoying part of the visa process is the need to provide an invitation (also called visa support) from a hotel or travel agency. If your hotel doesn't offer this service – most do but you'll usually have to pay for it – then you'll need to get in touch with a travel agency. You'll normally need to fill in a form online and give your planned travel dates, but you can leave generous room with these to allow yourself some flexibility. Invitations are normally processed within a week.

Applying for a Visa

To do things as cheaply as possible, get started on the visa process two months before you plan to travel. Once you've got your invitation you can apply for your visa at your local Russian consulate by dropping off all the necessary documents with the appropriate payment, or by mailing them (along with a self-addressed, postage-paid envelope for the return).

A more expensive but far easier option is to use a visa agency, who will deal with the consulate for you. Processing time ranges from 24 hours to two weeks, depending on how much you are willing to pay. When you receive the visa check it carefully – especially the expiry, entry and exit dates.

For more details on visas, see p234.

Guided Tours

Many first-time visitors to St Petersburg join a guided tour or two during their stay in the city. This can make things far easier and help to ease the nerves of anyone who might find exploring the city without speaking any Russian to be quite a challenge.

's Cathedral (p78)

Walking Tours

There is no shortage of walking tours in St Petersburg, the chief advantage of which is getting a local's perspective on the city. Even though distances are long, walking is a great way to discover courtyards, gardens, quirky sights and side streets that you might otherwise miss. Some operators will provide transport for walking tours as well, meaning that greater areas can be covered. Highly recommended operators include the following:

Peter's Walking Tours (☏812-943 1229; www.peterswalk.com; per person from R750; ☉Apr-Oct) Established in 1996, Peter Kozyrev's innovative and passionately led tours are highly recommended as a way to see the city with knowledgable locals. The Original Peterswalk is one of the favourites and leaves from Hostel Life (p182) at 10.30am daily from mid-April to late October. The choice of tours available with Peter's is enormous and includes a Friday-night pub crawl, a Rasputin Walk and a WWII and the Siege of Leningrad tour.

Sputnik Tours (www.sputnik8.com) This online tour agency is one with a difference: it acts as a market place for locals wanting to give their own unique tours of their city. Browse, select a tour, register and pay a deposit and then you get given the contact number of the guide. It's a superb way to meet locals you'd never meet otherwise.

St Petersburg Free Tour (www.petersburg freetour.com) The central offering of this tour company is its 10.45am daily free city tour, which departs from the Alexander Column on Palace Sq. But the company has plenty of other (not free but still reasonably priced) tours on offer, including metro tours, communist Leningrad and the Hermitage.

VB Excursions (☏812-380 4596; www.vb -excursions.com) Offers excellent walking tours with clued-up students on themes including Dostoevsky and Revolutionary St Petersburg. Its 'Back in the USSR' tour (R2300 per person) includes a visit to a typical Soviet apartment for tea and bliny.

Boat Tours

Boat is the ideal way to see such a watery city, though of course they only operate from April to October or so, as the river is frozen over for much of the winter. Most boats leave from the Moyka, Griboyedov Canal and Fontanka near to where Nevsky pr crosses them. There are dozens of operators, and many of them give very loud commentary (in Russian only) that might not exactly enhance your experience.

Anglo Tourismo (☑921-989 4722; www. anglotourismo.com; 27 nab reki Fontanki; 1hr tour adult/student R650/550; MGostiny Dvor) There's a huge number of companies offering cruises all over the historic heart, all with similar prices and itineraries. However, Anglo Tourismo is the only operator to run tours with commentary in English. Between May and September the schedule runs every 1½ hours between 11am and 6.30pm. From 1 June to 31 August there are additional night cruises. The company also runs free daily walking tours starting at 10.30am and lasting three hours.

Bus Tours

Given the range of far more pleasant ways to see the city, not to mention St Petersburg's gridlocked traffic, bus tours might not be immediately appealing, but the introduction of hop-on, hop-off buses means that they're an option. Alternatively, buy yourself a far cheaper local R25 bus ticket and improvise your own route around the city!

City Tour (☑812-718 4769; www.citytourspb.ru) The familiar red 'hop-on, hop-off' double-decker buses you'll see in most big cities in Europe are now well established in St Petersburg. They offer a useful service for anyone unable to walk easily, with buses running along Nevsky pr, passing the Hermitage, going over the Strelka to the Petrograd Side and then back to the historic centre. An adult day ticket costs R600, valid for as many trips as you like, and you can buy tickets when you board the bus.

Bike Tours

Seeing the city by bike is definitely a grand idea, and doing this on a tour can really be great. Several hostels offer bike tours, but the best established tours in town are those offered by Skatprokat (p229), whose White Nights bicycle tours (every Tuesday and Thursday from early June until late August) are a firm traveller favourite.

Other Tours

Transport enthusiasts will love the 'retro' tours given by the City Electrical Transport Museum, while less mobile travellers will appreciate the existence of Liberty's tours.

City Electrical Transport Museum (☑812-717 8229; Sredny pr 77; per person R130; ☉11.30am & 2pm Sat & Sun; MVasileostrovskaya) This museum runs weekend tours around St Petersburg on an old tram car from the 1930s. The tours take around two hours, and run across the Petrograd Side then via Sennaya and Kolomna before returning here. The tram leaves from the other side of the street to the museum, and tours on a similarly ancient trolleybus can also be arranged.

Liberty (Map p268; ☑812-232 8163; www. libertytour.ru; ul Polozova 12, Office 1; MPetrogradskaya) Specialising in wheelchair-accessible tours in and around St Petersburg, this unique-in-Russia company has specially fitted vans. It can also advise on accommodation and book hotels with rooms for travellers with disabilities.

Visiting on a Cruise

isiting St Petersburg by ferry *or as part of a cruise is an* *increasingly popular choice, as* *arriving this way automatically* *entitles you to enter Russia visa-* *free for up to 72 hours. This allows* *you to see St Petersburg without* *the visa headache and combine it* *with other cities in the Baltic.*

on the Spilled Blood (p77)

Visa-Free Travel

In order to benefit from the 72-hour visa-free travel rule, you simply have to arrive in St Petersburg by boat at one of the multiple ferry terminals, and have booked a tour with a licensed operator. You can either sleep on your boat, or pay for a hotel, but note that you are also obliged to leave St Petersburg by sea.

If you're on a cruise to St Petersburg, your operator will normally have arrangements in place with a local travel agency, whose tour you will be sold hard. Many cruise-ship passengers have reported being told that visitors need a Russian visa if they do not take the tour sold by the cruise ship. This is in fact not true at all, and any company offering shore excursions is sufficient to avoid the necessity of getting a visa.

Booking Tours

If you're arriving by ferry, **St Peter Line** (812-386 1147; www.stpeterline.com) offers a 'tour package', which is really just a bus transfer service into the city centre for €25 per person. These hourly buses run between the Sea Port and St Isaac's Cathedral, though you can get off at two other stops on Vasilyevsky Island too. There's no guided tour element, so once you get off the bus, you're free to roam around the city as you please.

It's often both cheaper and a far better experience if you opt out of the cruise-sold excursions, as they rarely offer the best way to spend your brief time in the city. To make the most of things, and to avoid being in an enormous group, consider booking a private tour from one of these shore excursion specialists:

DenRus (www.denrus.ru) This long-established shore excursion operator offers a number of different tours angled specifically towards cruise passengers. Tours can often be adapted to visitor needs and the guides are well trained, experienced and speak good English.

Red October (www.redoctober.ru) Operating for 15 years, this experienced tour agency specialises in one- to three-day shore excursions for cruise-ship passengers, including tailor-made programs for private groups.

IMAGE SOURCE / GETTY IMAGES ©

Ports of Arrival

There are a number of places where cruise ships arrive in St Petersburg, while all ferries from elsewhere in the Baltic arrive at the Sea Port on Vasilyevsky Island. Anyone on a river cruise from Moscow will arrive at the River Port (p227) in the south of the city, which is a short walk away from the Proletarskaya metro station (Line 3).

Marine Facade Terminal

The **Marine Facade Terminal** (Морской фасад; www.portspb.ru) at the far end of Vasilyevsky Island is a brand-new facility where most big cruise ships now dock in St Petersburg. It's not in the city centre, but all shore excursion operators have buses or cars for their passengers, and the journey to the Hermitage can be done in 30 minutes. The nearest metro station is Primorskaya, from where it's just two stops to Gostiny Dvor (Line 3) in the historic heart, but it's a good 30-minute walk away. Head down the main road from the Marine Facade, then once you've crossed Nalichnaya ul, take Novosmolenskaya nab and you'll reach the station.

Alternatively you can take a taxi. An official dispatch stand is in the arrivals area, with fixed rates to various places around town. You'll be given a slip of paper with the price you need to pay the driver: prices average R200 to R400 depending on where in the centre you want to go.

Sea Port

If you're arriving by ferry from Stockholm, Tallinn or Helsinki then you'll arrive at the **Sea Port** (Морской вокзал; ☎812-337 2060; www.mvokzal.ru; pl Morskoy Slavy 1) in the southern corner of Vasilyevsky Island. It's not served by the metro, so your easiest way into the city centre is to take a taxi. Drivers wait outside the terminal; negotiate with them. Again, prices average R200 to R400 depending on where in the centre you want to go.

An alternative option is to take bus 7 (R25) from the main road outside. The bus should have Pl Vosstaniya (Пл Восстания) written on it, and it goes all the way down Sredny pr, crosses the Neva at the Hermitage and then goes down Nevsky pr to Pl Vosstaniya.

St Peter Line (☎812-386 1147; www.stpeterline.com) offers a €25 'tour package' bus service that shuttles anyone taking it to St Isaac's Cathedral and back again every hour.

Other Ports

There are three other docks where cruise ships sometimes arrive in St Petersburg. Smaller cruise ships usually dock on either the English Embankment Passenger Terminal or the Lieutenant Schmidt Embankment Passenger Terminal. Neither terminal has much in the way of facilities, but both are centrally located and you're within easy walking distance from the sights of the historic heart.

One far less attractive possibility is docking at the **St Petersburg Sea Port** (Морской порт Санкт-Петербург; Map p270; www.seaport.spb.ru; Mezhevoy kanal 5), which is the main commercial and industrial port in the city. It's on Gutuyevsky Island and a long way from anything. It's technically possible to walk out of the port to the Narvskaya metro station, but reckon on a 30-minute walk through a fairly miserable industrial area. If you decide to walk, head up Obvodny Canal and then turn right onto Staropetrogovsky pr and you'll see Narvskaya metro station on pl Stachek.

Travelling to Moscow

Many visitors to St Petersburg combine their trip here with one to Moscow. Russia's two largest cities are superbly well connected to each other, with flights leaving at least every hour, Sapsan express trains during the day, slower overnight trains you can sleep on, and even slower boats.

Air

The following airlines fly from Pulkovo International Airport in St Petersburg to three different Moscow airports. Book in advance and you can get tickets as cheap as R2000 one-way, although normally prices are between R3000 and R4000.

Aeroflot (Map p260; www.aeroflot.ru) Flies between 25 and 30 times a day to all three Moscow airports.

Rossiya Airlines (Map p260; www.rossiya-airlines.com) Flies to Domodedovo Airport in Moscow and operates 10 flights per day between the two cities.

S7 Airlines (www.s7.ru) Operates seven flights per day between St Petersburg and Moscow Domodedovo Airport.

Transaero (www.transaero.ru) Operates three flights per day to both Domodedovo and Vnukovo Airports.

UTair (www.utair.ru) Operates four daily flights between St Petersburg and Vnukovo Airport.

Train

All trains to Moscow from St Petersburg depart from the Moscow Station (p227). Take your pick from the overnight sleeper trains or the super-fast Sapsan day trains. All train tickets can be bought online at www.rzd.ru, or from the machines at any station in St Petersburg.

Overnight

There are about 10 overnight trains travelling between St Petersburg and Moscow. Most depart between 10pm and 1am, arriving in the capital the following morning between 6am and 8am. On the more comfortable *firmeny* trains, a 1st-class *lyuks* (two-person cabin) runs from R5000 to R6000, while a 2nd-class *kupe* (four-person cabin) is R2000 to R3500. You will often have to pay extra for bed linen, although with some tickets this – and breakfast – is included.

Sapsan

These high-speed trains travel at speeds of 200km/h to reach Moscow in four to 4½ hours. There are six to eight daily departures. Comfortable 2nd-class seats are R2560 to R3800, while super-spacious 1st-class seats run from R5000 to R6000.

Boat

Boats from Moscow and elsewhere within Russia arrive at the River Port (p227), which is a short walk away from the Proletarskaya metro station.

See p228 for full details of operators that sell cruises to Moscow.

Museums & Galleries

St Petersburg is a city of museums and galleries, famed around the world for its world-class collection at the Hermitage, but also for the stellar Russian Museum and the new, yet already widely renowned Erarta Museum of Contemporary Art. Elsewhere, St Petersburg's smaller institutions focus on everything from the Arctic to zoology, via bread, toys, trams, trains, religion and vodka.

The Big Three

If you're only going to visit three museums, make it a triad of art galleries: the Hermitage, the Russian Museum and the Erarta Museum of Contemporary Art. The Hermitage needs no introduction – suffice to say that one of the greatest art collections on the planet should always be top of your must-see list. The lesser-known Russian Museum displays Russian art from the medieval times until the early 20th century and is the perfect counterpoint to the Hermitage's Western Art collection. Finally, though it only opened in 2010, the Erarta Museum of Contemporary Art is one of world's best collections of modern and contemporary Russian art and equally should not be missed.

New Additions

While many of St Petersburg's most august museums are bastions of tradition, things are being kept fresh and exciting by a glut of new arrivals. The suberb new Fabergé Museum, in a converted palace on the Fontanka, showcases the apex of Peter Carl Fabergé's jewellery making, and includes some 1500 of his unique creations. A rather different tone is set by the new and equally exciting Street Art Museum, in a plastic laminate factory in the suburb of Okhta, where the walls have become a canvas for some of Russia's most celebrated street artists. Finally, the brand-new Central Naval Museum in Kolomna, where an old collection of boats, models and paintings has been rejuvenated by an impressive new location, is superb and will appeal to anyone who loves boats and models.

The Best of the Rest

The best of the lesser-known museums include the fascinatingly macabre Kunstkamera, Peter the Great's private cabinet of curiosities (think babies in bottles); the gorgeously down-at-heel Museum of Decorative & Applied Arts; the Pushkin Flat-Museum, a veritable pilgrimage spot for Russians who still mourn the premature death of their national bard; and the excellent complex of museums at the Peter & Paul Fortress, the kernel of the 18th-century city and home to a good museum covering the history of the city.

Lonely Planet's Top Choices

Hermitage Everybody's first-choice museum will not fail to amaze even the most jaded traveller. (p54)

Russian Museum Visiting the city's stellar collection of Russian art over the centuries is a sublime experience. (p70)

Erarta Museum of Contemporary Art Trek out to this excellent survey of Soviet underground and contemporary Russian art. (p135)

Kunstkamera See Peter the Great's collection of curiosities, freaks and babies in jars. Not for the faint-hearted! (p134)

Fabergé Museum This new museum is a must for anyone interested in late imperial Russian jewellery. (p82)

Best Museums by Neighbourhood

Hermitage One of the world's most famous museums never fails to dazzle and amaze. (p54; Historic Heart)

Central Naval Museum Brand-new home for a long-established museum; must-see for boat lovers. (p103; Sennaya & Kolomna)

Museum of Decorative & Applied Arts This little-known gem of a museum contains thousands of beautiful objets d'art. (p117; Smolny & Vosstaniya)

Erarta Museum of Contemporary Art A unique showcase for modern Russian art, this superb museum is worth the trek to reach it. (p135; Vasilyevsky Island)

Peter & Paul Fortress Where the city began its life; this fortress contains several fascinating museums. (p144; Petrograd & Vyborg Sides)

Best Museums for Kids

Kunstkamera The ghoulish collection of babies in jars and other anatomical rarities will amaze older children. (p134)

Museum of Zoology Check out the stuffed mammoths here, as well as the thousands of other specimens on display. (p136)

Museum of Railway Technology Let the kids run wild around scores of steam trains, carriages and even a nuclear missile launcher. (p104)

Central Naval Museum Any kids interested in model-making will be in awe at this huge collection of model boats. (p103)

Best House Museums

Anna Akhmatova Museum at the Fountain House The unusual house-museum of St Petersburg's most famous modern poet is both tragic and uplifting. (p118)

Pushkin Flat-Museum 'Russia's most famous address' is the house in which its national bard died in 1837. (p83)

Dostoevsky Museum This gloomy museum is a sufficiently suitable place to explore Dostoevsky's troubled and brilliant life. (p120)

Derzhavin House-Museum A wonderful chance to visit an 18th-century mansion brought back to its original splendour. (p121)

Kirov Museum Take a look at how the Bolshevik elite lived in the 1930s, when Kirov was one of Russia's most powerful men. (p148)

NEED TO KNOW

Opening Days & Hours

Nearly all museums close at least one day a week. This tends to vary, although Monday and Tuesday are the most common days. Be aware that in addition to this, many museums close one day a month for cleaning; it's worth checking a museum's website for these details.

Language Issues

Things are getting better but very few museums have full signage in English. Audioguides, increasingly available in English, are a great way to understand a collection. Guided tours in English vary enormously in quality, and usually need to be booked in advance.

Ticket Prices

As a foreigner you will often be charged a 'foreigner price', anything from 50% to 100% more than the Russian price. That said, children, students and pensioners normally receive discounts on entrance fees, even as foreigners, so it's always worth asking.

ARKONT / GETTY IMAGES ©

Spinach crepes with salmon roe

Eating

There has never been a better time to eat out in St Petersburg. The range and quality of food available seem to increase year on year, making stereotypes about Russian food now seem like bizarre anachronisms. Petersburgers have well and truly caught the foodie bug, and while little of good quality is cheap in this town, the choice is bigger than ever.

Getting Serious about Food

St Petersburg has become a place where good food is prized and defined not by its high price tag but rather by the talents of the chef. Fresh ingredients, inventive combinations, the use of herbs and spices (other than the ubiquitous dill) and a wider range of flavours have finally come to the city's dining tables, and while there's still plenty of mediocre food out there, visitors today are truly spoiled for choice. We've never had an easier time recommending restaurants.

However, good places are rarely the most obvious, and you may have to reserve for the very best.

Modern Russian

Russian food, it's fair to say, has an image problem – and if you're not careful you can easily end up with dill-smothered soups, under-seasoned and over-cooked meats, and salads that are more mayonnaise than vegetable. But fret not: there is great Russian cooking to be had in St Petersburg now – both traditional and modern, and increasingly a combination of the two. Russian chefs have been rediscovering their own culinary history, and have been slowly moving away from the dozen or so standard offerings that are common on the country's menus. They're preparing rarer or even forgotten dishes such as venison and duck cooked in subtle and interesting ways and combined with herbs and fresh, organic vegetables.

Local Chains

There are a number of home-grown Russian restaurant chains that are well worth knowing about as they provide cheap and reliable eating options all over town. Chief among these is the national pie chain Stolle (Столле), a near-ubiquitous cafe where delicious, moist savoury and sweet pies are available to eat in and take away. It's a good-value spot for lunch or dinner. A few other chains to look out for are coffee and cake specialists Bushe (Буше) and Baltic Bread (Балтийский Хлеб), which does good sandwiches and pastries.

International Cuisine

There was a time when international cuisine in St Petersburg was limited to the odd Georgian or Italian place. Next came sushi in the late 1990s, which is universally adored by locals and can still be found on every corner (and even on the menu of many non-Japanese places!). But as Russians have travelled more and experienced more foreign cuisines, their tastes have widened and there's a healthy mixture of non-Russian cuisine available in St Petersburg today, running from Thai and Indian to American and even Lithuanian. These days the buzz word seems to be gourmet burgers, but that may change again soon: there's plenty of excellent French, German, Italian and pan-Asian food on the city's menus. More common, however, is the international menu, where Russian dishes, pizza, sushi and noodles all compete side by side for your attention. In many cases this means that all four are pretty average, but increasingly there are places that know what they're doing with multiple cuisines.

NEED TO KNOW

Price Ranges

The following price indicators represent the cost of a main course:

€   less than R500

€€   R500–1000

€€€   more than R1000

Opening Hours

Nearly all restaurants are open seven days a week, generally from around 11am or noon until at least 11pm. Many restaurants open 'until the last customer' – a fairly nonspecific term that means as long as someone is still ordering, they'll keep serving.

Reservations

The vast majority of restaurants don't require reservations, though they can be handy on Friday or Saturday evenings or for weekend breakfasts in popular places. Reservations are always recommended if you want to sit in a particular place, for example outside on the terrace. We note in individual reviews when it's a good idea to reserve a table.

Service

Service is improving but rarely tends to be very good outside fancy places where it often veers on the over-attentive. The main problem you'll have is that most waiting staff's English is limited.

Tipping

In little cafes and cheap eats, tipping is not expected, though you can easily round up the amount you pay if you're happy with the service. Anywhere more upmarket will usually expect a 10% tip.

English Menus

These are a lifeline for non-Russian speakers and are available in nearly all good restaurants, though they're often not available in cheaper cafes (and when they are, they are very badly translated). Bring along a sense of humour and adventure!

Vegetarian Options

There is now a very respectable variety of vegetarian cuisine on offer, both at mainstream restaurants and at an increasing number of meat-free places. Look out for vegetarian chains Troitsky Most and Ukrop, as well as individual restaurants such as Botanika (p121), Idiot (p107) and Samadeva (p89). Some non-vegetarian restaurants that offer plenty of choice for non-meat eaters include Marketplace (p85), Zoom Café (p89) and Mamaliga (p90). Fish is widely offered on menus, making an excellent alternative for pescatarians. During the 40 days before Orthodox Easter (*veliky post* in Russian), many restaurants also offer a Lent menu that is animal-free.

Like a Local

Locals still disappear to their local *stolovaya* (canteen) at lunchtime for a supremely cheap and social meal, albeit one that's rarely particularly exciting. These places, hangovers from the Soviet days, are usually not signposted and tend to be located in basements and courtyards, but if you stumble across one (look for the sign столовая), you're normally more than welcome to go in. Experiences don't come much more local than this, and you'll generally find yourself saving plenty of cash if you eat in such places. A sign of their enduring popularity is the recent reinvention of the *stolovaya* in such guises as Marketplace (p85) and Obed Bufet (p121): modern, attractive spaces that have taken the essential idea of a *stolovaya* and translated it into something appealing for the contemporary St Petersburg diner.

Eating by Neighbourhood

➡ **Historic Heart** Hidden gems among many mediocre places. (p85)

➡ **Sennaya & Kolomna** Has some of the city's best restaurants. (p105)

➡ **Smolny & Vosstaniya** Cool and innovative dining options abound. (p121)

➡ **Vasilyevsky Island** Great Russian and international dining. (p138)

➡ **Petrograd & Vyborg Sides** Some good choices on the Petrograd side. (p154)

Vegetable stall, Kuznechny Market (p130)

Lonely Planet's Top Choices

Teplo Charming, welcoming and eccentric, this great spot is a perennial favourite. (p106)

Yat Traditional charm in a country-cottage environment moments from the Hermitage. (p90)

Duo Gastrobar Super-stylish fusion food in an equally smart environment. (p121)

Dom Beat Retro-funky and eclectic, Dom Beat exudes cool and has a delicious menu. (p123)

Koryushka Stunning Neva views and a great menu featuring St Petersburg's beloved fish specialty. (p156)

Best by Budget

€

Marketplace A smart and great-value cafeteria-style place with oodles of choice and several outlets in the city. (p85)

Obed Bufet A wonderful new take on the Soviet canteen, boasting huge choice and swanky surroundings. (p121)

Soup Vino Friendly and stylish mini-cafe with gastro leanings; a great spot for a cheap lunch. (p89)

Dekabrist Well located for a post-Hermitage meal, this modern cafe is excellent value. (p106)

Duo Gastrobar One of our favourite spots, this place has cheap individual dishes realised with great creative flair. (p121)

€€

Chekhov Delicious Russian food served in a traditional dacha-style environment. (p156)

Romeo's Bar & Kitchen A superb new Italian restaurant that has quickly earned an excellent reputation. (p107)

Yat Dine on superior Russian cuisine in a faux-traditional-hut setting near the Hermitage. (p90)

Vinostudia An awesome place to eat and drink in style, with an enormous choice of wine by the glass. (p123)

Koryushka Come for the views and stay for the food at this smart Petrograd Side spot. (p156)

€€€

Sinhoto Super-stylish dining inside the Four Seasons Hotel where the food matches the refined surroundings. (p91)

MiX in St Petersburg The W Hotel's restaurant, helmed by Alain Ducasse, is one of the city's smartest tables. (p91)

Mansarda The dazzling views here don't distract you from the food at this impressive establishment. (p108)

Dom Dine in an environment of tsarist elegance at this new but serious restaurant. (p106)

Grand Cru Fabulously imaginative food is paired with a fantastic selection of wines by the glass. (p125)

Best for Breakfast

Zoom Café This cosy subterranean space in the heart of town serves up a mean Russian breakfast. (p89)

Grey's A pared back but elegant spot for weekend brunch or a simple weekday breakfast. (p123)

Idiot A favourite with tourists, the vegetarian Idiot provides an atmospheric venue in which to enjoy its famous brunch. (p107)

Teplo Now serving breakfast, St Petersburg's most charming restaurant just got even better. (p106)

Biblioteka With dining over several floors, you can choose your favourite spot for breakfast. (p89)

Best 24-Hour Eats

Khochu Kharcho This sprawling Georgian restaurant offers you the choice of a filling meal at any time of day. (p106)

Jean-Jacques Multiple outlets of this French favourite all remain open day in, day out. (p124)

Brynza Another Caucasian food outlet that never sleeps, Brynza can be found just off Nevsky pr. (p123)

Stolovaya No 1 Kopeika Enjoy round-the-clock access to the Russian dishes served up at this canteen. (p90)

Best for Atmosphere

Teplo Its name translates as 'warm', and you'll quickly understand why: this place feels like a home away from home. (p106)

Sadko With waiters who sing opera between courses, this is a favourite spot for post-Mariinsky dining. (p107)

Zoom Café Full of knick-knacks and charming clutter, Zoom has the feel of an eccentric friend's living room (p89) .

Vinostudia Wine flows and conversation buzzes at this low-key and friendly spot for wine lovers. (p123)

Botanika This restaurant's vegetarianism has translated into a zen-like calm you won't find elsewhere. (p121)

LONELY PLANET / GETTY IMAGES ©

Groboyedov (p127)

Drinking & Nightlife

'Drinking is the joy of the Rus. We cannot live without it.' With these words Vladimir of Kiev, father of the Russian state, is said to have rejected abstinent Islam on his people's behalf in the 10th century. And the grateful Russian people have confirmed old Vlad's assessment, as drinking remains an integral part of Russian culture and society.

Little Water

The word 'vodka' is the diminutive of *voda*, the Russian word for water, so it means something like 'a wee drop'. Russians sometimes drink vodka in moderation, but more often it's tipped down in swift shots, often followed by a pickle (snacking apparently stops you from getting drunk). It's very rare to get bad vodka in a restaurant, so do not fear if you don't recognise the brand name (there are many). However, if the vodka isn't served cold, send it back immediately.

Many visitors to St Petersburg are surprised to learn that *pivo* (beer) is actually Russia's most popular alcoholic drink. The market leader is Baltika, a Scandinavian joint-venture with Russian management, based in St Petersburg. Another very popular local brand is Vasileostrovskaya, named after Vasilyevsky Island, where it is brewed.

Where to Drink

Back in the day, the equivalent of the local pub was a *ryumochnaya*, which comes from the word *ryumka* (shot). These were pretty grim places, serving up *sto gramm* (100 grams), but not much else.

In recent years, St Petersburg's drinking possibilities have expanded exponentially. Now, drinkers can take their pick from wine bars, cocktail bars, pubs, sports bars, microbreweries and more. In summer months, there is an additional assortment of *letniye sady* (summer gardens) scattered around town. It's also perfectly acceptable to go into almost any restaurant and just order drinks.

Nightlife in St Petersburg

St Petersburg boasts a sophisticated array of live-music joints, jazz venues, dance clubs, karaoke places, stylish bars, British- and Irish-style pubs and even its fair share of hipster hang-outs. Undoubtedly the centre of the city's party culture is Dumskaya ul, a side street off Nevsky pr that has transformed into St Petersburg's unofficial drinking street. Indeed, after midnight at the weekends, it's a sight to see. For more bohemian venues, head to Vosstaniya and along the Fontanka, where you'll find lots of cool bars and clubs.

Cafes

A few Russian coffee-shop chains have followed their Western counterparts and opened up outlets on every corner. Rest assured, you will never be far from a Coffee House (Кофе Хауз), Ideal Cup (Идеальная Чашка) or Shokoladnitsa (Шоколадница), and you can even find well-known international brands such as Starbucks (Старбакс) and Costa Coffee. Most restaurants will do coffee to go as well, and quality is now exceptionally high across the city.

But the independent cafes earn far higher marks for atmosphere and artistry, and are well worth seeking out. There are about half a dozen or so serious coffee shops in Petersburg, where preparation methods include syphon and Chemex, and devotion to creating the perfect brew is nothing short of fanatical.

Drinking & Nightlife by Neighbourhood

→ **Historic Heart** An endless choice of smart cafes, cool bars and busy clubs centred on Dumskaya ul. (p91)

NEED TO KNOW

Opening Hours

Most pubs and bars are open very late indeed – typically from 6pm until 6am, although many use the cunningly unclear phrase 'until the last customer' (ie as long as you're still buying drinks, the staff will be there to serve them to you). Cafes are usually open from early in the morning until the late evening – typically from 8am to 10pm. Clubs open around 11pm and close around 7am, but many only open at weekends.

Service & Tipping

In most cafes and bars you'll be waited upon. Only in rougher, more crowded places will you usually have to go to the bar yourself. You'll rarely be expected to tip, unless you're in a very high-end place.

Legality

It's perfectly acceptable to drink in public in Russia, even on the way to work. Alcohol is legal on the street, but it's banned in the metro. The legal drinking age is 18 in Russia, though it's rarely enforced. Note that it is illegal for shops to sell any alcohol between 10pm and 11am – so buy drinks in advance or you'll have to drink in a bar or restaurant between these times.

Smoking

Russia introduced a nationwide smoking ban in mid-2014, and it's strictly enforced. You're unable to smoke in restaurants, cafes, bars or hotels, and can only now do so outside.

→ **Sennaya & Kolomna** Despite being decidedly quiet for the most part, there are a few excellent bars here. (p108)

→ **Smolny & Vosstaniya** The city's coolest district is the preferred haunt of hipsters, serious musicians and clubbers, particularly along the Fontanka, ul Zhukovskogo and Ligovsky pr. (p126)

→ **Vasilyevsky Island** This residential area isn't noted for nightlife, but there are a couple of great places on the island. (p141)

→ **Petrograd & Vyborg Sides** It's rather quiet after dark north of the Neva, but the Petrograd Side has a couple of interesting places to divert you. (p157)

Lonely Planet's Top Choices

Borodabar A hipster cocktail hang-out with committed mixologists. (p91)

Dead Poets Bar Little known but a superb and serious cocktail bar. (p126)

Union Bar & Grill Huge and thriving beard-heavy bar on Liteyny pr. (p126)

Dom Beat Retro-funky and eclectic, this is where to kick back with a cocktail in style. (p126)

Dyuni Come and join the fun in this hipster sandpit. (p127)

Best Cocktail Bars

Borodabar The mixologists really know their stuff at this hipster hang-out. Try their smoked old fashioned. (p91)

MiXup Bar The W Hotel's sleek bar is as much about the extraordinary views as the cocktails. (p92)

Dead Poets Bar Grown-up cocktail bar with plush upholstery and a fanatical approach to mixology. (p126)

Mayakovsky The intellectual vibe doesn't interfere with the hedonistic drink pouring at this homage to the poet. (p108)

Dom Beat Long-running lounge-bar-club where eclectic design and great music keep a cool crowd happy. (p126)

Best Bars by Neighbourhood

Radiobaby Come and meet the most convivial crowd in town at this ever-busy nightspot. (p92; Historic Heart)

Mayakovsky This otherwise quiet neighbourhood's sleek, secret speakeasy does great cocktails. (p108; Sennaya & Kolomna)

Union Bar & Grill With a huge bar and a New York vibe, look no further for weekend drinks. (p126; Smolny & Vosstaniya)

Buter Brodsky Effortlessly cool, beautifully designed and with a bunch of interesting drinks on the menu. (p141; Vasilyevsky Island)

Kamchatka One of the few drinking spots north of the river, Kamchatka is nevertheless a great one. (p157; Petrograd & Vyborg Sides)

Best St Petersburg Clubs

Barakobamabar Enjoy the outside bar and dance floor in the summer months at this friendly place. (p93)

More An eclectic range of music plays here, as well as live acts to keep things interesting. (p93)

Radiobaby Despite/because of its 'no techno, no house' rule, Radiobaby always has a great vibe. (p92)

Griboyedov This long-running bunker club remains a perennial favourite for clubbers in the city. (p127)

Kamchatka This shrine to Kino frontman Viktor Tsoy is a great place to hear new local groups. (p157)

Best for Beer

Grad Petrov Tour the on-site microbrewery before tasting its impressive creations in the bar. (p141)

Brúgge A shrine to Belgian beer where the sheer selection alone is reason enough to visit. (p141)

Brimborium Serving up artisanal ales and organic beers, this is the place for cool connoisseurs. (p127)

Terminal Bar Draw up a stool and select one of the many well-chosen beers on tap here. (p127)

Sidreria With 10 different ciders on tap and many more in bottles this a cider-lover's treat. (p92)

Best Bohemian Hang-outs

Borodabar Be sure to be sporting at least a stubble when you visit the very hip 'beard bar'. (p91)

The Hat Live jazz, cocktails and a boho vibe make for a great evening out. (p126)

Brimborium Drink ales, munch on homemade quiche and watch the lights change at this cool joint. (p127)

Stirka 40 Whether or not you bring your washing to be done, this low-key place is a winner. (p108)

Buter Brodsky Come for cocktails or homemade tinctures at what is easily the coolest bar on Vasilyevsky Island. (p141)

PETE SEAWARD / GETTY IMAGES ©

Performance at the Mariinsky Theatre (p101)

⭐ Entertainment

The classical performing arts are one of the biggest draws to St Petersburg. Highly acclaimed professional artists stage productions in elegant theatres around the city, many of which have been recently revamped and look marvellous. Seeing a Russian opera, ballet or classical music performance in a magnificent baroque theatre is a highlight of any trip.

The Glorious Mariinsky

The Mariinsky Theatre gave the world Nijinsky, Nureyev and Baryshnikov among many, many others, and is understandably every visitor's first choice for entertainment in St Petersburg. Under the artistic direction of Valery Gergiev, the theatre has gone from strength to strength, and the 2013 opening of the Mariinsky II (next door to the mid-19th-century main Mariinsky Theatre) has certainly put the institution back on the world map of great ballet and opera houses.

Tickets are easy to obtain online before you travel, and even during your stay, but it's recommended you book well in advance for the White Nights.

Ballet & Opera

Beyond the Mariinsky, there's no shortage of ballet and opera in St Petersburg; the next best are the Mikhailovsky (p94), the Alexandrinsky (p94), the Hermitage Theatre (p94) and the St Petersburg Opera (p110). The key is to ask locally for recommendations,

NEED TO KNOW

Prices

Expect to pay a minimum of R600 for ballet and opera tickets – these will usually be for a seat with a restricted view in 'the gods' (the upper balconies), and the price will rise by R400 to R600 with each floor lower you go. The very best seats in the house at the Mariinsky will go for up to R6000, while an average seat will go for R2500. Classical concerts will generally be cheaper than ballet and opera, but will remain pricey if they're held in prestigious venues such as the Shostakovich Philharmonia or the Mariinsky Concert Hall: reckon on paying R500 to R1500. Theatre tickets are far less expensive, starting from around R200 to R1000.

Performance Times

Most ballet, opera and theatre performances begin at 7pm or 7.30pm. Come in good time to absorb the atmosphere (woe betide you if you're late – you'll have to face the wrath of the fearsome babushkas who ensure order in the theatre). During the White Nights, many theatres have two evening performances to meet the enormous demand for tickets, so you may find you can get tickets for a second show at 9pm. As Russian theatregoers live for the socialising in the intervals, at which time the bars are packed out, there's always at least one interval during a performance, and sometimes two!

Etiquette

Definitely dress up for the ballet, opera or theatre: Russians are dolled up to the nines on these occasions, and you'll stick out like a sore thumb if you aren't. Don't wear jeans or trainers, and try at least to manage a smart shirt or dress.

as most educated Petersburgers can give you an idea of which productions are worth buying tickets for. Critics complain that the Russian renditions of well-known Western works often seem naive and over-stylised, so steer clear of Mozart. Far more likely to be good are productions of Tchaikovsky, Prokofiev, Rimsky-Korsakov or Shostakovich, all regulars on the playbills at most theatres.

Tickets

By far the easiest way to buy tickets is online through the theatre's own website; this also means you can book tickets from home, ensuring you get seats for shows you want to see when you're in St Petersburg. Last-minute tickets are generally easy to find, though, with the exception of the Mariinsky and anywhere during the White Nights: book well in advance in both cases. The standard way to buy tickets on the ground is from a theatre kiosk (театральная касса), which can be found all over the city; you can also buy them in person from the individual theatre box offices.

Classical Music

Orchestral music is taken very seriously in St Petersburg, and unsurprisingly so, as most of the Russian genre originated here. The Rimsky-Korsakov Conservatory (p110) is the beating heart of the classical music scene, and hosts concerts given by its students in both its Bolshoy Zal (Big Hall) and Maly Zal (Little Hall). Quality is superb, and can be matched only by that at the Shostakovich Philharmonia (p93), under the baton of maestro Yury Temirkanov, where concerts are given in two concert halls with the same name as those at the Conservatory.

Banya

If you're looking for a completely different and uniquely Russian experience, then head to your nearest *banya* (steam bath). Enter the *parilka* (steam room) stark naked and sit back and watch the mercury rise. To eliminate toxins and improve circulation, bathers beat each other (never too hard!) with a bundle of birch branches, known as *veniki*. It's actually an extremely pleasant sensation. When you can't take the heat, retreat. A public *banya* allows access to a plunge pool, usually filled with ice-cold water. The contrast in temperature is invigorating, energising and purifying. *Bani* are normally segregated by gender, unless you book a private one with friends.

Lonely Planet's Top Choices

Mariinsky Theatre The classic St Petersburg theatre oozes history and has a dazzling interior. (p109)

Mariinsky II Buy tickets to see inside Russia's newest opera and ballet house – it's quite the occasion. (p109)

Hermitage Theatre Watching a classical concert inside the Hermitage is a great experience. (p94)

Yusupov Palace Theatre This charming mini theatre was once the private stage of the Yusupovs. (p110)

Alexandrinsky Theatre See ballet and drama on the stage where Chekhov's *The Seagull* premiered. (p94)

Best Festivals

Stars of White Nights Annual festival showcases world premieres of opera and ballet. (p25)

Early Music Festival A musical festival aiming to revive forgotten masterpieces from the Middle Ages, the Renaissance and the baroque era. (p25)

Mariinsky Ballet Festival The cream of Russian ballet dancers showcase their talents. (p24)

Arts Square Winter Festival Stages classical and contemporary works, including symphonic music and opera. (p25)

Best Live-Music Venues

A2 St Petersburg's top live-music venue is this superb and

professionally run Petrograd Side place. (p157)

Cosmonaut Another large and modern venue for seeing live acts. (p128)

Kamchatka A homage to Kino's Viktor Tsoy, this club is where to see new local acts do their thing. (p157)

Fish Fabrique The ultimate St Petersburg music venue, this veritable institution is favoured by a bohemian crowd. (p128)

Best for Kids

St Petersburg State Circus Always a blast for children, this well-established circus puts on a great show! (p95)

Feel Yourself Russian Folk-show An excellent way to see traditional Russian folk dances performed with great flair. (p110)

Bolshoy Puppet Theatre St Petersburg's main puppet theatre has a program of shows aimed at children. (p128)

Demmeni Marionette Theatre Another excellent puppet theatre with a nationwide reputation, which does performances aimed at kids. (p95)

Best for Classical Music

Glinka Capella House The building alone is reason to visit this superb concert venue. (p94)

Rimsky-Korsakov Conservatory Breathe in the history at the home of so much of St Petersburg's great musical history. (p110)

Mariinsky Concert Hall A relatively recent addition to the city's concert halls, with fabulous acoustics. (p109)

Shostakovich Philharmonia Home to two world-famous symphony orchestras, this is a classic venue for the classics. (p93)

Best Small Theatres

Yusupov Palace Theatre Seeing a performance in the Yusupov's tiny but ornate private theatre is an unforgettable experience. (p110)

Hermitage Theatre The tsars' private theatre is a gorgeous treat for any music and ballet lover. (p94)

Maly Drama Theatre A small drama theatre that sometimes presents plays with English subtitles. (p128)

Priyut Komedianta Theatre An excellent small drama theatre featuring some of the best actors in the city. (p94)

Best Activities

Skatprokat Hires bikes and offers an excellent Sunday-morning bike tour of the city. (p229)

Petrovsky Stadium To see how football is a local religion, go along to see a Zenit football match. (p157)

Krugliye Bani One of the very best spots for a traditional Russian *banya* in St Petersburg. (p158)

Yelagin Island Escape the city's chaos by taking a trip to this Petrograd Side oasis of calm. (p158)

Shopping

St Petersburg's shopping scene may still lag behind Moscow's glitzy capitalist paradise, but it's a massive improvement on the past, with something for everyone hidden in an ever-increasing array of new shops and malls. If nesting dolls aren't your thing, you can enliven your souvenir shopping with pieces of Soviet chic, antiques, street fashion and contemporary arts and crafts.

Souvenirs

The city heaves with shops selling that most archetypal souvenir of Russia, the *matryoshka* (nesting doll). Other good souvenirs include amber jewellery, traditionally painted wooden eggs, vodka, Russian chocolates and porcelain, the last of which is available from one of Imperial Porcelain's many St Petersburg outlets.

Shopping Centres

Shopping centres, for so long considered rather Muscovite and tacky in St Petersburg, have finally become big business in the northern capital. Two recently opened palaces to consumerism are on either side of Pl Vosstaniya, right in the heart of the city. The sheer size of Galeria (p130) is something to behold, and with its international designer names as well as local brands it's definitely the easiest one-stop shop for retail therapy in St Petersburg. Nearby Nevsky Centre (p130) is smaller, but equally impressive, and houses the first true department store in the city, Stockmann.

Local Fashion

There's a small but enterprising fashion industry in St Petersburg with a few local designers blazing the trail and selling classy and creative clothing designs. While it has taken a long time for them to get any real recognition in a market obsessed with Euro-|pean labels, in the past few years it has become very fashionable to buy Russian fashion in Russia. The local fashion week, called 'Defile on the Neva', features local designers including Lilya Kissilenko, Natalya Soldatova and Tatyana Sulimina, all of whom have boutiques in the city.

Secondhand & Vintage

Sekond-khand (Секонд-ханд) is all the rage in St Petersburg, with fabrics and designs from the Soviet era now being very fashionable among the younger generations. Soviet chic is so in that it goes way beyond clothing – accessories, music, art and (let's face it) a lot of plain junk is on sale all over the city, simply because it's from that era. If you're into Soviet bric-a-brac, then head to Udelnaya Fair (p158) on a Sunday for a truly mind-blowing array of Soviet junk and the odd real treasure.

Shopping by Neighbourhood

→ **Historic Heart** The city's commercial heart positively throbs with shopping possibilities. (p95)

→ **Sennaya & Kolomna** This quiet neighbourhood offers some truly offbeat, quirky and arty shopping experiences. (p110)

→ **Smolny & Vosstaniya** Dominated by two enormous shopping centres, there's plenty of unique shopping here. (p128)

→ **Vasilyevsky Island** This area's highlight is the chance to buy contemporary art at Erarta. (p141)

→ **Petrograd & Vyborg Sides** You'll find St Petersburg's best flea market here. (p158)

Lonely Planet's
Top Choices

Taiga This cool collection of shops and businesses just moments from the Hermitage is well worth exploring. (p95)

Udelnaya Fair Find the gems among the junk at this amazing, sprawling place. (p158)

Dom Knigi This beautiful building is the city's most impressive bookshop. (p95)

Kupetz Eliseevs Glam deli and confectioners that's great for edible gifts. (p96)

Perinnye Ryady An arcade of art and craft shops where you'll find unique souvenirs. (p95)

Best Souvenirs

Northway The best place in town for choice in *matryoshki* (nesting dolls), and many other Russian souvenirs (p110) .

Tula Samovars A great selection of these typically Russian traditional hot-water dispensers. (p130)

Yakhont A good place to buy locally produced jewellery. (p97)

Military Shop Get your Russian army uniforms and other military paraphernalia here. (p95)

Udelnaya Fair Sort through mountains of Soviet kitsch at this huge flea market. (p158)

Best Fashion Shops

Day & Night Emporium of big-name brands and international fashion labels on the Petrograd Side. (p158)

Nevsky 152 A very fancy 'concept store' housing a number of international fashion brands under one roof. (p131)

8 Store Inside Taiga, this is a stylish boutique selling clothes and accessories from local designers. (p95)

Parfionova The Nevsky pr boutique of St Petersburg's original and most famous couturier. (p130)

Bat Norton Locally produced, bright, psychedelic and playful unisex street fashion. (p130)

Best Bookshops

Dom Knigi The city's largest bookshop is a sight in itself, with a huge range to choose from. (p95)

Staraya Kniga Pick your way through two centuries of old books. (p95)

Knizhnaya Lavka Pisatelei Long-standing bookshop with a social conscience. (p97)

Anglia The best English-language bookshop in St Petersburg. (p129)

Best Art Shopping

Dom Knigi Lots of art posters and books about the city's art history. (p95)

Erarta Commercial galleries here are a great place to buy contemporary Russian art. (p141)

Borey Art Centre Take the pulse of the local artistic underground here. (p129)

Sol-Art Attached to the next-door art school, this is a great place to buy paintings by local artists. (p129)

Art Re.Flex A contemporary art gallery well worth checking out for new up-and-comers as well as established names. (p130)

NEED TO KNOW

Opening Hours

Shop hours vary: most open seven days a week, typically from 10am to 9pm Monday to Friday, and from 10am to 7pm on weekends.

Credit Cards

In general, smarter, larger shops will nearly always take major credit cards, though an increasing number of smaller places and supermarkets now do too.

Caviar

It might be the glamorous face of Russian shopping, but the environmentally conscious will stay well clear of black caviar: sturgeon overfishing in the Caspian Sea has reached crisis levels and the international trade of caviar from wild sturgeon has been banned since 2006.

Explore St Petersburg

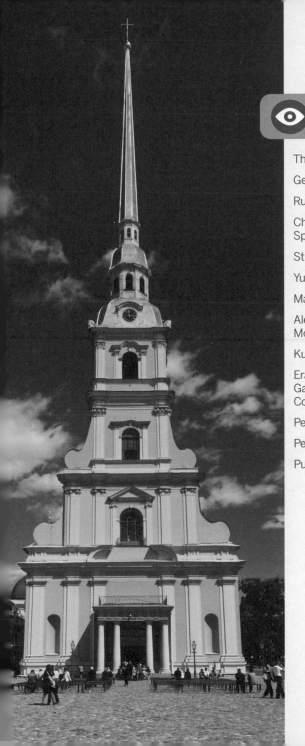

**ST PETERSBURG'S
TOP SIGHTS**

Neighbourhoods at a Glance

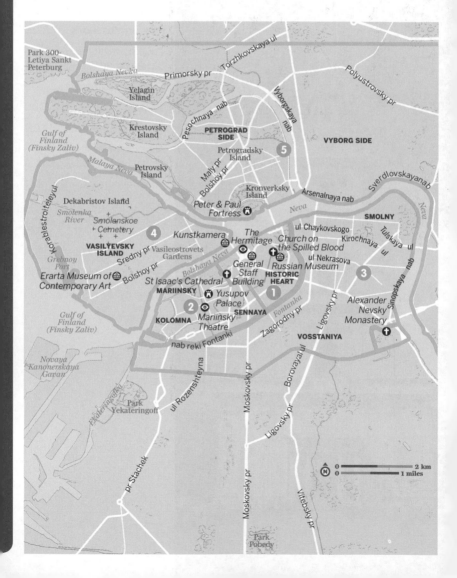

Park 300-Letiya Sankt Peterburg

Bolshaya Nevka

Primorsky pr

Torzhkovskaya ul

Polyustrovsky pr

Yelagin Island

Vyborgskaya nab

Krestovsky Island

Pesochnaya nab

PETROGRAD SIDE

VYBORG SIDE

Gulf of Finland (Finsky Zaliv)

Petrogradsky Island

5

Malaya Neva

Petrovsky Island

Maly pr

Bolshoy pr

Kronverksky Island

Sverdlovskayana b

Dekabristov Island

Smolenka River

Smolenskoe Cemetery

Peter & Paul Fortress

Neva

Arsenalnaya nab

Korablestroiteleyul

4

Kunstkamera

The Hermitage

ul Chaykovskogo

SMOLNY

Tulskaya ul

Kirochnaya ul

VASILYEVSKY ISLAND

Sredny pr

Vasileostrovets Gardens

Church on the Spilled Blood

Neva

Grebnoy Port

Bolshoy pr

Bolshaya Neva

General Staff Building

Russian Museum

ul Nekrasova

Sinopskaya nab

Erarta Museum of Contemporary Art

St Isaac's Cathedral

HISTORIC HEART

3

MARIINSKY

Yusupov Palace

1

Ligovsky pr

Alexander Nevsky Monastery

Gulf of Finland (Finsky Zaliv)

2

SENNAYA

Fontanka

KOLOMNA

Mariinsky Theatre

Zagorodny pr

VOSSTANIYA

nab reki Fontanki

Borovaya ul

Novaya Kanonerskaya Gavan

ul Rozenshteyna

Moskovsky pr

Ligovsky pr

Vitebsky pr

pr Stachek

Park Yekateringoff

Moskovsky pr

N 0   2 km
0   1 miles

Park Pobedy

❶ Historic Heart (p52)

The heart of the city is the area between the Neva and Fontanka Rivers. It is cut in two by Nevsky pr, the city's vast main avenue, and separated from Sennaya and Kolomna by Gorokhovaya ul. The most famous sights are packed together extraordinarily tightly here, including the Hermitage, Kazan Cathedral and Church on the Spilled Blood. It's a fast-paced, crowded part of the city and is its commercial as well as its tourist heart. The majority of the city's best hotels and restaurants can be found here, and whether you stay here or not, it's where you'll inevitably spend much of your time in St Petersburg.

❷ Sennaya & Kolomna (p98)

These two areas adjoin the Historic Heart and are almost as historic themselves, even though they're quite different from one another. Sennaya is centred on Sennaya Pl (the Haymarket), a traditionally poor area immortalised in Dostoevsky's *Crime and Punishment* and one that has somehow retained its seedy and down-at-heel air despite a big attempt to redevelop it. Kolomna is the largest of seven islands and a quiet, rather out-of-the-way place, although one steeped in history and great beauty. It contains the world-famous Mariinsky Theatre and more canals and rivers than any other part of the city.

❸ Smolny & Vosstaniya (p112)

This agglomeration of four districts (Smolny, Liteyny, Vosstaniya and Vladimirskaya) is also part of the city centre. The Smolny peninsula is a well-heeled residential district dominated by Smolny Cathedral, while next-door Liteyny is centred on Liteyny pr, a commercial street between Smolny and the Fontanka River. South of Nevsky pr are Vosstaniya and Vladimirskaya. Vosstaniya is the focus of St Petersburg's underground art and drinking scene, while Vladimirskaya, named after the stunning Vladimirsky Cathedral, is a mercantile district full of shopping, markets and a clutch of quirky museums.

❹ Vasilyevsky Island (p132)

The concentration of historic sights at Vasilyevsky Island's eastern edge was originally set to be the administrative heart of the city under Peter the Great, but the plan was never carried out and today the island is largely residential, with a uniform grid system and several busy shopping streets. The western edge of the island is more empty and industrial, but houses the fantastic new Erarta Museum of Contemporary Art, the main reason to come out here.

❺ Petrograd & Vyborg Sides (p142)

The Petrograd Side is a fascinating place that includes everything from the Peter and Paul Fortress to an impressive clutch of Style Moderne buildings lining its main drag. It also hosts St Petersburg's beautiful mosque, many fine museums and huge swaths of parkland on the Kirov Islands, the city's largest green lung. The Vyborg Side, home to the Finland Station (Finlyandsky vokzal), is famous for its role in Soviet history and can be a little bleak. That said, a walk around the ugly but interesting postindustrial landscape here will appeal to anyone with palace fatigue, and a few notable sights can make coming out here worthwhile.

Historic Heart

Neighbourhood Top Five

1 Surveying a millennium of global art and culture in the **Hermitage** (p54) and be dazzled by the gilded apartments of the Romanovs.

2 Gawping at the jewel-box-bright exterior of the **Church on the Spilled Blood** (p77), then being awestruck by the epic mosaics inside.

3 Getting to know the world's best collection of Russian art at the fantastic **Russian Museum** (p70).

4 Climbing the 262 steps to the golden dome of the monumental **St Isaac's Cathedral** (p78) for breathtaking views.

5 Taking a **cruise** (p97) on the rivers and canals of the historic heart, one of the best way to see this watery city!

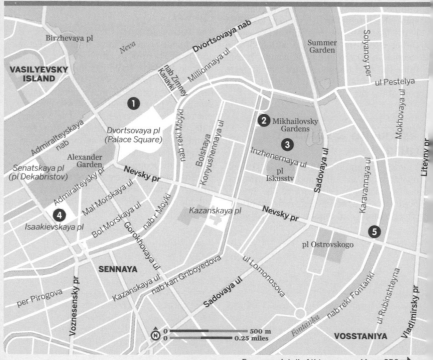

For more detail of this area see Map p256

Explore: Historic Heart

Radiating out from the golden spire of the Admiralty towards the Fontanka River, the historic heart has plenty of obvious attractions, including grand palaces, churches and museums, but also quirky gems like the Museum of Soviet Arcade Machines and a quartet of lovely parks. This is where you will be spending most of your time in St Petersburg, especially as the area is also blessed with great dining and drinking options.

For an unforgettable first impression, head straight to vast Palace Sq, where you'll see the Winter Palace, home to the Hermitage, in all its glory along with the amazing panorama of the General Staff Building and the great Neva River. From there, cherry-pick your way through the rest of the neighbourhood over a couple of days or so.

Nevsky pr, the city's main avenue, dominates every itinerary, and you'll find yourself back on its broad, busy pavements throughout your visit, whether you like it or not. Do try to spend some time off the main drag though, as this fascinating district deserves to be fully explored.

Local Life

→**Parks** The vast Mars Field (p83), Summer Garden (p80), Mikhailovsky Gardens (p82) and Alexander Garden (p82) are delightful green spaces for taking a breather from sightseeing to enjoy a picnic and do some sunbathing on sunny days.

→**Free art** Locals flock to the Hermitage (p54) on the first Thursday of each month when entrance is free, although the crowds can be huge!

→**Hang-outs** Check out the events, including free concerts, at anti-cafes such as Ziferberg (p92) and Miracle (p92); see if the Museum of Soviet Arcade Machines (p85) is holding one of its ping-pong DJ nights.

Getting There & Away

→**Metro** This neighbourhood is served by three metro stations: the interconnecting Nevsky Prospekt (Line 2) and Gostiny Dvor (Line 3), and Admiralteyskaya (Line 5) around the corner from the Hermitage.

→**Trolleybus** The number 7 bus, which runs the length of Nevsky pr, goes past Palace Sq and then crosses Dvortsovy most to Vasilyevsky Island.

→**Bus** Hop on bus 7, 10, 24, 27, 181 or 191 to save some footwork along Nevsky.

Lonely Planet's Top Tip

A great boon for time-challenged visitors, or those wanting to avoid daytime crowds – especially tour and school groups – has been the extension of opening hours until 9pm once a week at major city museums and galleries, including the Hermitage (Wednesday) and the Russian Museum (Thursday).

✕ Best Places to Eat

→ Yat (p90)

→ Marketplace (p85)

→ Jack & Chan (p85)

→ Gosti (p90)

For reviews, see p85➡

▼ Best Places to Drink

→ Radiobaby (p92)

→ Borodabar (p91)

→ Ziferberg (p92)

→ Sidreria (p92)

For reviews, see p91➡

⌂ Best Places to Shop

→ Taiga (p95)

→ Kupetz Eliseevs (p96)

→ Perinnye Ryady (p95)

→ Passage (p96)

For reviews, see p95➡

 TOP SIGHT
THE HERMITAGE

The geographic and tourism centrepiece of St Petersburg is one of the world's greatest art collections and usually most visitors' first stop in the city, even if it is simply to admire the baroque Winter Palace and the extraordinary ensemble of buildings that surround it. No other institution so embodies the opulence and extravagance of the Romanovs.

The Collection

Today, for the price of admission, anybody can parade down the grand staircases and across parquet floors, gawping at crystal chandeliers, gilded furniture and an art collection that cannot fail to amaze.

Since the move of the Impressionist, post-Impressionist and modern works to the new galleries of the General Staff Building (p68), the main Hermitage complex – which consists of five linked buildings: the Winter Palace, the Small Hermitage, the Old and New Hermitage and the State Hermitage Theatre – is now devoted to items from prehistoric times up until the mid-19th century.

The Western European Collection, in particular, does not miss much: Spanish, Flemish, Dutch, French, English and German art are covered from the 15th to the 18th centuries, while the Italian collection goes back all the way to the 13th century, including the Florentine and Venetian Renaissance, with priceless works by Leonardo da Vinci, Raphael, Michelangelo and Titian. A highlight is the enormous collection of Dutch and Flemish painting, in particular the spectacular assortment of works by Rembrandt, most notably his masterpiece *Return of the Prodigal Son.*

As much as you will see in the museum, there's about 20 times more in its vaults, part of which you can visit at the Hermitage Storage Facility (p152). Other branches of the mu-

DON'T MISS...

➡ Rembrandt (Room 254)
➡ Great Church
➡ Golden Rooms
➡ Peacock Clock

PRACTICALITIES

➡ Государственный Эрмитаж
➡ Map p256
➡ www.hermitage museum.org
➡ Dvortsovaya pl 2
➡ adult/student R400/ free, 1st Thu of month free, camera R200
➡ ⊘10.30am-6pm Tue & Thu-Sun, to 9pm Wed
➡ Ⓜ Admiralteyskaya

seum include the Menshikov Palace (p136) on Vasilyevsky Island, and the Imperial Porcelain factory (p129) in the south of the city.

Visiting the Hermitage

The Hermitage is a dynamic institution. Displays change, renovations continue, specific pieces go on tour, and temporary exhibitions occupy particular rooms, displacing whatever normally resides there, so be prepared for slight changes.

First-Floor Exhibits

To get here you'll need to go up to the 2nd floor and then down via the stairs between Rooms 153 and 156 or between Rooms 289 and 288.

Rooms 11–26: Prehistoric Artefacts

The prehistoric collection at the Hermitage contains thousands of artefacts dating as far back as the Palaeolithic era (500,000 to 12,000 BC). Most items were excavated from different regions of the USSR during the Soviet era. The following are the highlights:

➡ **Room 12** Carved petroglyphs (dating to 2000 BC) taken from the northeastern shores of Lake Onega after archaeological expeditions in 1935.

➡ **Rooms 13–14** Excavations of a burial mound in the northern Caucasus include the corpse of a nomadic chief, lavishly dressed and covered in jewels.

➡ **Room 26** This room contains mummified human corpses that are more than 2000 years old, as well as a fantastically reconstructed wooden cart.

Rooms 27–40 & 46–69: Ancient East

These excellent galleries present exhibits from Central Asia, Siberia and the Caucasus, dating as far back as the 10th century BC. Rooms 47 to 51 feature impressive 7th- and 8th-century relics from Panjakent in present-day Tajikistan, while Rooms 67 to 69 feature art and artefacts of the Golden Horde, which swept through Russia in the 13th and 14th centuries.

Rooms 89–91: Ancient Near East

These rooms house a very impressive collection of cuneiform texts from Babylon and Assyrian limestone reliefs.

Room 100: Ancient Egypt

This large hall houses an incredible collection of ancient Egyptian artefacts uncovered by Russian archaeologists. The display spans the Egyptian era from the Old Kingdom (3000–2400 BC) to the New Empire (1580–1050 BC). There are many painted sarcophagi and tombstones carved with hieroglyphics, as well as a fascinating mummy from the 10th century BC.

HERMITAGE TIPS

➡ If you reserve tickets online (www.hermitagemuseum.org) your printed-out voucher is not tied to any date. Walk straight into the Hermitage and collect your ticket without waiting in the main line.

➡ Alternatively pay at the computerised ticket machines in the main entrance courtyard and be sure to wait for your tickets to be printed at the end of the transaction (they come after the payment receipt).

➡ To take photographs you should buy the R200 ticket, although many people don't and checking within the museum is rare.

➡ If you leave jackets and bags in the cloakroom, be aware that you can't go back for anything without leaving the museum.

➡ Handbags and plastic bags are allowed in the Hermitage, but backpacks aren't.

There is good provision of toilets throughout the Hermitage – don't make the rookie mistake of thinking that those at the foot of the Jordan Staircase as you enter are the only ones available, as the lines (especially for women) can be very long indeed.

The Hermitage

A HALF-DAY TOUR

Successfully navigating the State Hermitage Museum, with its four vast interconnecting buildings and around 360 rooms, is an art form in itself. Our half-day tour of the highlights can be done in four hours, or easily extended to a full day.

Once past ticket control start by ascending the grand **Jordan Staircase** ❶ to Neva Enfilade and Great Enfilade for the impressive staterooms, including the former throne room St George's Hall and the 1812 War Gallery (Room 197), and the Romanovs' private apartments. Admire the newly restored **Great Church** ❷ then make your way back to the Neva side of the building via the Western Gallery (Room 262) to find the splendid **Pavilion Hall** ❸ with its view onto the Hanging Garden and the gilded Peacock Clock, always a crowd pleaser.

Make your way along the series of smaller galleries in the Large Hermitage hung with Italian Renaissance art, including masterpieces by **Da Vinci** ❹ and **Caravaggio** ❺. The Loggia of Raphael (Room 227) is also impressive. Linger a while in the galleries containing Spanish art before taking in the Dutch collection, the highlight of which is the hoard of **Rembrandt** ❻ canvases in Room 254.

Descend the Council Staircase (Room 206), noting the giant malachite vase, to the ground floor where the fantastic Egyptian collection awaits in Room 100 as well as the galleries of Greek and Roman Antiquities. If you have extra time, it's well worth booking tours to see the two special exhibitions in the **Gold Rooms** ❼ of the Treasure Gallery.

TOP TIPS

» **Queues** Reserve tickets online to skip the long lines.

» **Dining** Bring a sandwich and a bottle of water with you: the cafe is dire.

» **Footwear** Wear comfortable shoes.

» **Cloakroom** Bear in mind the only one is before ticket control, so you can't go back and pick up a sweater.

KEVIN OSBORNE / FOX FOTOS / GETTY IMAGES ©

Jordan Staircase
Originally designed by Rastrelli, in the 18th century this incredible white marble construction was known as the Ambassadorial Staircase because it was the way into the palace for official receptions.

The Gold Rooms
One of two sections of the Treasure Gallery, here you can see dazzling pieces of gold jewellery and ornamentation created by Scythian, Greek and ancient Oriental craftsmen.

IMAGE SOURCE / GETTY IMAGES ©

Great Church
This stunningly ornate church was the Romanovs' private place of worship and the venue for the marriage of the last tsar, Nicholas II, to Alexandra Feodorovna in 189

Rembrandt

A moving portrait of contrition and forgiveness, *Return of the Prodigal Son* (Room 254) depicts the biblical scene of a wayward son returning to his father.

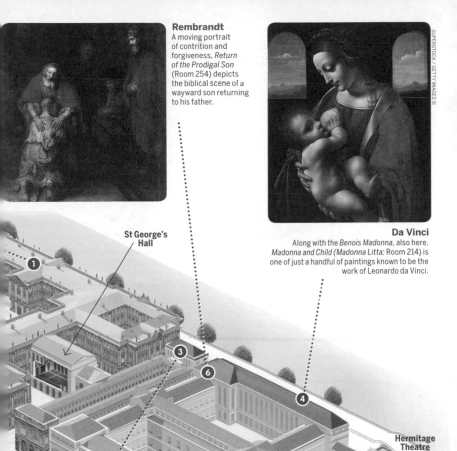

Da Vinci

Along with the *Benois Madonna*, also here, *Madonna and Child (Madonna Litta;* Room 214) is one of just a handful of paintings known to be the work of Leonardo da Vinci.

St George's Hall

Hermitage Theatre

Pavilion Hall

Apart from the Peacock Clock, the Pavilion Hall also contains beautifully detailed mosaic tables made by Italian and Russian craftsmen in the mid-19th century.

Caravaggio

The Lute Player (Room 237) is the Hermitage's only Caravaggio, and a work that the master of light and shade described as the best piece he'd ever painted.

THE HERMITAGE — FIRST FLOOR

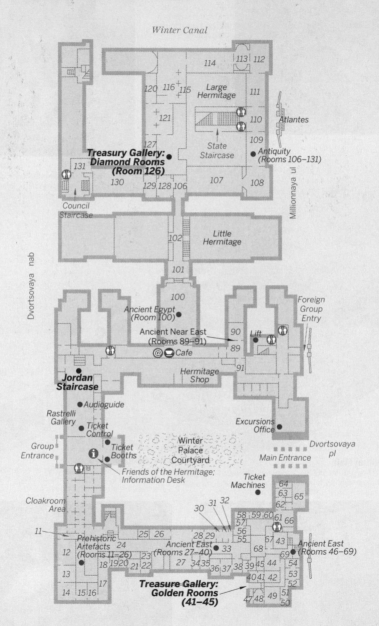

Winter Canal

114
113 112
120 116 115
Large Hermitage
111
121
Atlantes
127
State Staircase
110
109
Treasury Gallery: Diamond Rooms (Room 126)
Antiquity (Rooms 106–131)
131
130 129 128 106
107
108
Council Staircase

Dvortsovaya nab

Millionnaya ul

102
Little Hermitage
101
100
Ancient Egypt (Room 100)
Ancient Near East (Rooms 89–91)
90
Lift
89
@ Cafe
91
Foreign Group Entry

Hermitage Shop

Jordan Staircase
Audioguide
Rastrelli Gallery
Ticket Control
Excursions Office
Group Entrance
Ticket Booths
Winter Palace Courtyard
Dvortsovaya pl
i Friends of the Hermitage; Information Desk
Main Entrance
Cloakroom Area
Ticket Machines
64
63
62
65
11
25 26
30
31 32
58 59 60 61
57
56
55
66
Prehistoric Artefacts (Rooms 11–26)
24
28 29
27 34 35
33
57 43
68
Ancient East (Rooms 46–69)
69
12
18 19 20 21 22
23
36 37 38 39 45 44
54
53
13
17
40 41 42
52
14 15 16
Treasure Gallery: Golden Rooms (41–45)
47 48
49
51
50
Ancient East (Rooms 27–40)

Rooms 106–131: Antiquity

The Hermitage has more than 100,000 items from Ancient Greece and Rome, including painted vases, antique gemstones, Roman sculpture and Greek gold.

➡**Room 107** The Jupiter Hall is a sumptuous space with portraits of sculptors on the ceiling.

➡**Room 108** Designed by German neoclassicist von Klenze to imitate a Roman courtyard.

➡**Room 109** Peter I acquired the sculpture *Tauride Venus* from Pope Clement XI. This piece – a Roman copy of a Greek original – was the first antique sculpture ever brought to Russia.

➡**Room 111** Another impressive design by von Klenze, this one was intended to be a library (which explains the philosophers' profiles).

➡**Room 130** Hall of Twenty Columns, containing a fabulous collection of Greco-Roman clay urns.

Second-Floor Highlights

The 2nd floor houses many of the Hermitage's highlights, including its unbeatable Western European collection and its grandest state rooms.

Rooms 151–161: Russian Culture & Art

Most of the western wing of the Winter Palace contains the huge collection from ancient Rus (10th to 15th centuries) up through to the 18th century, including artefacts, icons, portraits and furniture.

➡**Rooms 151 & 153** This long corridor, with its vast clock, contains portraits of all the Russian tsars from Peter the Great to Nicholas II.

➡**Rooms 155–156** Moorish Dining Room and Rotunda.

➡**Rooms 157–162** The Petrovsky Gallery displays personal effects and equipment used by Peter the Great, as well as some beautiful early-18th-century furniture. Look for the ivory chandelier that was partly built by Peter himself.

➡**Room 161** In 1880 there was an attempt on the life of Alexander II in this room. A young revolutionary, Khalturin, planted a bomb in the room below. It killed 11 soldiers, although the tsar had wandered into another room at the time.

Rooms 175–189: Imperial Apartments

This series of rooms represents the private apartments of the last tsar, Nicholas II and the imperial family. Many of these rooms were completed in 1894, and they now show off elaborate 19th-century interiors.

➡**Room 178** Nicholas II spent much of his time in this wonderful Gothic library, topped with a sublime walnut ceiling.

➡**Room 181** The relatively small and intimate Pompeii dining room.

➡**Room 187** Griffin-motif furniture in this palace drawing room dates from 1805.

➡**Room 188** This small dining room is where the Provisional Government was arrested by the Bolsheviks in 1917.

➡**Room 189** Two tonnes of gorgeous green columns, boxes, bowls and urns have earned this room the name 'Malachite Hall', and it is one of the most striking rooms in the entire palace. The handiwork of architect Alexander Bryullov, it was completed in 1839. Three figurines on the wall represent Day, Night and Poetry. This was where the last meeting of the 1917 Provisional Government occurred, on the fateful nights of 25 and 26 October 1917; they were arrested soon after, in the Small Dining Room next door.

Rooms 190–192: Neva Enfilade

These grand ceremonial halls are often used for temporary exhibitions.

➡**Room 190** This Concert Hall was used for small soirées. The enormous ornate silver tomb was commissioned by Empress Elizabeth for the remains of Alexander Nevsky.

➡**Room 191** As many as 5000 guests could be entertained in the Great Hall (also called Nicholas Hall), the scene of imperial winter balls.

➡**Room 192** This ante-room was used for pre-ball champagne buffets.

Rooms 193–198: Great Enfilade

You'll find more staterooms here.

➡**Room 193** The Field Marshals' Hall is known for its military-themed chandelier and its portraits of seven of Russia's military leaders.

➡**Room 194** The Hall of Peter the Great contains his none-too-comfy throne.

➡**Room 195** This gilt Armorial Hall contains chandeliers engraved with the coat of arms of all the Russian provinces.

➡**Room 197** The 1812 War Gallery is hung with 332 portraits of Russian and Napoleonic war leaders.

➡**Room 198** St George's Hall served as the staterooms where the imperial throne used to sit. With white Carrara marble imported from Italy and floors crafted from the wood of 16 different tree species, it is a splendid affair.

Room 204: Pavilion Hall & Hanging Garden

The ceremonial Pavilion Hall is an airy white-and-gold room sparkling with 28 chandeliers. The south windows look on to Catherine the Great's hanging garden (under restoration), while the north overlooks the Neva. The amazing floor mosaic in front of the windows is a copy of that in the Roman bath of Otricoli (Ocriculum) near Rome.

Rooms 207–238: Italian Art

Covering 30-plus rooms, the Hermitage's collection of Italian art traverses the 13th to the 18th centuries. The highlights are certainly the works by the Renaissance artists: Leonardo da Vinci, Raphael, Giorgione and Titian. Look also for Botticelli, Caravaggio and Tiepolo.

➡**Room 207** The earliest example in this collection is *The Crucifixion,* painted by Ugolino di Tedice in the second half of the 13th century.

➡**Room 214** Of a dozen or so original paintings by da Vinci that exist in the world, two are here. The very different *Benois Madonna* (1478) and *Madonna Litta* (1490) are named after their last owners. For years, the latter was considered lost. However, in 1909, the Russian architect Leon Benois surprised the art world when he revealed that it was part of his father-in-law's collection.

➡**Room 217** Giorgione is one of the most mysterious painters of the Renaissance, as only a few paintings exist that are known for certain to be his work. A portrait of idealised beauty, *Judith* is said to represent the inseparability of life and death.

➡**Room 221** The work of Titian, the best representative of the Venetian school in the 16th century, is featured here: *Danaya* and *St Sebastian* are widely accepted as two of his masterpieces.

➡**Room 224** Accessed off this room is the Hermitage Theatre; there are lovely views from the connecting corridor over the Neva.

➡**Rooms 226–227: Loggia of Raphael** When Catherine the Great visited the Vatican she was so impressed that she commissioned Quarenghi to create this copy of a Vatican gallery; a team of Raphael's students re-created the master's murals on canvas. Note the occasional Russification on these versions: the two-headed eagle of the Romanov dynasty replaces the papal coat of arms.

➡**Room 229** Here you'll enjoy two pieces by Raphael, *The Holy Family* and *Madonna and Child,* as well as many pieces by his disciples This room contains the Hermitage's only piece by Michelangelo, a marble statue of a crouching boy.

➡**Rooms 237–238** These Italian Skylight Halls are bathed in natural light, which highlights the ornately moulded ceilings.

Rooms 239–240: Spanish Art

Ranging from the 16th to the 18th centuries, this collection includes the most noteworthy artists of this 'Golden Age' of Spanish painting: Murillo, Ribera and, of course, Velázquez. The collection also includes two remarkable paintings from the 16th century: the marvellous *St Peter and St Paul,* by El Greco; and *St Sebastian Cured by St Irene,* by Ribera.

Room 243: Knights' Hall

Nicholas I started collecting artistic weapons and armaments from around the world. Here is the Western European collection, featuring four impressive 16th-century German knights sitting atop their armoured horses.

Rooms 245–247: Flemish Art

These three rooms dedicated to 17th-century Flanders are almost entirely consumed by three artists: Peter Paul Rubens, Anthony Van Dyck and Frans Snyders.

RUSSIAN ARK

Wander with a ghost through 33 rooms of the Hermitage and 300 years of Russian history in *Russian Ark* (2002). Director Alexander Sokurov shot the movie in one continuous 96-minute take in the Winter Palace.

Rooms 289 and 304–308 comprise the private apartments of Tsar Alexander II. Most spectacular is Room 304, the Golden Drawing Room, which features a fabulous gilt ceiling and a marble fireplace with an intricate mosaic over the mantle.

PEACOCK CLOCK

The centrepiece of the Pavilion Hall (Room 204) is the incredible Peacock Clock, created by James Cox and gifted to Catherine the Great in 1781 by Grigory Potemkin. A revolving dial in one of the toadstools tells the time, and as it strikes the hour the automaton peacock spreads its wings and the toadstools, owl and cock come to life. A video beside the clock shows the action in close-up detail should you not be around for the once-weekly performance at 7pm on Wednesday.

THE HERMITAGE — SECOND FLOOR

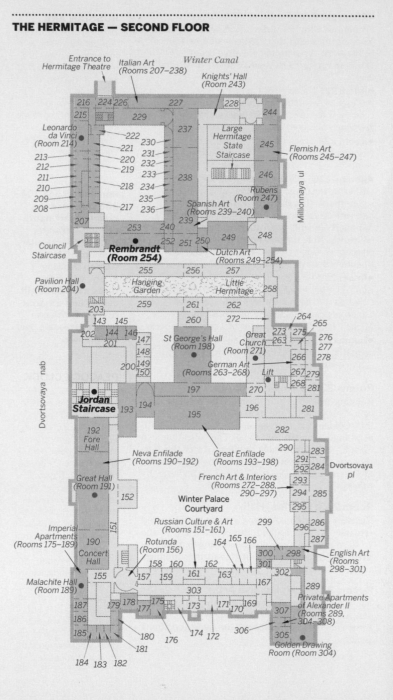

Entrance to Hermitage Theatre

Italian Art (Rooms 207–238)

Winter Canal

Knights' Hall (Room 243)

216 224 226   227   228   244

215

229   237

Leonardo da Vinci (Room 214)

222   230
221   231
220   232
219   233
218   234
217   235   236

213
212
211
210
209
208

Large Hermitage State Staircase

245

Flemish Art (Rooms 245–247)

246

Rubens (Room 247)

238

Spanish Art (Rooms 239–240)

239

Millionnaya ul

207

253   240   252   251   250   249   248

Council Staircase

Rembrandt (Room 254)

Dutch Art (Rooms 249–254)

255   256   257

Pavilion Hall (Room 204)

Hanging Garden

Little Hermitage

258

203

259   261   262

143   145

260   272   264   265

202   144   146

201   147

St George's Hall (Room 198)

Great Church (Room 271)

273   263   275   276

266   277
278

148
149
150

German Art (Rooms 263–268)

Lift

267   279
268   281

200

Dvortsovaya nab

197   270

193   194

Jordan Staircase

195   196   281

192 Fore Hall

Neva Enfilade (Rooms 190–192)

Great Enfilade (Rooms 193–198)

282   290   283

291   292   284

Dvortsovaya pl

Great Hall (Room 191)

152

French Art & Interiors (Rooms 272–288, 290–297)

293   294   285
295

151

Winter Palace Courtyard

296   286

Imperial Apartments (Rooms 175–189)

Russian Culture & Art (Rooms 151–161)

Rotunda (Room 156)

299   287

164   165   166

300   298

English Art (Rooms 298–301)

190 Concert Hall

158   160   162

301
302

Malachite Hall (Room 189)

155   157   159   161   163

167

289

Private Apartments of Alexander II (Rooms 289, 304–308)

303

307

187
186
185

179   178   177   175   173   171   170   169

306   305

180   176   174   172

181

Golden Drawing Room (Room 304)

184   183   182

Rooms 249–254: Dutch Art

Dating from the 17th and 18th centuries, the Dutch collection contains more than 1000 pieces. The 26 paintings by Rembrandt in Room 254 nearly outshine anything else in these rooms. The collection traces his career, starting with *Flora* and *The Descent from the Cross,* which are noticeably lighter but more detailed. His later work tends to be darker and more penetrating, such as the celebrated *The Return of the Prodigal Son.* Painted between 1663 and 1665, it arguably represents the height of Rembrandt's mastery of psychology in his paintings. The solemn baroque masterpiece is a moving portrait of unquestioning parental love and mercy.

Rooms 263–268: German Art

This small collection of German art ranges from the 15th to the 18th centuries. Among the earliest works here are five paintings by Lucas Cranach the Elder.

Room 271: Great Church

Due to reopen at the end of 2014 after a major renovation, this Rastrelli-designed chapel is one of the Winter Palace's most dazzling spaces, with a white and gilt dome and the ceiling painting *The Ascension of Christ* by Pyotr Basin.

Rooms 272–288 & 290–297: French Art & Interiors

These rooms trace the development of French art from the 15th to the 18th centuries, including tapestries, ceramics, metalwork and paintings. Look for rooms devoted to Nicholas Poussin, founder of French Classicism, and Claude Lorrain, master of the classical landscape. Room 282, Alexander Hall, is another testament to the victory over Napoleon in 1812.

Rooms 298–301: English Art

These rooms showcase 15th- to 18th-century English art. Highlights include *The Infant Hercules Strangling the Serpents,* by Sir Joshua Reynolds, which was commissioned by Catherine the Great to symbolise the growing strength of Russia. *Portrait of a Lady in Blue,* by Thomas Gainsborough, is perhaps the most famous piece in the collection.

Third-Floor Highlights

At the time of research, the plan was to move all of the Impressionist and Post-Impressionist works from the galleries on the 3rd floor across to the General Staff Building. Expect much of this floor to be closed for renovation.

Rooms 351–400: Oriental & Middle Eastern Culture & Art

These 50 rooms display ancient art from the Far East, including China and Tibet, Indonesia, Mongolia and India. Also on display are art and artefacts from Syria, Iran, Iraq, Egypt and Turkey.

THE TREASURE GALLERY

For lovers of things that glitter and the applied arts, the Hermitage's **Treasure Gallery** (Map p256; ☎812-571 8446; tour R300) should not be missed. These two special collections, guarded behind vault doors on the 1st floor, are open only by guided tour, for which you should either call ahead to reserve a place, or buy a ticket at the entrance. The **Golden Rooms** collection focuses on a hoard of fabulous Scythian and Greek gold and silver from the Caucasus, Crimea and Ukraine, dating from the 7th to 2nd centuries BC; the **Diamond Rooms** section has fabulous jewellery from Western Europe, and pieces from as far apart as China, India and Iran.

History of the Hermitage

When, in 1764, Catherine the Great purchased the art collection of Johann Gotzkowski, which contained a large number of works by Rubens, Rembrandt and Van Dyck, little did anyone suspect that this would form the basis of one of the world's most celebrated art museums, the repository of millions of artistic masterpieces from around the world.

A New Winter Palace

Some 30 years earlier, it was Empress Anna who engaged a young Bartolomeo Rastrelli to incorporate the existing royal buildings on the Neva into a proper palace. Her successor, the ever-extravagant Empress Elizabeth, wanted something grander so in 1754 she signed a decree ordering the creation of a winter palace, closely supervising its design and construction. Her inopportune death in 1761 occurred only a few months before the Winter Palace was finally completed, but her legacy has been confirmed by what is arguably St Petersburg's most strikingly beautiful palace.

Visitors and residents were wowed by the capital's newest addition: 'visible from a distance, rising above the rooftops, the upper storey of the new Winter Palace, adorned with a host of statues', as it was described by one 18th-century visitor to the capital. But the palace, of course, was a private residence. After the death of Empress Elizabeth, Peter III lived here for only three months before he was overthrown in a palace coup and replaced by Catherine the Great. This grand baroque building thenceforth became the official residence of the imperial family.

The Imperial Art Collection

Collecting art was an obsession for Catherine, who purchased some of the most extensive private collections in Europe, including those of Heinrich von Brühl, Lord Robert Walpole and Baron Pierre Crozat. By 1774 Catherine's collection included over 2000 paintings, and by the time of her death in 1796 that number had doubled.

Catherine and her successors didn't much care for Rastrelli's baroque interiors and had most of the rooms completely remodelled in classical style. To display her art, Catherine first had built the Small Hermitage and later the so-called Old Hermitage, and allowed prominent people to privately visit the collection on application. In the 1780s Giacomo Quarenghi added the Hermitage Theatre, which served as the private theatre for the imperial family; it is still used today although now for public performances.

The early 19th century saw the expansion of the collection, particularly in the field of classical antiquity, due both to the continued acquisition of

....

1. Jordan Staircase (Ambassadorial Staircase; p59)
2. Winter Palace (p54) exterior

other collections and rich finds being discovered in southern Russia. More acquisitions followed Russia's victory over Napoleon in 1812 and included the private collection of Napoleon's consort, Joséphine de Beauharnais.

In December 1837 a devastating fire broke out in the heating shaft of the Field Marshals' Hall; it burned for over 30 hours and destroyed a large portion of the interior. Most of the imperial belongings were saved, thrown out of windows or dragged outside to sit in the snow. Nicholas I vowed to restore the palace as quickly as possible, employing architect Vasily Stasov and thousands of workers to toil around the clock. Their efforts were not in vain, as the project was completed in a little over a year. Most of the classical interiors in the ceremonial rooms that we see today, including the Grand Hall, the Throne Room and the Armorial Hall, were designed by Stasov.

Russia's First Public Art Museum

While Peter the Great opened the Kunstkamera (p134), his private collection of curiosities, to the public in the early 18th century, it was Nicholas I who eventually opened the first public art museum in Russia. During a visit to Germany in 1838 he was impressed by the museums he saw in Munich – specifically, by the idea of buildings that were architectural masterpieces in themselves, designed specifically to house and preserve artistic masterpieces. He employed German architect Leo von Klenze and local boy Vasily Stasov to carry out such a project in the proximity of the Winter Palace. The result was the 'neo-Grecian' New Hermitage, adorned by statues and bas-reliefs depicting great artists, writers and other cultural figures. After 11 years of work, the museum was opened to the public in 1852.

1. Astronomy instruments, Kunstkamera (p134) 2. Palace Square, Alexander Column (p79) and the General Staff Building (p68)

At this time, the first director of the Hermitage was appointed and the collection as a museum, rather than the tsar's private gallery, began to take shape. Various further acquisitions in the late 19th and early 20th centuries meant that the Hermitage had truly arrived as a world-class museum. Particularly important caches of paintings included the two Leonardo da Vinci *Madonnas* (acquired in 1865 and 1914), Piotr Semionov-Tien-Shansky's enormous collection of Dutch and Flemish art, purchased in 1910, and the Stroganov collection of Italian old masters.

Expanding the Collection

It was the postrevolutionary period that saw a threefold increase in the Hermitage's collection. In 1917 the Winter Palace and the Hermitage were declared state museums, and throughout the 1920s and 1930s the Soviet state seized and nationalised countless valuable private collections, including those of the Stroganovs, Sheremetyevs, Shuvalovs, Yusupovs and Baron Stieglitz. In 1948 it incorporated the renowned collections of post-Impressionist and Impressionist paintings of Moscow industrialists Sergei Shchukin and Ivan Morozov, including works by Matisse and Picasso.

During WWII, Soviet troops in Germany and Eastern Europe appropriated enormous numbers of paintings that had belonged to private collectors. In 1995, after years of keeping the paintings in storage, the Hermitage finally put these works, including those by Monet, Degas, Renoir, Cézanne, Picasso and Matisse, on public display. In recent years, the museum has been building a collection of contemporary art that currently numbers around 1500 pieces, some of which are displayed in the General Staff Building (p68) – a tiny fraction of the three million items listed in the Hermitage's inventory.

GENERAL STAFF BUILDING

The east wing of this magnificent building, wrapping around the south of Dvortsovaya pl and designed by Carlo Rossi in the 1820s, marries restored interiors with contemporary architecture to create a series of galleries displaying the Hermitage's amazing collection of Impressionist and post-Impressionist works. Contemporary art is here, too, often in temporary exhibitions by major artists.

New Grand Enfilade

Entry to the galleries is via a new marble staircase, which doubles as an amphitheatre for musical performances. A 'New Grand Enfilade' of exhibition rooms has been created by throwing a glass ceiling over the building's interior courtyards, and 26 halls with historic decorative paintings have also been restored.

At the time of research, installation of all the artworks was underway and should be completed by the end of 2015 – the following is what is expected to be on display, although there could be slight changes to this, so if there's a work you particularly want to see check first with information here or at the main Hermitage.

DON'T MISS

➡ Monet
➡ Picasso
➡ Matisse
➡ *Black Square*, Kazimir Malevich

PRACTICALITIES

➡ Здание Главного штаба
➡ Map p256
➡ www.hermitage museum.org
➡ Dvortsovaya pl 6-8
➡ admission R100
➡ ⊙10.30am-6pm Tue & Thu-Sun, to 9pm Wed
➡ Ⓜ Admiralteyskaya

Barbizon School & Romanticism

Romanticism was the prevailing school of art in the 19th century and Delacroix is the most celebrated French Romantic painter of that time. Prime examples of his style can be seen in *A Moroccan Saddling a Horse* and *Lion Hunt in Morocco*.

The Barbizon School, named for the village where this group of artists settled, reacted against this romanticism, making a move towards realism. Gustave Courbet, Jean-Baptiste-Camille Corot, Théôdore Rousseau and Jean-François Millet are all represented.

Impressionists & Post-Impressionists

The Hermitage's collection of Impressionist and post-Impressionist paintings is arguably the best in the world: much of this artwork was displayed for the first time in the 1990s, when the museum revealed some fabulous pieces, kept secret since seizure by the Red Army from Germany at the end of WWII.

Among the paintings on display are those by Gauguin, including the primitive works that he created in Tahiti; Van Gogh's *Thatched Cottages* (1890) and the dreamy *Memory of the Garden at Etten* (1888); Cézanne's *Mont Sainte-Victoire, Lady in Blue* and *The Smoker;* Pissarro's *Blvd Montmartre* and *Sunny Afternoon* (1897); an early piece by Monet titled *Lady in a Garden* and his late-career masterpiece *Waterloo Bridge, Effect of Mist* (1903); and Renoir's iconic *Child With a Whip* (1885). There are also three sculptures by Rodin.

Russian Avant-Garde

Russian avant-garde art is not a strong point of the Hermitage (try the Russian Museum). That said, the General Staff Building displays a couple of Kandinsky's early works, as well as paintings by Kazimir Malevich. This is the permanent home of *Black Square* (1915), which went missing during the Soviet period, mysteriously reappearing in southern Russia in 1993. Oligarch Vladimir Potanin bought the painting for $US1 million and donated it to the Hermitage in 2002.

20th Century

There are over 40 paintings by Matisse and almost as many by Picasso on display. Henri Matisse was initially classified as a Fauvist, but he continued to paint in his own particular style, even as Fauvism declined in the early 20th century. Around this time, Matisse met Pablo Picasso and the two became lifelong friends. Picasso is best known as the founder and master of cubism; but again, his work spanned many styles.

A turning point for Matisse – and perhaps his most famous work – is *The Dance* (1910). The intense colours and the dancing nudes convey intense feelings of freedom. This panel – along with the accompanying *The Music* – was painted specifically for Russian businessman Sergei Shchukin. While these panels are certainly commanding, don't miss *The Red Room* and *Portrait of the Artist's Wife.*

Picasso's blue period is characterised by sombre paintings in shades of blue. When he was only 22, he painted *The Absinthe Drinker,* a haunting portrait of loneliness and isolation. The sensuous *Dance of the Veils* (1907) and *Woman with a Fan* (1908) are excellent representations of his cubist work, as are the ceramics on display here.

Inspired by Romanticism, a group of painters in the 1860s began experimenting with painting modern life and landscapes, endeavouring to capture the overall effect of a scene instead of being overly concerned with details. The new trend – radical in its time – was known as Impressionism.

BLACK SQUARE

Kazimir Malevich's *Black Square* is the most striking painting of the Petrograd avant-garde. Malevich created several variants of the simple black square against a white background throughout his career, of which this is the fourth and last. It was taken by many as a nihilistic declaration of the 'end of painting', causing both awe and outrage.

TOP SIGHT
RUSSIAN MUSEUM

Focusing solely on Russian art, from ancient church icons to 20th-century paintings, the Russian Museum's collection is magnificent and can easily be viewed in half a day. Although the collection is less overwhelming than that of the Hermitage, the masterpieces nonetheless keep on coming as you tour the Mikhailovsky Palace and the attached Benois Wing.

The Museum's Collection

Mikhailovsky Palace was designed by Carlo Rossi and built between 1819 and 1825. It was a gift for Grand Duke Mikhail (brother of Tsars Alexander I and Nicholas I) as compensation for missing out on the throne. Nicholas II opened it as a public gallery on 7 March 1898.

The museum originated from the collection begun by Tsar Alexander III, whose bust greets you on the magnificent main staircase; the collection now numbers around 400,000 pieces (the Russian Museum also manages several other palaces, plus the Mikhailovsky and Summer Gardens). On display are a superb range of ancient icons, paintings, graphic art, sculpture, folk, decorative and applied art. The collection of avant-garde works is particularly notable, including pieces by Nathan Altman, Natalya Goncharova, Kazimir Malevich and Alexander Rodchenko.

The museum's Benois Wing houses the modern collection as well as temporary exhibitions and was constructed between 1914 and 1919. It is now connected to the original palace and is accessible through an entrance on nab kanala Griboyedova.

DON'T MISS...

➡ *Peter I Interrogating Tsarevich Alexey in Peterhof* – Nicholas Ghe
➡ *Barge Haulers on the Volga* – Ilya Repin
➡ *The Last Day of Pompeii* – Karl Bryullov
➡ *Portrait of the Poetess Anna Akhmatova* – Nathan Altman

PRACTICALITIES

➡ Русский музей
➡ Map p256
➡ www.rusmuseum.ru
➡ Inzhenernaya ul 4
➡ adult/student R350/150, 4-palace ticket adult/child R600/300
➡ ⏱10am-6pm Wed & Fri-Sun, to 5pm Mon, 1-9pm Thu
➡ Ⓜ Nevsky Prospekt

Visiting the Russian Museum

Enter via the ground-floor entrance to the right of the main facade. Pick up a museum map before ascending the magnificent main staircase to the 1st floor, as this is where the chronological ordering of the exhibits from the 10th to the 20th century begins. Galleries close for restoration and rehangings from time to time, and works are sometimes loaned out, so be prepared for slight changes to the following.

Rooms 1–4: Religious Icons

The first four rooms of the museum encapsulate a succinct but brilliant history of Russian icon painting, including work from the three major schools of Russian icon painting: Novgorod, and Pskov. Room 2 has *St Nicholas and Scenes of His Life,* while Room 3 features Russian master Andrei Rublev's massive *Peter and Paul* as well as his *Presentation of Christ in the Temple.* Room 4 is notable in its departure from earlier styles. Compare *Old Testament Trinity with Scenes from Genesis* with the completely atypical *Our Father* (1669).

Rooms 5–7: Petrine & Post-Petrine Art

Peter was a great patron of the arts and almost single-handedly brought the Western eye to Russian painting, as witnessed by the massive jump in style from ecclesiastical to secular subjects between Rooms 4 and 5. The room includes three busts of Peter and two portraits.

Room 6 includes some charmingly odd canvases in very strange shapes as well as mosaic portraits of both Peter and Catherine the Great, as well as of Elizabeth I, Peter's daughter. The centre of the room is taken up by a huge portrait of the ill-fated Peter III, although look out for the impressive bust of Prince Menshikov. Room 7 has an amazingly ornate ceiling. The room houses a sculpture of *Empress Anna with an Arab Boy* and a few impressive tapestries, including one that depicts Peter the Great at the Battle of Poltava, his greatest military victory.

Rooms 8–11: The Rise of the Academy

These rooms display the early works of the St Petersburg Academy of Arts. These artists borrowed the European classical aesthetic for their work. Look for portraits in Rooms 8 and 10 (including two portraits and a full-sized sculpture of Catherine the Great) and biblical themes in Room 9.

Room 11 is the Rossi-designed White Hall, which was Grand Duke Mikhail's drawing room. Here, the interior is the art – in this case representing the Empire epoch. It's wonderfully ornate and shiny – a perfect place to host musical greats like Strauss and Berlioz, who performed here.

OTHER BRANCHES OF THE RUSSIAN MUSEUM

As well as the magnificent Mikhailovsky Palace, the Russian Museum also manages three other impressive palaces in the city centre, where you can view temporary exhibits, permanent collections and grand staterooms. These are the Marble Palace (p80), the Stroganov Palace (p79) and Mikhailovsky Castle (p80). A good-value joint ticket for all four venues can be used over three days. Of the palaces, the Marble Palace has the best art collection, while the Stroganov Palace has the best interiors.

RUSSIAN MUSEUM — FIRST FLOOR

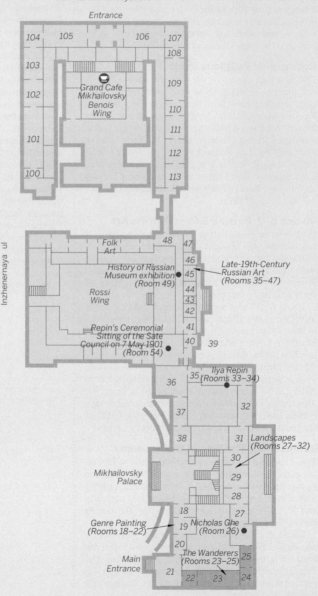

nab kanala Griboyedova

Entrance

104 105 106 107

108

103

Grand Cafe
Mikhailovsky
Benois
Wing

109

102

110

111

101

112

100 113

Inzhenernaya ul

Folk
Art

48 47

46

History of Russian
Museum exhibition
(Room 49)

45

Late-19th-Century
Russian Art
(Rooms 35–47)

44

Rossi
Wing

43

42

Repin's Ceremonial
Sitting of the Sate
Council on 7 May 1901
(Room 54)

41

40 39

Ilya Repin
(Rooms 33–34)

36 35

32

37

38 31

Landscapes
(Rooms 27–32)

30

Mikhailovsky
Palace

29

28

18 27

Genre Painting
(Rooms 18–22)

19

Nicholas Ghe
(Room 26)

20

Main
Entrance

The Wanderers
(Rooms 23–25)

25

21

22 23 24

khailovsky Palace

PETER I INTERROGATING TSAREVICH ALEXEY IN PETERHOF

The theme of this painting by Nicholas Ghe is the tumultuous relationship between Peter the Great and his son Alexey, whom he had imprisoned and tortured to death as he tried to extract information about 'plotters' against him. It expertly captures the gulf between the two men, and foreshadows Alexey's brutal end in the Peter & Paul Fortress. Although considered a masterpiece today, initially the painting was met with such critical coldness Ghe declared that art should not be for sale, became a follower of Tolstoy, bought a farm and began painting portraits for a pittance, believing everyone should be able to pay to preserve their image.

Rooms 12–17: Dominance of the Academy

By the early 19th century the Academy of Arts was more influenced by Italian themes, given the unfashionability of France. In Room 12 look for Vladimir Borovikovsky's magnificent *Catherine II Promenading in Tsarskoe Selo* and his *Portrait of Murtaza Kuli*. Room 13 is full of peasant subjects with uplifting titles such as *Peeling Beetroot*.

Room 14 is truly spectacular, including enormous canvases such as Karl Bryullov's incredible *The Last Day of Pompeii* and *The Crucifixion*, and Ivan Aivazovsky's terrifying *The Wave*.

Room 15 is also impressive, with the far wall made up of studies for Alexander Ivanov's masterpiece *The Appearance of Christ Before the People* (1837–57), which hangs in Moscow's Tretyakov Gallery. Ivanov spent 20 years on this work, but it was met with a negative critical reception. However, later generations appreciated the work, and even these studies, many of which mark a notable departure in terms of detail and representation.

Rooms 18–22: Genre Painting

At the turn of the 19th century, it became fashionable for 'genre painting' to look to themes from (an incredibly idealised) rural Russia, which you can see in Rooms 18 to 20. Room 21 contains some enormous canvases: *Phrina at the Poseidon Celebration in Elesium* by Genrikh Semiradsky, *Christian Martyrs at the Colosseum* by Konstantin Flavitsky and *Nero's Death* by Vasily Smirnov.

There are a couple of cafes in the Russian Museum, the best of which is the Grand Cafe Mikhailovsky (Map p256; 10am to 5pm Monday, Wednesday and Friday to Sunday, 1pm to 8pm Thursday; mains R300), in the Benois Wing, where you can enjoy a coffee and cake or a more substantial meal in a handsome Style Moderne–design salon.

RUSSIAN MUSEUM — SECOND FLOOR

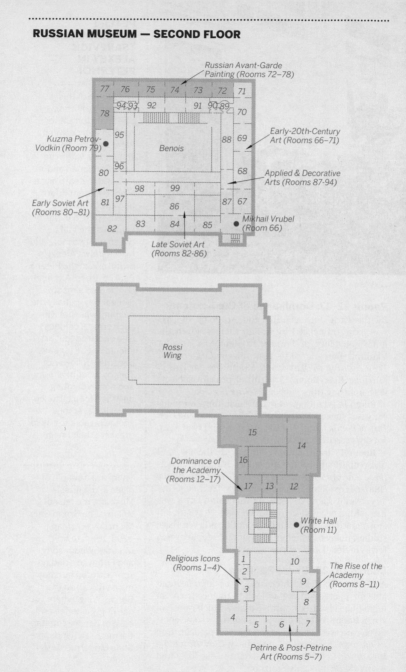

Russian Avant-Garde Painting (Rooms 72–78)

77 76 75 74 73 72 71

78 94 93 92 91 90 89 70

Kuzma Petrov-Vodkin (Room 79)

95 Benois 88 69

Early-20th-Century Art (Rooms 66–71)

96 68

80 Applied & Decorative Arts (Rooms 87-94)

98 99

Early Soviet Art (Rooms 80–81)

81 97 86 87 67

82 83 84 85

Mikhail Vrubel (Room 66)

Late Soviet Art (Rooms 82-86)

Rossi Wing

15 14

Dominance of the Academy (Rooms 12–17)

16

17 13 12

White Hall (Room 11)

Religious Icons (Rooms 1–4)

1 10

2

3 9

The Rise of the Academy (Rooms 8–11)

8

4 7

5 6

Petrine & Post-Petrine Art (Rooms 5–7)

Rooms 23–25: The Wanderers

At the time of research rooms 23 to 29 were closed for restoration. Usually, this is where you'll find works by the Wanderers (Peredvizhniki), a group of academy artists who saw their future outside the strict confines of that institution. They wandered among the people, painting scenes of realism that had never been seen before in Russian art. Prime examples include Nikolai Perov's *Hunters at Rest* and the scathing *Monastery Refectory*.

Room 26: Nicholas Ghe

Ghe's masterpiece, *Peter I Interrogating Tsarevich Alexey in Peterhof*, is usually here (at the time of research it was in room 19). Ghe's other work, such as *Christ and his Disciples Come into the Garden of Gethsemane* and *The Last Supper*, are equally dark.

Rooms 27–32: Landscapes

Contemporaries of the Wanderers, landscape artists such as Ivan Shishkin were still popular. These rooms also document the rise of populist art, which had a strong social conscience and sought to educate the public. The best examples of this are Vladimir Makovsky's *The Condemned* (Room 30) and Konstantin Savitsky's *To War* (Room 31).

Rooms 33–34: Ilya Repin

This room contains several masterpieces by Ilya Repin (1844–1930), one of Russia's most famous painters. The iconic *Barge Haulers on the Volga* is an incredible picture, as is *Cossacks Writing a Letter to the Turkish Sultan*. There is also his marvellous portrait of a barefoot Leo Tolstoy.

Rooms 35–47: Late-19th-Century Russian Art

These rooms display the large number of contradictory styles that were fashionable in St Petersburg before the explosion of the avant-garde. These include Vasily Surikov, a master of the historical painting that was in vogue in the late 19th century. His portrayals of *Yermak's Conquest of Siberia* and *Suvorov Crossing the Alps* (Room 36) are particularly romantic, but the lifelike rendition of Cossack rebel *Stepan Razin* (Room 37) is undoubtedly his most evocative.

Rooms 48–49: Antokolsky's Sculptures & Folk Art

Mark Antokolsky's statues *Ivan the Terrible* and *Death of Socrates* are on display either side of a souvenir stand. From here you enter the Benois Wing to your right or continue straight ahead for the comprehensive account of Russian folk art, a really lovely display featuring everything from kitchen

ILYA REPIN

One of Russia's greatest artists, Ilya Repin was born in Chuhuiv, now part of Ukraine. Originally a member of the Wanderers, he outgrew the movement and went on to produce key works of Russian realist and populist art. His masterpiece, *Barge Haulers on the Volga*, an unrivalled portrait of human misery and enslavement in rural Russia, shows why the early Soviet authorities held him in high regard as a model for the Socialist Realist painters to come equipment to giant carved house gables. Room 49 is a long corridor devoted to the museum's history showcasing old photos and posters from past exhibitions.

Room 54: Repin

Room 54 features Repin's enormous rendition of the *Ceremonial Sitting of the State Council on 7 May 1901, Marking the Centenary of Its Foundation*. Around the walls are individual portraits of its members.

Rooms 66–71: Early-20th-Century Art

Room 66 is the home of the father of modern Russian art, Mikhail Vrubel (1856–1910). Some of his ground-breaking works include *Epic Hero (Bogatyr)* and *Flying Demon*. Rooms 67 to 71 include works by an array of important early-20th-century painters including Kuzma Petrov-Vodkin, Nikolai Sapunin, Mikhail Nesterov and Boris Kustodiev, whose *Merchant's Wife at Tea* is perhaps the most well-known picture here.

Rooms 72–78: Russian Avant-Garde Painting

Between 1905 and 1917, the Russian art world experienced an explosion of creative inspiration that defied the stylistic categorisation that had existed before. Room 72 is home to Nathan Altman's gorgeous, semi-cubist *Portrait of the Poetess Anna Akhmatova*, painted in 1914, and it remains one of his most famous works even though Akhmatova apparently didn't care for it herself. In the same room is Altman's striking *Self Portrait* (1911). Room 74 contains primitivist paintings by artist couple Natalya Goncharova and Mikhail Larionov.

Futurism and suprematism, including works by Malevich – *Torso, Red Square (Painterly Realism of a Peasant Woman in Two Dimensions)* and *Black Square* – can be found in Rooms 75 to 76. Room 77 is devoted to constructivism and features works by Alexander Rodchenko and Vladimir Lebedev. Room 78 displays the bright, ethereal work of Pavel Filonov.

Room 79: Kuzma Petrov-Vodkin

Spanning two centuries and surviving the Russian Revolution, Kuzma Petrov-Vodkin (1878–1939) was a unique painter. His work conveys a dreamlike atmosphere, much of it with homoerotic overtones. See *Mother of God* (1914–15) and another *Portrait of Anna Akhmatova* (1922).

Rooms 80–81: Early Soviet Art

Most paintings from the Stalin era may have been censored beyond meaning, but there are some interesting portraits of daily life here, such as Alexander Samokhvalov's *Militarised Komsomol* (1932–33) and various pictures from WWII showing heroic resistance and national unity.

Rooms 82–86: Late Soviet Art

With Stalin gone and the 'thaw' under way in the 1950s, Soviet art recovered somewhat from the severity of socialist realism. Idealised images of rural life and peasants still feature very strongly, however. Look for Alexander and Pyotr Smolin's *Polar Explorers* (Room 83), a good example of the new Severe Style, and Dmitry Zhilinsky's *Under the Old Apple Tree*, showing three generations of a family.

Rooms 87–94: Applied & Decorative Arts

Works in these galleries range from a beautifully glazed ceramic fireplace by Mikhail Vrubel and other art nouveau–inspired pieces to Soviet-era textiles porcelain and textile printed with ingenous patterns made out of tiny tractors or planes.

TOP SIGHT
CHURCH ON THE SPILLED BLOOD

This is St Petersburg's most elaborate church, with a classic Russian Orthodox exterior and interior decorated with some 7000 sq metres of mosaics. Officially called the Church of the Resurrection of Christ, its far more striking colloquial name references the assassination attempt on Tsar Alexander II here in 1881.

Restored Beauty

Designed by architect AA Parland and the archimandrite Ignaty (a rector of the Troitse-Sergievsky Monastery), the church incorporates elements of 18th-century Russian architecture from Moscow and Yaroslavl, and is so lavish it took 24 years to build and went over budget by 1 million roubles – an enormous sum for the times. The candy-cake structure was consecrated in 1907 in memory of reformist Tsar Alexander II.

Decades of abuse and neglect during the Soviet era ended in the 1970s when restoration began. When the doors re-opened 27 years later on what is now a museum, visitors were astounded by the spectacular mosaics covering the walls and ceilings. Designs came from top artists of the day including Victor Vasnetsov, Mikhail Nesterov and Andrey Ryabushkin.

In the western apse, the assassination spot is marked by a canopy made of rhodonite and jasper. Near the exit is a small exhibit of photos showing parts of the restoration process.

The Exterior

The superbly polychromatic exterior of this Russian Revival marvel is unique in the city. The 20 granite plaques on the facade record, in gold letters, the main events of Alexander's reign. The mosaic panels about halfway up detail scenes from the New Testament, and the 144 mosaic coats of arms each represent the provinces, regions and towns of the Russian Empire of Alexander's time.

DON'T MISS...

➡ Taking a photo from the footbridge

➡ Canopy marking the assassination spot

➡ The mosaic murals

➡ The 20 granite plaques on the outside

PRACTICALITIES

➡ Церковь Спаса на Крови

➡ Map p256

➡ http://cathedral.ru

➡ Konyushennaya pl

➡ adult/student R250/150

➡ ⏱10.30am-6pm Thu-Tue

➡ Ⓜ Nevsky Prospekt

ST ISAAC'S CATHEDRAL

Named after St Isaac of Dalmatia, on whose feast day Peter the Great was born, this is one of the largest domed buildings in the world. Most people bypass the museum to climb the 262 steps to the *kolonnada* (colonnade) around the drum of the dome. The outlook to the four corners of the city is superb.

Controversial Design

French designer Auguste Montferrand began designing the cathedral in 1818, despite the fact that he was no architect. Local architects were outraged at the foreign upstart's commission and were quick to point out (correctly) a number of technical flaws in the plan.

The cathedral took so long to build (until 1858) that Nicholas I was able to insist on an even more grandiose structure than Montferrand had originally planned. More than 100kg of gold leaf was used to cover the 21.8m-high dome alone, while the huge granite pillars on the building's facade each weigh over 120 tonnes. There's a statue of Montferrand holding a model of the cathedral on the west facade, although Nicholas I denied the architect his dying wish, to be buried here, considering it too high an honour for a mere artisan.

Interior Decoration

The cathedral's lavish interior is decorated with 600 sq metres of mosaics, 16,000kg of malachite, 14 types of marble and an 816-sq-metre ceiling painting by Karl Bryullov. Look out for some interesting photographs of the cathedral throughout its history, including one of the park outside being used to grow cabbages during the Nazi blockade. Since 1990, after a 62-year gap, services have been held here on major religious holidays even though St Isaac's is officially classed as a museum.

DON'T MISS...

➡ Views from the dome
➡ Lavish interiors
➡ Display of historic photos
➡ Statue of Montferrand

PRACTICALITIES

➡ Isaakievsky Sobor
➡ Map p256
➡ www.cathedral.ru
➡ Isaakievskaya pl
➡ cathedral adult/ student R250/150, colonnade R150
➡ ⊙10.30am-6pm Thu-Tue, cathedral closed Wed, colonade 1st & 3rd Wed
➡ ⓂAdmiralteyskaya

👁 SIGHTS

HERMITAGE   MUSEUM
See p54.

GENERAL STAFF BUILDING   MUSEUM
See p68.

RUSSIAN MUSEUM   MUSEUM
See p70.

CHURCH ON THE SPILLED BLOOD   CHURCH
See p77.

ST ISAAC'S CATHEDRAL   MUSEUM
See left.

PALACE SQUARE   SQUARE
Map p256 (Дворцовая пл; Ⓜ Admiralteyskaya)
This vast expanse is simply one of the most striking squares in the world, still redolent of imperial grandeur almost a century after the end of the Romanov dynasty. For the most amazing first impression, walk from Nevsky pr, up Bolshaya Morskaya ul and under the triumphal arch.

In the centre of the square, the 47.5m **Alexander Column** was designed in 1834 by Montferrand. Named after Alexander I, it commemorates the 1812 victory over Napoleon.

On windy days, contemplate that the pillar is held on its pedestal by gravity alone!

The square's northern end is capped by the **Winter Palace** (Zimny Dvorets), a rococo profusion of columns, windows and recesses, topped by rows of larger-than-life statues. A residence of tsars from 1762 to 1917, it's now the largest part of the Hermitage (p54).

Curving an incredible 580m around the south side of the square is the Carlo Rossi–designed **General Staff Building** completed in 1829. The east wing (p68) now houses a branch of the Hermitage while the west wing is the headquarters of the Western Military District. The two great blocks are joined by a triumphal arch over Bolshaya Morskaya ul, topped by the *Chariot of Glory* by sculptors Stepan Pimenov and Vasily Demuth-Malinovsky, another monument to the Napoleonic Wars.

KAZAN CATHEDRAL   CHURCH
Map p256 (Казанский собор; http://kazansky-spb.ru; Kazanskaya pl 2; ⊘8.30am-7.30pm; Ⓜ Nevsky Prospekt) **FREE** This neoclassical cathedral, partly modelled on St Peter's in Rome, was commissioned by Tsar Paul shortly before he was murdered in a coup. Its 111m-long colonnaded arms reach out towards Nevsky pr, encircling a garden studded with statues.

Inside, the cathedral is dark and traditionally orthodox, with a daunting 80m-high dome. There is usually a queue of believers waiting to kiss the icon of Our Lady of Kazan, a copy of one of Russia's most important icons.

Look for the victorious Napoleonic War field marshal Mikhail Kutuzov (whose remains are buried inside the cathedral) and his friend and aide Mikhail Barclay de Tolly.

The cathedral's design reflects Paul's eccentric desire to unite Catholicism and Orthodoxy in a kind of 'super-Christianity' as well as his fascination with the Knights of Malta, of which he was a member.

STROGANOV PALACE   MUSEUM
Map p256 (Строгановский дворец; www.rusmuseum.ru; Nevsky pr 17; adult/student R300/150; ⊘10am-6pm Wed & Fri-Mon, 1-9pm Thu; Ⓜ Nevsky Prospekt) One of the city's loveliest baroque exteriors, the salmon pink Stroganov Palace was designed by court favourite Bartolomeo Rastrelli in 1753 for one of the city's leading aristocratic families. The building has been superbly

---

WITNESS TO HISTORY

Palace Sq has been the location for some of the most dramatic moments in St Petersburg's history. On Bloody Sunday (9 January 1905), tsarist troops fired on workers who were peaceably gathered in the square, sparking the 1905 revolution. And it was across Dvortsovaya pl that the storming of the Winter Palace took place during the 1917 October Revolution, an event re-enacted by Lenin and thousands of Red Guards in 1920 and later filmed in 1927 for Sergei Eisentstein's *October,* commissioned by the government to celebrate the 10th anniversary of the Bolshevik Revolution.

restored by the Russian Museum, and you can visit the impressive state rooms upstairs, where the Arabesque Dining Room, the Mineralogical Study and the Rastrelli Hall, with its vast frieze ceiling, are the obvious highlights.

Famously, the Stroganov's chef created here a beef dish served in a sour cream and mushroom sauce that became known to the world as 'beef stroganoff'.

MARBLE PALACE   PALACE

Map p256 (Мраморный дворец; www.rusmuseum.ru; Millionnaya ul 5; adult/student R350/150; ⊙10am-6pm Mon, Wed & Fri-Sun, 1-9pm Thu; MNevsky Prospekt) This branch of the Russian Museum features temporary exhibitions of contemporary art and a permanent display of paintings from the Ludwig Museum in Cologne that includes works by Picasso, Warhol, Basquiat and Liechtenstein. The palace, designed by Antonio Rinaldi, gets its name from the 36 kinds of marble used in its construction. Highlights include the Gala Staircase, made of subtly changing grey Urals marble; and the impressive Marble Hall, with walls of lapis lazuli and marble in a range of colours from yellow to pink.

Built between 1768 and 1785, the palace was a gift from Catherine the Great to Grigory Orlov for suppressing a Moscow rebellion. Outside it stands the equestrian statue of Alexander III.

MIKHAILOVSKY CASTLE   MUSEUM

Map p256 (Михайловский замок; www.rusmuseum.ru; Sadovaya ul 2; adult/student R300/150; ⊙10am-6pm Wed & Fri-Sun, 10am-5pm Mon, 1-9pm Thu; MGostiny Dvor) A branch of the Russian Museum, the castle is worth visiting for its temporary exhibitions, permanent display of art by foreigners working in Russia in the 18th and early 19th centuries as well as a few finely restored state rooms, including the lavish burgundy throne room of Tsar Paul I's wife Maria Fyodorovna.

Rastrelli's original fairy-tale wooden palace for Empress Elizabeth was knocked down in the 1790s to make way for this bulky edifice, a bizarre take on a medieval castle, quite unlike any other building in the city.

The son of Catherine the Great, Tsar Paul I, was born in the wooden palace and he wanted his own residence on the same spot. He specified a defensive moat as he (quite rightly) feared assassination. But this erratic, cruel tsar only got 40 days in his new abode before he was suffocated in his bedroom in 1801.

In 1823 the palace became a military engineering school (hence its Soviet-era name, Engineer's Castle, or Inzhenerny Zamok), whose most famous pupil was Fyodor Dostoevsky.

SUMMER GARDEN   PARK

Map p256 (Летний сад; ☎812-314 0374; nab reki Moyki; tours per group R1200; ⊙10am-10pm May-Sep, to 8pm Oct-Mar, closed Apr.; MGostiny Dvor) FREE Central St Petersburg's loveliest and oldest park, the Summer Garden can be entered either at the northern Neva or southern Moyka end. Early-18th-century architects designed the garden in a Dutch baroque style, following a geometric plan, with fountains, pavilions and sculptures studding the grounds. The ornate cast-iron fence with the granite posts was a later addition, built between 1771 and 1784.

MONUMENT TO ALEXANDER III

'I don't care about politics. I simply depicted one animal on another,' said sculptor Paolo Trubetskoy defending his equestrian statue of Alexander III when it was unveiled in 1909. Originally erected on pl Vosstaniya, the unflattering giant bronze of the stout, unpopular tsar caused a scandal among St Petersburg society, who were divided on its artistic merits. Alexander's son Nicholas II considered shipping it off to Irkutsk, but when rumours started that he wanted to send his dad into Siberian exile, he changed his mind.

In 1937 the statue was removed from pl Vosstaniya and sent to languish in an interior courtyard of the Russian Museum. In post-communist Russia, when the Marble Palace ceased to house the Lenin Museum, the statue was moved to the forecourt there, replacing Lenin's armoured car (which now can be seen at the Artillery Museum; p148).

REMEMBERING THE DECEMBRISTS

The square on which the Bronze Horseman statue of Peter the Great stands has two names. City maps list it as Senatskaya pl after the monumental Senate and Synod Buidling on the west side. However, it's also commonly known as pl Dekabristov (Decembrists' Sq) after the first attempt at a Russian revolution: the Decembrists' Uprising which occurred here on 14 December 1825.

The Decembrists were young officers who were inspired by radical ideas from France during the Napoleonic campaigns and wanted to introduce constitutional monarchy. Ineptly, they set up their protest on the same day as the swearing-in ceremony of the new tsar, Nicholas I. After repeated attempts by Nicholas' ministers to reason with the rebels, they were fired upon. Many officers and bystanders died as a result. Most of the leaders later ended up on the gallows or in Siberia.

The gardens functioned as a private retreat for Peter the Great (his modest **Summer Palace**, currently closed for renovations, is here) before becoming a strolling place for St Petersburg's 19th-century leisured classes. Only in the 20th century were commoners admitted.

There's a small museum in the garden, devoted to the few archaeological finds discovered during the garden's recent restoration.

BRONZE HORSEMAN   MONUMENT

Map p256 (Senatskaya pl; MSadovaya) The most famous statue of Peter the Great was immortalised as the Bronze Horseman in the epic poem by Alexander Pushkin. With his horse (representing Russia) rearing above the snake of treason, Peter's enormous statue was sculpted over 12 years for Catherine the Great by Frenchman Etienne Falconet. Its inscription reads 'To Peter I from Catherine II – 1782'.

Many have read significance into Catherine's linking of her own name with that of the city's founder: she had no legitimate claim to the throne and this statue is sometimes seen as her attempt to formalise the link (philosophical, if not hereditary) between the two monarchs. The significance of the inscription in both Latin and Cyrillic alphabets would not have been lost on the city's population, which was still in the process of Westernisation during Catherine's reign.

Despite completing his lifework here, Falconet departed Russia a bitter, angry man. Years of arguing with the head of the Academy of Fine Arts over the finer details of the sculpture had taken its toll, and he didn't even bother staying for the unveiling.

It's tradition for local newlyweds to be photographed here after their weddings, so expect to see plenty of jolly wedding parties.

RUSSIAN MUSEUM OF
ETHNOGRAPHY   MUSEUM

Map p256 (Российский Этнографический музей; ☑812-570 5421; www.ethnomuseum.ru; Inzhenernaya ul 4/1; adult/student R350/150, treasure room R250; ⊗10am-6pm Wed-Sun, to 9pm Tue; MGostiny Dvor) This excellent museum displays the traditional crafts, customs and beliefs of more than 150 cultures that make up Russia's fragile ethnic mosaic. It's a marvellous collection with particularly strong sections on the Jews of Russia, Transcaucasia and Central Asia, including rugs and two full-size yurts (nomads' portable tent-houses). Galleries are accessed either side of the magnificent 1000-sq-metre Marble Hall, flanked by rows of pink Karelian-marble columns, in which events and concerts are held.

You need to buy an extra ticket to view the treasure room, which has some great weapons and rare devotional objects.

WINTER PALACE OF PETER I   MUSEUM

Map p256 (Зимний дворец Петра Первого; www.hermitagemuseum.org; Dvortsovaya nab 32; admission R100; ⊗10.30am-5pm Tue-Sat, 10am-4pm Sun; MAdmiralteyskaya) Excavations beneath the Hermitage Theatre in the late 1970s revealed remains of the principal residence of Peter the Great, including a large fragment of the former state courtyard, as well as several suites of palace apartments. Some rooms have been restored to their appearance during Peter's era, complete with Dutch tiles and parquet floors, and are used to exhibit some of Peter's personal items from the Hermitage collection.

The cobbled courtyard has one of Peter's official carriages and a sledge. In the last room before you leave, don't miss the wax effigy of Peter made by Bartolomeo Rastrelli after the tsar died in the palace in 1725.

ADMIRALTY
NOTABLE BUILDING

Map p256 (Адмиралтейство; Admiralteysky proezd 1; MAdmiralteyskaya) The gilded spire of the Admiralty is a prime St Petersburg landmark, visible from Gorokhovaya ul, Voznesensky pr and Nevsky pr, as all of these roads radiate outwards from this central point. From 1711 to 1917, this spot was the headquarters of the Russian navy; now it houses the country's largest military naval college and is closed to the public.

The building itself was reconstructed between 1806 and 1823 to the designs of Andreyan Zakharov. With its rows of white columns and its plentiful reliefs and statuary, it is a foremost example of the Russian Empire style. Get a close look at the globe-toting nymphs flanking the main gate. Despite the spire's solid-`gold appearance, it's actually made from wood and was almost rotted through before restoration efforts began in 1996.

ALEXANDER GARDEN
PARK

Map p256 (Александровский сад; Admiralteysky pr; MAdmiralteyskaya) FREE Laid out from 1872 to 1874, these pleasant gardens, named after Alexander II, wrap around the Admiralty and are mentioned in Pushkin's famous verse novel *Eugene Onegin* as being a fashionable place for a stroll. They remain so, dotted with statues of Glinka, Lermontov, Gogol and other cultural figures, as well as a fountain that dates to 1879. Opposite St Isaac's Cathedral there's a very good **children's playground** within the garden.

MIKHAILOVSKY GARDENS
PARK

Map p256 (☉10am-10pm May-Sep, to 8pm Oct-Mar, closed Apr; MNevsky Prospekt) FREE Administered by the Russian Museum, these 8.7-hectare gardens are lovely and offer an impressive perspective of Mikhailovsky Palace. They are famous for their Style Moderne wrought-iron fence and gates, a profusion of metallic blooms and flourishes

---

◉ TOP SIGHT
FABERGÉ MUSEUM

Book by email at least five days in advance for one of the hour-long tours of the magnificently restored Shuvalovsky Palace, home to the largest collection of pieces manufactured by the jeweller Peter Carl Fabergé (including nine imperial Easter eggs) and fellow master craftsmen and women of prerevolutionary Russia.

Fabergé founded his jewellery business in St Petersburg in 1842. At its height he employed 700 people across many factories and in four shops in Russia and one in London. The tradition of tsars giving their wives jewelled Easter eggs began in 1885 when Alexander III commissioned the 37-year-old Fabergé to create a present for his Danish wife Maria Feodorovna. From 1897, the new tsar Nicholas II asked the jeweller to continue making the eggs for his mother, now the dowager empress, and his own wife Alexandra Feodorovna.

As dazzling as these baubles are they are just a prelude to a series of other lavishly decorated halls in which thousands of other pieces are displayed, including silver tea services, enamelled and jewelled cigarette cases and belt buckles, jade bowls and Russian Impressionist paintings. Look out for pieces by Fyodor Rückert, whose cloisonné enamel work is highly distinctive and beautiful.

DON'T MISS

➜ Imperial Easter eggs

➜ Fyodor Rückert cloisonné enamel pieces

PRACTICALTIES

➜ Map p256

➜ ☎812-333 2655

➜ www.fsv.ru/en/collection

➜ nab reki Fontanki 21

➜ tour R300

➜ ☉11am-7pm

➜ MGostiny Dvor

that wrap around one side of the Church on the Spilled Blood.

PUSHKIN FLAT-MUSEUM   MUSEUM

Map p256 (Музей-квартира А.С. Пушкина; ☑812-314 0006; www.museumpushkin.ru; nab reki Moyki 12; adult/student R250/100; ☺10.30am-5pm Wed-Sun; ⓂAdmiralteyskaya) Alexander Pushkin, Russia's national poet, had his last home here on one of the prettiest curves of the Moyka River. He only lived here four months, and died here after his duel in 1837. The little house is now the Pushkin Flat-Museum, which has been reconstructed to look exactly as it did in the poet's last days. You can only visit on a tour (run hourly on the hour), and these are given in Russian only.

On display are his death mask, a lock of his hair and the waistcoat he wore when he died.

ROSPHOTO STATE PHOTOGRAPHY CENTRE   GALLERY

Map p256 (Государственный центр фотографии (РОСФОТО); www.rosphoto.org; Bolshaya Morskaya ul 35; admission R100-200; ☺11am-7pm; ⓂAdmiralteyskaya) Showcases rotating exhibitions of photography, videography and other mixed media drawn from across Russia and around the world. It's definitely one of the best spaces for seeing contemporary photographic work in St Petersburg. Note the beautiful stained-glass windows on the stairwell of the handsome building the gallery is located in, which housed, prerevolution, an insurance company.

The gallery's well-stocked art bookshop and pleasant cafe are also worth a look.

ST PETERSBURG STATE MUSEUM OF THEATRE & MUSIC   MUSEUM

Map p256 (Санкт Петербургский музей театрального и музыкального искусства; ☑812-571 2195; www.theatremuseum.ru; Ostrovskogo pl 6; adult/child R200/100; ☺11am-7pm Thu-Mon, 1-9pm Wed; ⓂGostiny Dvor) Behind the Alexandrinsky Theatre, appropriately enough, you'll find this museum, a treasure trove of items relating to the Russian theatre including model sets, posters and costumes. A section aimed at children has great models of the Mariinksy stage and antique contraptions used to create effects like the sound of wind, rain and trains. There's also a graceful glass and metal automaton in the entrance hall that springs to life as people pass by.

KARL BULLA PHOTOGRAPHY STUDIO   GALLERY

&Map p256 (Фонд исторической фотографии им. Карла Буллы; ☑812-312 2083; www.bullafond.ru; 4th fl, Nevsky pr 54; admission R100; ☺10am-8pm; ⓂGostiny Dvor) Karl Bulla (1853–1929) was one of the city's most famous photographers and is immortalised in a life-sized **statue** on Malaya Sadovaya. Around the corner, his studio is still in operation at the top of this building where there's also a gallery of evocative black-and-white images of the city, shot by Bulla and his sons in the late 19th and early 20th century alongside photographic portraits of the likes of the Imperial family, Tolstoy and Chaliapin.

MUSEUM OF THE HISTORY OF POLITICAL POLICE   MUSEUM

Map p256 (Музей политической полиции; ☑812-312 2742; www.polithistory.ru; Gorokhovaya ul 2; adult/student R100/40; ☺10am-6pm Mon-Fri; ⓂAdmiralteyskaya) In the very same building that housed the tsarist and the Bolshevik secret-police offices, this small museum recounts the history of this controversial institution and includes one room that re-creates the office of Felix Dzerzhinsky, founder of the Cheka (Bolshevik secret police). Each of the remaining three rooms is devoted to the secret police during a different period of Russian history: the tsarist police, the Cheka and the KGB.

Exhibitions are heavy on photographs and documents, but some of them are fascinating. Some explanatory materials are available in English.

MARS FIELD   PARK

Map p256 (Марсово поле; nab Lebyazhey kanavki; ⓂNevsky Prospekt) Named after the Roman god of war and once the scene of 19th-century military parades, the grassy Mars Field is a popular spot for strollers, even though in the early 20th century it was used as a burial ground for victims and heroes of the revolution. At its centre, an **eternal flame** has been burning since 1957 in memory of the victims of all wars and revolutions in St Petersburg.

LUTHERAN CHURCH   CHURCH

Map p256 (☑812-312 0798; www.petrikirche.ru; Nevsky pr 22; ☺9am-9pm; ⓂNevsky Prospekt) **FREE** Tucked in a recess between Bolshaya and Malaya Konyushennaya uls is this lovely church, in the romantic-Gothic style, built for St Petersburg's thriving German community in the 1830s. It's distinguished by a four-column portico and topped with a discreet cupola. Concerts are also held here including free ones when the church organ is played.

There's an exhibition in the upstairs gallery about the city's German population and the church, which during Soviet times housed a swimming pool (the high diving board was placed in the apse).

BRODSKY HOUSE-MUSEUM   MUSEUM

Map p256 (Музей-квартира И.И. Бродского; www.nimrah.ru/musbrod; pl Iskusstv 3; adult/student R300/100; ⊙noon-7pm Wed-Sun; MNevsky Prospekt) This is the former home of Isaak Brodsky, Repin's favourite student and one of the favoured artists of the revolution (not to be confused with Joseph Brodsky, one of the least favourite poets of the same regime). Besides being a painter himself, Brodsky was also an avid collector, and his house-museum contains his collection of thousands of works, including lesser-known paintings by top 19th-century artists such as Repin, Levitan and Kramskoy.

ARMENIAN CHURCH OF
ST CATHERINE   CHURCH

Map p256 (Церковь Святой Екатерины; Nevsky pr 42; ⊙8am-6.30pm Mon-Fri, 9.30am-1.30pm Sat; MNevsky Prospekt) Continuing with a tradition of non-Orthodox churches being built on Nevsky pr, the Armenian merchant Ovanes Lazarian paid for the city's first Armenian church to be erected here in 1771. It was designed and built by German architect Georg Veldten and completed in 1780.

Restoration of the working church's ornate, intimate interior, which was destroyed during Soviet times, has recently been completed.

PLOSHCHAD OSTROVSKOGO   SQUARE

Map p256 (Площадь Островского; MGostiny Dvor) Created by Carlo Rossi in the 1820s and 1830s, this square is named for Alexander Ostrovsky (1823–86), a celebrated 19th-century playwright. An enormous **statue of Catherine the Great** (1873) stands amid the chess, backgammon and mah-jong players who crowd the benches here. At the Empress' heels are renowned statesmen of

the 19th century, including her lovers Orlov, Potemkin and Suvorov.

The most prominent building on the square is Rossi's neoclassical **Alexandrinsky Theatre**.

The square's west side is taken up by the **National Library of Russia**, St Petersburg's biggest, with some 31 million items, nearly a sixth of which are in foreign languages. To gain access for research purposes only you will need to bring your passport, registration documents for the city and either copies of your higher education certificates or proof of student status.

PLOSHCHAD LOMONOSOVA   SQUARE

Map p256 (MGostiny Dvor) Named after the great scientist Mikhail Lomonosov, this small square forms the southwestern end of the Carlo Rossi–designed ensemble and is the best spot from which to admire the ideal symmetrical proportions of ul Zodchego Rossi: the buildings on this street are 22m wide, 22m apart and 220m long.

The **Vaganova School of Choreography** at No 2 is the Mariinsky Ballet's training school, where Pavlova, Nijinsky, Nureyev and others learned their art.

From the square you can also admire **Most Lomonosova**, a stone drawbridge (no longer functioning) dating from 1787 with four Doric pavilions that housed the drawbridge mechanism.

PLOSHCHAD ISKUSSTV   SQUARE

Map p256 (Площадь Искусств; MNevsky Prospekt) In the 1820s and 1830s, Carlo Rossi designed pl Iskusstv (Arts Sq), named after the cluster of museums and concert halls that surrounds it, and the lovely Mikhailovskaya ul, which joins the square to Nevsky pr. There is invariably a pigeon perched atop the **statue of Pushkin**, erected in 1957, which stands in the middle of the tree-lined square.

KONYUSHENNAYA PLOSHCHAD   SQUARE

Map p256 (Конюшенная площадь; MNevsky Prospekt) Under wraps for restoration, the buildings along the north side of Stables Square is where the imperial court once kept its horses and transportation. Access is still possible to the **Church of the Saviour Not Made by Human Hand** (the classical building in the centre of stables with the Doric columns); this is where Pushkin's funeral service was held.

MUSEUM OF SOVIET ARCADE MACHINES

Giving new meaning to 'back in the USSR' this so-called **museum** (Map p256; http://15kop.ru; Konyushennaya pl 2; admission R350; ⊙11am-8pm; Ⓜ Nevsky Prospekt) is one of the city's most entertaining. Admission includes a stack of 15 *kopek* coins used to operate the 50-odd arcade machines in its collection which date to the Brezhnev era. Have great fun joining local kids and their nostalgic parents as they play games such as *Morskoi Boi* (Battleships), table ice hockey and *Repka*, based on a Russian fable about pulling a giant radish out the ground!

Hostels often have flyers offering a discount on admission. There's a pleasant cafe and at least once a month they host late-night DJ parties when ping-pong tables are rolled out to add to the fun.

The south side has been colonised by upmarket restaurants and bars, as well as the fun Museum of Soviet Arcade Machines, tucked away in the courtyard.

VORONTSOV PALACE HISTORIC BUILDING
Map p256 (Sadovaya ul 26; Ⓜ Gostiny Dvor) Opposite Gostiny Dvor, this palace (1749–57) is another noble town house by Rastrelli. From 1810 it was the most elite military school in the empire and is still used as a military school for young cadets. The palace is occasionally opened for concerts and such, details of which are posted out the front.

ANICHKOV PALACE PALACE
Map p256 (Аничков дворец; ☎812-314 9555; www.anichkov.ru; nab reki Fontanki; Ⓜ Gostiny Dvor) Built between 1741 and 1750, with input from a slew of architects, including Rastrelli and Rossi, the Anichkov Palace is now officially known as the St Petersburg City Palace of Youth Creativity. It's the location for around 1300 hobby classes and after-school clubs for over 16,000 children. There's a small museum inside, but it is only open sporadically for tours.

The palace was twice a generous gift for services rendered: Empress Elizabeth gave it to her favourite Count Razumovsky and later Catherine the Great presented it to Potemkin. This was also Tsar Nicholas II's favourite place to stay in St Petersburg – he far preferred the cosy interiors to the vastness of the Winter Palace.

AU PONT ROUGE HISTORIC BUILDING
Map p256 (nab reki Moyki 73-79; Ⓜ Admiralteyskaya) Dating from 1906–7, the one-time Esders and Scheefhaals department store has been beautifully restored, including the rebuilding of its cupola, destroyed in the 1930s so as not to clutter the view towards the Admiralty down Gorokhovaya ul. The glorious Style Moderne building, now dubbed Au Pont Rouge after the **Krasny most** (Red Bridge) it stands beside, is once again a department store.

🍴 EATING

The historic heart of St Petersburg is also its culinary heart: the range of options is generally excellent, though you'll do better to get off Nevsky pr itself, which tends to be pricey and of average quality (with a few notable exceptions). Keep an eye out for branches of the excellent bakery cafes Stolle and Bushe (p37) for cheap eats.

★MARKETPLACE RUSSIAN, INTERNATIONAL €
Map p256 (http://market-place.me; Nevsky pr 24; mains R200-300; ⊙9am-6am; 🛜✎; Ⓜ Nevsky Prospekt) The most central branch of this mini chain that brings a high-class polish to the self-serve canteen concept with many dishes cooked freshly on the spot to order. The hip design of the multi-level space is very appealing, making this a great spot to linger, especially if you indulge in one of the desserts or cocktails served on the 1st floor.

★JACK & CHAN INTERNATIONAL €
Map p256 (http://jack-and-chan.com; Inzhenernaya ul 7; mains R350; ⊙10am-midnight; 🛜; Ⓜ Gostiny Dvor) The name of the restaurant, a punning reference to Jackie Chan in Russian, neatly sums up the burger-meets-Asian menu at this fine and stylish casual diner. Try the sweet-and-sour fish and the prawn-and-avocado salad with glass noodles.

St Petersburg's Bridges

A city threaded with canals and rivers needs bridges. St Petersburg has made a virtue of this necessity, crafting bridges that are both practical and beautiful to look at. Here are a few of our favourites:

Anichkov most (Аничков мост)

Named after its engineer and featuring rearing horses at all four corners, the striking ornamentation of this bridge symbolises humanity's struggle with and taming of nature.

Bankovsky most (Банковский мост)

This charming footbridge is suspended by cables emerging from the mouths of golden-winged griffins. The name comes from the Assignment Bank (now a further-education institute), which stands on one side of the bridge.

1. ankovsky most **2.** Anichkov most **3.** Lviny most

Lviny most (Львиный мост)

Another suspension footbridge over Griboyedov Canal, this one is supported by pairs of regal lions, hence its name.

Panteleymonovsky most (Пантелеймоновский мост)

At the confluence of the Moyka and the Fontanka, this beauty features lamp posts bedecked with the double-headed eagle and railings adorned with the coat of arms.

1-y Inzhenerny most (Первый Инженерный мост)

While there is no shortage of adornment on the cast-iron bridge leading to Mikhailovsky Castle, the highlight is the Chizhik-Pyzhik, the statue of the little bird that hovers over the Moyka.

Troitsky most (Троицкий мост)

Opened in 1903, this Franco-Russian co-design is a Style Moderne classic. Like most other spans across the Neva it is a drawbridge, raised every evening during the shipping season at designated times to allow the passage of river traffic.

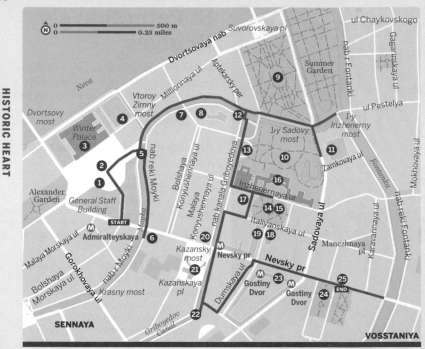

Neighbourhood Walk
Historic Heart

START DVORTSOVAYA PL (Ⓜ NEVSKY PROSPEKT)
END KUPETZ ELISEEVS (Ⓜ GOSTINY DVOR)
LENGTH 2KM; TWO HOURS

Approach ❶ **Palace Square** (p79) from Bolshaya Morskaya ul. Turning the corner from Nevsky pr, behold the ❷ **Alexander Column**, framed under the triumphal arch. Ahead is the ❸ **Hermitage** (p54); don't miss the colossal ❹ **atlantes** holding aloft the portico fronting the Large Hermitage.

At the ❺ **Moyka River** look northwest for a view of the Neva; to the south is the lavish ❻ **Stroganov Palace** (p79). Head north along nab reki Moyki to No 12, final residence of Russia's most celebrated poet and now the ❼ **Pushkin Flat-Museum** (p83).

❽ **Konyushennaya ploshchad** (p84) is dominated by the 18th-century court stables. Formerly the imperial guard parade grounds, ❾ **Mars Field** (p83) became a burial ground for revolution and civil war victims. South is the shady canal-side

❿ **Mikhailovsky Gardens** (p82) and southeast is ⓫ **Mikhailovsky Castle** (p80). Near the intersection of the Moyka and Kanal Griboyedova, ⓬ **Teatralny most** gives a spectacular perspective on the ⓭ **Church on the Spilled Blood** (p77).

Centred on a ⓮ **statue of Pushkin**, ⓯ **ploshchad Iskusstv** (p84) is ringed by institutions including the ⓰ **Russian Museum** (p70), ⓱ **Mikhailovsky Theatre** (p94) and ⓲ **Shostakovich Philharmonia** (p93), as well as the historic ⓳ **Belmond Grand Hotel Europe** (p180).

The Style Moderne ⓴ **Singer Building** (p96), on the corner of Nevsky and the canal, provides a contrast to the formidable ㉑ **Kazan Cathedral** (p79) opposite. Behind it, ㉒ **Bankovsky most** is the city's most picturesque bridge.

Crowds pour out of the metro station at ㉓ **Gostiny Dvor**. The National Library of Russia, Alexandrinsky Theatre and Anichkov Palace surround ㉔ **ploschad Ostrovskogo** (p84). Finish up at one of the cafes at the grand food hall ㉕ **Kupetz Eliseevs** (p96).

BIBLIOTEKA
INTERNATIONAL €

Map p256 (www.ilovenevsky.ru; Nevsky pr 20; mains R250-450; ⊙cafe/restaurant 8am-1am, bar 5pm-5am; ⊛; MNevsky Prospekt) You could spend the better part of a day here. Ground floor is a waiter-service cafe where it's difficult to avoid being tempted by the cake and dessert display by the door; next up is a more formal restaurant; and on the top floor there's a multi-roomed lounge bar with live music and DJs late into the night.

Also here are a couple of quirky stalls selling flowers and nutty nibbles, and a bookshop.

ZOOM CAFÉ
EUROPEAN €

Map p256 (www.cafezoom.ru; Gorokhovaya ul 22; mains R300-450; ⊙9am-midnight Mon-Sat, from 11am Sat, from 1pm Sun; ⊛◪▣✦; MNevsky Prospekt) A perennially popular cafe (expect to wait for a table at peak times) with a funky feel and an interesting menu, ranging from Japanese-style chicken in teriyaki sauce to potato pancakes with salmon and cream cheese. Well-stocked bookshelves, a range of board games and adorable cuddly toys encourage lingering.

SOUP VINO
MEDITERRANEAN €

Map p256 (◪812-312 7690; www.supvino.ru; Kazanskaya ul 24; mains R310-410; ⊙noon-11pm; ◪▣; MNevsky Prospekt) This tiny place is a foodie dream. Fresh daily specials such as artichoke salad and gazpacho complement a large range of freshly made soups. There are also several pasta dishes and delicious panini that can be taken away or enjoyed in the cute, wood-heavy premises.

PELMENIYA
RUSSIAN €

Map p256 (Пельмения; nab reki Fontanki 25; mains R300; ⊙11am-11pm; ⊛▣; MGostiny Dvor) All kinds of dumplings are on the menu here – Georgian *khinkali,* Uzbek *manti,* Ukrainian *varenyky* and of course the eponymous *pelemni* – prepared fresh in a pleasant, contemporary design space near the main boat-tour dock.

CHAIKI
ITALIAN €

Map p256 (Чайки; www.chaykibar.ru; nab reki Moyki 19; mains R350; ⊙noon-midnight; ⊛; MAdmiralteyskaya) Whitewashed brick walls and a lime green bike (seemingly a currently obligatory piece of decor for all local hipster joints!) set the tone for this relaxed basement cafe-bar which does excellent pizza and decent salads. Wash the food down with locally made sweet-cherry or ginger cider.

POTATOES WITH MUSHROOMS
INTERNATIONAL €

Map p256 (Картофель с грибами; http://vk.com/streetfoodspb; Gorokhovaya ul 12; mains R240-360; ⊙11am-11pm Sun-Thu, to 2am Fri & Sat; ⊛◪; MAdmiralteyskaya) This is a good spot for a good-value, light bite, such as its various *kapsalon* dishes (a Dutch-style meal in a tin bowl). The potato pancakes are excellent and there's a nice line in cocktails and wine too.

UKROP
VEGAN €

Map p256 (www.cafe-ukrop.ru; Malaya Konyushennaya ul 14; mains R200-300; ⊙9am-11pm; ⊛◪; MNevsky Prospekt) Proving that veggie, vegan and raw food can be inventive and tasty as well as wholesome, Ukrop (meaning dill) also makes an effort with its bright and whimsical craft design, which includes swing seats and lots of natural materials.

There's also a branch on **ul Marata** (Укроп; Map p260; ul Marata 23; ⊙9am-11pm; ⊛◪▣; MMayakovskaya).

CLEAN PLATES SOCIETY
INTERNATIONAL €

Map p256 (Общество чистых тарелок; http://cleanplates.ru; Gorokhovaya ul 13; R350-500; ⊙noon-2am; ⊛▣; MAdmiralteyskaya) Burgers, curry, borsch and burritos all get a look in on this stylish and relaxed restaurant's menu. The horseshoe bar and the inventive cocktail and drinks list are its prime attractions.

TROITSKY MOST
VEGETARIAN €

Map p256 (www.t-most.ru; nab reki Moyki 27; mains R200-300; ⊙9am-11pm; ⊛◪▣; MAdmiralteyskaya) This is the most central branch of the excellent vegie-cafe chain. It serves up the same excellent fare, including great vegetarian lasagne, in a cosy interior.

SAMADEVA
VEGETARIAN €

Map p256 (www.samadevacafe.ru; Kazanskaya ul 10; mains R200-300; ⊙9am-11pm; ⊛◪▣; MNevsky Prospekt) The food isn't the tastiest vegetarian fare you'll find in the city, but this self-proclaimed 'philosophical cafe' provides a blissful break from the sightseeing grind and has a daily schedule of yoga classes in the studio above.

STOLOVAYA NO 1 KOPEIKA
RUSSIAN €

Map p256 (Столовая No. 1 Копейка; Nevsky pr 25; mains R25-50, set lunch R99; ⊙24hr; MNevsky Prospekt) We doubt there are cheaper places to eat this well on Nevsky – no wonder the lines are long at this self-serve canteen in a cheerfully decorated basement. It's standard Russian dishes but all are freshly prepared and available around the clock.

PELMENY BAR
RUSSIAN €

Map p256 (Пельмени Бар; ✆812-570 0405; Gorokhovaya ul 3; mains R300; ⊙11am-11pm, from noon Sat & Sun; ⏰; MAdmiralteyskaya) No surprises for what this kitschy cafe special-ises in; its traditional dumplings (*pelmeni*) come stuffed with beef, pork, salmon or mushrooms. Choose a soup or a salad as a starter, and you've got a filling and good-value meal.

PIROGOVOY DVORIK
BAKERY €

Map p256 (Пироговой дворик; www.pirogov-dvorik.ru; nab kanala Griboyedova 22; pies R50-100; ⊙10am-11pm; MNevsky Prospekt) For those on a serious budget, this bargain-basement version of Stolle is ideal for a cheap lunch. Even the pie fillings are al-most identical to Stolle's, but for a fraction of the price (and charm!).

PYSHKI
DONUTS €

Map p256 (Пышки; Bolshaya Konyushennaya ul 25; donuts R12; ⊙9am-10pm; MNevsky Prospekt) Join the babushkas and families lining up for the greasy, sugar-dusted donuts and milky coffee (R18) sold at Soviet-era prices at this institution, in business since 1958. Little appears to have changed since that time – nor will it as local government has protected it as a landmark.

★YAT
RUSSIAN €€

Map p256 (Ять; ✆812-957 0023; http://eatinyat.com; nab reki Moyki 16; mains R500; ⊙11am-11pm; ⏰🐾; MAdmiralteyskaya) Perfectly placed for eating near to the Hermitage, this country-cottage-style restaurant has a very appeal-ing menu of traditional dishes, which are presented with aplomb. The *shchi* soup is excellent and it offers a tempting range of flavoured vodkas. There's also a fab kids area with pet rabbits for them to feed.

Hand-painted crockery items are avail-able for sale and make excellent souvenirs.

★GOSTI
RUSSIAN €€

Map p256 (Гости; http://gdegosti.ru; Malaya Morskaya ul 13; mains R500-600; ⊙9am-mid-night; ⏰; MAdmiralteyskaya) Whether you drop by for bakery treats and its homemade teas, or for a full meal of delicious and well-presented Russian classics you can't go wrong at Gosti. Friendly service, a comfy, cosy and colourful interior on two levels, and live piano music on some nights all add to its considerable charm.

ARKA
RUSSIAN, INTERNATIONAL €€

Map p256 (www.arka.spb.ru; Bolshaya Kon-yushennaya ul 27; mains R600; ⊙9am-6am; ⏰; MNevsky Prospekt) Sip your drink at the 13m-long bar that runs down to a double-storey restaurant at the rear. This sophis-ticated place keeps long hours and covers many bases, from a pastry and coffee for breakfast to a main meal (the Russian food is good) to house-made chocolates.

The same menu is served in the neigh-bouring **Teatr** (Map p256; Bolshaya Kon-yushennaya ul 27; ⊙9am-6pm; ⏰; MNevsky Prospekt), a serene whitewashed space named after the theatre that anchors the building.

MAMALIGA
CAUCASIAN €€

Map p256 (www.ginzaproject.ru; ul Kazans-kaya 2; mains R550; ⊙10am-midnight; ⏰🐾📱; MNevsky Prospekt) This stylish, bright and spacious cafe has wooden floors, deeply distressed walls and understated old-world furnishings. Its mouth-watering pictorial menu covers a wide range of dishes from the Caucasus.

YEREVAN
ARMENIAN €€

Map p256 (✆812-703 3820; http://erivan.ru; nab reki Fontanki 51; mains R500-1000; ⊙noon-mid-night; ⏰; MGostiny Dvor) Top-class Armenian restaurant, with an elegant ethnic design and delicious traditional food made with ingredients it promises are from 'ecologi-cally pure' regions of Armenia. Live tradi-tional music is performed after 8pm.

TERRASSA
EUROPEAN €€

Map p256 (✆812-937 6837; www.terrassa.ru; Kazanskaya ul 3a; mains R600-1000; ⊙11am-1am, from noon Sat & Sun; ⏰🐾📱; MNevsky Prospekt) Sleek and buzzing, Terrassa is cen-tred on its namesake terrace, which boasts unbelievable views (open only in warmer months). Inside you can watch the chefs, busy in the open kitchen, preparing fresh fusion cuisine that exhibits influences from Italy, Asia and beyond.

You'll usually need reservations to sit on the terrace, but you can just drop by and hope to get lucky.

KILIKIA
ARMENIAN €€

Map p256 (☑812-327 2208; www.kilikia.spb.ru; nab kanala Griboyedova 40; mains R200-600; ☺10.30am-6am; ▣; ▥Sennaya Pl) An excellent option for the late-night munchies, Kilikia is famous for its shashlyk, which is the real thing – deliciously seasoned, fresh meat served with a range of traditional Armenian dishes. There's live music between 8pm and 11pm each night.

CAFÉ KING PONG
ASIAN €€

Map p256 (www.kingpong.ru; Bolshaya Morskaya ul 16; mains R500; ☺noon-midnight; ▣▣▣; ▥Admiralteyskaya) This fun pan-Asian diner, occupying sleek and luminous premises with a retro-glamorous feel just off Nevsky, offers a large menu of very-good-quality dishes taking in dim sum, noodles, soups and rice dishes. There are also plenty of vegie options.

PATISSERIE GARÇON
FRENCH €€

Map p256 (www.garcon.ru; nab kanala Griboedova 25; mains R400-600; ☺10am-11pm; ▥Nevsky Prospekt) Convenient branch for the city's best-value French bistro-cafe, providing a relaxed Parisienne atmosphere to enjoy decent coffee, fresh bakes and light meals. There's another **branch** (Map p256; Malaya Morskaya ul 20; ☺10am-11pm; ▥Admiralteyskaya) a hop from St Isaac's Cathedral.

TANDOORI NIGHTS
INDIAN €€

Map p256 (☑812-312 8772; http://tandoorinightsspb.com; Voznesensky pr 4; meals R600-800; ☺noon-11pm; ▣▣▣; ▥Admiralteyskaya) One of the city's most authentic Indian restaurants offering a mix of traditional and modern recipes in a range of spice levels. It's a great choice for vegetarians.

MIX IN ST PETERSBURG
INTERNATIONAL €€€

Map p256 (☑812-610 6166; www.wstpetersburg.com; Voznesensky pr 6; mains R1000-2200; ☺noon-3pm & 7pm-midnight; ▣▣; ▥Admiralteyskaya) French cookery star Alain Ducasse is the man behind this slick and creative kitchen attached to the W Hotel. Sublime yet simple dishes tend to be French

in essence with an international or Russian edge. A nice touch is the vegetarian set meal, a great deal at R700/1100 for two/three courses. Service and atmosphere are both top-notch.

SINHOTO
ASIAN €€€

Map p256 (www.fourseasons.com/stpetersburg/dining/restaurants/sinhoto; Four Seasons Hotel Lion Palace, Admiralteysky pr; mains R1000; ☺4-11pm; ▣▣; ▥Admiralteyskaya) Classic dishes, with creative twists, from Singapore, Hong Kong and Tokyo (hence the SinHoTo name) are served in the Four Season's luxurious and contemporarily styled restaurant. A Singaporean chef is in charge, ensuring the chicken rice is excellent at least (we also liked the dumplings).

If this doesn't appeal, the hotel has a lovely winter garden for meals and afternoon tea and the gentleman's-club-like Xander bar, with a double-sided central fireplace – the perfect place to hole up on a wintery night.

BAKU
AZERI €€€

Map p256 (☑812-941 3756; www.baku-spb.ru; Sadovaya ul 12/23; mains R600-1600; ☺noon-midnight; ▣▣▣; ▥Gostiny Dvor) Baku's lavish decor – tiled walls, arched doorways and throw pillows – whisks you to Azerbaijan. Try Azeri shashlyk, traditional *plov* (rice and lamb spiced with cumin and raisins), as well as delicious *kutab* (thin pancakes stuffed with different fillings).

Service is deferential, and there's an upstairs room if you don't fancy the nightly live music downstairs.

🍸 DRINKING & NIGHTLIFE

★BORODABAR
COCKTAIL BAR

Map p256 (Kazanskaya ul 11; ☺6pm-6am; ▣; ▥Nevsky Prospekt) Boroda means 'beard' in Russian, and sure enough you'll see plenty of facial hair and tattoos in this hipster cocktail hang-out. Never mind, as the mixologists really know their stuff – we can particularly recommend their smoked old fashioned, which is infused with tobacco smoke, and their colourful (and potent) range of shots.

★RADIOBABY

BAR, CLUB

Map p256 (www.radiobaby.com; Kazanskaya ul 7; ⊘6pm-6am; MNevsky Prospekt) FREE Go through the arch at Kazanskaya 5 (not 7 – that's just the street address), turn left through a second arch and you'll find this super-cool barnlike bar on your right. It's divided into several different rooms, there's a 'no techno, no house' music policy, table football, a relaxed crowd and an atmosphere of eternal hedonism. After 10pm each night, the place becomes more a club than a bar.

★ZIFERBERG

ANTI-CAFE

Map p256 (http://ziferburg.ziferblat.net; 3rd fl, Passage, Nevsky pr 48; 1st/subsequent hr per min charge R2/1, max charge R360; ⊘11am-midnight Sun-Thu, to 7am Fri & Sat; 🛜; MGostiny Dvor) Occupying much of the 3rd-floor gallery of Passage is this anti-cafe with a range of quirky, boho-hipster decorated spaces, some intimate, others very social. There's an excellent range of activities to enjoy with your coffee or tea, from board games and movies to concerts by classical-music students, particularly on the weekends.

MIRACLE

ANTI-CAFE

Map p256 (☏812-570 1314; http://itsamiracle.ru; Moshkov per 4; 1/2hr R150/200; ⊘1pm-1am; 🛜; MAdmiralteyskaya) There's a very warm welcome at this charming pay-by-the-hour cafe. In summer there's outdoor seating in the courtyard as well as two comfy interiors. Check the website for details of regular events such as music concerts and talks.

SIDRERIA

BAR

Map p256 (http://vk.com/sidreria; Karavannaya ul 6; ⊘6pm-midnight Sun-Thu, to 2am Fri & Sat; 🛜; MGostiny Dvor) It's all about apples at this fun, slickly-designed bar with at least 10 different ciders on tap alongside many others in bottles. Sample ciders made not only from apples but also pears, cherries and blueberries. For a side snack it offers hot dogs and you can choose what music to listen to while you drink from its big selection of LP records.

PIFF PAFF

BAR

Map p256 (www.pifpafbar.com; nab kanala Griboyedova 31; 🛜; MNevsky Prospekt) It's a happening bar, it serves a mean burger and there's a hairdressers at the back – should you fancy a new 'do' part-way through the night. Oh, and there's a foosball (table football) table, if conversation flags and you fancy a bit of hand-twisting action.

DOUBLE B

CAFE

Map p256 (Дабл би; http://vk.com/doublebspb; Millionnaya ul 18; ⊘9am-10pm Mon-Fri, 11am-10pm Sat & Sun; 🛜; MAdmiralteyskaya) The young baristas are friendly and take their coffee brewing seriously at this serene hipster hang-out, with specially roasted beans from Ethiopia, Costa Rica and Kenya and methods including Aeropress and drip. They also do various artisan teas.

KOFYE NA KUKHNYE

CAFE

Map p256 (Кофе на Кухне; nab reki Fontanki 13; ⊘10am-11pm Mon-Fri, 11am-11pm Sat & Sun; 🛜; MGostiny Dvor) Go on, spoil yourself with one of the vegan-friendly muffins and other baked goodies at 'Coffee in the Kitchen', where there's a wide choice of the ways in which your cup of joe is prepared. It's a comfy space with a rainbow-coloured communal table in the back.

KOPEN

BAR

Map p256 (Bolshaya Konyushennaya pl 2; ⊘6pm-3am; 🛜; MNevsky Prospekt) There are several flash, face-control-operating clubs in this courtyard ('face control' is the common practice of denying entry based on appearance) – and then there's Kopen, which is much more democratic and fun. In warmer months patrons linger outside but the double-height interior is a fine hang-out too and has a DJ to set the mood.

BELOCHKA & MIELOFON

BAR

Map p256 (http://vkontakte.ru/belochkami; Bankovsky per 3; ⊘6pm-6am; MSennaya Pl) Cool, friendly and relaxed, this basement bar is a little tricky to find: walk past Friends Hostel into the courtyard behind it, take the first right and listen for music to work out the door. There are two low-slung rooms, one with a bar, busy dance floor and DJ, the second with the ubiquitous table football and plenty of comfy sofas.

MIXUP BAR

BAR

Map p256 (www.wstpetersburg.com; W Hotel, Voznesensky pr 6; ⊘1pm-midnight Sun-Thu, to 2am Fri & Sat; 🛜; MAdmiralteyskaya) The W's superb cocktail bar offers fantastic city views from its Antonio Citterio–designed lounge area to be enjoyed over top-notch libations. One floor up is the MiXup Terrace (May to September), an outdoor space with seating in cosy cabanas and views straight onto St Isaac's Cathedral.

BARAKOBAMABAR
BAR, CLUB

Map p256 (http://barbarakobama.ru; Konyush-ennaya pl 2; ☺6pm-6am; ⓂNevsky Prospket) In the summer months there's a great outdoor bar and dance floor, while inside there are a couple of cosy bars and a hookah lounge spread over two floors, both always full of beautiful young things. It's right at the back through the complex at Konyushennaya pl 2 – walk through the courtyard and continue to veer right.

MORE
CLUB

Map p256 (Мope; http://vk.com/thinkofsea; Malaya Morskaya ul 20; cover R300; ☺6-11.45pm Thu & Sun, 6pm-6am Fri & Sat; ⓂAdmiralteyskaya) The entrance to this barn-like club is tucked away, up the psychedelic aquarium-decorated stairs, to the left of the courtyard. It often has live-music gigs by bands and alt-rock singers at the weekends, for which there is a cover charge. DJs keep the vibe veering from chilled to pumped and dancing at other times.

MOD CLUB
BAR, CLUB

Map p256 (www.modclub.info; nab kanala Griboye-dova 5; cover R150-300; ☺6pm-6am; ⓂNevsky Prospekt) A popular spot for students and other indie types who appreciate the fun and friendly atmosphere, the groovy mix of music (live and spun) and added entertainment such as novus tables (a billiards-type game that is increasingly popular in Russia). Laid-back and great fun, this is a solid choice for a night out.

GOLUBAYA USTRITSA
GAY BAR

Map p256 (www.boyster.ru; ul Lomonosova 1; ☺7pm-6am; ⓂNevsky Prospekt) Loud, lewd and lots of fun, this is the coolest gay place in town. Take your pick from the main bar, where the uninhibited crowd is often quite literally hanging from the rafters, the *Priscilla, Queen of the Desert* karaoke bar, or the other upstairs bars and dancefloors.

Meaning 'Blue Oyster', the bar is named after the leather bar that featured in the 1980s *Police Academy* movies, but is as unlike it as vinyl is to velvet.

CENTRAL STATION
GAY BAR

Map p256 (www.centralstation.ru; ul Lomonosova 1/28; cover after midnight R100-300; ☺6pm-6am; ⓂNevsky Prospekt) Huge, with several bars and dance floors, as well as a men-only dark room, this is a stalwart of the St Petersburg gay scene. There are events on throughout the week, including after-hours parties (from 5am to 10am). Music is mainly at the pop and house end of the spectrum and there's usually plenty of topless eye candy gyrating at weekends.

BERMUDY BAR DISCO
BAR

Map p256 (Bankovsky per 6; ☺6pm-6am; ⓂSen-naya Ploshchad) Resurrecting the time-|honoured St Petersburg practice of dancing on the tables, this friendly bar does indeed become more of a disco than a bar after midnight. With low prices, good cocktails, table football and a trashy, fun atmosphere, Bermudy is an anything-goes destination if you want a late night.

POISON
KARAOKE

Map p256 (ul Lomonosova 2; ☺6pm-7am; ⓂNevsky Prospekt) While Datscha, Fidel and Belgrad around the corner on Dumskaya still pull in the crowds, the current hit among the many dive bars crammed into this shabby-chic block is this one, specialising in rock-and-roll karaoke. Lubricate your vocal chords with cheap beers (R120) and Pop Idol your way through song selections stretching from A-ha to Led Zep. There are a few other branches around town.

CAFE-BAR PRODUCKTY
CAFE

Map p256 (Продукты; nab reki Fontanky 17; ☺2pm-2am Sun-Thu, to 6am Fri & Sat; ⓂGostiny Dvor) Retro movie posters, mix-and-match furniture and a working jukebox provide the hipster wrapper for this relaxed cafe-bar serving both hot drinks and cool cocktails.

☆ ENTERTAINMENT

SHOSTAKOVICH PHILHARMONIA
CLASSICAL MUSIC

Map p256 (www.philharmonia.spb.ru; ⓂNevsky Prospekt) Under the artistic direction of world-famous conductor Yury Temirkanov, the Philharmonia represents the finest in orchestral music. The Bolshoy Zal on pl Iskusstv is the venue for a full program of symphonic performances, while the nearby Maly Zal hosts smaller ensembles. Both venues are used for numerous music festivals, including the superb **Early Music Festival** (www.earlymusic.ru).

MIKHAILOVSKY OPERA & BALLET THEATRE
OPERA, BALLET

Map p256 (☑812-595 4305; www.mikhailovsky. ru; pl Iskusstv 1; MNevsky Prospekt) While not quite as grand as the Mariinsky (p101), this illustrious stage still delivers the Russian ballet or operatic experience, complete with multitiered theatre, frescoed ceiling and elaborate concerts. Pl Iskusstv (Arts Sq) is a lovely setting for this respected venue, which is home to the State Academic Opera & Ballet Company.

It's generally easier and cheaper to get tickets to the performances staged here than those at the Mariinsky.

HERMITAGE THEATRE
BALLET

Map p256 (www.hermitageballet.com; Dvortsovaya nab 34; online tickets $160; MAdmiralteyskaya) This intimate neoclassical theatre, designed by Giacomo Quarenghi and once the private theatre of the imperial family, stands on the site of the original Winter Palace of Peter I. Book early if you'd like to see a ballet (usually classics such as *Swan Lake* and *Giselle*) in this intimate space. Access to the theatre is via an entrance to the Large Hermitage on Dvortsovaya nab.

The Russian Ballet Theatre company who perform here also have shows at the **Palace Theatre** (Map p256; Italiyanskaya ul 13; MGostiny Dvor) and **Aurora Palace Theatre** (Map p264; Pirogovskskaya 5/2; MPloschad Lenina).

GLINKA CAPELLA HOUSE
CLASSICAL MUSIC

Map p256 (☑812-314 1058; www.glinka-capella. ru; nab reki Moyki 20; MAdmiralteyskaya) This historic hall was constructed for Russia's oldest professional choir, the Emperor Court Choir Capella, founded in 1473. Originally based in Moscow, it was transferred to St Petersburg upon the order of Peter the Great in 1703. These days, performances focus on choral and organ music.

ALEXANDRINSKY THEATRE
THEATRE

Map p256 (☑812-710 4103; www.alexandrinsky. ru; pl Ostrovskogo 2; MGostiny Dvor) This magnificent venue is just one part of an immaculate architectural ensemble designed by Carlo Rossi. The theatre's interior oozes 19th-century elegance and style, and it's worth taking a peek even if you don't see a production here.

This is where Anton Chekhov premiered *The Seagull* in 1896; the play was so badly received on opening that the playwright fled to wander anonymously among the crowds on Nevsky pr. Chekov is now a beloved part of the theatre's huge repertoire, ranging from Russian folktales to Shakespearean tragedies.

BOLSHOY DRAMA THEATRE
THEATRE

Map p256 (BDT; ☑812-310 9242; http://bdt.spb. ru; nab reki Fontanki 65; MSennaya Ploshchad) The BDT, which will celebrate its centenary in 2019, has a reputable repertoire and is a good place to see Russian drama. Recently renovated, it is one of the city's grandest theatres, and its location on the Fontanka River is delightful.

KOMISSARZHEVSKAYA THEATRE
THEATRE

Map p256 (☑812-315 5355; www.teatrvfk.ru; Italiyanskaya ul 19; MGostiny Dvor) Named after Vera Komissarzhevskaya, a great actress who gained her reputation as leading lady in Vsevolod Meyerhold performances during the late 19th century, this theater is known for its modern treatment of classic plays.

PRIYUT KOMEDIANTA THEATRE
THEATRE

Map p256 (☑812-310 3314; www.pkteatr.ru; Sadovaya ul 27/9; MSennaya Ploshchad) This delightful theatre's name means 'the actor's shelter' and it does a pretty good job of fulfilling its role, providing refuge for some of the city's best up-and-coming directors and producers. It was founded by actor Yury Tomashevsky in the late 1980s, when the city turned over a defunct cinema that the group still uses.

KINO&TEATR ANGLETER
CINEMA

Map p256 (Кино&Театр Англетер; ☑812-494 5063; www.angleterrecinema.ru; Angleterre Hotel, Malaya Morskaya ul 24; MAdmiralteyskaya) This new cinema inside the Angleterre Hotel is one of the best places in the city to see movies in their original language, with subtitles rather than dubbing. The program, which includes several different features every day, focuses on current arthouse releases.

AVRORA
CINEMA

Map p256 (www.avrora.spb.ru; Nevsky pr 60; MGostiny Dvor) Opening in 1913 as the Piccadilly Picture House, this was the city's most fashionable cinema in the early years of Russian film, and it has retained its position pretty consistently ever since. Today most premieres (to which you can nearly always buy tickets) take place here. Foreign films are dubbed into Russian, though sometimes you'll find the odd subtitled one.

Renamed the more Soviet-sounding Avrora in 1932, it was here that a young Dmitry Shostakovich played piano accompaniment to silent movies.

DOM KINO
CINEMA

Map p256 (☑812-314 5614; www.domkino.spb.ru; Karavannaya ul 12; ⓂGostiny Dvor) One of the handful of cinemas in the city where you can see foreign films and some higher-brow Hollywood productions with subtitles, as well as arty Russian movies. It is also where the British Council holds its British Film Festival. Despite a refit, the whole place remains remarkably Soviet in a charming way.

DOM 7
JAZZ

Map p256 (http://vk.com/dom_7; nab kanala Griboyedova 7; ⓝnoon-midnight Sun & Tue-Thu, to 5am Fri & Sat; ⓂNevsky Prospekt) This low-key Russian restaurant and bar has very popular live jazz sets at 9pm and 11.30pm on Friday and Saturday, when it's practically standing room only.

DEMMENI MARIONETTE THEATRE
PUPPET THEATRE

Map p256 (☑812-571 2156; www.demmeni.ru; Nevsky pr 52; ⓂGostiny Dvor) Around since 1917, this venue under the arches on central Nevsky is the city's oldest professional puppet theatre. Mainly for children, shows are well produced and professionally performed.

ST PETERSBURG STATE CIRCUS
CIRCUS

Map p256 (☑812-570 5390; www.circus.spb.ru; nab reki Fontanki 3; ⓂGostiny Dvor) While Russia's oldest permanent circus complex (built in 1877) undergoes renovation of its roof for a couple of years, the shows will happen in a big top elsewhere in the city; check the website for details. Circus troupes and artists from other cities and countries perform shows here too.

 **SHOPPING**

⭐TAIGA
FASHION

Map p256 (Тайга; http://space-taiga.org; Dvortsovaya nab 20; ⓝ1-9pm; 🔊; ⓂAdmiralteyskaya) Like several other of Piter's trendy hangouts, Taiga keeps a low profile despite its

prime location close by the Hermitage. The warren of small rooms in the ancient building are worth exploring to find cool businesses ranging from a barber to guitar workshop. **8 Store** (Map p256; 8-store.ru; Dvortsovaya nab 20; ⓝ1-9pm; ⓂAdmiralteyskaya) is one of the best, a stylish boutique stacked with clothes and accessories by local designers.

Also check out **Books & More** (Map p256; www.facebook.com/booksandmore.ru/info; Dvortsovaya nab 20; ⓂAdmiralteyskaya), Sewing Corp for cute vintage and original designs, and the atelier of fashion designer Liza Odinokikh.

PERINNYE RYADY
ARTS & CRAFTS

Map p256 (Периные ряды, арт-центр; ☑812-440 2028; www.artcenter.su; Dumskaya ul 4; ⓝ10am-8pm; ⓂNevsky Prospekt) Scores of arts-and-craft stores can be found in this arcade in the midst of Dumskaya ul, amongst them Collection, with a wide range of painted works, several by members of the Union of Artists of Russia, and Pionersky Magazin, specialising in Soviet-era memorabilia, where you're guaranteed to find a bust of Lenin and colourful propaganda and art posters.

There's also a small exhibition space here (adult/student R300/200).

DOM KNIGI
BOOKSHOP

Map p256 (www.spbdk.ru; Nevsky pr 28; ⓝ9am-1am; 🔊; ⓂNevsky Prospekt) A stalwart of the city's bookshops, Dom Knigi is housed in the wonderful, whimsical Singer Building. On the ground floor you'll find lots of English-language coffee-table books that make good souvenirs.

STARAYA KNIGA
BOOKSHOP

Map p256 (Старая книга; Nevsky pr 3; ⓝ10am-7pm; ⓂAdmiralteyskaya) This long-established antique bookseller is a fascinating place to rummage around. The stock ranges from fancy, mint-edition books to secondhand, well-worn Soviet editions, maps and art (in the section next to the art supplies shop). It's a great place to look for an unusual, unique souvenir. Find it in the courtyard off the main road.

MILITARY SHOP
MILITARY

Map p256 (Товар для военных; www.voentorg spb.ru; Sadovaya ul 26; ⓝ10am-8pm; ⓂGostiny Dvor) In a city where there are men in uniform on every street corner, this is where

HISTORIC SHOPS OF NEVSKY PROSPEKT

Nikolai Gogol described it as 'Petersburg's universal channel of communication' in his story *Nevsky Prospekt*. Some 300 years on from its creation, little has changed. Nevsky remains the city's most famous street, running 4.7km from the Admiralty to the Alexandr Nevsky Monastery, from which it takes its name. Taking a stroll along it is an essential St Petersburg experience and is particularly special at dusk as the low light casts shadows and picks out silhouettes from the elegant mix of architecture.

The inner 2.5km to Moscow Station (Moskovsky vokzal) is the city's prime shopping drag and pulses with street life. Here you'll find baroque palaces, churches in a range of denominations, all manner of entertainments and above all shops, some historic in their own right. Following are the mains ones:

Singer Building (Map p256; Nevsky pr 28; MNevsky Prospekt) The former headquarters of the Singer sewing-machine company, which opened a factory in the Russian capital in 1904, is one of St Petersburg's most marvellous edifices. Designed by Pavel Suzor, and topped with a glass cupola and globe held up by two female sculptures, it also housed the American consulate and offices of other American businesses in the city. During Soviet times it was known as Dom Knigi (House of the Book) and there's still a good bookshop (p95) there now, as well as the pleasant **Cafe Singer** (Map p256; Nevsky pr 28; ⊙9am-11pm; ☏; MNevsky Prospekt), with superb views of the Kazan Cathedral, and the offices of vk.com, Russia's equivalent to Facebook.

Bolshoy Gostiny Dvor (Большой Гостиный Двор; Map p256; http://bgd.ru; Nevsky pr 35; ⊙10am-10pm; MGostiny Dvor) One of the world's first indoor shopping malls, the 'Big Merchant Yard' dates from between 1757 and 1785 and stretches 230m along Nevsky pr (its perimeter is more than 1km long). This Rastrelli creation is not as elaborate as some of his other work, finished as it was by Vallin de la Mothe in a more sober neoclassical style. Facing the arcade's northwest corner is the clock tower of the former Town Duma, the seat of the prerevolutionary city government. By the turn of the 20th century, Gostiny Dvor had reached its zenith and contained over 170 shops. Today, it has been eclipsed by other more luxurious and modern shopping complexes, but remains a major landmark and is useful for general souvenir shopping.

Passage (Пассаж; Map p256; www.passage.spb.ru; Nevsky pr 48; ⊙10am-9pm; MGostiny Dvor) Built between 1846 and 1848, this arcade has a glass roof spanning the entire block from Nevsky to Italiyanskaya ul. Dostoevsky wrote a story about a man who was swallowed by a crocodile in Passage, after a live crocodile was exhibited here in 1864. Look for the small exhibition area on the 1st floor with historical photos and other items related to the arcade. The handsomely restored ground floor has several good souvenir and antique shops. On the top floor (which in the early 20th century was a gay cruising site) you'll find the anti-cafe Ziferberg (p92) and youth fashion outlet **Freedom Store** (http://freedomstore.ru).

Kupetz Eliseevs (Map p256; http://kupetzeliseevs.ru; Nevsky pr 56; ⊙10am-10pm; ☏; MGostiny Dvor) In same year that the Singer Building was erected, further along Nev-sky wealthy merchant Grigory Eliseevs was busy having his own Style Moderne stunner constructed. Eliseevs Brothers was already a highly successful food emporium with several branches – this would be their flagship and little expense or design flourish was spared. Huge plate-glass windows gave glimpses into a dazzling interior of stained glass, chandeliers, polished brass and a giant pineapple palm. The building's exterior was no less lavish and was graced with four allegorical sculptures representing industry, trade and commerce, art and science. The building also included a theatre, which is still functioning. Recently renovated Kupetz Eliseevs is once again St Petersburg's most elegant grocery store, selling plenty of branded goods from blends of tea to caviar and handmade chocolates, as well as delicious freshly baked breads, pastries and cakes. Kids will love watching the animatronic figures in the window display and there are pleasant cafes on the ground floor and in the former wine cellar.

you can get yours (the uniform that is!). Buy stripey sailor tops, embroidered badges, big boots, camouflage jackets and snappy caps at decent prices. Look for the circular green and gold sign with 'Military Shop' written in English; the entrance is in the courtyard.

MANUFACTORY 812   FASHION

Map p256 (www.facebook.com/manufactory812; Bolshaya Morskaya ul 14; ⊙10am-8pm; ⓂAdmiralteyskaya) Buy a St Petersburg souvenir that's also a fashion statement. There's some neat graphic design at play on the youthful T-shirts, sweatshirts and hoodies sold in this small boutique.

KNIZHNAYA LAVKA PISATELEI   BOOKSHOP

Map p256 (Книжная лавка писателей; http://lavka-pisateley.ru; Nevsky pr 66; ⊙10am-10pm; ⓂGostiny Dvor) Apart from selling mainly Russian books, this long-established business also has posters, prints and reproductions of antique maps that make for interesting souvenirs, as well as T-shirts, mugs and bags that help the local charity Homeless.ru.

VINISSIMO   FOOD & DRINK

Map p256 (☑812-571 3405; www.bonvin.ru; nab kanala Griboyedova 29; ⊙noon-9pm Mon-Sat; ⓂNevsky Prospekt) With low ceilings and exposed brickwork, this little wine cellar is an atmospheric place to pick out a *bon vin*. There is no shortage of *grands crus* and pricey reserves if you are shopping for a special occasion, but head to the sale rack in the centre of the store for excellent bargain-priced French, Spanish and Italian wines.

YAKHONT   JEWELLERY

Map p256 (Яхонт; Bolshaya Morskaya ul 24; ⊙10am-8pm; ⓂNevsky Prospekt) From this building, Carl Fabergé dazzled the imperial family and the rest of the world with his extraordinary bespoke designs. Yakhont has no link to the Fabergé family, but it is carrying on the tradition anyway. This long, dark salon provides an impressive showcase of the work.

DLT   DEPARTMENT STORE

Map p256 (www.dlt.ru; Bolshaya Konyushennaya ul 21-23; ⊙10am-10pm; ⓂNevsky Prospekt) This historic department store is a temple to prestige fashion and beauty brands, all of them foreign. The interior, with twin atriums, is amazing but the only people you are likely to see are bored shop assistants and security guards – actual paying customers are conspicuously absent.

GRAND PALACE   SHOPPING CENTRE

Map p256 (Гранд Палас; www.grand-palace.ru; Nevsky pr 44; ⊙11am-9pm; ⓂGostiny Dvor) This palatial shopping centre is nothing less than grand and glittering. The biggest names in fashion may have moved on to Bolshaya Konyushennaya ul, but the Grand Palace remains home to Sonia Rykiel and Swarovski, not to mention the fanciest free toilets in the city.

APRAKSIN DVOR   MARKET

Map p256 (http://apraksindvor.piter-center.ru/; Sadovaya ul 30; ⊙10am-7pm; ⓂGostiny Dvor) There's been a market here since the 18th century. The gritty Dostoevsky-style warren of stalls is chaotic and offers mainly cheap clothes, shoes and leather goods, as well as food and snacks beloved by the multi-ethnic traders who work here. Look for a fab Chinese grocery and cafe on the upper floor of the Korpus 27 block.

🏃 ACTIVITIES

ANGLO TOURISMO   BOAT TRIPS, WALKING

(☑8-921-989 4722; www.anglotourismo.com; 27 nab reki Fontanki; 1hr tour adult/student R650/550; ⓂGostiny Dvor) There's a huge number of companies offering cruises all over the historic heart, all with similar prices and itineraries. However, Anglo Tourismo is the only operator to run tours with commentary in English. Between May and September the schedule runs every 1½ hours between 11am and 6.30pm. From 1 June to 31 August there are also additional night cruises.

The company also runs free daily walking tours starting at 10.30am and lasting three hours.

LAVRUSHKA   COOKING COURSE

Map p256 (☑812-942 4928; www.lavrushka.org/; nab reki Moyki 81; courses 1-3hr R1400-3100; ⓂAdmiralteyskaya) Offering courses in English in which you get hands-on experience at cooking Russian culinary classics including bliny, *pelmeni*, various soups and – of course – beef stroganoff. The kitchens are modern and the location handily central, so you can combine a few hours cooking here with other sightseeing.

Sennaya & Kolomna

SENNAYA | KOLOMNA

Neighbourhood Top Five

1 Seeing a dazzling Russian ballet or opera classic at the iconic **Mariinsky Theatre** (p101) or the impressive new **Mariinsky II** (p109) next door.

2 Marveling at the interiors and hearing tales of Rasputin's grizzly end at the impressive **Yusupov Palace** (p100).

3 Visiting perhaps St Petersburg's single prettiest church, the sky-blue and gold **Nikolsky Cathedral** (p104), surrounded by canals and charming gardens.

4 Reliving one of the most famous murders in literature in and around **Sennaya Ploshchad** (p102), where Dostoevsky set his classic *Crime and Punishment*.

5 Taking a journey into Russia's impressive maritime history at the superb **Central Naval Museum** (p103).

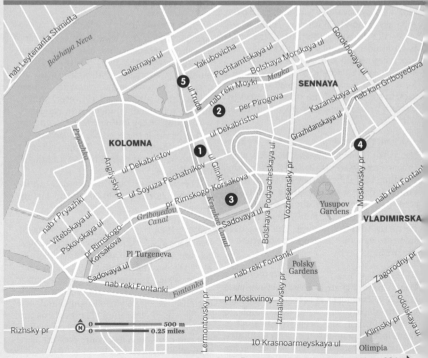

For more detail of this area see Map p264

Explore: Sennaya & Kolomna

Sennaya and Kolomna are two very different areas directly to the west of Nevsky pr, both wedged between the Fontanka and Neva Rivers. Sennaya, focused on the eponymous Sennaya pl (Haymarket), is one of the city's busiest commercial neighbourhoods and is also rather rundown. The poverty so vividly brought to life in Dostoevsky's *Crime and Punishment* may no longer be evident here any more, but you'll immediately notice that this is a poorer, scruffier part of town than the historic heart, with few of the embellishments.

Kolomna, named after the largest of the seven islands that make up the neighbourhood, is by contrast something of a sleepy village in the heart of the city. With no metro station and surrounded on three sides by water, it's a beautiful and relaxed quiet spot that also includes the world-famous Mariinsky Theatre and the abandoned island of New Holland, in the slow process of being transformed into an enormous cultural centre. A new metro station by the Mariinsky Theatre is promised, and this could certainly enliven what remains a bit of a backwater at St Petersburg's heart.

Local Life

→**Canal life** Sennaya and Kolomna are home to some of the prettiest stretches of canal in the city, well away from the crowds. Check out the gorgeous Kryukov Canal, the far ends of the Griboyedov Canal and the Fontanka River.

→**Free concerts** Check out the Maly Zal (small hall) at the Rimsky-Korsakov Conservatory (p110), where you'll often see fantastic-quality free concerts from students and alumni.

→**Transport issues** Get to know the bus and *marshrutka* (fixed route minibus) routes if you're going to be spending any time in Kolomna, where there's no metro and distances on foot can be very long.

Getting There & Away

→**Metro** Sennaya is served by the interconnecting Sennaya Ploshchad (Line 2), Spasskaya (Line 4) and Sadovaya (Line 5) stations, the city's biggest interchange, entrances to which are all on Sennaya pl. Kolomna is not served by the metro at all at the time of writing, though an extension to the Mariinsky is planned. Currently the nearest stations are those on Sennaya pl or Admiralteyskaya station in the historic heart.

→**Bus** Bus 3 connects the Mariinsky with Nevsky pr via Bolshaya Morskaya ul, while trolleybus 5 connects pl Truda with Nevsky pr via Konnogvardeysky bul.

Lonely Planet's Top Tip

Book ahead of time to see the ballet or opera performance you're interested in at the Mariinsky Theatre (www.mariinsky.ru), especially during the White Nights, when performances of popular productions sell out months in advance. You can book and pay for tickets on the website, and then collect them at the box office before the performance, which is much better than trying to find what's available once you're in town.

✕ Best Places to Eat

→ Mansarda (p108)
→ Romeo's Bar & Kitchen (p107)
→ Teplo (p106)
→ Khochu Kharcho (p106)

For reviews, see p105 ➡

☕ Best Places to Drink

→ Mayakovsky (p108)
→ Stirka 40 (p108)
→ Real Deal's Old School Bar (p109)
→ Dom (p106)

For reviews, see p108 ➡

⊙ Best Palaces

→ Yusupov Palace (p100)
→ House of Music (p105)
→ Old Yusupov Palace (p103)
→ Rumyantsev Mansion (p104)

For reviews, see p100 ➡

 TOP SIGHT
YUSUPOV PALACE

This spectacular palace on the Moyka River has some of the best 19th-century interiors in the city, in addition to a fascinating and gruesome history. The palace's last owner was Prince Felix Yusupov, at one time the richest man in Russia. Most notoriously, the palace is where Grigory Rasputin was murdered in 1916.

Amazing Interiors

The palace was built by Vallin de la Mothe in the 1770s, but the current interiors date from a century later, when it became the residence of the Yusupov family. The palace interiors are sumptuous and rich, with many halls painted in different styles and decked out with gilded chandeliers, silks, frescoes, tapestries and some fantastic furniture. Your visit begins on the 2nd floor, which features an amazing ballroom (the White Column Room), banquet hall, the delightful Green Drawing Room and the ornate rococo private theatre. The tour continues on the ground floor, where you will see the fabulous Turkish Study (used by Felix as a billiards room), the Prince's study and the Moorish Drawing Room, among many other rooms.

The Mad Monk

In 1916 Rasputin was murdered here by Felix Yusupov and some fellow plotters, who considered the Siberian mystic to have become too powerful. If you want to see the room where Rasputin's murder began (he was poisoned and shot to no avail, finally succumbing to drowning) you have to pay for an extra tour, which takes place at 1.45pm daily except Sunday. There are only 20 tickets available each day, so come in good time to secure a place. The tour is in Russian only. The admission price to the palace includes an audio tour in English.

DON'T MISS

➡ White Column Room
➡ Private theatre
➡ Oak Dining Room
➡ Rasputin tour

PRACTICALITIES

➡ Юсуповский дворец
➡ Map p264
➡ ☎812-314 9892
➡ www.yusupov-palace.ru
➡ nab reki Moyki 94
➡ adult/student/child incl audioguide R500/380/280, Rasputin tour adult/student R300/180
➡ ⊙11am-5pm
➡ ⓂSadovaya

MARIINSKY THEATRE

The Mariinsky Theatre has played a pivotal role in Russian ballet ever since it was built in 1859 and remains one of Russia's most loved and respected cultural institutions. Its pretty green-and-white main building on aptly named Teatralnaya pl (Theatre Square) is a must for any visitor wanting to see one of the world's great ballet and opera stages.

A Glittering History

The building you see today opened its doors in 1860, and was named in honour of Maria Alexandrovna, the wife of Tsar Alexander II. Since its inception, the Mariinsky has seen some of the world's greatest musicians, dancers and singers on its stage. Petipa choreographed his most famous works here, including *Swan Lake* and *The Nutcracker*, and the premieres of Tchaikovsky's *The Queen of Spades* and Prokofiev's *Romeo & Juliet* were held here. The Soviets initially closed the Mariinsky down, but as the renamed Kirov Ballet it became a major force in promoting the Soviet Union abroad, and is still the main reason that ballet and Russia remain synonymous worldwide.

Performance

The best way to experience the building as its designers intended is to see an opera or ballet here (see p109). Outside performance times you can wander into the theatre's foyer and maybe peep into its lovely auditorium. Private tours are sometimes available – ask at the main ticket office if these are running during your visit. As well as the main Mariinsky Theatre, there is also the brand-new, world-class Mariinsky II next door, a 2000-seat, six-stage theatre that marks the Mariinsky's arrival in the 21st century.

DON'T MISS

➡ Russian 'champagne' during show intervals
➡ White Nights Festival
➡ Small Mariinsky II performances

PRACTICALITIES

➡ Мариинский театр
➡ Map p264
➡ ☎812-326 4141
➡ www.mariinsky.ru
➡ Teatralnaya pl
➡ ⊙box office 11am-7pm
➡ Ⓜ Sadovaya

👁 SIGHTS

👁 Sennaya

More infamous than famous, this neighbourhood is named for the once derelict Haymarket (Sennaya pl), which was the centre of Dostoevskian St Petersburg. Sennaya was home to the poor workers and peasants who were new arrivals in the city, living in rat-infested basements and sleeping 10-to-a-room in shifts.

In honour of the city's tercentennial celebrations in 2003, Sennaya pl received a massive overhaul, being modernised and sanitised almost beyond recognition. But the chaos around the square has not subsided, and the alleyways and waterways to the north still evoke the very moodiness and social decay that Fyodor Dostoevsky portrayed so vividly.

SENNAYA PLOSHCHAD   SQUARE

Map p264 (Сенная площадь; Ⓜ Sennaya Ploshchad) Immortalised by Dostoevsky, who lived all over the neighbourhood and set *Crime and Punishment* here, St Petersburg's Haymarket was once the city's filthy underbelly. Indeed, until a much-needed facelift just over a decade ago, the square was overloaded with makeshift kiosks and market stalls, which made it a magnet for the homeless, beggars, pickpockets and drunks. Despite the square's big clean-up in 2003, Sennaya Polshchad retains a fundamental insalubriousness. Be on your guard walking around here at night.

The peripatetic Dostoevsky, who occupied some 20 residences in his 28-year stay in the city, once spent a couple of days in debtors' prison in what is now called the Senior Officers' Barracks, just across the square from the Sennaya Ploshchad metro station.

Alyona Ivanovna, the elderly moneylender murdered in *Crime and Punishment,* lived a few blocks west of here, at nab kanala Griboyedova 104. Her flat would have been No 74, in the courtyard on the 3rd floor.

DOSTOEVSKY HOUSES   HISTORIC BUILDINGS

Map p264 (Kaznacheyskaya ul 7; ☺ closed to the public; Ⓜ Sennaya Ploshchad) Dostoevsky lived in three flats on this tiny street alone. From 1861 to 1863, he lived at No 1. In 1864 he spent one month living in the faded red building at No 9, before moving to No 7. Here, he lived from 1864 to 1867 and wrote *Crime and Punishment;* indeed, the route taken by the novel's antihero Raskolnikov to murder the old moneylender passed directly under his window.

RASKOLNIKOV HOUSE   HISTORIC BUILDING

Map p264 (Дом Раскольникова; Stolyarny per 5; ☺ closed to the public; Ⓜ Sennaya Ploshchad) This innocuous house on the corner of Stolyarny per (called 'S... lane' in the book) is one of two possible locations of the attic apartment of Rodion Raskolnikov, protagonist of Dostoevsky's *Crime and Punishment.* Those who claim this is the place go further, saying that Rodion retrieved the murder weapon from a street-sweeper's storage bin inside the tunnel leading to the courtyard.

The house is marked by a sculpture of Dostoevsky. The inscription says something to the effect of 'The tragic fate of the people of this area of St Petersburg formed the foundation of Dostoevsky's passionate sermon of goodness for all mankind'. Other Dostoevsky connoisseurs argue that it would be more appropriate if Raskolnikov's attic apartment was located further down the street at No 9, which is otherwise unmarked.

RAILWAY MUSEUM   MUSEUM

Map p264 (Музей железнодорожного транспорта; www.railroad.ru/cmrt; Sadovaya ul 50; adult/student & child R200/100; ☺ 10.30am-5.30pm Sun-Thu; Ⓜ Sadovaya) This museum near Sennaya pl is a must for train-set fans and modellers. It houses a collection of scale locomotives and model railway bridges, often made by the same engineers that built the real ones. The oldest such collection in the world, the museum dates to 1809, 28 years before Russia had its first working train! There are free Russian-language guided tours of the museum every hour on the hour.

Look out for the fantastic map of Russia hanging above the main museum staircase showing all the train lines in the country, which almost makes up for the total lack of signage in English.

YUSUPOV GARDENS   PARK

Map p264 (Юсуповский сад; Sadovaya ul; ☺ sunrise-sunset; Ⓜ Sadovaya) West of Sennaya pl along Sadovaya ul you'll find the charming Yusupov Gardens, a pleasant park with a big lake in the middle. The flower-filled grounds are a popular place to stroll, sit and sunbathe. The building set back behind the gardens is the **Old Yusupov Palace** (Map p264), not to be confused with the Yusupov Palace on the Moyka River. The Old Yusupov Palace is closed to the public and is used mainly for official receptions.

TRINITY CATHEDRAL   CATHEDRAL

Map p264 (Троицкий собор; Izmailovsky pr 7a; ☉9am-7pm Mon-Sat, 8am-8pm Sun, services 10am daily & 5pm Fri-Sun; MTekhnologichesky Institut) The Trinity Cathedral boasts stunning blue cupolas emblazoned with golden stars. A devastating fire in 2006 caused the 83m-high central cupola to collapse, but it has been fully restored and now looks even better than it did before. Construction of the vast cathedral began in 1828, according to a design by Vasily Stasov. The cathedral was consecrated in 1835 and functioned as the chapel for the Izmailovsky Guards, who were garrisoned next door.

In honour of the Russian victory in the Russo-Turkish War in 1878, the memorial Column of Glory was constructed out of 128 Turkish cannons. (The present monument was erected on the north side of the cathedral in 2003: it is an exact replica of the original, which was destroyed by Stalin.)

The cathedral was famed for its immense collection of icons, as well as several silver crosses dating from the 18th and 19th centuries. After the revolution, most of these treasures were looted, the ornate interiors were destroyed and the cathedral was finally closed in 1938.

Trinity Cathedral was returned to the Orthodox Church in 1990, but the interior is decidedly bare, especially compared with its previous appearance. It was here that Fyodor Dostoevsky married his second wife, Anna Snitkina, in 1867.

⊙ Kolomna

YUSUPOV PALACE   PALACE
See p100.

MARIINSKY THEATRE   THEATRE
See p101.

CENTRAL NAVAL MUSEUM   MUSEUM

Map p264 (Центральный военно-морской музей; ☎812-303 8513; www.navalmuseum.ru; pl Truda; admission R250, camera R200; ☉11am-6pm Wed-Sun; MAdmiralteyskaya) Following a move to this beautifully repurposed building opposite the former shipyard of New Holland, the Central Naval Museum has moved into the 21st century and is now one of St Petersburg's best history museums. The superb, light-bathed building houses an enormous collection of models, paintings and other artefacts from three centuries of Russian naval history, including *botik*, the small boat known as the 'grandfather of the Russian navy' – stumbling across it in the late 17th century was Peter the Great's inspiration to create a Russian maritime force.

The real attraction here is the superb collection of model boats, some of which are simply extraordinary in size and detail. There's sadly little signage in English, so it's worthwhile booking a tour in English (R1500, book in advance) if you're interested in really understanding what you're seeing. The entrance to the museum is opposite New Holland on nab Kryukova kanala.

GRAND CHORAL SYNAGOGUE   SYNAGOGUE

Map p264 (Большая хоральная синагога; ☎812-714 4332; http://eng.jewishpetersburg.ru; Lermontovsky pr 2; ☉8am-8pm Sun-Fri, services 10am Sat; MSadovaya) FREE Designed by Vasily Stasov, the striking Grand Choral Synagogue opened in 1893 to provide a central place of worship for St Petersburg's growing Jewish community. Its lavishness (particularly notable in the 47m-high cupola and the decorative wedding chapel) indicates the pivotal role that Jews played in imperial St Petersburg. The synagogue was fully revamped in 2003. Visitors are welcome except on the Sabbath and other holy days. Men and married women should cover their heads upon entering.

Also on-site are the **Small Synagogue** (☉11am-4pm Mon-Thu, 11am-1pm Fri & Sun), the Jewish restaurant Lechaim and Kosher Shop (p110). In summer, the synagogue also hosts performances with a Jewish cantor and other musicians performing *chaaznut* and *klezmer* music. The synagogue organises English-language tours of the building, as well as longer tours of 'Jewish St Petersburg', all of which need to be organised in advance; see the website.

NIKOLSKY CATHEDRAL
CATHEDRAL

Map p264 (Никольский собор; Nikolskaya pl 1/3; ⊘9am-7pm; MSadovaya) FREE Surrounded on two sides by canals, this ice-blue cathedral is one of the most picture-perfect in the city, beloved by locals for its baroque spires and golden domes. It was one of the few churches that continued to work during the Soviet era, when organised religion was effectively banned. Nicknamed the Sailor's Church (Nicholas is the patron saint of sailors), it contains many 18th-century icons and a fine carved wooden iconostasis, though visitors are limited to only a small area of the church's interior.

A graceful bell tower overlooks the Griboyedov Canal, which is crossed by Staro-Nikolsky most. From this bridge, you can see seven other bridges, more than from any other spot in the city.

NABOKOV MUSEUM
MUSEUM

Map p264 (Музей Набокова; www.nabokovmuseum.org; Bolshaya Morskaya ul 47; ⊘11am-6pm Tue-Fri, noon-5pm Sat & Sun; MAdmiralteyskaya) FREE This 19th-century town house was the suitably grand childhood home of Vladimir Nabokov, infamous author of *Lolita* and arguably the most versatile of 20th-century Russian writers. Here Nabokov lived with his wealthy family from his birth in 1899 until the revolution in 1917, when they left the country. Nabokov artefacts on display include family photographs, first editions of his books and parts of his extensive butterfly collection, as well as rooms given over to temporary exhibits.

The house features heavily in Nabokov's autobiography *Speak, Memory*, in which he refers to it as a 'paradise lost'. Indeed, he never returned, dying abroad in 1977. Aside from the various Nabokov artefacts, there's actually relatively little to see in the museum itself, save for some charming interiors (don't miss the gorgeous stained-glass windows in the stairwell, which are not technically part of the museum, but staff will often allow you to take a peek), and the Green Dining Room, which was being renovated at the time of writing.

RUMYANTSEV MANSION
MUSEUM

Map p264 (Особняк Румянцева; www.spbmuseum.ru; Angliyskaya nab 44; adult/student R150/80; ⊘11am-6pm Thu-Tue; MAdmiralteyskaya) History buffs should not miss this oft-overlooked but superb local museum. Part of the State Museum of the History of St Petersburg, the mansion contains an exhibition of 20th-century history, including displays devoted to the 1921 New Economic Policy (NEP), the industrialisation and development of the 1930s, and the Siege of Leningrad during WWII. Exhibitions are unusual in that they depict everyday life in the city during these historic periods. Each room has an explanatory panel in English.

The museum is housed in the majestic 1826 mansion of Count Nikolai Petrovich Rumyantsev, a famous diplomat, politician and statesman, as well as an amateur historian whose personal research library became the basis for the Russian State Library in Moscow. The history of the mansion and its owners is fascinating in itself, and the few restored staterooms at the front of the house suggest that daily life for the Rumyantsev family was an opulent affair.

WORTH A DETOUR

MUSEUM OF RAILWAY TECHNOLOGY

Trainspotters should hasten to view the impressive collection of decommissioned locomotives at the **Museum of Railway Technology** (Музей железнодорожной техники; nab kanala Obvodnogo 118; adult/child R100/50; ⊘10am-5pm Wed-Sun Apr-Oct, 11am-4pm Nov-Mar; ♿; MBaltiyskaya), behind the former Warsaw Station, now an entertainment complex called Warsaw Express. Some 75 nicely painted and buffed engines and carriages dating back to the late 19th century are on display, as well as a mobile intercontinental nuclear-missile launcher that looks like the unlikely secret weapon of a 1960s Bond villain. This is a fantastic option for kids, though for some killjoy reason it's only possible to enter a couple of trains. There's full English signage throughout, though. To get here from the metro, turn right onto the canal and then right again just before you pass the former Warsaw Station.

RUSSIAN VODKA MUSEUM
MUSEUM

Map p264 (Музей русской водки; www.vodka-museum.su; Konnogvardeysky bul 4; admission with/without tour R350/170, unguided/guided tasting tour R350/500; ⊗noon-7pm; MᴀAdmiralteyskaya) This excellent private museum tells the story of Russia's national tipple in an interesting and fun way, from the first production of 'bread wine' to the phenomenon of the modern international vodka industry, complete with waxwork models and some very cool bottles. You can guide yourself through the exhibit, or be accompanied by an English-speaking guide who'll liven things up a bit. If you'd like to sample the exhibits too, take a **tasting tour**. There's an excellent restaurant (p108) in the same building, and if you eat there, you can get a discount on museum entry.

MANEGE CENTRAL EXHIBITION HALL
EXHIBITION HALL

Map p256 (Центральный выставочный зал Манеж; ☑81-314 8859; www.manege.spb.ru; Isaakievskaya pl 1; admission R100-300; MᴀAdmiralteyskaya) Formerly the Horse Guards' Riding School, this large white neoclassical building was constructed between 1804 and 1807 from a design by Giacomo Quarenghi. It now houses rotating art and commercial exhibitions, often featuring contemporary and local artists. Check the website to see what's on while you're in town. Opening hours depend on what's on.

NEW HOLLAND
HISTORIC BUILDINGS

Map p264 (Новая Голландия; www.newhollandsp.ru; cnr nab kanala Kryukova & Bolshaya Morskaya ul; MᴀSadovaya) This triangular island has been closed to the public for the majority of the last three centuries, and its structures appear to be little more than ruins at present. Its fortunes are slowly changing, however, and it has been taken over by the city authorities who are slowly transforming the island into an arts and entertainment centre. While the island remains closed at the time of writing, parts of it have been open over recent summers, so may be possible to visit during your stay.

In Peter's time, the complex was used for shipbuilding (its name refers to the place where he learned the trade). In the 19th century a large basin was built in the middle of the island. Here experiments were conducted by scientist Alexey Krylov in an attempt to build a boat that couldn't be capsized. In 1915 the navy built a radio transmitter here – the most powerful in Russia at the time – but it's been derelict and inaccessible ever since. If you walk by, look out for the impressive red-brick-and-granite arch, designed by Jean-Baptiste Vallin de la Mothe in the late 18th century, one of the city's best examples of Russian classicism.

In its new form, the island is expected to house exhibition spaces, a children's centre, educational facilities, shops, a cinema and even a hotel. Check the website to see if the recent summer openings (for concerts, markets, public art and sports events) are still ongoing before the island's completion, which is due by 2018.

HOUSE OF MUSIC
PALACE

Map p264 (Дом музыки; ☑812-400 1400; www.spdm.ru; nab reki Moyki 211; tour R350; MᴀSadovaya) This fabulous and fully restored mansion on the Moyka River belonged to Grand Duke Alexey, the son of Alexander II. The wrought-iron-and-stone fence is one of its most stunning features, with the Grand Duke's monogram adorning the gates. Tours of the house usually leave once or twice a week, but the dates vary and tickets often sell out in advance, so check the website. Another way to visit the interior is to see a concert here.

The palace was built in 1895 by Maximilian Messmacher, and each facade represents a different architectural style. The interior is equally diverse, and since renovation has housed the House of Music (Dom Muzyki), where popular classical concerts (R250 to R300) are regularly held in the building's English Hall. Guided tours are given only in Russian and German.

✕ EATING

✕ Sennaya

TESTO
ITALIAN €

Map p264 (Тесто; www.testogastronomica.ru; per Grivtsova 5/29; mains R250-500; ⊗11am-11pm; ⛭⏎⚹; MᴀSennaya Ploshchad) This pleasant little place is good value and yet takes Italian cookery very seriously. Choose from a wide range of homemade pastas and top them with your favourite sauce, whether tomato-based bolognese or a rich, creamy salmon sauce. A few options for soup, salad and pizza round out the menu, but the pasta is the main focus.

SUMETA
CAUCASIAN €

Map p264 (Сумета; ul Yefimova 5; mains R200-400; ⊙11am-11pm; ✎🚭; MSpasskaya) Even if you've never had Dagestani food, you'll see plenty of familiar Caucasian dishes in this friendly place, from Lula kebab (minced-meat kebab) to fried eggplant with garlic and walnuts in sour cream. The house speciality here is *khinkali,* a delicious, juicy meat dumpling. Try the pumpkin *chudu* (large pancake) or the selection of Caucasian wines for something new.

★KHOCHU KHARCHO
GEORGIAN €€

Map p264 (Хочу харчо; Sadovaya ul 39/41; mains R500-1200; ⊙24hr; 🛜✎🚼; MSennaya Ploshchad) This sparkling, friendly and capacious offering right on the Haymarket effortlessly outshines the generally dire offerings to be found elsewhere in this area. A delicious fully photographic menu of comfort food awaits, focused on Mingrelian (West Georgian) cooking, meaning that you can expect calorific *khachapuri* (cheese-stuffed bread), *khinkali* (dumplings), and of course the eponymous *kharcho,* a beef, rice, tomato and walnut soup.

This is the best thing that has happened Sennaya pl for years.

OH! MUMBAI
INDIAN €€

Map p264 (Per Grivtsova 2; mains R350-670; ⊙noon-11pm; 🛜✎🚭; MAdmiralteyskaya) Incense infused but pleasantly bright and popular with a young crowd who come here as much to drink as to eat, Oh! Mumbai provides a modern take on Indian food in a city with plenty of old-school, somewhat cliché-ridden establishments from the subcontinent. The menu includes curries, tandoors and a delicious selection of vegetarian options.

Service is very polite and staff speak English.

KARAVAN
CENTRAL ASIAN €€

Map p264 (Караван; www.caravan2000.ru; Voznesensky pr 46; mains R300-1000; ⊙11am-1am; 🚭; MSadovaya) Despite the kitschy decor (think stuffed camel in the corner), Karavan is a superb Central Asian restaurant with a lovely location overlooking the Fontanka River. Open grills line the dining room, giving an optimum view (and scent) of the kebabs that are on the menu.

It's not strictly Central Asian cookery on offer though, with shrimp grilled in cognac and seabass both on the menu. Service is attentive and efficient.

★DOM
RUSSIAN €€€

Map p264 (Дом; ✎812-930 7272; nab reki Moyki 72; mains R500-1500; ⊙noon-11pm Sun-Thu, 1pm-1am Fri & Sat; 🛜🚭; MAdmiralteyskaya) This magnificent addition to the local dining scene is housed in the former home of the Decembrist Ryleev, and what a house it is! All white tablecloths, polished wood floors and scattered objets d'art, it's rather like dining in the home of a wealthy friend. The contemporary Russian cookery is superb, and service couldn't be more attentive or polite.

Taking up the entire ground floor, the restaurant is divided into several dining rooms, a glorious library and a very smart bar. Sample dishes include pumpkin fritters with Siberian salmon roe, roast hare with stewed vegetables and deer fillet with warm pear, while the wine list is voluminous. This is an excellent choice for a thoughtfully prepared and beautifully presented meal in sumptuous surroundings.

✕ Kolomna

DEKABRIST
MODERN EUROPEAN €

Map p264 (www.decabrist.net; ul Yakubovicha 2; mains R300-500; ⊙8am-11pm; 🚭🛜🚭; MAdmiralteyskaya) A decent-value, modern and stylish cafe just moments from St Isaac's Cathedral, Dekabrist sounds like it might be too good to be true. The menu is simple but eclectic, and includes burgers, grilled salmon, pork schnitzel, felafel and a range of salads and desserts, while the two-floor space is comfortable and sociable, even if the lighting is borderline interrogatory.

★TEPLO
MODERN EUROPEAN €€

Map p264 (✎812-570 1974; www.v-teple.ru; Bolshaya Morskaya ul 45; mains R250-650; ⊙9am-midnight; 🚭🛜✎🚭; MAdmiralteyskaya) This much-feted, eclectic and original restaurant has got it all just right. The venue itself is a lot of fun to nose around, with multiple small rooms, nooks and crannies. Service is friendly and fast (when it's not too busy) and the peppy, inventive Italian-leaning menu has something for everyone. Reservations are usually needed, so call ahead.

The restaurant is full of unexpected props, from table football to a child's play room. Dishes come from all over the world and there's plenty of vegetarian choice, as well as breakfasts served daily from 9am to noon.

ROMEO'S BAR & KITCHEN
ITALIAN €€

Map p264 (www.romeosbarandkitchen.ru; Pr Rimskogo-Korsakova 43; mains R400-1000; ⊙9am-midnight; ⊜⏰📶; MSadovaya) This stylish Italian-run restaurant on one side of the charming Kryukov Canal offers a full menu of traditional Italian cooking, from its large fish selection to main courses such as osso busco with mashed potatoes and calf's liver with spinach. Ask for its pizza menu (R300 to R500), as it's separate from the main one. Breakfast is served daily until noon.

SADKO
RUSSIAN €€

Map p264 (📞812-903 2373; www.sadko-rst.ru; ul Glinki 2; mains R400-1000; 📶🚻; MSennaya Ploshchad) Serving all the Russian favourites, this impressive restaurant's decor combines traditional Zhostovo floral designs and Murano glass chandeliers with a slick contemporary style. It's popular with theatregoers (reservations are recommended in the evenings in the high season), as it's an obvious pre– or post–Mariinsky Theatre dining option. The waiters, all music students at the nearby Conservatory, give 'impromptu' vocal performances.

There's a great children's room and a full children's menu to boot, so families are very well catered for.

ENTRÉE
FRENCH €€

Map p264 (Nikolskaya pl 5; sandwiches R240-500, mains R450-650; ⊙noon-midnight Mon-Fri, 11am-midnight Sat & Sun; ⏰📶; MSadovaya) Charming Entrée comes in two parts: the cafe-cum-deli to the right has a chessboard floor, rustic decor, delicious cakes and sandwiches and, for some reason, Michael Douglas' signature scrawled on the wall. To the right is a far more formal restaurant with a classic but clever French menu and a huge wine list.

Service could be a little friendlier, but otherwise this place is a great find in an otherwise rather desolate stretch of the city centre. Breakfast (blink and you miss it!) is served from 11am to 1pm on the weekend.

GRAF-IN
INTERNATIONAL €€

Map p264 (www.graf-in.com; Konnogvardeysky bul 4; mains R400-1000; ⊙11am-midnight Sun-Thu, to 4am Fri & Sat; ⏰📶; MAdmiralteyskaya) This smart, funky but informal restaurant offers an international selection of food focused mainly on Modern European cooking, with sections of the menu devoted to Josper, pasta and Asian food, among others. The dishes are prepared in the glass-walled kitchen and are all beautifully presented, while the art-direction budget attracts a young and chic crowd.

STROGANOFF STEAK HOUSE
STEAK €€

Map p264 (📞812-314 5514; www.stroganoffsteakhouse.ru; Konnogvardeysky bul 4; mains R400-3000; ⏰📶🚻; MAdmiralteyskaya) Beef lovers can indulge their habit at this 12,000-sq-metre restaurant, the city's biggest. Thanks to clever design, though, it doesn't feel overwhelmingly large or impersonal, with the huge space divided into six stylish yet informal dining spaces. The steaks menu is impressive and there's a large list of side orders, salads and other main courses to choose from as well.

There's a fun children's playroom here, making it good for young families.

MIGA
KOREAN €€

Map p264 (Мига; Lermontovsky pr 6; mains R400-1200; ⊙noon-midnight; ⏰📄📶; MSadovaya) The authentic (read: no frills) Korean restaurant is a great find in this quiet residential neighbourhood. There's a wide-ranging, pictorial menu that includes delicious *bulgogi* (Korean beef barbecue), *bossam* (spicy pork belly) and *bajon* (seafood pancakes), as well as perennial favourite *bibimbap*. Service is fast and friendly, and there's a private banqueting room for groups.

IDIOT
VEGETARIAN €€

Map p264 (nab reki Moyki 82; mains R300-1000, brunch R410; ⊙11am-1am; ⊜⏰📄📶; MSennaya Ploshchad) Something of an expat favourite, the Idiot is a charming place and has been providing brunch for travellers for years now. Insidiously vegetarian (you may not even notice that there's no meat on the menu, as there's plenty of fish), the friendly basement location is all about atmosphere, relaxation and fun (encouraged by the complimentary vodka coming with each meal).

The cosy subterranean space, the antique furnishings and crowded bookshelves make it an extremely pleasant place to come to eat or drink.

CROCODILE INTERNATIONAL €€
Map p264 (Крокодил; Galernaya ul 18; mains R400-850; ⊘12.30pm-midnight; 🖥📶; MAdmiralteyskaya) This pleasant place is a good lunch or dinner choice. Enjoy a dimly lit but artsy interior (including a piano just waiting to be played) and an interesting, eclectic menu with dishes such as eel soup, salmon steaks, duck legs, veal fillet in grape sauce and lamb cooked in a white-wine sauce and star anise.

MANSARDA INTERNATIONAL €€€
Map p264 (Мансарда; ☑812-946 4303; www.ginza.ru; ul Pochtamskaya 3; mains R500-1400; ⊘noon-midnight; ➡🖥📶; MAdmiralteyskaya) It's all about glass at the rooftop restaurant of the Gazprom building. This impressive place definitely has the best views in town and you can almost touch the dome of St Isaac's Cathedral from the best tables (book in advance). Yet despite the fixation, the food is no afterthought, with a delicious range of international cooking and a superb winelist on offer.

To get here, enter the Gazprom building and take the dedicated lift to the top floor.

RUSSIAN VODKA ROOM NO 1 RUSSIAN €€€
Map p264 (www.vodkaroom.ru; Konnogvardeysky bul 4; mains R400-1600; 🖥📶; MAdmiralteyskaya) This charming, welcoming place is the restaurant of the Russian Vodka Museum (p105), but it's good enough to be a destination in its own right. The interior enjoys a grand old-world dacha feel, as does the menu: rack of lamb in pomegranate sauce, stewed veal cheeks and whole fried Gatchina trout take you back to imperial tastes and tsarist opulence.

As you'd expect there's a huge vodka list (shots R100 to R500) and the knowledgable staff will help you match your meal to one of the many bottles they sell.

🍷 DRINKING & NIGHTLIFE

🍷 Sennaya

★SMALLDOUBLE CAFE
Map p264 (www.smalldouble.com; Kazanskaya ul 26; ⊘8.30am-10pm Mon-Fri, 11am-10pm Sat & Sun; 🖥; MSennaya Ploshchad) Taking coffee very seriously, friendly and handily located Smalldouble offers Aeropress, Chemex and syphon brews, as well as the good old-fashioned espresso machine. The locals love it, and it always seems to be abuzz with young creatives getting their caffeine fix. A small menu runs from breakfast and salads to sandwiches (R250 to R280) and a gorgeous array of cakes.

STIRKA 40 BAR
Map p264 (Стирка; Kazanskaya ul 26; ⊘11am-midnight Sun-Thu, to 4am Fri & Sat; 🖥; MSennaya Ploshchad) This friendly joint, the name of which means 'washing', has three washing machines, so you can drop off a load and have a few beers while you wait. A novel idea, though one few people seem to take advantage of. Its small and unassuming layout makes it a great place for a quiet drink with a cool young crowd.

SCHUMLI CAFE
Map p264 (www.schumli.ru; Kazanskaya ul 40; ⊘9.30am-10pm Mon-Fri, from noon Sat & Sun; 🖥; MSennaya Ploshchad) With its large range of coffees, sumptuous selection of cakes and (best of all) freshly made Belgian waffles, this small but friendly cafe is a great place to regain flagging energy when wandering around the city. There's a rather garish upstairs dining room if you want a full meal (mains R150 to R500), but the excellent coffee is the real reason to come.

🍷 Kolomna

★MAYAKOVSKY COCKTAIL BAR
Map p264 (www.mayakovskybar.su; Pochtamtsky per 5; ⊘noon-last customer Mon-Fri, from 4pm Sat; MAdmiralteyskaya) Despite its overabundance of disco balls, Mayakovsky lives up to its self-given description of 'intelligent bar'. There's a very adult cocktail menu (try a superb Karamazov: Martini Rosso, Be-

cherovka, Bacardi, lemon and cinnamon), red velvet bar stools, a jazz soundtrack and a dark and moodily lit lounge where you can also eat from an impressive international menu.

There are regular enough literary and poetic evenings to justify the bar's name, while they're few and far enough between to make it unlikely your cocktail drinking will be interrupted.

REAL DEAL'S OLD SCHOOL BAR BAR

Map p264 (nab Admiralteyskogo kanala 27; ⊙6pm-last customer; ☎; ⓂAdmiralteyskaya) In a bunkerlike location in front of New Holland, this cool and creative two-room space is a haven for vinyl lovers (think soul, funk, blues, ska) and live performances (local groups take the stage each weekend). There's also a dance floor for when things get busy, and table football to play. Drinks are cheap and the crowd is friendly.

 **ENTERTAINMENT**

MARIINSKY THEATRE OPERA, BALLET

Map p264 (Мариинский театр; ☑812-326 4141; www.mariinsky.ru; Teatralnaya pl 1; R1000-6000; ⓂSadovaya) St Petersburg's most spectacular venue for ballet and opera, the Mariinsky Theatre is an attraction in its own right. Tickets can be bought online or in person, but they should be bought in advance during the summer months. The magnificent interior is the epitome of imperial grandeur, and any evening here will be an impressive experience.

Known as the Kirov Ballet during the Soviet era, the Mariinsky has an illustrious history, with troupe members including such ballet greats as Nijinsky, Nureyev, Pavlova and Baryshnikov. In recent years the company has been invigorated by the current Artistic and General Director Valery Gergiev, who has worked hard to make the company solvent while overseeing the construction of the impressive and much-needed second theatre, the Mariinsky II, across the Kryukov Canal from the company's green-and-white wedding cake of a building. It is rumoured that the Mariinsky Theatre will close at some point in the near future for a full (and, again, much-needed) renovation, so visit the Mariinsky's faded grandeur while you can.

MARIINSKY II THEATRE

Map p264 (Мариинский II; ☑812-326 4141; www.mariinsky.ru; ul Dekabristov 34; tickets R300-6000; ⊙ticket office 11am-7pm; ⓂSadovaya) Finally opening its doors in 2013 after more than a decade of construction, legal wrangles, scandal and rumour, the Mariinsky II is a showpiece for Petersburg's most famous ballet and opera company. It is one of the most technically advanced music venues in the world, with superb sightlines and acoustics from all of its 2000 seats.

There's no denying that the modern-yet-not-modern-enough-to-be-interesting exterior is no great addition to St Petersburg's magnificent wealth of buildings. Inside, it's a different story though. The interior is a beautifully crafted mixture of back-lit onyx, multilevel public areas between which staircases, lifts and escalators weave, limestone walls, marble floors and Swarovski chandeliers. The simple yet superbly designed auditorium boasts plenty of leg room, three stages that can be combined to form one and an orchestra pit that can hold no fewer than 120 musicians. Serious music fans should come here to see a state-of-the-art opera and ballet venue, while anyone curious to see the results of a decade of building work will also not leave disappointed. As well as the main auditorium, there are also several smaller venues within the venue (Prokofiev Hall, Stravinsky Foyer, Shchedrin Hall, Mussorgsky Hall), all of which host regular concerts that can be a cheaper alternative to seeing a performance in the main hall.

MARIINSKY CONCERT HALL CLASSICAL MUSIC

Map p264 (Мариинский концертный зал; www.mariinsky.ru; ul Dekabristov 37; tickets R600-1500; ⊙ticket office 11am-8pm; ⓂSadovaya) Opened in 2007, this concert hall is a magnificent multifaceted creation. It manages to preserve the historic brick facade of the set and scenery warehouse that previously stood on this spot, while the modern main entrance, facing ul Dekabristov, is all tinted glass and angular lines, hardly hinting at the beautiful old building behind.

Its array of classical orchestral performances is superb, but be aware that it's a modern venue, and won't provide your typical 'night at the Mariinsky' atmosphere.

RIMSKY-KORSAKOV CONSERVATORY
CLASSICAL MUSIC

Map p264 (Консерватория имени Н. А. Римского-Корсакова; ☎812-312 2519; www.conservatory.ru; Teatralnaya pl 3; tickets R200-2000; MSadovaya) This illustrious music school was the first public music school in Russia. The Bolshoy Zal (Big Hall) on the 3rd floor is an excellent place to see performances by up-and-coming musicians throughout the academic year, while the Maly Zal (Small Hall) often hosts free concerts from present students and alumni; check when you're in town for what's on.

Founded in 1862, the Conservatory counts Pyotr Tchaikovsky among its alumni and Nikolai Rimsky-Korsakov among its former faculty. Dmitry Shostakovich and Sergei Prokofiev are graduates of this institution, as are countless contemporary artistic figures, such as Mariinsky artistic director Valery Gergiev.

YUSUPOV PALACE THEATRE
THEATRE

Map p264 (Театр Юсуповского дворца; ☎812-314 9883; www.yusupov-palace.ru; nab reki Moyki 94; tickets R500-3000; MSadovaya) Housed inside the outrageously ornate Yusupov Palace, this elaborate yet intimate venue was the home entertainment centre for one of the city's foremost aristocratic families. While you can visit the theatre when you tour the palace, seeing a performance here is a treat, as you can imagine yourself the personal guest of the notorious Prince Felix himself.

The shows are a mixed bag – usually a 'Gala Evening' that features fragments of various Russian classics.

ST PETERSBURG OPERA
THEATRE

Map p264 (Санкт-Петербургская Опера; ☎812-312 3982; www.spbopera.ru; ul Galernaya 33; tickets R500-2000; MAdmiralteyskaya) Housed in the sumptuous (and dare we say, rather bizarre) former home of Baron von Derviz, the St Petersburg Opera performs regular operas in its intimate and grandly lavish former ballroom. With just 187 seats, you're guaranteed a good view of the Russian, Italian and German classics, even if the quality can't compare to other more established opera houses in the city.

FEEL YOURSELF RUSSIAN FOLKSHOW
DANCE

Map p264 (☎812-312 5500; www.folkshow.ru; Nikolayevsky Palace, ul Truda 4; ticket incl drinks & snacks R2900; ☺box office 11am-9pm, shows 7pm & in high season 9pm; MAdmiralteyskaya) Terrible title, but not a bad show of traditional Russian folk dancing and music. The two-hour performance features four different folk groups, complete with accordion, balalaika and Cossack dancers. It's worth attending to get a look inside the spectacular Nikolayevsky Palace, if nothing else.

🛍 SHOPPING

NORTHWAY
SOUVENIRS

Map p264 (Angliyskaya nab 36/2; ☺9am-8pm; MAdmiralteyskaya) There is quite simply no bigger collection of *matryoshki* (nesting dolls), amber, fur and other Russian souvenir staples than that on offer at this very impressive and stylish shop right on the Neva embankment. Look no further for Russian gifts to take home.

MARIINSKY ART SHOP
SOUVENIRS

Map p264 (www.mariinsky.ru; Mariinsky Theatre, Teatralnaya pl 1; ☺11am-6pm performance days, also open during interval; MSadovaya) Opera and ballet lovers will delight at the theatre-themed souvenirs for sale in the Mariinsky gift shop. None of it is cheap, but the selection is impressive. Also on sale: a comprehensive collection of CDs, DVDs, books and posters that you won't find elsewhere.

MIR ESPRESSO
FOOD & DRINK

Map p264 (Мир Эспрессо; www.mirespresso-spb.ru; ul Dekabristov 12/10; ☺9am-8pm Mon-Fri, 10am-8pm Sat & Sun; MSadovaya) Come for the aroma and stay for the amazing coffee from all over the world. There are espresso machines and every type of coffee maker and caffeine-related accessory.

SENNOY MARKET
FOOD & DRINK

Map p264 (Moskovsky pr 4; ☺8am-7pm; MSennaya Ploshchad) Cheaper and less atmospheric than Kuznechny Market (p130), Sennoy Market is also centrally located. You'll find fruit and vegies, as well as fresh-caught fish and fresh-cut meat, which makes it a useful spot for self-caterers.

KOSHER SHOP
FOOD & DRINK

Map p264 (www.jewishpetersburg.ru; Lermontovsky pr 2; ☺Sun-Fri 10am-7pm; MSadovaya) Serving St Petersburg's Jewish community, the Kosher Shop is conveniently located next to the Grand Choral Synagogue. Although its emphasis is on hard-to-find kosher food, the shop also sells books about Judaism in many languages, plus Jewish music and art.

GALLERY OF DOLLS   SOUVENIRS

Map p264 (Галерея кукол; Bolshaya Morskaya ul 53/8; admission R50; ⊙noon-7pm Tue-Sat; ⓂSennaya Ploshchad) Featuring ballerinas and babushkas, clowns and knights, this gallery depicts just about every fairy-tale character and political persona in doll form. The highly creative figures are more like art than toys and make unusual souvenirs (although they're admittedly an acquired taste).

🏃 SPORTS & ACTIVITIES

KAZACHIYE BANI   BANYA

Map p264 (Казачие бани; www.kazbani.ru; Bolshoy Kazachy per 11; communal sauna per hr R100-300, private sauna per hr R600-1300;

⊙24hr; ⓂPushkinskaya) Following a trend that is occurring throughout the city, the communal *banya* (hot bath) is something of an afterthought here. The vast majority of the venue is given over to very swanky, private *bani,* which are an excellent option for a group of up to 10 people. The cheaper communal *banya* is good value though.

Tuesday, Thursday and Saturday are for women; Wednesday, Friday and Sunday are for men.

RENTBIKE   CYCLING

Map p264 (☑812-981 0155; www.rentbike.org; ul Yefimova 4a; per day from R400; ⊙24hr; ⓂSennaya Ploshchad) This centrally located company rents out well-maintained bikes at good rates. It will also deliver to your hotel for free if you're staying in the city centre. You'll need to leave a passport or ID card with them with a deposit of R2000 per bike.

The place is a little tricky to find, off ul Yefimova and through two car parks; see the website for details.

Smolny & Vosstaniya

SMOLNY | LITEYNY | VLADIMIRSKAYA | VOSSTANIYA

Neighbourhood Top Five

1 Exploring the beating heart of Orthodox St Petersburg in the complex of churches at the **Alexander Nevsky Monastery** (p114) and seeing the last resting place of many of Russia's greatest artists in the atmospheric cemeteries.

2 Taking in the spectacular powder blue and white exterior of Rastrelli's baroque **Smolny Cathedral** (p116).

3 Savouring the superb collection of gorgeous objects at the **Museum of Decorative & Applied Arts** (p117).

4 Visiting the **Cathedral of the Transfiguration Of Our Saviour** (p116) and **Vladimirsky Cathedral** (p120), two of St Petersburg's least known but most charming churches.

5 Seeing the room where Fyodor Dostoevsky wrote *The Brothers Karamazov* at the fascinating **Dostoevsky Museum** (p120).

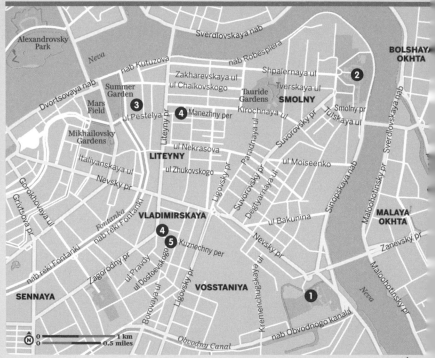

For more detail of this area see Map p260

Explore: Smolny & Vosstaniya

This area, bisected by the second half of Nevsky pr, breaks down into four districts: Smolny, Liteyny, Vosstaniya and Vladimirskaya. An extremely varied place, it contains the closest thing St Petersburg has to a creative hub, as well as its political and diplomatic heart.

The Liteyny and Smolny districts sit side by side east of the historic heart, tucked inside a swooping curve of the Neva River on its left bank. These neighbourhoods take their names from the industries that once dominated this area: *liteyny* means 'foundry' and *smol* means 'tar', although these evocative names hardly capture the atmosphere of these quaint but quiet neighbourhoods today. Smolny is the well-heeled seat of local government and home to most of the consulates in the city, while Liteyny is centred on Liteyny pr, a busy traffic artery, but is quiet and residential as soon as you get onto the side streets.

On the south side of Nevsky the neighbourhood of Vladimirskaya is dominated by the grand, onion-domed Vladimirsky Cathedral. This is a busy, commercial area full of shops, restaurants and quirky museums.

Nevsky pr continues east to pl Vosstaniya (Uprising Sq), so called because the February Revolution began here in 1917. This large area contains industrial wasteland, as well as St Petersburg's busiest railway terminus, the Moscow Station (Moskovsky Vokzal). Nevsky pr ends at pl Alexandra Nevskogo, named after the city's patron saint. On this square stands the ancient and revered Alexander Nevsky Monastery. Vosstaniya has a seedy, poor feel, but is the closest St Petersburg has to a creative and alternative culture hub, with art galleries, bars and clubs.

Local Life

→**Creative kicks** Make the most of being in St Petersburg's most creative area: enjoy an exhibition at Loft Project ETAGI, installations at the Rizzordi Art Foundation and shop at Tkachi.

→**Shop till you drop** Two of the city's biggest shopping centres are here: Galeria and Nevsky Centre.

→**Park life** When the weather is fine, join locals in the Tauride Garden, one of Petersburg's most lovely and laid-back green spaces.

Getting There & Away

→**Metro** Access by Ploshchad Vosstaniya/Mayakovskaya, Vladimirskaya/Dostoevskaya, Ploshchad Alexandra Nevskogo, Chernyshevskaya and Ligovsky Prospekt.

→**Bus** Handy for getting up or down Nevsky pr, dozens of buses and trolleybuses run this route, including buses 24 and 191, which run the entirety of Nevsky.

Lonely Planet's Top Tip

Avoid hanging around the entrance to the Moscow Station on pl Vosstaniya. It's a favoured police hang-out for document checks and, in some cases, shakedowns. You're unlikely to have problems (if you have your passport with you), but it's just a pain and best avoided.

Best Places to Eat

→ Grand Cru (p125)
→ Duo Gastrobar (p121)
→ Mechta Molokhovets (p122)
→ Schengen (p121)
→ Vinostudia (p123)

For reviews, see p118→

Best Places to Drink

→ Mishka (p126)
→ Union Bar & Grill (p126)
→ Dyuni (p127)
→ Dom Beat (p126)
→ The Hat (p126)

For reviews, see p126→

Best Museums

→ Museum of Decorative & Applied Arts (p117)
→ Anna Akhmatova Museum at the Fountain House (p118)
→ Museum of the Defence & Blockade of Leningrad (p118)
→ Dostoevsky Museum (p120)

For reviews, see p116→

SMOLNY & VOSSTANIYA

TOP SIGHT
ALEXANDER NEVSKY MONASTERY

Named after the patron saint of St Petersburg who led the Russian victory over the Swedes in 1240, the Alexander Nevsky Monastery is the city's oldest and most eminent religious institution. Today it is a working monastery that attracts scores of devout believers, as well as being the burial place of some of Russia's most famous artistic figures.

Founding the monastery in 1710, Peter the Great sought to link St Petersburg to the historic battle against the Swedes, and thus to underscore Russia's long history with the newly captured region. Even though the site of Nevsky's victory was further upstream by the mouth of the Izhora River, the monastery became the centre of the Nevsky cult and his remains were transferred here from Vladimir in 1724, and remain the most sacred item in the cathedral here. In 1797 the monastery became a *lavra,* the most senior grade of Russian Orthodox Christian monasteries, and a status awarded only to one other monastery in the country.

You can wander for free around most of the grounds and churches, but you must buy tickets to enter the two most famous cemeteries.

Cemeteries

Coming into the monastery complex, you'll first arrive at the Tikhvin and Lazarus Cemeteries, burial place to some of Russia's most famous names. You'll find Dostoevsky, Tchaikovsky, Rimsky-Korsakov, Borodin and Mussorgsky within the walls of the **Tikhvin Cemetery** (Map p260) (also called the Artists' Necropolis), which is on your right af-

DON'T MISS...

➡ Seeing the greats in the Tikhvin Cemetery
➡ The iconostasis in the Trinity Cathedral
➡ Alexander Nevsky Gardens
➡ The Nikolsky Cemetery

PRACTICALITIES

➡ Монастырь Александра Невскаого
➡ Map p260
➡ www.lavra.spb.ru
➡ Nevsky pr 179/2
➡ cemeteries admission R150, pantheon R100
➡ ⊘ grounds 6am-11pm (8am-9pm winter), churches 6am-9pm, cemeteries 9.30am-9pm (11am-4pm winter), pantheon 11am-5pm Tue & Wed, Fri-Sun
➡ Ⓜ Ploshchad Aleksandra Nevskogo

ter you enter the monastery's main gate. Across the way in the **Lazarus Cemetery** (Map p260), or 18th Century Cemetery, you'll find even more atmospheric graves, though fewer famous names – look out for polymath Mikhail Lomonosov, as well as the graves of the St Petersburg architects Quarenghi, Stasov and Rossi.

The cemeteries are now part of the rather misleadingly named State Museum of Urban Sculpture (also known as the Russian National Pantheon), which also has an exhibit inside the **Annunciation Church**, where you'll find the tombs of many minor royals and tsarist generals.

Monastery Complex

The monastery itself is within a further wall beyond the cemeteries. The centrepiece is the classical **Trinity Cathedral** (Map p260), which was built between 1776 and 1790. Hundreds crowd in here on 12 September to celebrate the feast of St Alexander Nevsky, whose remains are in the silver reliquary by the elaborate main iconostasis, which you'll find to the right of the main altar, under a red and gold canopy.

Behind the cathedral is the **Nikolsky Cemetery** (Map p260), a beautiful spot with a little stream running through it, where more recently deceased Petersburgers can be found, including former mayor Anatoly Sobchak and murdered Duma deputy Galina Starovoytova.

Opposite the cathedral is the 1775–78 **Metropolitan's House** (Map p260), the official residence of the spiritual leader of St Petersburg's Russian Orthodox community. In the surrounding grounds is a smaller cemetery where leading Communist (ie atheist) Party officials and luminaries are buried. On the far right of the grounds facing the canal is St Petersburg's **Orthodox Academy** (Map p260), one of only a handful in Russia (the main one is at Sergiev Posad, near Moscow).

NEW EXHIBITION HALL

Also on the grounds of the monastery is the New Exhibition Hall, which holds temporary exhibits of local artists' work. Enter from outside the monastery walls off Pl Alexandra Nevskogo.

Anyone wanting to visit the Trinity Catheral should dress respectfully (no shorts, or sleeveless tops, for example) and women should cover their heads before entering.

FOR FREE

Even if you don't want to pay to enter the famous cemeteries or the Annunciation Church, you can wander the beautiful monastery grounds and visit the Trinity Cathedral for free.

 SIGHTS

⊙ Smolny & Liteyny

SMOLNY CATHEDRAL
CHURCH

Map p260 (Смольный собор; ☎812-577 1421; pl Rastrelli 3/1; adult/student/child R150/90/50, bell tower R100, general ticket R200; ⊙10.30am-6pm Thu-Tue; ⓂChernyshevskaya) If baroque is your thing, then look no further than the sky-blue Smolny Cathedral, an unrivalled masterpiece of the genre that ranks among Bartolomeo Rastrelli's most amazing creations. The cathedral is the centrepiece of a convent mostly built to Rastrelli's designs between 1748 and 1757. His inspiration was to combine baroque details with the forest of towers and onion domes typical of an old Russian monastery. There's special genius in the proportions of the cathedral (it gives the impression of soaring upwards), to which the convent buildings are a perfect foil.

In stark contrast, the interior is a disappointingly austere plain white as Rastrelli fell from favour before he was able to begin work on it. Today the cathedral is no longer a working church, but serves instead as a concert hall and exhibition space. If you're lucky there may well be rehearsals for concerts going on while you visit, to which you're welcome to listen, otherwise it's not really worth paying to enter the cathedral itself.

However, it's definitely worth paying to climb the 277 steps to one (or both) of the two 63m-high bell towers for stupendous views over the city.

SMOLNY INSTITUTE
HISTORIC BUILDING

Map p260 (Смольный институт; pl Proletarskoy Diktatury 3; ⊙closed to the public; ⓂChernyshevskaya) Built by Giacomo Quarenghi between 1806 and 1808 as a school for aristocratic girls, the Smolny Institute was thrust into the limelight in 1917 when it became the headquarters for the Bolshevik Central Committee and the Petrograd Soviet. From here, Trotsky and Lenin directed the October Revolution, and in the **Hall of Acts** (Aktovy zal) on 25 October, the All-Russian Congress of Soviets conferred power on a Bolshevik government led by Lenin.

The Smolny Institute served as the seat of Soviet power until March 1918, when the capital was relocated to Moscow. In 1934

the powerful Leningrad Party chief Sergei Kirov was assassinated in its corridors, on orders from Stalin, ridding the Soviet leader of a perceived rival and simultaneously providing the perfect pretext for the notorious Leningrad purges. Today St Petersburg's governor continues to run the city from here.

TAURIDE PALACE & GARDENS
PARK

Map p260 (Таврический дворец и сад; ⊙8am-8pm, to 10pm May-Jul, closed Apr; ⓂChernyshevskaya) Catherine the Great had this baroque palace built in 1783 for Grigory Potemkin, a famed general and her companion for many years of her life. Today it is home to the Commonwealth of Independent States and is closed to the public. The gardens, on the other hand, are open to all; once the romping grounds of the tsarina, they became a park for the people under the Soviets, and their facilities include a lake, several cafes and an entertainment centre.

The palace was named aft er Tavria (another name for Crimea, the region that Potemkin conquered), and was a thank-you present to Potemkin from Catherine. Catherine's bitter son, Paul I, turned the palace into a barracks after his ascension to the throne in 1796, which ruined most of the lavish interiors. Between 1906 and 1917 the State Duma, the Provisional Government and the Petrograd Soviet all met here; in the 1930s it housed the All-Union Agricultural Communist University, a fate that would have no doubt horrified Catherine the Great.

CATHEDRAL OF THE TRANSFIGURATION OF OUR SAVIOUR
CATHEDRAL

Map p260 (Спасо-преображенский собор; Preobrazhenskaya pl; ⊙8am-8pm; ⓂChernyshevskaya) The interior of this marvellous 1743 cathedral, which has been beautifully restored and repainted both outside and in, is one of the most gilded in the city. The grand gates bear the imperial double-headed eagle in vast golden busts, reflecting the fact that the cathedral was built on the site where the Preobrazhensky Guards (the monarch's personal protection unit) had their headquarters. Architect Vasily Stasov rebuilt the cathedral from 1827 to 1829 in the neoclassical style. It is dedicated to the victory over the Turks in 1828–29; note the captured Turkish guns in the gate surrounding the cathedral.

BOLSHOY DOM
HISTORIC BUILDING

Map p260 (Большой дом; Liteyny pr 4; ⊘closed to the public; MChernyshevskaya) Noi Trotsky's monolithic design for the local KGB headquarters (and currently the St Petersburg headquarters of the Federal Security Service, or FSB, its successor organisation) is referred to by everyone as the 'Bolshoy Dom' ('Big House'). It's a fierce-looking block of granite built in 1932 in the late-constructivist style and was once a byword for fear among the people of the city: most people who were taken here during the purges were never heard from again.

Employees who have worked here include Vladimir Putin during his KGB career. The Bolshoy Dom made the news in 2010, when the subversive art collective Voina (War) drew a 65m-long penis on the nearby Liteyny Bridge, which, when the bridge was raised, made a very clear statement towards the FSB.

ANNA AKHMATOVA MONUMENT
MONUMENT

Map p260 (Памятник Анне Ахматовой; nab Robespierre; MChernyshevskaya) This moving statue of St Petersburg's most famous 20th-century poet was unveiled in 2006, across the river from the notorious Kresty holding prison, to mark the 40th anniversary of Akhmatova's death. The location is no coincidence – Kresty Prison was where Akhmatova herself queued for days in the snow for news of her son after his multiple arrests during Stalin's terror.

The inscription on the monument comes from her epic poem 'Requiem' (1935–40), in which she describes life during the purges. It reads: 'That's why I pray not for myself/ But for all of you who stood there with me/ Through fiercest cold and scorching July heat/Under a towering, completely blind red wall.'

MONUMENT TO THE VICTIMS OF POLITICAL REPRESSION
MONUMENT

Map p260 (Памятник жертвам политических репрессий; nab Robespierre; MChernyshevskaya) This gruesome piece of sculpture by Russian artist Mikhail Shemyakin was unveiled in 1995, shortly after the end of the Soviet Union. The scultpure is centred on two sphinxes, both of which look, from one side, like beautiful creatures. However, view them from the other side (facing the infamous Kresty Prison across the water) and it's clear the beauty has been corrupted

beyond recognition and half the face is a mere skull.

Lines of writing from many of the Soviet system's victims are engraved on the monument's granite base. It's a sad and deeply moving place.

MUSEUM OF DECORATIVE & APPLIED ARTS
MUSEUM

Map p260 (Музей декоративного и прикладного искусства; www.spbghpa.ru; Solyanoy per 15; adult/student R100/50, tour in Russian R200; ⊘11am-5pm Tue-Sat; MChernyshevskaya) Also known as the **Stieglitz Museum**, this fascinating establishment is as beautiful as you would expect a decorative arts museum to be. An array of gorgeous objects is on display, from medieval furniture to 18th-century Russian tiled stoves and contemporary works by the students of the Applied Arts School, also housed here. This museum is less visited than some of its counterparts in the city, but the quiet atmosphere only adds to its appeal.

In 1878 the millionaire Baron Stieglitz founded the School of Technical Design and wanted to surround his students with world-class art to inspire them. He began a collection that was continued by his son and was to include a unique array of European and Oriental glassware, porcelain, tapestries, furniture and paintings. It eventually grew into one of Europe's richest private collections. Between 1885 and 1895, a building designed by architect Maximilian Messmacher was built to house the collection and this building also became a masterpiece. Each hall is decorated in its own unique style, including Italian, Renaissance, Flemish and baroque. The Terem Room, in the style of the medieval Terem Palace of Moscow's Kremlin, is an opulent knockout.

After the revolution the school was closed, the museum's collection redistributed to the Hermitage and the Russian Museum, and most of the lavish interiors brutally painted or plastered over and even destroyed (one room was used as a sports hall). The painstaking renovation continues to this day, despite receiving no state funding.

Just finding the museum can be tricky; enter through the academy building (the second entrance as you walk up Solyanoy per from ul Pestelya). Tell the guard that you want to go to the museum (v moozáy), then go up the main staircase, turn right at the top, walk through two halls and then go down the staircase to your left. All signs are in Russian only. Once you've visited the museum, it's perfectly possible to wander around the grand halls and corridors of the Applied Arts School: if you continue the way you came to get to the museum and turn right you'll get to the school's main hall, with its signature skylights, where exhibitions of students' work are often held.

MUSEUM OF THE DEFENCE & BLOCKADE OF LENINGRAD   MUSEUM

Map p260 (Музей обороны и блокады Ленинграда; www.blokadamus.ru; Solyarnoy per 9; adult/student R300/150; ⊘10am-5pm Thu-Mon, 12.30-9pm Wed; MChernyshevskaya) The grim but engrossing displays here contain donations from survivors, propaganda posters from the blockade period and many photos depicting life and death during the siege. An audio guide in English was about to be made available at the time of research, which will compensate for the lack of English signage elsewhere in the museum.

This museum opened just three months after the blockade was lifted in January 1944 and boasted 37,000 exhibits, including real tanks and aeroplanes. But three years later, during Stalin's repression of the city, the museum was shut, its director shot, and most of the exhibits destroyed or redistributed. Not until 1985's *glasnost* (openness) was an attempt made once again to gather documents to reopen the museum; this happened in 1989.

ANNA AKHMATOVA MUSEUM AT THE FOUNTAIN HOUSE   MUSEUM

Map p260 (Музей Анны Ахматовой в Фонтанном Доме; www.akhmatova.spb.ru; Liteyny pr 51; adult/child R80/40; ⊘10.30am-6.30pm Tue & Thu-Sun, noon-8pm Wed; MMayakovskaya) Housed in the south wing of the Sheremetyev Palace, this touching and fascinating literary museum celebrates the life and work of Anna Akhmatova, St Petersburg's most famous 20th-century poet. Akhmatova lived here from 1924 until 1952, as this was the apartment of her common-law husband Nikolai Punin. The apartment is on the 2nd floor and is filled with mementos of the poet and correspondence with other writers.

A visit to this peaceful and contemplative place is also an interesting chance to see the interior of an (albeit atypical) apartment from the early to mid-20th cen-

tury, even if relatively few pieces of original furniture have survived. Particularly moving is the study where, in her own words, Akhmatova 'quite unexpectedly' started her masterpiece *Poem Without a Hero* in 1940, and her living room where the poet had a famous all-night conversation with British diplomat Isaiah Berlin during the height of Stalinism, an event that has become legendary in Russian literary history. There are information panels in English in each room, as well as a R200 audio guide available in English.

Admission also includes the Josef Brodsky American Study. Brodsky did not live here, but his connection with Akhmatova was strong. For lack of a better location, his office has been re-created here, complete with furniture and other artifacts from his adopted home in Massachusetts. Funds are currently being collected to open a Josef Brodsky Museum at the poet's former home a few blocks away on Liteyny pr.

When coming to the museum, be sure to enter from Liteyny pr, rather than from the Fontanka River, where the main palace entrance is, as it's not possible to reach the museum from there.

SHEREMETYEV PALACE   MUSEUM

Map p260 (Шереметьевский дворец; ⌨812-272 4441; www.theatremuseum.ru; nab reki Fontanki 34; admission R300; ⊘11am-7pm Thu-Mon, 1-9pm Wed; MGostiny Dvor) Splendid wrought-iron gates facing the Fontanka River guard the entrance to the Sheremetyev Palace (built 1750–55), now a branch of the **State Museum of Theatre & Music**, which has a collection of musical instruments from the 19th and 20th centuries. The Sheremetyev family was famous for the concerts and theatre performances they hosted at their palace, which was a centre of musical life in the imperial capital.

Upstairs, the rooms have been restored, although the management can't quite seem to decide whether it's a museum of instruments or a palace: the rooms, while impressive, have never fully recovered from years of neglect under the Soviets, when the building was used to house the Arctic & Antarctic Institute. The instruments on display are impressive though, including pianos belonging to Tchaikovsky, Glinka and Nicholas II. The ground floor is given over to an enormous collection of more instruments, but it's only visitable on a Russian-language guided tour on Thursday, Saturday or Sunday.

THE SOVIET SOUTH
....

Sprawling southern St Petersburg was once planned to be the centre of Stalin's new Leningrad, and anyone interested in Stalinist architecture should make the easy trip down here to the Moskovskaya metro station for a wander around and to see a clutch of sights all within easy walking distance.

Right outside the metro station you'll see the **House of Soviets** (Дом советов; Moskovsky pr 212; ☺closed to the public; ⓂMoskovskaya), a staggeringly bombastic Stalinist beauty. Planned to be the central administrative building of Stalin's Leningrad, it was built with the leader's neoclassical tastes in mind. Begun by Noi Trotsky in 1936, it was not finished until after the war, by which time the architect had been purged. Nonetheless, this magnificently sinister building is a great example of Stalinist design, with its columns and bas-reliefs and an enormous frieze running across the top. Today it houses the Moskovsky Region's local administration.

Due south from here down Moskovsky pr is the striking **Monument to the Heroic Defenders of Leningrad** (Монумент героическим защитникам Ленинграда; www.spbmuseum.ru; pl Pobedy; adult/student R120/70; ☺10am-6pm Thu-Mon, to 5pm Tue; ⓂMoskovskaya). Centred around a 48m-high obelisk, the monument, unveiled in 1975, is a sculptural ensemble of bronze statues symbolising the city's encirclement and eventual victory in WWII. On a lower level, a second bronze ring 40m in diameter surrounds a very moving sculpture standing in the centre. Haunting symphonic music creates a sombre atmosphere to guide you downstairs to the underground exhibition in a huge, mausoleum-like interior. Here, the glow of 900 bronze lamps creates an eeriness matched by the sound of a metronome (the only sound heard by Leningraders on their radios throughout the war save for emergency announcements), showing that the city's heart was still beating. Twelve thematically assembled showcases feature items from the war and siege. An electrified relief map in the centre of the room shows the shifting front lines of the war.

Finally, if all this Soviet architecture makes you yearn for something a little more traditional, then wander back north past the House of Soviets, turn right onto ul Tipanova and then left into ul Lensoveta and you'll see the beautiful **Chesme Church** (Чесменская церковь; http://chesma.spb.ru; ul Lensoveta 12; admission free; ☺10am-7pm; ⓂMoskovskaya), one of the city's most wonderful buildings. This red-and-white Gothic beauty looks not unlike a candy cane, with long, vertical white stripes giving the impression that it's shooting straight up from the earth like a mirage. Designed by Yury Felten, it was built between 1777 and 1780 in honour of the Battle of Chesme (1770). The church's remote location is due to the fact that Catherine was on this spot when news arrived of her great victory over the Turks. Ever capricious, Catherine ordered that a shrine be built on the spot to preserve this great moment in Russian history. It now seems particularly incongruous with its surroundings, as Stalin's planned city centre has since grown up around it.

☉ Vladimirskaya & Vosstaniya

ALEXANDER NEVSKY MONASTERY MONASTERY
See p114.

PUSHKINSKAYA 10 ART GALLERY
Map p260 (Арт-Центр Пушкинская 10; www.p-10.ru; Ligovsky pr 53; ☺4-8pm Wed-Sun; ⓂPloshchad Vosstaniya) This now legendary locale is a former apartment block – affectionately called by its street address despite the fact that the public entrance is actually on Ligovsky pr – that contains studio and gallery space, as well as music clubs Fish Fabrique (p128) and Fabrique Nouvelle (p128), plus an assortment of other shops and galleries. It offers a unique opportunity to hang out with local musicians and artists, who are always eager to talk about their work.

WORTH A DETOUR

ART SAFARI

For a splash of adventure combined with contemporary art, head out to the **Rizzordi Art Foundation** (☑812-643 0483; www.rizzordi.org; 4th floor, Kurlyandskaya ul 49; ⊙noon-8pm during exhibits; Ⓜ Baltiyskaya) FREE, the most exciting contemporary-art venue in the city to date. Opened in summer 2011, this impressive factory conversion is worth seeing in itself; it's a huge space taking up the top two floors of a disused 19th-century brewery. Very interesting temporary exhibits from local up-and-coming artists are showcased here, although there can be gaps between shows, so do call or email ahead to confirm the space is open. Half the adventure is just getting to the site (not to mention the incredible postindustrial wasteland you have to travel through). It's a 30-minute walk from Baltiyskaya metro, or you can take bus 49 from Sennaya pl towards Dvinskaya ul and get off at Kurlyandskaya ul, the second stop after you cross the Fontanka River. Other good contemporary galleries worth checking out include **K-Gallery** (Map p260; ☑812-273 0056; www.kgallery.ru; nab reki Fontanki 24; Ⓜ Gostiny Dvor) and **Marina Gisich Gallery** (Map p264; ☑812-314 4380; www.gisich.com; nab reki Fontanki 121; ⊙11am-7pm Mon-Fri, noon-5pm Sat; Ⓜ Sadovaya), both of which are on the Fontanka.

LOFT PROJECT ETAGI   CULTURAL CENTRE

Map p260 (Лофт проект ЭТАЖИ; www.loftpro jectetagi.ru; Ligovsky pr 74; ⊙noon-10pm; Ⓜ Ligovsky Prospekt) This fantastic conversion of the former Smolninsky Bread Factory has plenty to keep you interested, including many of the original factory fittings seamlessly merged with the thoroughly contemporary design. There are several galleries and exhibition spaces, lots of shops, a hostel, a bar and a cafe with a great summer terrace all spread out over five floors.

While it's true that ETAGI has become much more of a commercial than an artistic venture in recent years, it's still a good place to take the pulse of St Petersburg's contemporary art scene and a good environment to meet a young and creative crowd. In summer months the roof of the building is open (R250), with comfortable furniture to lounge on while overlooking the city. Enter through the doors to one side of the main gate and you'll find ETAGI in the courtyard.

VLADIMIRSKY CATHEDRAL   CATHEDRAL

Map p260 (Владимирский собор; Vladimirsky pr 20; admission free; ⊙8am-6pm, services 6pm daily; Ⓜ Vladimirskaya) This fantastic, five-domed cathedral, ascribed to Domenico Trezzini, is the namesake of this neighbourhood. Incorporating both baroque and neoclassical elements, the cathedral was built in the 1760s, with Giacomo Quarenghi's neoclassical bell tower added later in the century. Over the centuries the congregation has included Dostoevsky, who lived around the corner. The cathedral was closed in 1932 and the Soviets turned it into an underwear factory, but in 1990 it was reconsecrated and has resumed its originally intended function.

These days it is one of the busiest cathedrals in town, as evidenced by the hordes of babushkas and beggars outside. Nonetheless, it's worth weaving your way through the outstretched hands to admire the cathedral's interiors (upstairs). The baroque iconostasis was originally installed in the private chapel of the Anichkov Palace, but was transferred here in 1808. For an impressive perspective on the onion domes, have a drink in the 7th-floor Raskolnikov bar of the Hotel Dostoevsky across the road.

DOSTOEVSKY MUSEUM   MUSEUM

Map p260 (Литературно-мемориальный музей Ф.М. Достоевского; www.md.spb. ru; Kuznechny per 5/2; adult/student R160/80, audio tour R200; ⊙11am-6pm Tue-Sun, 1-8pm Wed; Ⓜ Vladimirskaya) ⌖ Fyodor Dostoevsky lived in flats all over the city, mostly in Sennaya, but his final residence is this 'memorial flat' where he lived from 1878 until he died in 1881. The apartment remains as it was when the Dostoevsky family lived here, including the study where he wrote *The Brothers Karamazov,* and the office of Anna Grigorievna, his wife, who recopied, edited and sold all of his books.

Two rooms of the museum are devoted to his novels; literature fans will want to pay close attention to the map of Dostoevsky's St Petersburg, which details the locations of characters and events in his various works. A rather gloomy sculpted likeness of the man himself (as if there's any other kind) is just outside the nearby Vladimirskaya metro station.

DERZHAVIN HOUSE-MUSEUM   MUSEUM

Map p264 (Музей-усадьба Державина; nab reki Fontanki 118; adult/student R80/40; ⊙10am-6pm Wed & Fri-Mon, noon-8pm Thu; MTekhnologichesky Institut) This grand old St Petersburg residence was the home to court poet Gabriel Derzhavin (1743–1816), one of Russia's greatest early writers, and someone who recognised the genius of Alexander Pushkin during Pushkin's own childhood. Having been divided into some 60 communal apartments under the Soviets, the mansion was fully renovated in 2003 and is now a charming museum. The focus of the house is Derzhavin's own study, with its three secret entrances.

EATING

Smolny & Liteyny

★DUO GASTROBAR   FUSION €

Map p260 (☏812-994 5443; www.duobar.ru; ul Kirochnaya 8a; mains R200-500; ⊙1pm-midnight, to 2am Fri & Sat; ⊕; MChernyshevskaya) This light-bathed place, done out in wood and gorgeous glass lampshades, has really helped put this otherwise quiet area on the culinary map. Its short fusion menu excels, featuring such unlikely delights as passionfruit and gorgonzola mousse and salmon with quinoa and marscarpone. There are also more conventional choices such as risottos, pastas and salads.

Run by two chefs who have worked all over the city, Duo is a great place to experiment with new flavours and combinations in a pleasant and friendly atmosphere. This is also a great spot for coffee and cake during the afternoon. There was no English menu or wi-fi at the time of research, but hopefully these oversights will be rectified soon. It's usually a good idea to reserve a table.

OBED BUFET   CAFETERIA €

Map p260 (Обед Буфет; 5th fl, Nevsky Centre, Nevsky pr 114; mains R100-200; ⊙10am-11pm; ⊕⑦; MMayakovskaya) Just what St Petersburg needs: a well-run, central and inviting cafeteria run by the city's most successful restaurant group. Here you'll find an extraordinary range of salads, soups, sandwiches, pizzas and meat dishes. There even a 50% discount noon and after 9pm, making this a superb deal (come at 9pm for the latter though, otherwise there will be no food left).

JAKOV   BAKERY €

Map p260 (Яков; www.jakovspb.ru; ul Chernyshevskogo 3; cakes from R150; ⊙9am-8pm; ⊕; MChernyshevskaya) This fantastic cake shop is a real treat for the well-heeled residents of the Smolny. Beautifully presented pastries, tarts, macaroons and handmade chocolates await, and while most people take them away, you can eat in and enjoy a coffee here too.

CITY GRILL EXPRESS   BURGERS €

Map p260 (ul Vosstaniya 1; burgers R150-350; ⊙10am-11pm; ⊕⑦⑩; MPloshchad Vosstaniya) This deceptively large place is a serious burger joint that remains affordable and comfortable. A great place for a pit-stop burger around the hectic pl Vosstaniya, they cook the burgers right in front of you.

SCHENGEN   INTERNATIONAL €€

Map p260 (Шенген; ☏812-922 1197; ul Kirochnaya 5; mains R400-850; ⊙11am-midnight; ⑦⑩; MChernyshevskaya) A breath of fresh air just off Liteyny pr, Schengen represents local aspirations to the wider world. The menu is truly international, has a Mac & Cheese section, chili con carne, Thai green curry and Norwegian trout fillet on it, and is served up in a cool and relaxing two-room space where efficient staff glide from table to table.

Food is of very high quality and there's a 20% discount until 3.30pm on weekdays.

BOTANIKA   VEGETARIAN €

Map p260 (Ботаника; www.cafebotanika.ru; ul Pestelya 7; mains R200-500; ⊙11am-midnight; ⊕⑦✍⑩; MChernyshevskaya) Enjoying perhaps the friendliest and most laid-back atmosphere of any restaurant in St Petersburg, this vegetarian charmer wins on all counts. The menu takes in Russian, Indian, Italian and Japanese dishes, all of which are very well realised, service is friendly, there's no loud TV on, English is spoken and there's even a playroom and menu for the kids.

FRANCESCO ITALIAN €€

Map p260 (Suvorovsky pr 47; mains R500-2000; ⏱9am-1am Mon-Fri, noon-1am Sat & Sun; 🖥📱; ⓂChernyshevskaya) Made to feel like a large family home, this charmingly decorated Italian restaurant comes complete with birds in cages, sideboards full of crockery and old photographs on the wall. The service is very good, food is excellent and there's an altogether lovely atmosphere.

MOSKVA INTERNATIONAL €€

Map p260 (Москва; ☎812-640 1616; www.moskvavpitere.ru; 6th fl, Nevsky Centre, Nevsky pr 114; mains R400-1600; ⏱10am-1am; 🍴✳🖥📱📶; ⓂPloshchad Vosstaniya) On the top floor of the Nevsky Centre shopping mall on St Petersburg's main street, Moskva has a handy location and tons of space. The pictorial menu is incredibly large: whatever you're in the mood for, you'll find it here, including a children's playroom. The best seats are on the terrace overlooking the city outside, but you'll need to reserve ahead for these.

MESTO ASIAN €€

Map p260 (Место; Tverskaya ul 20; mains R450-1100; ⏱noon-11pm; 🖥; ⓂChernyshevskaya) 'The place' offers a variation on its original venue on the Petrograd Side; this time it's all about Asian cuisine: sushi, maki, rolls, gyoza (dumplings) and a selection of hot dishes too. This is all served up in very sleek and rather dark premises designed to appeal to the Smolny political classes. One of the few quality restaurants in the area.

SUNDUK INTERNATIONAL €€

Map p260 (Сундук; www.cafesunduk.ru; Furshtatskaya ul 42; mains R300-1000; ⏱10am-midnight Mon-Fri, from 11am Sat & Sun; 🍴🖥📱; ⓂChernyshevskaya) This self-termed 'art cafe' is tucked into a tiny basement, its two rooms crowded with mismatched furniture, musical instruments, carefully posed mannequins and lots of other junk (or 'art'), creating a bohemian atmosphere. The European menu has a hearty selection of meat and fish, with plenty of Russian classics, plus the odd Asian dish to spice things up.

There is live music nightly at 8.30pm.

GIN NO TAKI JAPANESE €€

Map p260 (www.ginnotaki.ru; pr Chernyshevskogo 17; mains R300-1200; ⏱9am-1am Mon-Fri, from 11am Sat & Sun; 🖥📱📱; ⓂChernyshev-skaya) In a city awash with wannabe Japanese restaurants, this large and lively operation is one of the most authentic, with a wide range of sushi, sashimi, kebabs, tempura and bento boxes. A photo menu makes ordering no hassle at all, and the homemade beer is an excellent accompaniment to any meal.

★MECHTA MOLOKHOVETS RUSSIAN €€€

Map p260 (Мечта Молоховец; ☎812-929 2247; www.molokhovets.ru; ul Radishcheva 10; mains R1450-1800; ⏱noon-11pm Mon-Fri, 2-11pm Sat & Sun; ✳🖥📱; ⓂPloshchad Vosstaniya) Inspired by the cookbook of Elena Molokhovets, the Russian Mrs Beeton, the menu at 'Molokhovets' Dream' covers all the classics from borsch to beef stroganoff, as well as less frequently seen dishes such as goose breast in forest berry sauce and veal cutlets in mushroom ragu. Whatever you have here, you can be sure it's the definitive version.

Start with berry *kissel,* a delicious sweet soup of brambles and wine, and don't bypass the speciality, *koulibiaca,* a golden pastry pie of fish or rabbit. This place is something of an institution locally and takes its food very seriously. Reservations are a good idea in the evenings.

PALKIN RUSSIAN €€€

Map p260 (Палкинъ; ☎812-703 5371; www.palkin.ru; Nevsky pr 47; mains R1000-4000; ⏱noon to 1am; 🖥📱📶; ⓂMayakovskaya) Following a beautiful refit this historic restaurant, first opened in 1871, is back to thrill a new generation of diners. This is the place in town for a blow-out meal, so bring your credit card and prepare yourself for a gastronomic experience that would have been recognisable to past guests, such as Tchaikovsky and Chekhov. Reservations are advised.

✕ Vladimirskaya & Vosstaniya

BGL CAFE & MARKET BAGELS €

Map p264 (nab reki Fontanki 96; bagels R50-250; ⏱11am-11pm; 🍴🖥📱📱) Finally, somewhere decent to enjoy freshly filled bagels! This cool little cafe is popular with a young

A GIFT TO YOUNG HOUSEWIVES

The most popular cookbook in 19th-century Russia was called *A Gift to Young House-wives*, a collection of favourite recipes and household-management tips that turned into a bestseller. The author, Elena Molokhovets, a housewife herself, was dedicated to her 10 children, to the Orthodox Church, and to her inexperienced 'female compatriots' who might need assistance keeping their homes running smoothly.

This book was reprinted 28 times between 1861 and 1914, and Molokhovets added new recipes and helpful hints to each new edition. The last edition included literally thousands of recipes, as well as pointers on how to organise an efficient kitchen, how to set a proper table and how to clean a cast-iron pot.

Molokhovets received an enormously positive response from readers who credited her with no less than preserving their family life. The popular perception of the time was that a wife's primary responsibility was to keep her family together, and keeping her husband well fed seemed to be the key. As one reader wrote, 'a good kitchen is... not an object of luxury. It is a token of the health and well-being of the family, upon which all the remaining conditions of life depend'. Molokhovets included some of these letters in later editions as testimony to her work.

The classic cookbook was never reprinted during the Soviet period. The details of sumptuous dishes and fine table settings, let alone questions of etiquette and style, would certainly have been considered bourgeois by the Soviet regime. Yet still, copies of this ancient tome survived, passed down from mother to daughter like a family heirloom. Today, the book reads not only as a cookbook, but also as a lesson in history and sociology.

and worldly crowd, and has a great location overlooking the Fontanka River. Good lunch deals (until 4pm) make this a great lunch stop, with good coffee and cake on offer too. Bagels to go are also available, and unfilled ones are also for sale.

GREY'S
BISTRO €

Map p260 (www.greys-bistro.ru; Konnaya ul 5/3; mains R200-300; ⊙9.30am-11.30pm Mon-Fri, from noon Sat & Sun; ▣☎; ⓂPl Vosstaniya) The name may be literal (the walls are an understated light grey that complements the dark timber floors and stylish lighting), but this is actually an exciting new arrival to a pleasant but rather quiet neighbourhood. Serving a good selection of breakfast items, plus a small but appealing array of bistro food (salads, couscous, meat grills), Grey's is a chic winner.

BRYNZA
CAUCASIAN €

Map p260 (Брынза; Pushkinskaya ul 1; mains R200-500; ⊙24hrs; ☎⓪; ⓂMayakovskaya) This spacious, great-value place serves up your typical Caucasian and Crimean fare; it specialises in the Crimean Tatar dish *chebureki* (a fried meat turnover) but has a huge selection of grills, salads, soups and *khachapuri* (Georgian cheese bread).

There's a helpful pictorial menu and even a cash machine on-site.

★VINOSTUDIA
ITALIAN €€

Map p260 (☎812-380 7838; www.vinostudia.com; ul Rubenshteina 38; mains R350-700; ☎⚲⓪⛶) Another superb addition to ul Rubenshteina's impressive eating options, Vinostudia is a serious and passionately run *enoteca*. All wine is available by the glass (R130 to R350) and the staff are knowledgable and friendly. There's a good Italian-leaning menu, with dishes such as grilled tiger shrimp, calamari and duck breast rounding out more traditional fare.

Its brick walls mean that it can be rather loud come weekend evenings, when the place is busy and reservations are a good idea. The whitewashed walls, large glass wine cooler and industrial touches all add to the atmosphere.

DOM BEAT
INTERNATIONAL €€

Map p260 (Дом Быта; www.dombeat.ru; ul Razyezzhaya 12; mains R300-500; ☎⚲⓪; ⓂLigovsky Prospekt) As if naming St Petersburg's coolest bar, lounge and restaurant after a Soviet all-purpose store and then dressing the model-gorgeous staff in tailored pastiches of factory uniforms wasn't a solid enough start, the sleek, retro-humorous interior, sumptuous menu and great atmosphere add up to make this one of the best eating choices in town.

As well as great breakfasts (served until 7pm), there's a wide choice of dishes ranging from top-notch Asian cuisine (Thai red curry, chicken tikka masala) to modern takes on Russian meals and international bar food. Portions aren't huge, though, but dishes are affordable enough to order a couple if you're hungry.

TASTE TO EAT   RUSSIAN €€

Map p260 (Вкус Поесть; nab reki Fontaki 82; mains R300-600; ☺noon-11pm Sun-Thu, 2pm-1am Fri & Sat; ☎) This very impressive new establishment has breathed some much-needed life into the beautiful but somewhat moribund Fontanka Embankment. With its concrete floors, exposed bricks and comfy leather seating, it looks gorgeous, while its interesting contemporary take on Russian cuisine and large wine room featuring an international selection with a focus on good Russian wines, won't disappoint either.

POLYANKA   EUROPEAN €€

Map p260 (Полянка; ul Kolokolnaya 10; mains R200-600; ☺10am-11pm; ✷🅿) A real find, this well-thought-through, charming place has got lots going for it: the menu for a start is varied and interesting (try the duck and goats cheese salad) and features everything from rare steak to cheesecake served as a main course with chicken (surprisingly excellent). The friendly, English-speaking staff are very keen to advise you.

ZIG ZAG   EUROPEAN €€

Map p264 (www.zigzag.spb.ru; Gorokhovaya ul 59/92; mains R400-700; ☺noon-11pm, to midnight Fri & Sat; ☎🅿; MPushkinskaya) This gorgeous place is rather unfortunately hidden away from the rest of the city in its sunken premises, but inside it's an effortlessly cool vibe with lots of retro furniture and charming staff. The menu is excellent too, running from burgers (including a lamb burger in a mint-yoghurt sauce and rabbit burger) to Swedish, Moroccan and Provençal dishes.

JEAN-JACQUES   FRENCH €€

Map p260 (Жан-Жак; www.jan-jak.com; ul Marata 10; mains R300-600; ☺24hrs; ☎🅿; MMayakovskaya) This is the most conveniently located of the several St Petersburg branches of this smart French bistro. With a pleasant terrace outside and a burgundy and hunter green

interior that could be that of your favourite Parisian cafe, this restaurant has a typically delicious brasserie menu, from *magret de canard* to boeuf bourguignon.

There's also lots of affordable wine available by the glass. There are other branches near **ploshchad Alexandra Nevskogo** (Жан-Жак; Map p260; www.jan-jak.com; Nevsky pr 166; ☺24 hrs; MPl Alexandra Nevskogo) and on both **Vasilyevsky Island** (Жан-Жак; Map p270; 7-aya liniya 24; ☺24hrs; MVasileostrovskaya) and the Petrograd Side (p157). All branches are open 24 hours.

★GREEN ROOM   RUSSIAN €

Map p260 (Ligivosky pr 74; mains R120-200; ☺9am-11pm Sun-Thu, to 3am Fri & Sat; ☎🍴🅿; MLigovsky Prospekt) The in-house cafe of the super cool Loft Project ETAGI, this place is on the 3rd floor (from the street go through the courtyard). The centrepiece here is a fantastic summer terrace, which is a gorgeous place to eat and drink. Inside it's an airy, cool cafe space with a menu that's simple, tasty and excellent value.

SCHASTYE   ITALIAN €€

Map p260 (Счастье; ☎812-572 2675; www.schastye.com; ul Rubinshteyna 15/17; mains R350-800; ☺9am-11pm, til last customer Fri & Sat; ☎🍴🅿; MMayakovskaya) 'Happiness' comes in several forms here: a multi-roomed venue full of cosy nooks and crannies to huddle up in, an expansive Italian menu, delicious pastries and sweets piled up on plates around the place, and lavish and thoroughly warm (if somewhat random) decor (think jars full of pasta and photo frames with stock shots of family members).

Breakfast is served daily until noon, and brunch until 6pm on weekends. There are a two further branches of Schastye that serve as cafes. These can be found on **Nevsky prospekt** (Счастье; Map p260; Nevsky pr 55; ☺10am-11pm; MMayakovskaya) and in the Angleterre Hotel on **Isaakievskaya pl** (Счастье; Map p256; ul Malaya Morskaya 24; ☺9am-11pm Sun-Thu, to 2am Fri & Sat; ☎; MAdmiralteyskaya).

MOPS   THAI €€

Map p260 (www.mopscafe.ru; ul Rubinshteyna 12; mains R500-1000; ☺2pm-1am Sun-Wed, to 3am Thu-Sat; ☎🍴🅿; MMayakovskaya) The first and only dedicated Thai restaurant in the city is a visual treat: the elegant street-level dining room is all white painted floorboards and linen tablecloths and embellished with gorgeous Thai furniture, while inside the feel is dark and moody. Whichever vibe you want to go with, it makes for a stylish place to eat out.

The enormous pictorial menu offers a mouth-watering selection of Thai classics. There's a 20% discount between 2pm and 5pm during the week, which makes it very reasonable.

BISTRO GARÇON FRENCH €€
Map p260 (www.garcon.ru; Nevsky pr 95; mains R450-850; ⊘10am-midnight; ⌂⃝; ⓜPloshchad Vosstaniya) This gorgeous little bistro is smart and unpretentious, with low lighting, upscale but still charming decor and professional staff. Prices are reasonable given the excellent standard of the cooking and service. While this is the main restaurant of the group in town, you can find its bakeries and patisseries, which serve up excellent sandwiches and cakes, all over St Petersburg.

YUZU ASIAN €€
Map p260 (www.yuzubar.ru; Suvorovsky pr 51; mains R550-1100; ⌂⃝⃝⃝; ⓜChernyshevskaya) This sleek place offers gourmet versions of classic Asian dishes, with the odd Russian one thrown in for good measure. Beef in sweet and sour sauce sits next to stewed rabbit with savoy cabbage, while tom yum soup complements chicken broth. DJs play at the bar and the menu is on iPads, just in case you need further context.

CAT CAFÉ GEORGIAN €€
Map p260 (Кафе Кэт; Stremyannaya ul 22/3; mains R250-800; ⊘noon-11pm; ⌂⃝⃝; ⓜMayakovskaya) With vines hanging from the ceiling to evoke the Caucasian countryside, this popular and reliable restaurant dishes up Georgian favourites such as hearty *khinkali* (meat dumplings), decadent *khachapuri* and delectable rolled aubergine with walnuts. It's reasonably priced, run by a friendly husband-and-wife team and has a helpful photographic menu.

POT ARTHUR INTERNATIONAL €€
Map p260 (Порт Артур; www.portartur-spb.ru; Zvenigorodskaya ul 12/17; mains R400-1000; ⊘noon-1am, to 2am Fri-Sun; ⌂⃝; ⓜZvenigorodskaya) Its name may be a bizarre one, as Port Arthur was the scene of one of Russia's most humiliating naval defeats, but everything else about this plush gentleman's club–style venue is welcome: there's a large menu of international cuisine, a grand circular bar and live music Thursday to Saturday at 9pm.

★GRAND CRU FINE DINING €€€
Map p260 (Великий Крю; www.grandcru.ru; nab reki Fontanki 52; mains R800-2000; ⊘noon-11pm; ⌂⃝⃝⃝) This wine emporium may function as a shop, but its excellent gastronomic restaurant is no afterthought; it's a beautifully decorated space with moody red lighting, timber floors and big windows. The menu is ambitious and expensive, with dishes such as rabbit with millet risotto and beetroot mousse presented on slabs of black slate and paired with a wine.

The only drawback is that there is no wine list, meaning you have to select the bottle with the sommelier and then (unless you're an oligarch), check the price of each one before committing. Otherwise the service is very professional and the standard of both food and wine is highly impressive. Don't miss the superb bruschetta.

NA ZDOROVYE!

'To your health!' is what Russians say when they throw back a shot of vodka. But this pronouncement hardly suffices as a proper toast in a public forum or an intimate drinking session among friends. A proper toast requires thoughtfulness and sincerity.

A few themes prevail. The first toast of the night often acknowledges the generosity of the host, while the second usually recognises the beauty of the ladies present. In mixed company, you can't go wrong raising your glass to international friendship (*za mezhdunarodnuyu druzhbu*) or world peace (*za miravoy mir*). But in all cases, the toast requires a personal anecdote or a profound insight, as well as a bit of rambling preamble to make it meaningful.

In Russia, drinking vodka is a celebration of life in all its complexity – the triumph, the tragedy and the triviality. A toast is a vocalisation of that celebration, so say it like you mean it. And drink it in the same way – *zalpom!* (bottoms up!)

🍷 DRINKING & NIGHTLIFE

🍷 Smolny & Liteyny

★UNION BAR & GRILL   BAR

Map p260 (Liteyny pr 55; ⊘6pm-4am Sun-Thu, to 6am Fri & Sat; 🛜; ⓂMayakovskaya) The Union is a glamorous and fun place, characterised by one enormous long wooden bar, low lighting and a New York feel. It's all rather adult, with a serious cocktail list and designer beers on tap. It's crazy at the weekends, but quiet during the week, and always draws a cool 20- and 30-something crowd.

There's a full food menu and the beard and tattoo levels often reach Williamsburg/Shoreditch levels, quite a feat for fusty old St Petersburg.

★THE HAT   JAZZ CLUB

Map p260 (ul Belinskogo 9; ⊘7pm-5am; ⓂGostiny Dvor) The wonderfully retro-feeling Hat is a serious spot for jazz and whiskey lovers, who come for the nightly live music and the cool-cat crowd that makes this wonderfully designed bar feel like it's been transported out of 1950s Greenwich Village. A very welcome change of gear for St Petersburg's drinking options, but it can be extremely full at weekends.

MISHKA   BAR

Map p260 (Мишка; www.miskhabar.ru; nab reki Fontanky 40; ⊘6pm-2am Mon-Thu, 2pm-6am Fri-Sun; 🛜; ⓂGostiny Dvor) Hipster ground zero in St Petersburg is this two-room basement place that is massively popular with a cool student crowd. The front room is hectic, smoky and becomes a dance floor later in the evening, while the quiet, nonsmoky back room is a chill-out area. DJs spin nightly and there's a big cocktail list.

DEAD POETS BAR   COCKTAIL BAR

Map p260 (ul Zhukovskogo 12; ⊘2pm-2am; 🛜; ⓂMayakovskaya) This very cool place is an adult's cocktail bar, with a sophisticated drinks menu and an almost unbelievable range of spirits stacked along the long bar and served up by a committed staff of mixologists. It's more of a quiet place, with low lighting, a jazz soundtrack and plenty of space to sit down.

COFFEE STATION   CAFE

Map p260 (ul Nekrasova 26; ⊘8am-10.30pm; 🛜; ⓂMayakovskaya) Hidden away (quite literally – the owners took down their street sign as they feared that they were becoming too popular!), this gorgeous place is a haven for anyone serious about coffee. With a wide selection of beans and preparation methods, including clever drippers, this is the best coffee you'll find this side of the Fontanka.

FREEDOM   ANTI-CAFE

Map p260 (Nevsky pr 88; per hour R2; ⊘noon-midnight Mon-Thu, to 6am Fri & Sat, to 2am Sun; 🛜; ⓂMayakovskaya) Another very popular anti-cafe in a courtyard off Nevsky pr, Freedom is spacious and friendly and full of rooms where you can play games, watch TV, hang out and meet like-minded boho types.

BAR 812   COCKTAIL BAR

Map p260 (www.bar812.ru; ul Zhukovskogo 11; ⊘6pm-1am Mon-Thu, to 4am Fri & Sat; 🛜; ⓂMayakovskaya) The brass bar here is one of the most popular in the city (not to mention one of the more pricey). With cocktails named Pussy Talker and Male of the Species, it's a popular pick-up joint and is always heaving at weekends, while it's surprisingly laid back and relaxed during the week.

🍷 Vladimirskaya & Vosstaniya

★DOM BEAT   COCKTAIL BAR

Map p260 (Дом Быта; www.dombeat.ru; ul Razyezzhaya 12; ⊘noon-6am; 🛜; ⓂLigovsky Prospekt) The big draws at this place are the superb cocktails and wide drinks menu. Funky '70s interior, a cool crowd and tables cleared for dancing later in the evening make it a great spot.

ZIFERBLAT   ANTI-CAFE

Map p260 (Циферблат; ☎8-960-285 6946; www.ziferblat.net; 2nd fl, Nevsky pr 81; per min R2; ⊘11am-midnight Mon-Thu, to 7am Fri & Sat, to midnight Sun; 🛜; ⓂPloshchad Vosstaniya) A charming multi-room 'free space' that has started a worldwide trend, Ziferblat is the original anti-cafe in St Petersburg. Coffee, tea, soft drinks and biscuits are included as you while away your time playing computer games, reading, watching movies and just hanging out with the arty young locals who frequent its cosy rooms.

WORTH A DETOUR

ST PETERSBURG FROM ABOVE

The top floor of the Soviet-era Azimut Hotel, one of the city's biggest eyesores, is now also home to the fantastic **Sky Bar** (Map p264; 18th fl, Hotel Azimut, Lermontovsky pr 43/1; ⊗5pm-1am; 🛜; MBaltiyskaya), quite simply the best place to get a bird's-eye view of the city. Taking up much of the 18th floor, the bar has plenty of space to sit back and enjoy the incredible view of the historic centre through its vast floor-to-ceiling windows. As well as cocktails and coffee, there's also a full food menu. Even the nearest metro is some distance away, however, so it's best to wander here along the Fontanka from the centre.

BRIMBORIUM   BAR

Map p260 (ul Mayakovskogo 22-24; ⊗1pm-last customer; 🛜; MMayakovskaya) When you see the smart, intellectual crowd here you'll understand why the bar's name is a casual reference to Faust. Brimborium is a charming, upscale place, with excellent designer ales on tap, a mixologist approach to cocktail making, delicious quiche on sale and different coloured wall projections that switch over throughout the night, changing the atmosphere.

DYUNI   BAR

Map p260 (Дюны; Ligovsky pr 50; ⊗4pm-midnight, to 6am Fri & Sat; 🛜; MPloshchad Vosstaniya) What looks like a small suburban house sits rather incongruously here amid repurposed warehouses in this vast courtyard. There's a cosy indoor bar and a sand-covered outside area with table football and ping pong, which keeps the cool kids happy all night in the summer months. To find it, simply continue in a straight line from the courtyard entrance.

TERMINAL BAR   BAR

Map p260 (ul Rubinshteyna 13a; ⊗4pm-last customer; 🛜; MDostoevskaya) A slice of New York bohemia on one of the city's most happening streets, Terminal is great for a relaxed drink with friends, who can spread out along the length of the enormous bar, while great music (and live piano from anyone who can play) fills the long, arched room under the grey vaulted ceilings. One of our favourites.

CAFE MITTE   CAFE

Map p260 (ul Rubinshteyna 27; ⊗10am-11pm Mon-Fri, from midday Sat & Sun; 🛜; MDostoevskaya) Named after one of Berlin's coolest districts, this friendly and casual cafe is a great place for a strong coffee, excellent cake, breakfast or a sandwich. If you get bored, there's even a Berlin-style photo booth in here to immortalise your visit.

GRIBOYEDOV   CLUB

Map p260 (Грибоедов; www.griboedovclub.ru; Voronezhskaya ul 2a; cover R200-400; ⊗noon-6am; 🛜; MLigovsky Prospekt) Griboyedov is hands down the longest-standing and most respected music club in the city. Housed in a repurposed bomb shelter, this one was founded by local ska collective Dva Samolyota. It's a low-key bar in the early evening, gradually morphing into a dance club later in the night.

☆ ENTERTAINMENT

JFC JAZZ CLUB   JAZZ

Map p260 (☎812-272 9850; www.jfc-club.spb.ru; Shpalernaya ul 33; cover R100-500; ⊗7-11pm; MChernyshevskaya) Very small and very New York, this cool club is the best place in the city to hear modern, innovative jazz music, as well as blues, bluegrass and various other styles (see the website for a list of what's on). The space is tiny, so book a table online if you want to sit down.

PETROVICH   LIVE MUSIC

Map p260 (Петрович; www.petrovich-piter.ru; ul Marata 56-58; 🛜; MLigovsky Pr) Styling itself a club-restaurant, Petrovich, a long-running Moscow institution that has made its way to St Petersburg, is actually more of a music and dancing venue. The extraordinary place is crammed with Soviet paraphernalia and the reason to come is to hear the nightly live music (usually Soviet songs) and join in the fun. There is no cover charge.

Saturdays is a Soviet dance night with obligatory participation – you have been warned!

CABARET
GAY CLUB

Map p260 (Кабаре; www.cabarespb.ru; Razyezzhaya ul 43; cover R200-500; ⊙11pm-6am Thu-Sat; MLigovsky Prospekt) This latest incarnation of a gay club that has been going in various forms for over a decade is a great place for a campy, old-school experience, complete with a very popular drag show featuring lip-synching drag queens who come on stage at 2.30am each club night and impersonate Russian and international stars. Lots of silly fun, but massively popular.

RED FOX JAZZ CAFÉ
JAZZ

Map p260 (Красный лис; ☑812-275 4214; www.rfjc.ru; ul Mayakovskogo 50; cover R100-200; ⊙10am-11am Mon-Fri, from 1.30pm Sat, from 4.30pm Sun; MChernyshevskaya) The fun and friendly Red Fox Jazz Café is a subterranean space that showcases various jazz styles in the old-fashioned 1920s to '50s sense: big band, bebop, ragtime and swing. Sunday changes it up with a jam session, featuring anybody who wants to participate. The menu is extensive and affordable and you can reserve a table for free.

Music starts at 8.30pm.

FISH FABRIQUE
LIVE MUSIC

Map p260 (www.fishfabrique.spb.ru; Ligovsky pr 53; ⊙3pm-6am, concerts from 8pm Thu-Sun & sometimes on other days; ☎; MPloshchad Vosstaniya) There are St Petersburg institutions and then there's Fish Fabrique, the museum of local boho life that has been going for two decades. Here, in the dark underbelly of Pushkinskaya 10, artists, musicians and counterculturalists of all ages meet to drink beer and listen to music.

Nowadays, the newer **Fabrique Nouvelle** (⊙3pm-late) in the same courtyard hosts concerts nightly, while the old Fish Fabrique has them just at weekends, but whichever one you're in, you're sure to rub shoulders with an interesting crowd.

COSMONAUT
LIVE MUSIC

(Космонавт; www.cosmonavt.su; ul Bronnitskaya 24; ☎; MTekhnologichesky Institut) This fantastic conversion of a Soviet-era cinema in a rather nondescript part of town is a great venue for medium-sized concerts and a good place to see live acts in St Petersburg. There's air-conditioning throughout, which is a godsend in summer, and a very comfortable VIP lounge upstairs, with seating throughout.

JAZZ PHILHARMONIC HALL
JAZZ

Map p260 (www.jazz-hall.spb.ru; Zagorodny pr 27; cover R500-1500; ⊙concerts 7pm Wed-Sun, Ellington Hall concerts 8pm Tue, Fri & Sat; MVladimirskaya) Founded by legendary jazz violinist and composer David Goloshchokin, this venue represents the more traditional side of jazz. Two resident bands perform straight jazz and Dixieland in the big hall, which seats up to 200 people. The smaller Ellington Hall is used for occasional acoustic performances. Foreign guests also appear doing mainstream and modern jazz; check the website for details.

SMOLNY CATHEDRAL
CLASSICAL MUSIC

Map p260 (Смольный собор; www.cathedral.ru; pl Rastrelli 3/1; tickets R500-1000; MChernyshevskaya) The beautiful Smolny Cathedral makes a great venue for classical concerts. While not as attractive as some of the other concert halls in the city (and certainly not as ornate as its gorgeous exterior), it is still an atmospheric place to watch a performance.

BOLSHOY PUPPET THEATRE
PUPPET THEATRE

Map p260 (Большой театр кукол; www.puppets.ru; ul Nekrasova 10; tickets R250-600; MChernyshevskaya) This 'big' puppet theatre is indeed the biggest in the city, and has been active since 1931. The repertoire includes a wide range of shows for children and for adults.

MALY DRAMA THEATRE
THEATRE

Map p260 (Малый драматический театр; www.mdt-dodin.ru; ul Rubinshteyna 18; MVladimirskaya) Also called the Theatre of Europe, the Maly is St Petersburg's most internationally celebrated theatre. Its director Lev Dodin is famed for his long version of Fyodor Dostoevsky's *The Devils,* as well as Anton Chekhov's *Play Without a Name,* which both toured the world to great acclaim. It's also one of the few theatres that does performances with subtitles.

🛍 SHOPPING

Smolny and Liteyny, mostly residential neighbourhoods, do not offer too much in the way of shopping, but both are arty, intellectual places, as evidenced by the proliferation of galleries and bookshops. As Nevsky pr continues east past the Fontanka River towards

pl Vosstaniya, it continues to be lined with boutiques and culminates with two enormous shopping centres.

TKACHI   SHOPPING CENTRE
(Ткачи; www.tkachi.com; nab Obvodnogo kanala 60; Ⓜ Obvodny Kanal) In an otherwise derelict part of town, 'Weavers' is an impressive conversion of a warehouse into a 'creative space', which more often than not in St Petersburg means shops and cafes with a vague nod in the direction of art. On the ground floor you'll find gifts, clothes, bikes and electronics, while the 5th floor is a huge exhibition space and restaurant.

OFF   SECONDHAND
(www.offoffoff.ru; nab Obvodnogo kanala 60; ◷noon-9pm; Ⓜ Obvodny Kanal) Inside the Tkachi 'Cultural Space' is this paradise for anyone after some Soviet accessories, vintage jackets and secondhand clothes of varying styles. The friendly owner may take it upon herself to find just the right outfit for you – and she clearly knows what she's doing judging by her own unique appearance.

PHONOTEKA   MUSIC
Map p260 (Фонотека; www.phonoteka.ru; ul Marata 28; ◷10am-10pm; Ⓜ Mayakovskaya) This cool store will thrill anyone interested in music and cinema, as it sells a very cool range of vinyls from all eras (it's particularly strong on rare Soviet discs), a great selection of CDs from around the world and a discerning choice of film and documentary on DVD, making it an excellent place to buy Russian films.

ANGLIA   BOOKS
Map p260 (nab reki Fontanki 30; ◷10am-8pm Mon-Fri, from 11am Sat, noon-7pm Sun; Ⓜ Gostiny Dvor) The city's only dedicated English-language bookshop has a large selection of contemporary literature, classics, dictionaries, history and travel writing. It also hosts small art and photography displays, organises book readings and generally is a cornerstone of expat life in St Petersburg.

WAGNER   ANTIQUES
Map p260 (Вагнер комиссионный магазин; ul Mayakovskogo 17; ◷10am-7pm; Ⓜ Mayakovskaya) It's rather generous to call this basement gem an antiques shop – much of the stock is more garage-sale worthy, but there are still some very cool bits and pieces. Everything from Soviet kitchen items and movie posters to old books and antique lamps can be found here if you look hard enough.

BOREY ART CENTRE   ART
Map p260 (Борей Артцентр; www.borey.ru; Liteyny pr 58; ◷noon-8pm Tue-Sat; Ⓜ Mayakovskaya) There is never a dull moment at this underground (in both senses of the word) art gallery. In the front room, you'll see some fairly mainstream stuff for sale, but the back rooms always house creative contemporary exhibitions by local artists. The bookshop is one of the best in town for books on art and architecture.

SOL-ART   ART
Map p260 (www.solartgallery.com; Solyanoy per 15; ◷10am-6pm; Ⓜ Chernyshevskaya) In the sumptuous surroundings of the Museum of Decorative & Applied Arts, this is a great place to buy contemporary local art.

IMPERIAL PORCELAIN   HOMEWARES
(Императорский Фарфор; www.ipm.ru; pr Obukhovsky Oborony 151; ◷10am-8pm; Ⓜ Lomonosovskaya) Dating back to the mid-18th century, this is the company that used to make tea sets for the Russian royal family.

WORTH A DETOUR

MUSEUM OF THE IMPERIAL PORCELAIN FACTORY

Run as an outpost of the Hermitage Museum, the superb **Museum of the Imperial Porcelain Factory** (www.ipm.ru; pr Obukhovsky Oborony 151; admission R150; ◷10am-7pm Mon-Fri; Ⓜ Lomonosovskaya) has a stellar display of the various designs the factory has produced over the centuries and will appeal to anyone interested in this very Russian handicraft. Among the collection you'll find everything from bespoke dinner services used by the tsars to unique constructivist tea sets created in the 1920s, indicative of the factory's versatility in serving its various political masters. There's also a discounted porcelain shop here (see above) where big savings can be made compared to the factory's cit-centre outlets.

Formerly known as Lomonosov China, the company continues to produce innovative designs – the speciality being contemporary takes on traditional themes. The stuff is expensive, but the quality is high and the designs can be spectacular.

This factory outlet is far-flung but offers discounted prices that are significantly cheaper than those you'll find at the city-centre outlets. To get here, turn left out of the metro station and walk under the bridge. Turn left on the embankment and you'll see the factory ahead.

IMAGINE CLUB   MUSIC

Map p260 (www.imagine-club.com; ul Zhukovskogo 20; ◎10am-8pm) St Petersburg's largest record shop, and by record we do actually mean vinyl as well as CDs, is a great place to buy some quality Russian music souvenirs. LPs from all over the former Soviet Union can be found here, as well as an impressive choice of imports from Western Europe and the US.

BAT NORTON   CLOTHING

Map p260 (www.batnorton.com; nab reki Fontanki 50; 10am-7pm; MDostoevskaya) This local street-wear brand has the tagline 'made in Russia' and its bright, psychedelic and playful unisex clothing is popular with a cool, younger crowd.

ART RE.FLEX   ART

Map p260 (www.artreflex.ru; pr Bakunina 5; ◎noon-7pm Tue-Sat; MPloshchad Vosstaniya) This contemporary gallery is unique, showcasing artists of all ages, genres and experience levels. So its exhibitions mix the work of up-and-coming artists with more established names. It displays painting, graphics and sculpture, in an attempt to highlight the most interesting trends in contemporary art.

RUSSKAYA STARINA   ANTIQUES

Map p260 (Русская старина; ul Nekrasova 6; ◎11am-9pm, from noon Sun; MMayakovskaya/ Chernyshevskaya) This fascinating place is a repository of local antiques and has a wide range of stock running from furniture and paintings to medals and samovars. It's well worth a look through, and the low-pressure sales technique invites browsing.

PARFIONOVA   CLOTHING, ACCESSORIES

Map p260 (Парфёнова; www.parfionova.ru; Nevsky pr 51; ◎noon-8pm; MMayakovskaya) Tatyana Parfionova was the first St Petersburg couturier to have her own fashion house back in the 1990s, when the New Russians turned up their noses at anything that was not straight from Paris or Milan. Now this local celebrity showcases her stuff at her Nevsky pr boutique, where you'll find her striking monochromatic prét-à-porter designs as well as her famous crimson scarves.

TULA SAMOVARS   SOUVENIRS

Map p260 (Тульские самовары; www.samovary.ru; per Dzhambula 11; MZvenigorodskaya) Nearly all samovars (metal containers holding boiling water) in Russia are made in the town of Tula, south of Moscow, but this beautiful showroom is the place in St Petersburg to buy a truly unique souvenir of your visit. The samovars range from small, simple designs to enormous and elaborate ones with precious stones and other embellishments.

KUZNECHNY MARKET   MARKET

Map p260 (Кузнечный рынок; Kuznechny per 3; ◎8am-8pm; MVladimirskaya) The colours and atmosphere of the city's largest fruit and vegetable market are a wonderful experience: the vendors will ply you with free samples of fresh fruits, homemade *smetana* (sour cream) and sweet honey. However, bargain hard – prices can start off very high, especially when it's clear you're not Russian.

GALERIA   SHOPPING CENTRE

Map p260 (Галерия; www.galeria.spb.ru; Ligovsky pr 30a; ◎10am-11pm; MPloshchad Vosstaniya) This extraordinary place has rather changed everything for shopping in St Petersburg – there are probably as many shops here as elsewhere in the entire city centre. Spread over five floors, with around 300 shops (including H&M, Gap, Marks & Spencer and Zara), this really is a one-stop shop for pretty much all your shopping needs.

NEVSKY CENTRE   SHOPPING CENTRE

Map p260 (Невский Центр; www.nevskycentre.ru; Nevsky pr 112; ◎10am-11pm; MPloshchad Vosstaniya) Nevsky Centre is a smart and central multifloor shopping centre. It houses some 70 shops over seven floors, including the city's largest department store, Stockmann, which includes the excellent basement Stockmann supermarket. Elsewhere there's a food court and lots of independent fashion and furnishing stores.

NEVSKY 152   FASHION
Map p260 (www.nevsky152.ru; Nevsky pr 152; ⊗noon-8pm) This is a one-stop 'concept store' for big name international fashion brands in St Petersburg, as the liveried doorman will make abundantly clear. Come here for boutiques from such names as Chanel, Fendi and Armani.

AUCHAN   HYPERMARKET
(Ашан; www.auchan.ru; ul Borovaya 47; ⊗8.30am-11pm; ⓂObvodny Kanal) If you can't find something anywhere else in the city, then head for this conveniently located hypermarket, just a short walk from Obvodny Kanal metro. You'll find a huge range of food, clothing, household products and far, far more.

IMPERIAL PORCELAIN   HOMEWARES
Map p260 (Императорский Фарфор; www.ipm.ru; Vladimirsky pr 7; ⊗10am-8pm; ⓂVladimirskaya) This is the convenient city-centre location of the famous porcelain factory that once made tea sets for the Romanovs. If you're determined to get a bargain, head out to the factory outlet (p129) where prices are far cheaper. There's a second **city centre branch** (Map p260; Nevsky pr 160; ⊗10am-9pm; ⓂPloshchad Vosstaniya) on the other side of pl Vosstaniya.

RUSSKY LYON   LINEN
Map p260 (Русский лён; Pushkinskaya ul 3; ⊗11am-8pm; ⓂPloshchad Vosstaniya) Russia has a long tradition of producing fine-grade linen; this small chain of shops with five branches around the city sells quality tableware and fashions made from the cloth, in both traditional and contemporary designs.

🏃 SPORTS & ACTIVITIES

MYTNINSKIYE BANI   BANYA
Map p260 (Мытнинские бани; www.mybanya.spb.ru; Mytninskaya ul 17-19; per hr R100-200; ⊗8am-10pm Fri-Tue; ⓂPloshchad Vosstaniya) Unique in the city, Mytninskiye Bani is heated by a wood furnace, just like the log-cabin bathhouses that are still found in the Russian countryside. It's actually the oldest communal *banya* (hot bath) in the city, and in addition to a *parilka* (steam room) and plunge pool, the private 'lux' *banya* includes a swanky lounge area with leather furniture and a pool table.

DEGTYARNIYE BATHS   BANYA
Map p260 (Дегтярные бани; www.d1a.ru; Degtyarnaya ul 1a; per hr R400-1425; ⊗8.30am-10pm; ⓂPloshchad Vosstaniya) These modern baths are divided up into mixed, men's and women's sections, or you can book private unisex *banyi* of varying degrees of luxury. Book ahead, though, as they are often full. English is spoken and the website has a helpful English-language guide to how to take a *banya* for novices.

SKATPROKAT   CYCLING
Map p260 (☎812-717 6838; www.skatprokat.ru; Goncharnaya ul 7; per day from R400; ⊗11am-8pm; ⓂPloshchad Vosstaniya) This outfit offers rental bicycles that include brand-new mountain bikes by the Russian company Stark. You'll need to leave either R2000 and your passport, or R7000 as a deposit per bike. If you are in town for a while, this place also sells secondhand bikes and does repairs. It also offers excellent Saturday- and Sunday-morning bike tours of the city.

Vasilyevsky Island

Neighbourhood Top Five

1 Taking in one of the best views of the city from the historic **Strelka** (p136), the spit of land that crowns Vasilyevsky Island and boasts flaming rostral columns during national holidays.

2 Exploring Peter the Great's private collection of anatomical oddities at the ghoulish **Kunstkamera** (p134).

3 Checking out St Petersburg's best modern-art museum, the huge **Erarta Museum of Contemporary Art** (p135), where you'll see Russian works from the late Soviet and post-Soviet era.

4 Visiting the fascinating **Menshikov Palace** (p136), St Petersburg's first stone building.

5 Hearing tales of Soviet exploration in the Arctic aboard the retired **Ice-breaker Krasin** (p137).

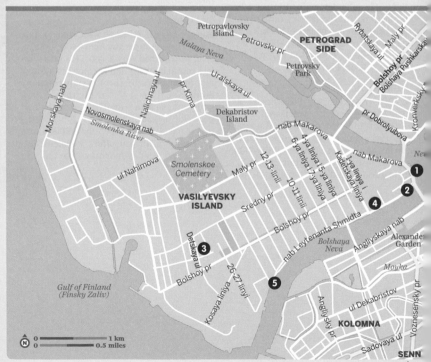

For more detail of this area see Map p270 ➡

Explore: Vasilyevsky Island

Peter the Great originally intended this large triangular island to be the heart of his city. As such, it is among the oldest neighbourhoods in St Petersburg, especially the eastern tip known as the Strelka (meaning 'tongue of land'), which is crammed with institutions, museums and the sprawling campus of St Petersburg State University.

Further back from the Strelka, the island is an orderly, residential place, with a grid system of wide roads full of shops, restaurants and cafes. It makes for a pleasant base for travellers, with fast connections to the centre and a good choice of eating options.

The northern and western end of the island is rather postindustrial and remote, with the city's ferry port and the LenExpo exhibition centre blighting the landscape. However, in the past few years regeneration has come, with the fantastic Erarta Museum of Contemporary Art well and truly putting the area on the map for more inquisitive travellers.

Local Life

➡ **Bridge advice** If you're staying on Vasilyevsky Island, remember that in the summer months the bridges go up at night and you can't cross. Dvortsovy most stays up all night (1.25am to 4.50am), but Blagoveshchensky most has a short break and is crossable from 2.45am until 3.10am.

➡ **Cool street** Hang with the locals on 6-ya and 7-ya liniya, the main pedestrian and commercial street of Vasilyevsky Island. Full of cafes, bars, restaurants and shops, this is where to escape the tourist crowds at the Strelka.

Getting There & Away

➡ **Metro** Vasilyevsky Island is served by two metro stations, both on Line 3. By far the most useful is Vasileostrovskaya, at the island's heart, while Primorskaya serves the far-flung northwestern corner of the island.

➡ **Bus** The number 7 bus goes between Primorskaya and pl Vosstaniya, via Nalichnaya ul, all of Bolshoy pr and Nevsky pr. Trolleybus 10 and 11 run similar routes.

➡ **Marshrutka** From Vasileostrovskaya metro station, the following *marshrutky* (fixed route minibuses) zip to the far end of Sredny pr: K30, K44, K62, K120.

Lonely Planet's Top Tip

This tip might sound slightly nuts, but trust us. If you're heading to Vasileostrovskaya metro station from the city centre during rush hour, be sure to get on the very last carriage (ie the one at the back end of the train), as this is nearest to the escalator when you arrive at the station. The platform at this very busy station is always swamped with people and you'll have to wait for minutes before being able to get on the escalator unless you use this sneaky trick.

✕ Best Places to Eat

➡ Restoran (p140)
➡ Na Kukhnye (p140)
➡ Buter Brodsky (p140)
➡ Casa del Myaso (p140)
➡ Gintarus (p140)

For reviews, see p138 ➡

🍷 Best Places to Drink

➡ Buter Brodsky (p140)
➡ Helsinki Bar (p141)
➡ Birzha Bar (p141)
➡ Brúgge (p141)
➡ Grad Petrov (p141)

For reviews, see p141 ➡

👁 Best Museums

➡ Erarta Museum of Contemporary Art (p135)
➡ Kunstkamera (p134)
➡ Museum of Zoology (p136)
➡ Menshikov Palace (p136)

For reviews, see p134 ➡

TOP SIGHT
KUNSTKAMERA

Also known as the **Museum of Ethnology and Anthropology**, the Kunstkamera was the city's first museum and was founded in 1714 by Peter himself. It is famous largely for its ghoulish collection of monstrosities, preserved 'freaks', two-headed mutant foetuses, deformed animals and odd body parts, all collected by Peter with the aim of educating the notoriously superstitious Russian people.

Babies in Bottles

Peter wanted to demonstrate that malformations were not the result of the evil eye or sorcery, but rather caused by 'internal damage as well as fear and the beliefs of the mother during pregnancy' – a marginally more enlightened view. This fascinating place is an essential St Petersburg sight, although not one for the faint-hearted. Think twice about bringing young children here and definitely give the Kunstkamera a wide berth if you are pregnant yourself. Indeed, where else can you see specimens with such charming names as 'double-faced monster with brain hernia'?

The Rest of the Collection

The famous babies in bottles make up just a small part of the enormous collection, which also encompasses some wonderfully kitsch dioramas exhibiting rare objects and demonstrating cultural practices from all over the world. The 3rd floor of the museum is given over to an exhibition about polymath Mikhail Lomonosov, with a re-creation of his study-laboratory. The top floors of the museum are only open as part of a guided tour (in English, for up to four people R2700, call in advance to book), and include the great Gottorp Globe, a rotating globe and planetarium all in one.

DON'T MISS

➡ The stuffed pangolin
➡ Skeletons of Siamese twins
➡ Gottorp Globe
➡ Skeleton of the Giant Bourgeois

PRACTICALITIES

➡ Кунсткамера
➡ Map p270
➡ www.kunstkamera.ru
➡ Tamozhenny per
➡ adult/child R250/50
➡ ⊙11am-7pm Tue-Sun
➡ Ⓜ Admiralteyskaya

TOP SIGHT ERARTA MUSEUM & GALLERIES OF CONTEMPORARY ART

This fantastic contemporary-art museum has made Vasilyevsky Island a destination in itself. Opened in 2010 and housed in a stunningly converted neoclassical Stalinist building, it is spread over five floors and is focused on the permanent collection of some 2000 works of Russian art produced between the 1950s and the present day. It also has a good restaurant and a cafe.

Permanent Collection

The permanent collection is an excellent survey of the past half-century of Russian art, and is particularly strong on late Soviet underground art. It's all terribly sleek and beautifully presented. An extension to display its ever-growing permanent collection is planned.

Erarta Galleries

One unusual feature of this museum is the inclusion of several floors of commercial galleries in the same building, where the work on display is also on sale. This tends to be contemporary installation, painting, video art and sculpture by Russian artists, and is worth checking out. Your ticket includes entrance to the entire permanent collection and the first three floors of the temporary exhibits, but those on the upper floors are an extra R150 each.

Tours & Interactive Installations

The museum offers very good tours in English (R3000 for a group of up to 20, museum tickets must also be bought); book ahead at excursion@erarta.com. Several 15-minute interactive audiovisual experiences, 'U Space Installations', are also on offer (R200 for up to five people).

DON'T MISS
....
➡ *A Plank Bed*, Savely Lapitsky
➡ *USSR*, Yegeny Sarasov
➡ *Night Shift*, Nikolai Vikulov
➡ *The Great Bear*, Rinat Voligamsi

PRACTICALITIES
....
➡ Музей современного искусства Эрарта
➡ Map p270
➡ www.erarta.com
➡ 29-ya Liniya 2
➡ adult/under 21 R450/300
➡ ⊘10am-10pm Wed-Mon
➡ Ⓜ Vasileostrovskaya then bus 6 or 7, or trolley-bus 10 or 11 from the opposite side of the road

◉ SIGHTS

KUNSTKAMERA
MUSEUM

See p134.

ERARTA MUSEUM OF CONTEMPORARY ART
MUSEUM

See p135.

STRELKA
LANDMARK

Map p270 Among the oldest parts of Vasilyevsky Island, this eastern tip is where Peter the Great wanted his new city's administrative and intellectual centre to be. In fact, the Strelka became the focus of St Petersburg's maritime trade, symbolised by the colonnaded Customs House (now the Pushkin House). The two rostral columns, archetypal St Petersburg landmarks, are studded with ships' prows and four seated sculptures representing four of Russia's great rivers: the Neva, the Volga, the Dnieper and the Volkhov.

These were oil-fired navigation beacons in the 1800s and their gas torches are still lit on some holidays, which makes for a breathtaking sight. The Strelka has one of the best views in the city, with the Peter & Paul Fortress to the left and the Hermitage, the Admiralty and St Isaac's Cathedral to the right.

MUSEUM OF ZOOLOGY
MUSEUM

Map p270 (Зоологический музей; www.zin.ru; Universitetskaya nab 1; adult/student R200/70, Thu free; ⊙11am-6pm Wed-Mon; ⓂAdmiralteyskaya) One of the biggest and best of its kind in the world, the Museum of Zoology was founded in 1832 and has some amazing exhibits, including a vast blue whale skeleton that greets you in the first hall. The highlight is unquestionably the 44,000-year-old woolly mammoth thawed out of the Siberian ice in 1902, although there are a further three mammoths, including a baby one – all incredible finds.

On top of the extraordinarily comprehensive collection of beasts from around the globe, upstairs you'll also find thousands of categorised insects, as well as a live **insect zoo** (adult/student R100/50), a favourite with kids.

TWELVE COLLEGES
UNIVERSITY

Map p270 (Двенадцать коллегий; Mendeleevskaya liniya 2; ⓂVasileostrovskaya) Completed in 1744 and marked by a statue of scientist-poet Mikhail Lomonosov (1711–65), the 400m-long Twelve Colleges is one of St Petersburg's oldest buildings. It was originally meant for Peter's government ministries, but it is now part of the university, which stretches out behind it. Within these walls populist philosopher Nikolai Chernyshevsky studied, Alexander Popov created some of the world's first radio waves and a young Vladimir Putin earned a degree in law.

This is also where Dmitry Mendeleev invented the periodic table of elements, and the building now contains the small **Mendeleev Museum** (Map p270; Mendeleevskaya liniya 2; ⊙11am-3pm Mon-Fri) **FREE**. His cozy study has been lovingly preserved and you can see his desk (where he always stood rather than sat) and some early drafts of the periodic table.

Also of interest here is the **University Sculpture Garden** (Map p270; Universitetskaya nab 11; ⊙8am-5pm; ⓂAdmiralteyskaya) **FREE**, which can be accessed from the main entrance here, or from the University's Philology Faculty. Here there's a whimsical collection of sculptures from different artists including monuments to figures as disparate as Ho Chi Minh, Vladimir Nabokov and Tomáš Masaryk. You may need to show your passport to gain entry.

MENSHIKOV PALACE
MUSEUM

Map p270 (Государственный Эрмитаж-Дворец Меншикова; www.hermitagemuseum.org; Universitetskaya nab 15; admission R100; ⊙10.30am-6pm Tue-Sat, to 5pm Sun; ⓂVasileostrovskaya) The first stone building in the city, the Menshikov Palace was built to the grandiose tastes of Prince Alexander Menshikov, Peter the Great's closest friend and the first governor of St Petersburg. It is now a branch of the Hermitage and while only a relatively small part of the palace is open to visitors, it's well worth coming here to see the impressively restored interiors.

Menshikov was of humble origins (he is said to have sold pies on the streets of Moscow as a child), but his talent for both organisation and intrigue made him the second-most important person in the Russian Empire by the time of Peter's death in 1725. His palace, built mainly between 1710 and 1714, was the city's smartest residence at the time (compare it to Peter the Great's tiny Summer Palace across the river). Peter used the palace for official functions and its interiors are some of the oldest and best preserved in the city.

The 1st floor displays some stunning Dutch tilework, intended to fortify the rooms against humidity to help ease Menshikov's tuberculosis. Original furniture and the personal effects of Menshikov are on display, and each room has a fact sheet in English explaining its history. Vavara's Chamber is particularly evocative of how the aristocracy lived during Peter's time, while the impressive Walnut Study also stands out.

The main room in the palace is the magnificent Grand Hall, where balls and banquets were held, including the now-infamous reception for Peter's dwarf wedding, in which Peter and his court sniggered as some 70-odd dwarfs from all over Russia attended the marriage of Peter's favourite dwarf and the subsequent drunken party.

ACADEMY OF ARTS MUSEUM   MUSEUM

Map p270 (Музей Академии Художеств; www.nimrah.ru; Universitetskaya nab 17; adult/student R300/150, photos R500; ⊙11am-7pm Wed-Sun; ⓂVasileostrovskaya) Two 3500-year-old sphinxes guard the entrance of the Russian Academy of Arts, and art lovers should not miss the museum of this time-tested institution, which contains works by students and faculty since the academy's founding in 1857.

This is the original location of the academy, where boys would live from the age of five until they graduated at age 15. It was an experiment to create a new species of human: the artist. For the most part, it worked; many great Russian artists were trained here, including Ilya Repin, Karl Bryullov and Anton Losenko. But the curriculum was designed with the idea that the artist must serve the state, and this conservatism led to a reaction against it. In 1863 some 14 students left to found a new movement known as the Wanderers (Peredvizhniki), which went on to revolutionise Russian art.

Nonetheless, the Academy of Arts has many achievements to show off, including numerous studies, drawings and paintings by academy members. On the 3rd floor you can examine the models for the original versions of Smolny Cathedral, St Isaac's Cathedral and the Alexander Nevsky Monastery. When you enter through the main door take the flight of stairs on your left up to the 2nd floor, where you can buy tickets.

TEMPLE OF THE ASSUMPTION   CHURCH

Map p270 (Успенское подворье монастыря Оптина пустынь; cnr nab Leytenanta Shmidta & 14-ya liniya; ⊙8am-8pm; ⓂVasileostrovskaya)

FREE This stunning 1895 neo-Byzantine church was built by architect Vasily Kosyakov on the site of a former monastery. It was closed during the Soviet period, and from 1957 the building became the city's first – and very popular – year-round skating rink. The 7.7m, 861kg metal cross on the roof was only replaced in 1998. Following a wonderful renovation, the church is looking superb again; do go inside to see the murals and icons covering the interior.

C-189 SUBMARINE MUSEUM   MUSEUM

(Музей подводной лодки С-189; ☑8-904-613 7099; www.museum-s-189.ru; cnr nab Leytenanta Shmidta & 16-ya liniya; adult/student R300/200; ⊙11am-7pm Wed-Sun; ♿; ⓂVasileostrovskaya) This Whiskey Class Soviet submarine was built in 1954, and – incredibly, once you've looked around inside – served in the Soviet navy until 1990. It has been renovated, repainted and can be visited if a big cruise ship is not docked at the next-door Lieutenant Schmidt Passenger Terminal.

Climbing into the interior, you can see the cramped living quarters, the engine room, look through the still-working periscope and see where the torpedoes were loaded and fired.

ICEBREAKER KRASIN   MUSEUM

Map p270 (Ледокол Красин; www.krassin.ru; cnr nab Leytenanta Shmita & 23-ya liniya; adult/student R300/150, photos R300; ⊙10am-6pm Wed-Sun; ⓂVasileostrovskaya) The *Krasin*, built in 1917, has a history almost as volatile as the 20th century itself. The Arctic icebreaker was decommissioned in 1971, and can now be visited on a guided tour that leaves every hour on the hour from 11am to 5pm. Call ahead to book a tour in English or French. Special tours of the engine room (over 14s only) are available at 1pm and 3pm on Saturday and Sunday.

The *Krasin* was captured by the British in 1918, returned to the Soviet Union two years later and took part in a large number of Arctic missions and rescues in her long career. The *Krasin* is also the last surviving ship of the infamous PQ-15 convoy that sent aid from Britain to the USSR during WWII.

PEOPLE'S WILL D-2 SUBMARINE MUSEUM   MUSEUM

Map p270 (Музей подводной лодки Д-2 Народоволец; Shkipersky protok 10; adult/student R350/200, photos R100; ⊙11am-5pm Wed-

Sun; MPrimorskaya) The *People's Will (Naro-dovolets)* D-2 Submarine was one of the first six diesel-fuelled submarines built in the Soviet Union and has been wonderfully preserved in this purpose-built museum. The sub itself saw action between 1931 and 1956, and sank five German ships during WWII. Today you can wander around its well-preserved (yet totally antiquated) interior and look at its equipment and weaponry. There's also a small museum containing photos, models and paintings of other submarines, including the ill-fated *Kursk*.

CITY ELECTRICAL TRANSPORT
MUSEUM
MUSEUM

Map p270 (Городской музей электронного транспорта; ☏812-321 9891; Sredny pr 77; admission R260; ◷10am-5pm Tue-Sun; MVasileostrovskaya) This museum is the place to come if you love the trams and trolleybuses of St Petersburg, though its collection of machines from the early 20th century to the present day can only be visited on a Russian-speaking excursion (included in the entry price). These 1½ hour tours leave at 10am, 11.30am, 2pm and 4pm Tuesday to Sunday. The museum offers retro tram trips around the city (R130, two hours), which leave at 11.30am and 2pm from the street outside.

GEOLOGICAL MUSEUM
MUSEUM

Map p270 (Геологический музей; Sredny pr 74; ◷10am-4pm Mon-Fri; MVasileostrovskaya) FREE Located in the upper floors of the All-Russian Geological Science and Research Institute, this huge museum contains thousands of fossils, rocks and gems. The centrepiece of the museum is a huge map of the Soviet Union made entirely of precious gems, which won the Paris World Exposition Grand Prix in 1937. On entering the building, call 7446 on the house phone, and say you'd like to visit the museum *('ya ha-choo pasyeteet moozáy')* and someone will escort you.

METRO MUSEUM
MUSEUM

Map p270 (Музей метро; www.metro.spb.ru/muzei.html; ul Odoevskogo 29; ◷10am-noon & 1-5pm Mon-Thu, until 3pm Fri; MPrimorskaya) FREE Bring your passport with you to access this small but interesting museum, which recounts the history of St Petersburg's metro. Sadly there's no signage in English, so this is strictly for enthusiasts, but there are nice touches, such as a metro escalator taking you between floors and a

metro car and cab you can enter to 'drive' your own train.

On arrival go directly to the pass office in the corner of the entrance hall to get a pass that will allow you to enter the metro's HQ.

PUSHKIN HOUSE
MUSEUM

Map p270 (Дом Пушкина; ☏812-328 0502; www.pushkinskijdom.ru; nab Makarova 4; adult/student R300/150, tour R1400; ◷11am-5pm Mon-Fri; MVasileostrovskaya) The old customs house, topped with statues and a dome, is home to the Institute of Russian Literature. Fondly called Pushkin House, the handsome building contains a small literary museum with dusty exhibits on Tolstoy, Gogol, Lermontov and Turgenev, as well as a room dedicated to the writers of the Silver Age. Call in advance for an English-language tour.

✕ EATING

Vasilyevsky Island offers plenty of choice for the discerning diner. There's a particular glut of places near the Strelka and around the metro station Vasileostrovskaya.

MARKETPLACE
CANTEEN €

Map p270 (www.market-place.me; 7-ya liniya 34/2; mains R100; ◷8.30am-11pm; 🛜✎; MVasileostrovskaya) This chain of cafeteria-style restaurants has a popular outlet on Vasilyevsky Island's main commercial strip. With appealing, light-bathed dining areas, a large choice of excellent-value salads, soups, meat dishes and desserts and with friendly service to boot, this spotless place is a lifeline for students and anyone after a low-cost lunch. There's also a cafe downstairs.

CARDAMOM
INDIAN €

Map p270 (Кардамон; www.cardamom-bar.ru; 1-ya liniya 18; mains R250-500; ◷noon-11pm; 🛜✎▯; MVasileostrovskaya) The lacklustre decor may not instantly endear you to this Indian-run place, but its popularity with locals and visiting Indians says a great deal. The English-speaking owner will make you feel very welcome and the selection of delicious baltis, vindaloos, *kadhai* and biriyanis is impressive.

IMPERATOR
RESTAURANT
EASTERN EUROPEAN €

Map p270 (Ресторан Император; Universitet-skaya nab 5; mains R200-500; ◷11am-11pm; 🛜▯;

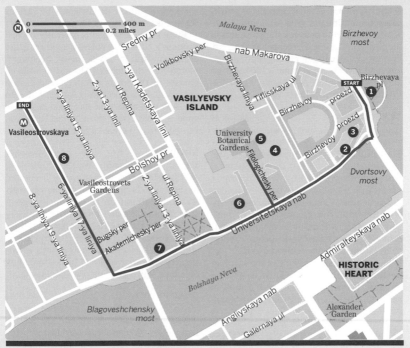

🏃 Neighbourhood Walk
Vasilyevsky Island

START STRELKA (Ⓜ ADMIRALTEYSKAYA)
END 6-YA LINIYA I 7-YA LINIYA (Ⓜ VASILE-
OSTROVSKAYA)
LENGTH 2KM; TWO HOURS

The eastern nose of Vasilyevsky Island, the ❶ **Strelka** (p136), boasts an unparalleled panorama, looking out over the Peter & Paul Fortress, the Hermitage, the Admiralty and St Isaac's Cathedral. A recent addition is the fountain in the middle of the Neva.

The ❷ **Kunstkamera** (p134), was Russia's first museum, set up by Peter to dispel common superstitions about illness and disease. The collection of deformed foetuses and animals is impressive, if a little disturbing. Next door is the equally impressive ❸ **Museum of Zoology** (p136).

Domenico Trezzini built the magnificent ❹ **Twelve Colleges** (p136), now St Petersburg State University, in 1722. The emperor based his bureaucracy here; separate entrances for each ministry signified their independence, while the unified facade highlighted collective goals. It is now part of the university, housing the ❺ **Mendeleev Museum** (p136) among others. Behind these buildings, the grounds contain the beautiful university botanical gardens and a quirky collection of sculptures.

Peter originally gifted the entirety of Vasilyevsky Island to his best friend, Prince Menshikov, who proceeded to build the fabulous ❻ **Menshikov Palace** (p136) on the north bank of the Neva. Menshikov's humble origins gave him a taste for opulence, and the interior has the best-preserved Petrine decor in the city.

The ❼ **Academy of Arts Museum** (p137) houses 250 years' worth of artistic expression. On display are works by academy students and faculty over the years, as well as temporary exhibitions. A beautiful old library is open for visiting researchers.

Pedestrian-friendly ❽ **6-ya liniya i 7-ya liniya** is one of the city's most pleasant places to sit at a sidewalk cafe and watch the world go by. Check out the charming Church of St Andrew, before sampling the goods at one of the sweet cafes.

VASILYEVSKY ISLAND

Ⓜ Admiralteyskaya) Given its expensive nearby competition, this is a great deal and a convenient lunch stop between the museums of the Strelka. The meaty menu has Russian, Eastern European and Caucasian standards and there's a good-value R200 business lunch (noon to 4pm). Add to that a pleasant summer terrace and this is a winner.

★ RESTORAN   RUSSIAN €€

Map p270 (Ресторанъ; www.elbagroup.ru/restoran; Tamozhenny per 2; mains R500-1000; ⊘noon-11pm; 🛜🅿; Ⓜ Admiralteyskaya) After 15 years on the scene, this excellent place is still going strong. Stylish and airily bright, Restoran is somehow formal and relaxed at the same time. The menu manages to combine the best of *haute russe* cuisine with enough modern flare to keep things interesting: try duck baked with apples or whole baked sterlet in white wine and herbs.

In winters fire roar, while in the summer the thick stone walls make for an oasis from the heat. Do not miss the superb Napoleon dessert, or the interesting selection of quality Russian wines.

★ NA KUKHNYE   EUROPEAN €€

Map p270 (На Кухне; ☎812-321 3806; nab Leytenanta Shmidta 43; mains R300-700; Ⓜ Vasileostrovskaya) This innovative place has just seven tables in its sun-bathed, whitewashed dining room, and an impressive handwritten menu of organic food featuring dishes such as risotto with white mushrooms, duck breast with caramelised apples and sea bass with asparagus and cream sauce. There's a daily cookery class at 7pm (R750), which can be arranged in English with advance booking.

In fact, any dish can be prepared by guests at any time of day, for a small surcharge. Chefs oversee your attempt in the open plan kitchen, making this a unique chance to try out your culinary skills in a professional environment.

BUTER BRODSKY   EUROPEAN €€

Map p270 (Бутер Бродский; www.bbbar.su; nab Makarova 16; mains R450-750; 🛜; Ⓜ Vasileostrovskaya) Just when you thought you'd go through life without visiting a Josef Brodsky theme restaurant, along comes Buter Brodsky (the name is a pun on the Russian word for sandwich, *buterbrod*), a super stylish, if unlikely, addition to Vasilyevsky Island's eating scene. The menu runs from

smørrebrød (open sandwiches) to various set meals of salads and soups.

But it's the decor that is particularly cool: Brodksy's (literally) chiseled features stare down on you from where they've been hammered into the cracked old walls, while elements of the historic building have been preserved and gorgeously integrated into the design. Shabby chic has never looked so good, and with *smørrebrød* at just R250, you can be sure of a great-value lunch as well.

GINTARUS   LITHUANIAN €€

Map p270 (Sredny pr 5; mains R350-1000; 🛜🅿; Ⓜ Vasileostrovskaya) Sumptuously decorated in dark woods and enjoying a very homely feel, this Lithuanian restaurant is a great spot for a smart and interesting meal. Try the excellent *zeppelins* (potato dumplings with various fillings), and if Lithuanian cuisine doesn't exactly get your mouth watering, try the range of other dishes, including delicious soups and lots of grilled meats.

GRAD PETROV   GERMAN €€

Map p270 (Градъ Петровъ; www.die-kneipe.ru; Univesitetskaya nab 5; meals R500-1200; ⊘noon-1am; 🛜🅿; Ⓜ Admiralteyskaya) Despite the laughable wax figure of a barely recognisable Pushkin with a quill in his hand at the entrance, 'Peter's City' is a classy German restaurant with an impressive menu and cozy decor. There's a separate bar where you can drink home-brewed Pilsners and Weizens, while the menu is all about meat and particularly sausages.

See if you can manage the 1m-long Thüringer, served with onion sauce and red cabbage. Ask also for a free tour of the on-site microbrewery. There's live music Wednesday to Saturday from 8pm.

SAKARTVELO   GEORGIAN €€

Map p270 (Сакартвело; 12-ya liniya 13; mains R300-750; 🛜🅿; Ⓜ Vasileostrovskaya) This is Vasilyevsky Island's best Georgian restaurant – a friendly place on a residential backstreet, where sumptuous Caucasian feasts are served up at any time of day, backed up by live music most evenings.

CASA DEL MYASO   STEAKHOUSE €€€

Map p270 (Каса-дель Мясо; www.we-love-meat.ru; Birzhevoy pr 6; mains R700-2200; 🛜🅿; Ⓜ Admiralteyskaya) This is Petersburg's best steakhouse, a place where a semi-fanatical anti-vegetarian stance is in evidence, but where you're guaranteed a great slab of meat. Try the Rossini Burger, which has been awarded *Time Out St Petersburg*'s 'best burger' gong, or just choose from a huge selection of various cuts of beef. Its stylish, brick-walled subterranean premises is another plus.

🍷 DRINKING & NIGHTLIFE

BUTER BRODSKY   BAR
Map p270 (www.bbbar.su; nab Makarova 16; ⊘noon-midnight; 🛜; ⓂVasileostrovskaya) This super-funky and beautifully designed bar, a homage to local poet Josef Brodsky, is one of the coolest spots to drink on the island. As well as offering a full cocktail menu, wine list and selection of nonalcoholic drinks, there is also its range of home-made spirits and tinctures.

HELSINKI BAR   BAR
Map p270 (www.helsinkibar.ru; Kadetskaya liniya 31; ⊘noon-2am, to 6am Sat & Sun; 🛜; ⓂVasileostrovskaya) A slice of neighbouring Finland in the heart of St Petersburg, Helsinki is another very cool place to drink on the island. The vibe is retro, with vinyl-spinning DJs, '70s Finnish ads on the walls, vintage furniture and Finnish home cooking. This is a great late-night option if you're staying locally and don't want to worry about the bridges.

BIRZHA BAR   BAR
Map p270 (Биржа Бар; ☑931-340 2299; www.birjabar.ru; Birzhevoy per 4; ⊘noon-3am; 🛜; ⓂVasileostrovskaya) A striking two-part painting of Jim Morrison hangs on the wall of this cool and spacious bar where DJs spin discs and there are occasional concerts and stand-up comedy nights. Eight beers on tap and plenty of other alcoholic concoctions will keep you in a happy mood.

BRÚGGE   PUB
Map p270 (www.inbrugge.ru; nab Makarova 22; ⊘noon-2am; 🛜; ⓂVasileostrovskaya) If the idea of going to a 'Belgian gastronomic pub' makes your eyes roll, you're in good company, but this pleasant basement space overcomes its heavy-handed marketing with cozy leather booths, a comfortable bar to sit at and over 20 Belgian beers on tap. There's also a great menu, including fresh White Sea mussels, French oysters and meaty mains.

GRAD PETROV   MICROBREWERY
Map p270 (www.die-kneipe.ru; Universitetskaya nab 5; ⊘noon to last customer; ⓂVasileostrovskaya) Fresh-brewed lager, Weizen, Pilsner, Dunkel and Hefeweizen – it's reason enough to stop by this upmarket microbrewery on Vasilyevsky Island. To top it off, the outdoor tables offer amazing views of St Isaac's Cathedral and the Admiralty across the Neva River.

BOOTLEGGER'S   BAR
Map p270 (www.bootleggers-spb.com; Birzhevoy proezd 2; ⊘noon-11pm Sun-Thu, to 3am Fri & Sat; 🛜; ⓂVasileostrovskaya) Vaulted ceilings and contemporary furnishings make this bar a handy hang-out for beers (11 types on tap), whiskey (70 brands) and other alcoholic beverages to wash down pizza and other European dishes. DJs and live music are other pluses.

☆ ENTERTAINMENT

KURYOKHIN MODERN ART CENTRE   ARTS CENTRE
Map p270 (☑812-322 0094; www.kuryokhin.net; 93 Sredny pr; ⓂVasileostrovskaya, then bus 6 or 7, or trolleybus 10 or 11 from other side of road) This cultural centre, in a clapped-out but atmospheric old cinema, is named after Sergey Kuryokhin (1954–96), a legend of the Russian contemporary-arts and music scene. SKIF, an international music and arts festival, is held here in May and other avant-garde performances and exhibitions happen throughout the year.

A major renovation is planned that will make the venue twice as large but keep the original cinema hall intact.

🛍 SHOPPING

ERARTA   ART
Map p270 (Эрарта; www.erarta.com; 29-aya liniya 2; ⊘10am-10pm Wed-Mon; ⓂVasileostrovskaya, then bus 6 or 7, or trolleybus 10 or 11 from the opposite side of the road) The superb Erarta Museum of Contemporary Art has several excellent shops in it, including its excellent gift shop, a well-stocked art bookshop and commercially run galleries where art is for sale. Definitely one of the best places to buy contemporary Russian art as well as creative and unique gifts.

Petrograd & Vyborg Sides

PETROGRADSKY ISLAND | KIROVSKY ISLANDS | VYBORG SIDE

Neighbourhood Top Five

1 Seeing the graves of the Romanovs, climbing the bell tower for stunning views and enjoying the museums and exhibits scattered around the **Peter & Paul Fortress** (p144).

2 Sneaking a behind-the-scenes look at one of the world's top museums at the **Hermitage Storage Facility** (p152).

3 Spending a day relaxing on charming, wooded **Yelagin Island** (p152) – perfect for walking, picnicking, boating and sunbathing.

4 Being dazzled by the industrial-scale creativity at the **Street Art Museum** (p154) and **Red Banner Textile Factory** (p147).

5 Making a detour to the historic **Sampsonievsky Cathedral** (p153) for one of the city's most beautiful church interiors.

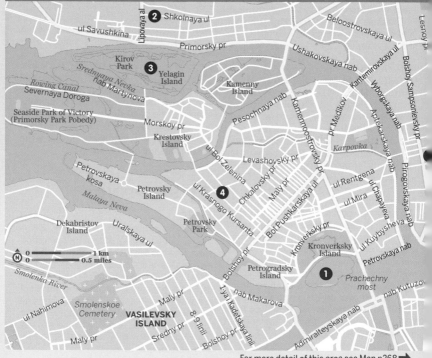

For more detail of this area see Map p268 ➡

Explore: Petrograd & Vyborg Sides

Peter's city was first founded on the Petrograd Side and it's a fascinating place packed with historical sites, stunning Style Moderne architecture and a couple of great live-music venues. It includes little Zayachy Island, home to the Peter & Paul Fortress, St Petersburg's most historic complex, as well as the Kirovsky Islands (Yelagin, Krestovsky and Kamenny), three charming, wooded Neva delta islands that are predominantly given over to parks and recreation areas.

North of the islands, on the right bank of the Neva River, the Vyborg Side is a sprawling area of industry and massive apartment blocks stretching from the Gulf of Finland to Okhta, east of the Neva as it bends around Smolny towards the Alexander Nevsky Monastery. The main attractions are scattered, but include worthwhile ones such as the Hermitage Storage Facility and new Street Art Museum, as well as one of the city's best bathhouses.

Local Life

➡ **Parks** If the weather's good, join the locals as they take to the Kirovsky Islands for fairground rides, boating, sunbathing and cycling through the woods – it's a total escape from the city just three metro stops from the city centre.

➡ **Street art** Check out the creative daubs of street artists on the walls around the shuttered Red Banner Textile Factory and the giant murals near Chkalovskaya metro (p147).

➡ **Strip off** Stand next to the serious sunbathers tanning against the fortress walls or on the beach at Zayachy Island. For a year-round tropical holiday, splash around with crowds at Piterland waterpark (p158).

Getting There & Away

➡ **Metro** The Petrograd Side is served by Gorkovskaya and Petrogradskaya on Line 2, and by Sportivnaya, Chkalovskaya and Krestovsky Ostrov on Line 5. The Vyborg Side has some 20 metro stations on it, mainly serving far-flung residential areas.

➡ **Bus** Bus 10 runs from the Vyborg Side at Chyornaya Rechka, down Bolshoy pr on the Petrograd Side and on into the historic heart.

➡ **Tram** Tram 6 provides a handy link between pl Lenina and Vasilyevsky Island via Kronverksky pr on the Petrograd Side while tram 40 is also useful for traversing the Petrograd Side to Chyornaya Rechka.

➡ **Marshrutka** *Marshrutka* (fixed route minibus) 346 runs the length of Bolshoy pr and then turns left onto Kamennoostrovsky pr and on to the Vyborg Side.

Lonely Planet's Top Tip

Don't miss the Petrograd Side or Vyborg Side if you'd like to see the real St Petersburg – a far cry from the uniform beauty of the historic heart. The Petrograd Side is a good place to see the everyday life of the middle classes in the city and, while the Vyborg Side around pl Lenina is a vision of a post-industrial nightmare, your average Joes live in the Soviet housing estates further along the metro line – travel to the end of lines 1 or 2 and you'll see real city life.

✖ Best Places to Eat

➡ Mesto (p156)

➡ Chekhov (p156)

➡ Koryushka (p156)

➡ Semeinye Traditsy (p156)

For reviews, see p154➡

⊙ Best Parks & Gardens

➡ Yelagin Island (p152)

➡ Kamenny Island (p152)

➡ Botanical Gardens (p148)

➡ Maritime Victory Park (p152)

For reviews, see p147➡

⊙ Best Museums

➡ Hermitage Storage Facility (p152)

➡ Museum of Political History (p147)

➡ Commandant's House (p145)

➡ Kirov Museum (p148)

For reviews, see p147➡

PETER & PAUL FORTRESS

Housing a cathedral, a former prison and various exhibitions, this large defensive fortress on Zayachy Island is the kernel from which St Petersburg grew into the city it is today. History buffs should definitely schedule a visit here. There are also panoramic views from atop the fortress walls, at the foot of which lies a sandy riverside beach, a prime spot for sunbathing.

Having captured this formerly Swedish settlement on the Neva, Peter set to turn the outpost into a modern Western city starting with the Peter & Paul Fortress in 1703. It has never been utilised in the city's defence – unless you count incarceration of political 'criminals' as national defence.

Today, the fort makes for a fascinating half-day outing. The main entrance is across the **Ioannovsky Bridge** at the island's northeast end; there's also access via the **Kronwerk Bridge**, which is within walking distance of Sportivnaya metro station.

SS Peter & Paul Cathedral

All of Russia's prerevolutionary rulers from Peter the Great onwards (except Peter II and Ivan VI) are buried inside this **cathedral** (Map p268; adult/student R250/130; ⊙10am-6pm Mon & Thu-Sat, 10am-5pm Tue, 11am-6pm Sun), which has a magnificent baroque interior quite different from other Orthodox churches. Peter I's grave is at the front on the right of the iconostasis. In 1998 the remains of Nicholas II and his family – minus Alexey and Maria – were interred in the Chapel of St Catherine to the right of the entrance.

DON'T MISS...

➡ SS Peter & Paul Cathedral

➡ Trubetskoy Bastion

➡ Commandant's House

➡ Neva Panorama

➡ The beach

PRACTICALITIES

➡ Петропавловская крепость

➡ Map p268

➡ www.spbmuseum.ru

➡ grounds free, exhibitions adult R60-150, student R40-80

➡ ⊙grounds 8.30am-8pm, exhibitions 11am-6pm Mon & Thu-Sun, 10am-5pm Tue

➡ Ⓜ Gorkovskaya

The 122.5m-high **bell tower** (Map p268; adult/student R250/150; ⊘11am-5.30pm May-Sep) is the city's second-tallest structure after the television tower. At the base there is a small exhibition about the renovation of the tower in 1997, as well as an up-close inspection of the bell-ringing mechanism. The main reason to climb all these steps, of course, is for the magnificent 360-degree panorama. Tickets for guided tours (in Russian only) are sold at the boathouse information centre; if you're happy to look around on your own then buy your ticket inside the cathedral.

The Trubetskoy Bastion

Evocative use of the original cells for displays about the former political prisoners of **Trubetskoy Bastion** (Map p268; adult/student R150/80; ⊘11am-6pm Mon & Thu-Sun, 10am-5pm Tue) – who included the likes of Maxim Gorky, Leon Trotsky, Mikhail Bakunin and Fyodor Dostoevsky – make this the best of the fort's clutch of exhibitions. Short biographies in English of the various inmates are posted on the doors.

Peter the Great's son was tortured to death here and, after the 1917 revolution, the communists continued to use the prison for former aristocrats and counterrevolutionaries until 1924, when it was turned into a museum.

The Commandant's House & Neva Gate

The fascinating museum in the **Commandant's House** (Map p268; adult/student R110/70; ⊘11am-6pm Mon & Thu-Sun, to 5pm Tue) charts the history of the St Petersburg region from medieval times to 1918. What starts as a fairly standard-issue plod through the city's history really comes alive once you're upstairs, with modern, interactive exhibits, even though there's still a lack of explanations in English.

In the south wall is the **Neva Gate**, a later addition (1787), where prisoners were loaded on boats for execution or exile. Notice the plaques here showing water levels of famous (and obviously devastating) floods. Outside there are fine views of the whole central waterfront, including the Hermitage.

Along the wall, to the left, a painting of a blue walrus marks the territory of the **Walrus Club**, the crazy crew that chops a hole in the iced-over Neva each winter so they can take a dip. Swimmers, known as *morzhi* (walruses), claim the practice eliminates muscle pains, boosts energy and even improves libido. This is not an exclusive club — all are invited to take the plunge!

PETER THE GREAT STATUE

Between the cathedral and the Senior Officers' Barracks is Mikhail Shemyakin's Peter the Great statue, which depicts him seated with strangely proportioned head and hands. When the statue was unveiled in 1991 it caused outrage among the city's citizens, for whom Peter remains a saintly figure. Local lore has it that rubbing his right forefinger will bring good luck.

Within the fortress grounds, you can grab a snack at the *stolovaya* (canteen) Leningradskoye Kafe (mains R300; open 10am to 8pm Thursday to Tuesday), but a far nicer option is Koryushka (p156), at the southwestern end of Zayachy Island.

POSTERN & NEVA PANORAMA

A separate ticket gains you access to both the Postern, a 97.4m passage hidden in the fortress walls, and the Neva Panorama (adult/student R250/200; open 10.30am to 7pm Thursday to Tuesday), a walkway atop the walls which concludes at Naryshkin Bastion. At noon every day a cannon is fired from here, a tradition dating back to Peter the Great's times.

PETROGRAD & VYBORG SIDES PETER & PAUL FORTRESS

PETER & PAUL FORTRESS

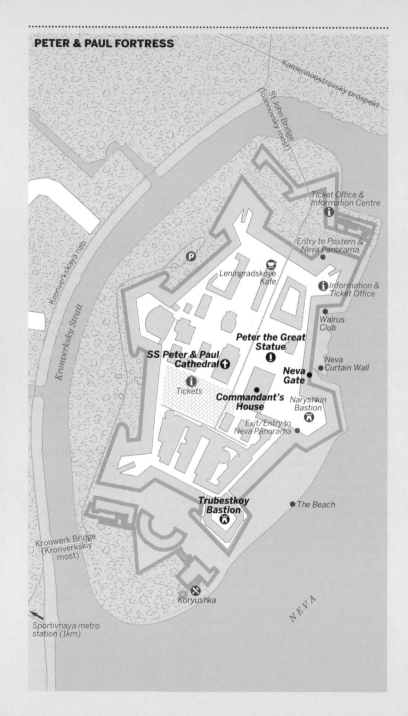

Kamennoostrovsky prospekt

St John Bridge
(Ioannovsky most)

Ticket Office &
Information Centre

Entry to Postern &
Neva Panorama

Leningradskoye
Kafe

Information &
Ticket Office

Kronverkskaya nab

Kronverksky Strait

Walrus
Club

Peter the Great
Statue

SS Peter & Paul
Cathedral

Neva
Curtain Wall

Neva
Gate

Tickets

Commandant's
House

Naryshkin
Bastion

Exit/Entry to
Neva Panorama

The Beach

Trubestkoy
Bastion

Kronwerk Bridge
(Kronverkskiy
most)

Koryushka

NEVA

Sportivnaya metro
station (1km)

 SIGHTS

◉ Petrogradsky Island

During WWI, the city of St Petersburg changed its name to the less Germanic 'Petrograd'. At this time, the large island north of Zayachy became a fashionable place to live, and the name stuck to the island, if not the city. Today, this fabulous district boasts distinctive Style Moderne architecture, a lively commercial district and plenty of refreshing, uncrowded, green space.

MUSEUM OF POLITICAL HISTORY MUSEUM

Map p268 (Музей политической истории России; ☑812-313 6163; www.polithistory.ru; ul Kuybysheva 4; adult/student R150/60; ⊙10am-6pm Fri-Tue, to 8pm Wed; ⓂGorkovskaya) The elegant Style Moderne Kshesinskaya Palace (1904) is a highly appropriate location for this excellent museum – one of the city's best – covering Russian politics in scrupulous detail up to contemporary times.

The palace, previously the home of Mathilda Kshesinskaya, famous ballet dancer and one-time lover of Nicholas II in his pre-tsar days, was briefly the headquarters of the Bolsheviks, and Lenin often gave speeches from the balcony.

Of special note are the rare satirical caricatures of Lenin that were published in magazines between the 1917 revolutions (the same drawings a few months later would have got the artist imprisoned or worse). By contrast, the Lenin memorial room is unchanged since Soviet days, with an almost religious atmosphere. You can visit Lenin's one-time office where he worked between the February and October Revolutions.

PETER'S CABIN HISTORIC BUILDING

Map p268 (Домик Петра Великого; Petrovskaya nab 6; adult/student R200/70; ⊙10am-6pm Wed, Fri-Mon, 1-9pm Thu; ⓂGorkovskaya) This charming log cottage, protected within a stone building, is St Petersburg's oldest surviving structure. The wooden cabin itself was supposedly built in three days in May 1703 for Peter to live in while he supervised the construction of the fortress and city. Feeling more like a shrine than a museum, the cabin confirms Peter's love for the simple life with its unpretentious, homely feel, visibly influenced by the time he spent in Holland.

It has long been a sentimental site for St Petersburg. During WWII, Soviet soldiers would take an oath of allegiance to the city here, vowing to protect it from the Germans, before disappearing to the front. After the Siege of Leningrad, this was the first museum to reopen to the public.

Look out for the bronze bust of Peter by Parmen Zabello in the garden.

MOSQUE MOSQUE

Map p268 (Соборная мечеть; ☑821-233 9819; http://dum-spb.ru/kontakty; Kronverksky pr 7; ⊙7am-9pm; ⓂGorkovskaya) Built 1910-14, this beautiful working mosque was modelled on

---

LOCAL KNOWLEDGE

CHKALOVSKAYA

Taking its name from Valery Chkalov (1904–1938), the legendary aircraft test pilot who pioneered the polar air route from Russia to North America, Chkalovskaya is an up-and-coming Petrograd Side area with ample rewards for casual strollers. Start by searching out the small park and giant **wall mural** (Map p268; cnr Chkalovsky pr & Pionerskaya ul; ⓂChkalovskaya) dedicated to Chkalov and other Russian scientists and explorers.

Next head up Pionerskaya ul to the **Red Banner Textile Factory** (Трикотажная фабрика Красное Знамя; Map p268; Pionerskaya ul 53; ⓂChkalovskaya) FREE, a grand relic of Soviet constructivist architecture. Street artists have commandeered walls around the abandoned industrial space to create an outdoor gallery of technicolour images, mainly along Korpusnaya ul.

Walk to the end of this street, then turn left to find the Style Moderne gem **Leuchtenberg House** (Map p268; Bolshaya Zelenina ul 28; ⓂChkalovskaya), so called because it once belonged to the duke of Leuchtenberg, great-grandson of Tsar Nicholas I. Cross the street to take in the full glory of the mosaic frieze spread across the upper story of the facade, the key decorative feature of the architect Theodor von Postels. Returning to Chkalovskaya metro station along Bolshaya Zelenina ul you'll pass several appealing spots to eat or drink, including Blizkie Druzya (p154).

Samarkand's Gur-e Amir Mausoleum. Its azure dome and minarets are stunning and prominent in the city's skyline. Outside of prayer times, if you're respectfully dressed (women should wear head covering, men long trousers), you can walk through the gate at the northeast side and ask the guard for entry – the interior is equally lovely. If you're allowed in, remove your shoes, do not talk and do not take photos.

KIROV MUSEUM
MUSEUM

Map p268 (Музей Кирова; www.kirovmuseum. ru; Kamennoostrovsky pr 26/28; admission R120; ⊙11am-6pm Thu-Tue; MPetrogradskaya) Leningrad party boss Sergei Kirov was one of the most powerful men in Russia in the early 1930s. His decidedly unproletarian apartment is now a fascinating museum showing how the Bolshevik elite really lived: take a quick journey back to the days of Soviet glory, including choice examples of 1920s technology, such as the first-ever Soviet-produced typewriter and a conspicuously noncommunist GE fridge, complete with plastic food inside. Many of Kirov's personal items are on display and his office from the Smolny Institute has been fully reconstructed in one of the rooms.

Kirov lived here for 10 years until his murder at Stalin's behest in 1934, which sparked a wave of deadly repression in the country. A gory but reverential display shows the clothes he was wearing when killed. The tiny hole in the back of his cap is where he was shot (blood stains intact) and the torn seam on his jacket's left breast is where doctors tried to revive his heart.

BOTANICAL GARDENS
GARDEN

Map p268 (Ботанический сад; ☑812-372 5464; http://botsad-spb.com; ul Professora Popova 2; adult/child R220/110; ⊙grounds 10am-6pm Tue-Sun May-Sep, greenhouse 11am-4pm Tue-Sun year round; MPetrogradskaya) On eastern Aptekarsky (Apothecary) Island, this was once a garden of medicinal plants (founded by Peter the Great himself in 1714) that gave the island its name. Today the botanical gardens contain 26 greenhouses on a 22-hectare site. It is a lovely place to stroll and a fascinating place to visit – and not just for botanists.

At the turn of the 20th century, these were the second-biggest botanical gardens in the world, behind London's Kew Gardens. However, 90% of the plants died during WWII, which makes the present collec-

tion all the more impressive (you will recognise the 'veterans' by their war medals).

A highlight is the tsaritsa nochi (*Selenicereus pteranthus*), a flowering cactus that blossoms only one night a year, usually in mid-June. On this night, the gardens stay open until morning for visitors to gawk at the marvel and sip champagne.

Entry to the gardens is on the corner of Aptekarsky per and nab reki Karpovki

ALEXANDROVSKY PARK
PARK

Map p268 (⛭; MGorkovskaya) This leafy park, laid out in 1845, wraps in an arc around the Kronverk moat and Artillery Museum. It's too close to traffic to ensure a peaceful escape but, if you have kids in tow, it harbours a few attractions worth considering, the best of which is the **Planetarium** (Планетарий; Map p268; ☑812-233 2653; www.planetary-spb. ru; adult/child R350/150; ⊙10.30am-6pm), offering shows throughout the day, an observatory and several different display halls.

Although the **Leningradsky Zoo** (Ленинградский зоопарк; Map p268; www. spbzoo.ru; adult/child R400/150; ⊙10am-6pm; ⛭) has had remarkable success in breeding polar bears in captivity (over 100 have been born here since 1993), the enclosures for most animals are cramped; kids will like it but animal-loving adults may be distressed.

Also inside the park is **Mini St Petersburg**, mini sculptures of the city's landmarks that make for a fun photo opportunity.

ARTILLERY MUSEUM
MUSEUM

Map p268 (Музей Артиллерии; ☑812-610 3301; www.artillery-museum.ru; Alexandrovsky Park 7; adult/student R300/150; ⊙11am-6pm Wed-Sun; ⛭; MGorkovskaya) Housed in the fort's original arsenal, across the moat from the Peter & Paul Fortress, this fire-powered museum chronicles Russia's military history, with examples of weapons dating all the way back to the Stone Age. The centrepiece is Lenin's armoured car, which he rode in triumph from the Finland Station (Finlyandsky vokzal). Even if you are not impressed by guns and bombs, who can resist climbing around on the tanks and trucks that adorn the courtyard?

CRUISER AURORA
MUSEUM

Map p268 (Крейсер Аврора; ☑812-230 8440; www.aurora.org.ru; Petrovskaya nab; ⊙10.30am-4pm Tue-Thu, Sat & Sun; ⛭; MGorkovskaya) FREE Moored on the Bolshaya Nevka, the *Aurora* had a walk-on part in the communist revolution. On the night of 25 October 1917, its crew fired a blank round from the forward gun as a signal for the start of the assault on the Winter Palace. Restored and painted in pretty colours, it's a living museum that swarms with kids on weekends.

Launched in 1901, the *Aurora* saw action in the Russo-Japanese War and was sunk by German bombs in WWII. Inside you can view the crew's quarters as well as communist propaganda and a collection of friendship banners from around the world.

SIGMUND FREUD MUSEUM OF DREAMS
MUSEUM

Map p268 (Музей сновидений Фрейда; ☑812-380 7650; www.freud.ru; Bolshoy pr 18a; ☺noon-5pm Tue, Sat & Sun; Ⓜ Sportivnaya) FREE This odd conceptual exhibition, based on abstractions and ideas, not artefacts, is an outgrowth of the Psychoanalytic Institute that houses it. The two-room exhibition aims to stimulate your subconscious as you struggle to read the display symbolising what Freud himself would have dreamt. Illustrations of Freud's patients' dreams and quotations line the hall. English is spoken.

CHALIAPIN HOUSE MUSEUM
MUSEUM

Map p268 (Дом-музей Шаляпина; ☑812-234 1056; www.theatremuseum.ru; ul Graftio 2b; adult/student R150/75; ☺11am-7pm Thu-Sun, 1-9pm Wed; Ⓜ Petrogradskaya) Opera buffs will want to visit this house-museum where the great singer Fyodor Chaliapin (1873–1938) lived before fleeing the Soviet Union in 1922. The kindly babushkas will happily play some of the singer's recordings for you as you peruse his personal effects. Check online for details of concerts held here.

TOY MUSEUM
MUSEUM

Map p268 (Музей игрушки; nab reki Karpovki 32; adult/child R270/90; ☺11am-6pm Tue-Sun; Ⓜ Petrogradskaya) This charming, privately run museum presents its pan-Russian collection in three sections – folk toys, factory toys and artisanal toys. Examples of the last include toys made in Sergiev Posad, home of the ubiquitous *matryoshka* (nesting doll), a creation often assumed to be far older than it is, being created for the first time only in the 19th century.

YELIZAROV MUSEUM
MUSEUM

Map p268 (Музей-квартира Елизаровых; ☑812-235 3778; flat 24, ul Lenina 52; adult/student R200/100; ☺10am-6pm Thu-Sun, 1-9pm Wed; Ⓜ Chkalovskaya) Lenin's wife's family lived in this apartment-turned-museum and Vladimir Ilyich himself laid low here before the revolution while organising the workers. The delightful turn-of-the-20th-century fittings have been preserved intact, including a telephone that still bears Lenin's home phone number. By the look of things, Lenin had a very bourgeois time of it.

The apartment building, which is known locally as the 'boat house' due to its external similarities to a large cruise liner, was built in 1913 at the height of St Petersburg's lust for Style Moderne. Tap in 24 at the front door and then go up the stairs to the 3rd floor when you're buzzed in.

PETERSBURG AVANT-GARDE MUSEUM
MUSEUM

Map p268 (Музей петербургского авангарда; ☑812-234 4289; www.spbmuseum.ru/exhibits_and_exhibitions/92/1344/; ul Professora Popova 10; adult/student R70/50; ☺11am-5pm Mon & Thu-Sun, to 4pm Tue; Ⓜ Petrogradskaya) Also known as the House of Matyushin, this small museum occupies a charming grey-painted wooden cottage dating from the mid-19th century that was once the home of avant-garde artist Mikhail Matyushin (1861–1934). The exhibition here relates to Matyushin's work and that of his coterie.

CHAEV MANSION
ARCHITECTURE

Map p268 (ul Rentgena 9; ☺8am-2pm & 3-9pm Mon-Fri, 9am-2pm Sat; Ⓜ Petrogradskaya) FREE This elegant mansion, constructed in 1907 for the engineer SN Chaev, is now occupied by a public clinic. It combines neoclassical and art nouveau motifs and has a beautifully preserved interior.

◉ Kirovsky Islands

This is the collective name for the three outer delta islands of the Petrograd Side – Kamenny, Yelagin and Krestovsky. Once marshy forests, the islands were granted to 18th- and 19th-century court favourites and developed into elegant playgrounds. Still mostly parkland, they are leafy venues for picnics, river sports and White Nights' cavorting, as well as home to St Petersburg's super rich.

The metro station Krestovsky Ostrov provides easy access to both Krestovsky and Yelagin Islands; for Kamenny you can walk across the bridge from metro station Chyornaya Rechka on the Vyborg Side.

150

1. Pushkin statue by Mikhail Anikushin in front of a mural by Maria Engelke, Pushkinskaya **2.** Narvskaya **3.** *The Foundation of the Admiralty* (A. Bistrov, 2011), Admiralteyskaya **4.** Avtovo

GREG BALFOUR EVANS / ALAMY ©

Metro Art

Beautiful interior design is not just for palaces and galleries in St Petersburg – it is also found across the city's metro system. Red Line 1, the first to be opened in 1955, is particularly striking for its station designs, but other newer stations also have artistic flourishes.

Admiralteyskaya

The city's deepest metro station features mosaics about the formation of the Russian fleet under Peter the Great.

Avtovo

Marble-and-cut-glass-clad columns hold up the roof, while a relief of soldiers stands in the temple-like entrance.

Baltiyskaya

There's a wavy motif on the mouldings along the ceiling and a vivid marble mosaic at the end of the platform depicting the volley from the *Aurora* in 1917.

Kirovsky Zavod

The decoration takes its inspiration from oil wells and industry. A scowling bust of Lenin is at the end of the platform.

Narvskaya

Features a fantastic sculptured relief of Lenin and rejoicing proletariat over the escalators, as well as carvings of miners, engineers, sailors, artists and teachers on the platform columns.

Pl Vosstaniya

Lenin and Stalin are depicted together in the roundels at either end of the platform. Look out for Lenin on a tank and Lenin with the Kronshtadt sailors.

Pushkinskaya

A statue of the poet stands at the end of the platform and a moulding of his head is above the escalators. Nip outside to view the nearby Style Moderne Vitebsk Station.

Tekhnologichesky Institut

The southbound platform has reliefs of famous Russian scientists, the northbound one lists dates of Russia's major scientific achievements along the columns.

YELAGIN ISLAND ISLAND

Map p268 (http://elaginpark.org; admission Mon-Fri free, Sat, Sun & public holidays adult/student R70/30; ☺6am-11pm; ⓐ; ⓂKrestovsky Ostrov) This island is one giant park, free of traffic and a serene place to wander. It was attractively landscaped by the architect Carlo Rossi, and its centrepiece, also by Rossi, is the beautiful restored **Yelagin Palace** (Yelagin ostrov 1; adult/child R150/75; ☺10am-6pm), which Alexander I commissioned for his mother, Empress Maria. The gorgeous interiors, with detailed murals and incredible inlaid-wood floors, are furnished with antiques.

At the palace it's possible to arrange temporary hire of period costumes in which to have your photos taken – it's a really fun thing for children and families to do together. Concerts are also held here on Wednesday evenings. Other nearby estate buildings host temporary exhibitions too.

The rest of the island is a lovely network of paths, greenery, lakes and channels. At the northern end of the island, you can rent row boats to explore the ponds or in-line skates to explore the paths; in winter it's an ideal setting for sledding, skiing and skating. At the west end, a plaza looks out to the Gulf of Finland: sunsets are resplendent from here.

KAMENNY ISLAND ISLAND

Map p268 (ⓂChyornaya Rechka) Century-old dachas (country cottages) and mansions, inhabited by very wealthy locals, line the wooded lanes that twist their way around Kamenny (Stone) Island. The island is punctuated by a series of canals, lakes and ponds, and is pleasant for strolling at any time of year. At its east end, the **Church of St John the Baptist** (built 1776–81) has been charmingly restored.

Behind it, Catherine the Great built the big, classical **Kamennoostrovsky Palace** (Map p268) for her son; at the time of research it was under restoration.

For years a dead oak, supposedly planted by Peter the Great, stood in the middle of the Krestovka embankment. It has been removed and replaced with a young, healthy tree, but it is still known as **Peter's Tree**.

KRESTOVSKY ISLAND ISLAND

Map p268 (ⓐ; ⓂKrestovsky Ostrov) The biggest of the three northern islands, Krestovsky consists mostly of the vast **Maritime Victory Park** (Приморский парк Победы; Map p268; www.primparkpobedy.ru; Krestovsky pr; ⓂKrestovsky Ostrov), dotted with sports fields; at the far western end the giant **Ze-**

TOP SIGHT
HERMITAGE STORAGE FACILITY

Guided tours of the Hermitage's state-of-the-art restoration and storage facility provide a superb reason for coming out to northern St Petersburg. You'll be led through a handful of vaults dedicated to different aspects of the museum's vast collection. This is not a formal exhibition, but guides are knowledgable and the examples chosen for display (paintings, furniture and carriages) are wonderful.

The highlight is undoubtedly the gorgeous wool and silk embroidered Turkish ceremonial tent, presented to Catherine the Great by the Sultan Selim III in 1793. Beside it stands an equally impressive modern diplomatic gift: a massive wood carving of the mythical garuda bird, given by Indonesia to the city for its 300th anniversary.

Other notable displays are ancient icons and frescoes; selections from the collection of 3500 canvases by Russian artists down the ages; giant hanging tapestries that can be moved simultaneously to a musical accompaniment; a hall of imperial carriages; and a depository with all kinds of furniture – a veritable imperial IKEA!

The storage facility is directly behind the big shopping centre opposite the metro station – look for the enormous golden-yellow glass facility decorated with shapes inspired by petroglyphs.

DON'T MISS

→ Turkish ceremonial tent
→ Tapestries
→ Medieval frescoes

PRACTICALITIES

→ Реставрационно-хранительский центр Старая деревня
→ Map p268
→ ☎812-340 1026
→ www.hermitage museum.org
→ Zausadebnaya ul 37a
→ tours R200
→ ☺tours 11am, 1pm, 1.30pm & 3.30pm Wed-Sun
→ ⓂStaraya Derevnya

nit Stadium, under construction for years, is scheduled to be ready in time for the 2018 FIFA World Cup.

At the main entrance opposite the metro station you can rent bikes and in-line skates. Also here is **Divo Ostrov** (Map p268; www.divo-ostrov.ru; admission free, rides R50-300; ⊙noon-7pm; 🚗; MKrestovsky Ostrov), a Disney-style amusement park with exciting fairground rides that kids will adore.

⊙ Vyborg Side

SAMPSONIEVSKY CATHEDRAL   CATHEDRAL

Map p268 (Сампсониевский собор; www.cathedral.ru; Bolshoy Sampsonievsky pr 41; ⊙10am-6pm Thu-Tue; MVyborgskaya) FREE This light-blue baroque cathedral dates from 1740, and having been repainted and restored to its original glory both inside and out, glistens like a pearl amid a gritty industrial area. Its most interesting feature is the calendar of saints, two enormous panels on either side of the nave, each representing six months of the year, where every day is decorated with a mini-icon of its saint(s). The enormous silver chandelier above the altar is also something to behold, as is the stunning baroque, green-and-golden iconostasis. Don't miss the frieze of a young Peter the Great, on the wall behind you when you face the main iconostasis.

This is also believed to be the church where Catherine the Great married her one-eyed lover Grigory Potemkin in a secret ceremony in 1774.

BUDDHIST TEMPLE   TEMPLE

Map p268 (Буддистский Храм; ☏812-239 0341; www.dazan.spb.ru; Primorsky pr 91; ⊙10am-7pm Thu-Tue; MStaraya Derevnya) Another in the city's collection of grand religious buildings is this beautiful functioning *datsan* (temple) where respectful visitors are welcome. The main prayer hall has lovely mosaic decoration and there's a cheap and cheerful cafe in the basement. The temple was built between 1909 and 1915 at the instigation of Pyotr Badmaev, a Buddhist physician to Tsar Nicholas II. Money was raised from all over Russia, and as far afield as Thailand and England, by various Buddhist organisations; it even gained the support of the Dalai Lama in Lhasa.

In the 1930s the communists shut the temple, arrested many of the monks and used the building as a military radio station. In the 1960s it was taken over by the Zoological Institute and used as laboratories. Thankfully, however, the damage was not particularly profound and the *datsan* was returned to the city's small Buddhist community in 1990. Services are held at 7pm.

PISKARYOVSKOE CEMETERY   CEMETERY

(Пискарёвское мемориальное кладбище; www.pmemorial.ru; pr Nepokoryonnikh 72; ⊙9am-9pm May-Oct, to 6pm Nov-Apr; MPloshchad Muzhestva) The main burial place for the victims of the Nazi blockade in WWII is a stark and poignant memorial to the tragedy. Some half a million people were laid to rest here between 1941 and 1943, during the siege. From metro station Ploshchad Muzhestva, take *marshrutka* 123 in the direction of Ladozhskaya metro, which passes by the entrance to the cemetery.

Originally, this area was just an enormous pit where unnamed and unmarked bodies were dumped. In 1960 the remodelled cemetery was opened and has been an integral part of the city's soul ever since. Every year on Victory Day (9 May) the cemetery is packed out with mourners, many of whom survived the blockade or lost close relatives to starvation.

FINLAND STATION   HISTORIC BUILDING

Map p268 (Финляндский вокзал; pl Lenina 6; MPloshchad Lenina) Rebuilt in the '70s in rectilinear Soviet style, Finland Station (Finlyandsky vokzal) endures as a place of historical significance, where Lenin arrived in 1917 after 17 years in exile abroad. Here he gave his legendary speech from the top of an armoured car. After fleeing a second time he again arrived here from Finland, this time disguised as a railway fireman, and the locomotive he rode in is displayed on the platform.

Walk out onto the square that still bears Lenin's name and you'll see a marvellous statue of the man himself at the far end.

SITE OF PUSHKIN'S DUEL   HISTORICAL SITE

(Место дуэли Пушкина; Kolomyazhsky pr; MChyornaya Rechka) Russia's poetic genius, Alexander Pushkin, was fatally wounded in a duel here with the Frenchman Georges d'Anthès on 8 February 1837. A granite monument marks the alleged spot, today a small park surrounded by fast-moving traffic.

From the metro station at Chyornaya Rechka, walk down Torzhkovskaya ul and turn left at the first light on Novosibirskaya

STREET ART MUSEUM

At the time of research, the workers at the laminated plastics factory Slopast in the industrial zone of Okhta, a 20-minute bus ride east of Ploshchad Lenina, were the first, fortunate audience for what is shaping up to be one of Russia's contemporary-art highlights. A graffiti party held in 2011 in one of the complex's abandoned workshops was the spark to the grand idea of creating a **Street Art Museum** (☑812-448 1593; www.streetartmuseum.ru; shosse Revolutsii 84, Okhta; ⓂPloshchad Lenina, then bus 137 or 530).

Covering 11 hectares and with 150,000–200,000 sq metres of walls, Slopast is practically the perfect postindustrial canvas for street artists. The factory has a busy production schedule but on a far smaller footprint of its site than during Soviet times. But it's not just the currently abandoned parts of the complex that are set for a spray-canned artistic facelift. Some of the workshops are already decorated with epic works by the likes of top Russian streets artists Timothy Radya, Kirill Kto and Nikita Nomerz, as well as the Spanish artist Escif. Before he died in 2013, Pasha 183, frequently referred to as Russia's Banksy because of his anonymity, also contributed 'Walls Don't Sleep', a beautiful monochrome mural based on an image of Soviet factory workers.

Public tours started in mid-2014 and the aim is that by 2016 the complex will have some 70 works of varying formats, the former boilerhouse will become an exhibition space, while the resin factory will be a concert venue and a skateboard park.

ul. Walk straight to the end of the road, cross the train tracks and enter the park.

 EATING

★ STARAYA DEREVNYA RUSSIAN €
Map p268 (Старая деревня; ☑812-431 0000; www.sderevnya.ru; ul Savushkina 72; mains R300-500; ⊙1-10pm; ⓂChyornaya Rechka) A tiny, family-run hideaway with an intimate atmosphere and delectable food. Try old Russian recipes such as beef in plum and nut sauce. The small size of the restaurant guarantees personal service, but reservations are a must. From the metro, take any tram down ul Savushkina and get off at the third stop.

BLIZKIE DRUZYA BAKERY, CAFE €
Map p268 (Близкие друзья; ul Bolshoy Zelenina 16; mains R200; ⊙9am-11pm; 🛜; ⓂChkalovskaya) Meaning 'Best Friends', this is the most comfy of several pleasant cafes and bars opening up along this street. It's perfect for a light meal of soup or a quiche. The bakery has savoury and sweet creations, including pastel-coloured meringue and macaroons.

CHAK-CHAK TATAR €
Map p268 (Чак-Чак; www.kafe-chakchak.ru; ul Kuybysheva 30; snacks from R50; ⊙9am-9pm Mon-Fri, 11am-11pm Sat, 11am-9pm Sun; 🛅; ⓂGorkovskaya) Named after the honey-dipped pastry chak chak, this is a conveni-

ent spot to sample Tatar snacks such as ech-pochmak (beef and potato pies) and kosh tele (crispy pastry coated in powdered sugar). The cafe also offers more substantial dishes including soups and the rice pilaf plov.

TROITSKY MOST VEGETARIAN €
Map p268 (Троицкий Мост; www.t-most.ru; Kamennoostrovsky pr 9/2; mains R300; ⊙9am-11pm; 🖉; ⓂGorkovskaya) The original branch of this chain of excellent vegetarian cafes is located just a few blocks north of the bridge for which it is named.

LE MENU VEGETARIAN €
Map p268 (http://le-menu.ru; Kronverksky pr 79; mains R300; ⊙9am-11pm; 🛜🖉🛅; ⓂGorkovskaya) This cafe is brought to you by the passionate vegetarians who run veg chain Troitsky Most. There's near-identical fare here; the only difference is the more sophisticated setting – all wooden floorboards and chandeliers for those who appreciate meatless meals in style. Fish is also on the menu.

PELMENIYA INTERNATIONAL €
Map p268 (Kronveksky pr 55; dumplings R140-450; ⊙11am-11pm; 🛜🛅; ⓂGorkovskaya) A second branch of this appealing contemporarily styled dumpling bar that's good for an inexpensive, filling meal.

FUNKY KITCHEN INTERNATIONAL €
Map p268 (☑812-983 0880; www.fun-ki.com; Bolshoy pr 88; mains R350-400; ⊙10am-midnight

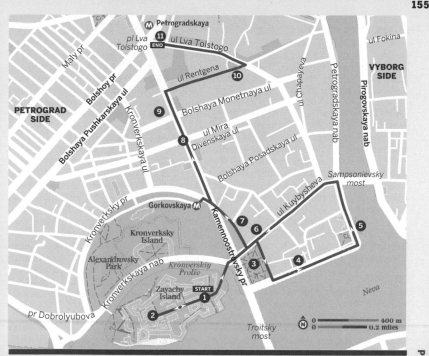

🏃 Neighbourhood Walk
Architectural Tour of Petrograd Side

START PETER & PAUL FORTRESS
(Ⓜ GORKOVSKAYA)
END ROSENSHTEIN APARTMENT BUILDING
(Ⓜ PETROGRADSKAYA)
LENGTH 1.5KM; TWO HOURS

The Petrograd Side is an architectural treasure trove with buildings ranging from the time of St Petersburg's inception up to contemporary times. Start with a quick tour of the city's first defensive installation, the **① Peter & Paul Fortress** (p144). Don't miss the splendid **② SS Peter & Paul Cathedral** (p144), the last resting place of Peter the Great and almost every tsar since.

The central square of Peter's early city, **③ Troitskaya ploshchad** (Trinity Sq) once had as its centrepiece Trinity Cathedral, where Peter attended Mass. The cathedral was destroyed soon after the 1917 revolution but a small chapel remains on the spot.

On Petrovskaya nab, **④ Peter's Cabin** (p147) is the wooden hut that was the tsar's first modest home in the city; and, off the island's eastern tip, the **⑤ Cruiser Aurora** (p148) is a legendary battleship which saw service in the Russo-Japanese War.

Return to Kamennoostrovsky pr via ul Kuybysheva, passing the Style Moderne palace of ballerina Mathilda Kshesinskaya that houses the **⑥ Museum of Political History** (p147), and the **⑦ Mosque** (p147), coated in dazzling mosaics of aquatint tiles.

Continue north along Kamennoostrovsky pr and look for architectural gems around **⑧ Avstriyskaya ploshchad**, with its castlelike edifices. Further along, if you want to get an idea of what one of these grand Style Moderne apartment blocks looks like inside, visit the **⑨ Kirov Museum** (p148).

Ul Rentgena offers up more beauties: note the decoration on No 4 and make sure you do a full circle of the freestanding **⑩ Chaev Mansion** (p149), which exhibits great geometric precision in its design.

Follow ul Lva Tolstogo towards the metro and you'll pass the **⑪ Rosenshtein Apartment Building**. Designed by Andrey Belogrud, this mash-up of neoclassical and neo-Gothic styles now houses a theatre.

Mon-Sat, 11am-midnight Sun; ⊖🛜🚫; MPetro-gradskaya) This hip restaurant-bar makes much of its balls – by which it means rissoles of meat, fish or chickpea (felafel), or chocolate and other sweet things. They're tasty but come in small portions so you should order several different dishes if you're hungry.

⭐MESTO
INTERNATIONAL €€

Map p268 (📞812-405 8799; Kronverksky pr 59; mains R400-600; ⏱11am-midnight; 🛜🚫; MGorkovskaya) Art deco fittings, a beautiful glass and marble counter and upholstered benches you could almost fall asleep on are a good start. The menu is eccentric but interesting: Anglophile shepherd's pie, chateaubriand and beef Wellington are supplemented by creative dishes such as green gazpacho and pumpkin and prawn soup. Portions are not huge but very tasty. Live piano playing Friday and Saturday from 7pm.

⭐CHEKHOV
RUSSIAN €€

Map p268 (Чехов; 📞812-234 4511; http://res taurant-chekhov.ru; Petropavlovskaya ul 4; mains R590-1110; ⏱noon-11pm; 🚫; MPetrogradskaya) Despite a totally nondescript appearance from the street, this restaurant's charming interior perfectly recalls that of a 19th-century dacha and makes for a wonderful setting for a delicious meal. The menu (not to mention the staff's attire) is very traditional and features lovingly prepared Russian classics such as 'fresh beef...stroganoff style'.

KORYUSHKA
RUSSIAN, GEORGIAN €€

Map p268 (Корюшка; 📞812-917 9010; http://gin zaproject.ru/SPB/Restaurants/Korushka/About; Petropavlovskaya krepost 3, Zayachy Island; mains R500; ⏱noon-midnight; 🛜🚫♿; MGorkov-ksaya) Lightly battered and fried *koryushka* (smelt) is a St Petersburg speciality every April, but you can eat the small fish year-round at this relaxed, sophisticated restaurant. There are plenty of other very appealing Georgian dishes on the menu to supplement the stunning views across the Neva.

SEMEINYE TRADITSY
RUSSIAN €€

Map p268 (Семейные традиции; 📞812-405 9413; Kronversky pr 65; mains R250-600; ⏱11am-11pm; 🛜🚫♿; MGorkovskaya) Meaning 'family traditions', there are plenty of child-friendly touches to this convivial place where the service truly is friendly. They serve the kind of heart-warming food your Russian mum would make, including homemade pickles and plenty of vegetarian dishes.

BABJIB
KOREAN €€

Map p268 (http://vk.com/babjib; ul Kuibisheva 7; mains R500; ⏱11am-11pm; 🛜🚫; MGorkovskaya) Be transported to contemporary Seoul at this delightful cafe serving up a tantalising menu of Korean classics such as *bibimbap* (rice salad), *gimbap* (sushi-style rolls) and various spicy stews. As is traditional the meals come with an assortment of hearty side dishes – so don't over order. The business lunch for R150 is a steal.

TBILISO
GEORGIAN €€

Map p268 (Тбилисо; 📞812-232 9391; Sytnin-skaya ul 10; mains R400-600; ⏱noon-midnight; MGorkovskaya) A beloved institution, and decidedly upscale as far as Georgian restaurants go, Tbiliso has a great interior with tiled tables and big booths, made more private by intricate latticework between them. The food is top-notch, with classics such as *khachapuri* (cheese bread) and chicken *tabaka* (flattened chicken cooked in spices) sumptuously prepared, and there's a huge range of wines.

MAKARONNIKI
ITALIAN €€

Map p268 (Макаронники; www.makaronniki.ru; pr Dobrolyubova 16; mains R300-1000; ⏱noon-1.30am; 🛜🚻🚫; MSportivnaya) The location of this trendy, charming place (the roof of a business centre) actually seems incidental – don't expect any life-changing views from here. However, the menu of modern Italian food, from pasta and pizza to rabbit served with cabbage and osso bucco, plus a laidback and whimsical feel make Makaronniki a place worth searching out.

VOLNA
INTERNATIONAL €€

Map p268 (Волна; www.volna.su; Petrovskaya nab 5; mains R300-600; ⏱noon-midnight; 🛜🚫; MGorkovskaya) Opposite Peter's Cabin, this sleek, laid-back lounge-restaurant has a great terrace perfect for a relaxed lunch over a bottle of wine. The menu ranges from risotto, salads and pasta to a selection of Asian dishes from the wok.

SALKHINO
GEORGIAN €€

Map p268 (Салхино; 📞821-232 7891; Kron-verksky pr 25; mains R300-600; ⏱11am-11pm; 🛜🚻🚫; MGorkovskaya) Pastel-coloured walls are adorned with paintings by local artists, and the menu of home-cooked Georgian meals, served in big portions, will keep everyone happy.

FLAMAND ROSE
BELGIAN €€

Map p268 (www.flamandrose.ru; Malaya Posadskaya ul 7/4; mains R750; ⊙11am-11pm; 🕿; MGorkovskaya) Above an interior-design shop, this darkly beautiful cafe-bar, dominated by a magnificent glass chandelier, specialises in Belgian cuisine and beers. The waffles are delish as are other sweet delights such as *tarte tatin*. Breakfast is also served up until 2pm.

MARI VANNA
RUSSIAN €€

Map p268 (☑812-230 5359; www.marivanna.ru; ul Lenina 18; mains R400-800; ⊙noon-10pm; 🕿; MPetrogradskaya) Like stepping into the parlour of your favourite, eccentric Russian relations, Ginza Project's original Mari Vanna now has branches across Russia, London and the US. You'll pay a slight premium for classic dishes such as borsch and *pelmeni* but it's all done so well you won't care.

JEAN-JACQUES
FRENCH €€

Map p268 (Жан-Жак; www.jan-jak.com; Bolshoy pr 54/2; mains R300-600; ⊙24hr; 🕿🈂; MPetrogradskaya) Chain offering excellent, affordable bistro fare including breakfast (served all day on weekends), as well as a huge selection of French wines.

PROBKA
ITALIAN €€€

Map p268 (☑911-922 7727; www.probka.org; pr Dobrolyubova 6; mains R300-1450; ⊙restaurant noon-midnight, cafe 8.30am-6pm Mon-Fri; 🕿; MSportivnaya) One of the city's top Italian operations, Probka oozes Milanese sophistication and is popular with suits from the building's Gazprom offices. Note that the Probka cafe inside the complex serves a very similar menu but is a bit cheaper.

🍷 DRINKING & NIGHTLIFE

It's slim pickings for drinking and nightlife this side of the Neva. There are a couple of places worth mentioning, mainly for coffee breaks while you're wandering the Petrograd Side.

COFFEE ROOM ST PETERSBURG
CAFE

Map p268 (http://vk.com/coffeeroom; Kamenoostrovsky pr 22; ⊙9am-11pm; MGorkovskaya) The Petrograd Side branch of this quirky chain of hipster cafe-bars – like the others it's arty and a very pleasant place to cool your feet.

VOLKONSKY
CAFE

Map p268 (www.wolkonsky.com; Kamennoostrovsky pr 8; ⊙8am-11pm; 🕿; MGorkovskaya) One of the more upmarket of the city's bakery-cafe chains, Volkonsky offers reviving brews and tempting confections.

☆ ENTERTAINMENT

A2
LIVE MUSIC

Map p268 (☑812-309 9922; http://a2.fm; pr Medikov 3; tickets from R1000; MPetrogradskaya) With capacity for 4000 and an exciting, eclectic line-up of DJs and live music, this is one of the best venues for contemporary sounds in the city. It also runs its own radio station.

KAMCHATKA
CLUB

Map p268 (www.clubkamchatka.ru; ul Blokhina 15; cover R200-300; MSportivnaya) A shrine to Viktor Tsoy, the late Soviet-era rocker who worked as caretaker of this former boilerhouse bunker with band mates from Kino. Music lovers flock here to light candles and watch a new generation thrash out their stuff. The line-up is varied and it's worth dropping by if only for a quick drink in this highly atmospheric place; find it tucked in a courtyard off the street.

BALTIC HOUSE
THEATRE

Map p268 (Балтийский дом; www.baltichouse.spb.ru; Alexandrovsky Park 4; MGorkovskaya) This large venue hosts an annual festival of plays from the Baltic countries, as well as Russian and European plays and a growing repertoire of experimental theatre.

PETROVSKY STADIUM
SPORTS

Map p268 (Спортивный комплекс Петровский; www.petrovsky.spb.ru; Petrovsky ostrov 2; MSportivnaya) Until the new stadium on Krestovsky Island is finally finished, this is the home ground of Zenit, St Petersburg's top football team. Games are well worth attending.

SIBUR ARENA
SPORTS

(http://siburarena.com; 8 Futbolnaya alleya, Krestovsky Ostrov; MKrestovsky Ostrov) This new 7000-seat stadium is home to local basketball team **BK Spartak** (www.bc-spartak.ru) who play here from October to April. The complex also houses a pool, gym and hotel.

🛍 SHOPPING

While the Petrograd Side has far fewer shopping options than the historic heart, it is nonetheless an inviting place to shop, its foothpaths lined with food shops, clothing boutiques and the odd speciality shop.

★ **UDELNAYA FAIR**   FLEA MARKET

(Удельная ярмарка; Skobolvesky pr, Vyborg Side; ⊗8am-5pm Sat & Sun; ⓂUdelnaya) This treasure trove of Soviet ephemera, pre-revolutionary antiques, WWII artefacts and bonkers kitsch from all eras is truly worth travelling for. Exit the metro station to the right and follow the crowds across the train tracks. Continue beyond the large permanent market, which is of very little interest, until you come to a huge area of independent stalls, all varying in quality and content.

The sheer size of the place means you'll really have to comb it to find the gems.

DAY & NIGHT   FASHION

Map p268 (www.day-night.ru; Malaya Posadskaya ul 6; ⊗11am-8pm; ⓂGorkovskaya) Looking like the set of *Alien* designed by Stella McCartney, this out-there boutique is one of St Petersburg's premier fashion experiences. Inside you'll find an absolutely top range of international designers for both men and women. Bring your credit card.

SYTNY MARKET   MARKET

Map p268 (Sytninskaya pl 3/5; ⊗8am-6pm; ⓂGorkovskaya) This colourful Petrograd Side market sells everything from vegetables, fruit, meat and fish inside to electronics, clothing and knick-knacks outside. Its name means 'sated market', quite understandably.

RUSSKY LYON   LINEN

Map p268 (Русский лён; www.linorusso.ru; Kronverskaya ul 1; ⊗11am-8pm; ⓂGorkovskaya) Branch of the good-quality Russian linen store.

MODEL SHOP   SOUVENIRS

Map p268 (Artillery Museum, Alexandrovsky Park 7; ⊗11am-6pm Wed-Sun; ⓂGorkovskaya)

Inside the Artillery Museum (though you don't need to pay for entry to get access to the shop), this is a must for fans of model planes, trains and automobiles. There's a good range of mainly Russian models in stock.

🏃 SPORTS & ACTIVITIES

KRUGLIYE BANI   BANYA

(Circle Baths; 📞8-964-368 2521; ul Karbysheva 29a; communal per person R20-190, luxe per person R400; ⊗communal baths 8am-10pm, luxe baths 9am-10pm Fri-Wed; ⓂPl Muzhestva) One of the city's best *bani* (hot baths) is opposite the metro; look for the round building across the grassy traffic island. Rates at the communal baths rise towards the weekend. The luxe baths (only open to women on Wednesday and Saturday) also grant you access to the heated circular open-air pool. There are private facilities too.

PITERLAND   WATER PARK

(http://piterland.ru; Primorsky pr 72, Vyborg Side; adult/child from R1000/700; ⊗10am-10.30pm; ⓂStaraya Derevnya) It's eternal summer under the giant dome of this superb aquapark accessed through a shopping mall facing onto the Gulf of Finland. The most fun is to be had slipping down the water slides twisting out of a giant pirate ship. There's also a wide range of styles of *banya* to sample, as well as a wave pool.

Buses and *marshrutky* run here from either Staraya Derevnya or Chyornaya Rechka metro stations.

YELAGIN ISLAND   OUTDOORS

Map p268 (http://elaginpark.org; ice skating per hr R150-250; ⊗ice skating 11am-9pm; ⓂKrestovsky Ostrov) This car-free island becomes a winter wonderland in colder temperatures, with sledding, cross-country skiing and ice skating. Skis and skates are both available for hire. In summer months, it's a great place to rent in-line skates as there is no traffic to contend with.

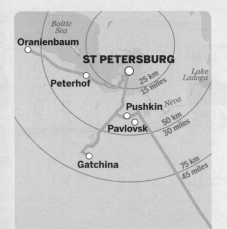

Day Trips from St Petersburg

Peterhof p160

The most popular day trip from St Petersburg is to Peter the Great's spectacular summer palace and grounds on the Gulf of Finland, easily reached from central St Petersburg by hydrofoil from outside the Admiralty.

Pushkin & Pavlovsk p165

Tsarskoe Selo (in the town of Pushkin) and Pavlovsk are two beautiful palaces and grounds next door to one another. This is a great day trip to see the summer palaces of Catherine the Great and Paul I.

Gatchina p169

The leafy park at Gatchina is one of the wildest and most beautiful of all the tsarist palace grounds, while the huge palace itself is an interesting and impressive place to explore.

Oranienbaum p170

Beyond Peterhof is Prince Menshikov's vast estate, which has some truly lovely gardens and is a great place to wander, especially since a recent renovation has brought the Great Palace back to its former glory.

TOP SIGHT
PETERHOF ПЕТЕРГОФ

The fountains are incredible, the palace is a stunner and the grounds are great for walking, so it's no surprise that Peter the Great's summer palace is usually the first-choice day trip for visitors to St Petersburg. Peterhof is no secret, however, so come early in the day or out of season to enjoy it without the crowds.

Peter's Summer Palace

Hugging the Gulf of Finland 29km west of St Petersburg, Peterhof, the 'Russian Versailles', is a far cry from the original cabin Peter the Great had built here to oversee construction of the Kronshtadt naval base. Peter liked the place so much he built a villa, Monplaisir, here and then a whole series of palaces and ornate gardens. Peterhof was renamed Petrodvorets (Peter's Palace) in 1944 but has since reverted to its original name. The palace and buildings are surrounded by leafy gardens and a spectacular ensemble of gravity-powered fountains.

What you see today is largely a reconstruction since Peterhof was a major casualty of WWII. Apart from the damage done by the Germans, the palace suffered the worst under Soviet bombing raids in December 1941 and January 1942 because Stalin was determined to thwart Hitler's plan of hosting a New Year's victory celebration here.

The Lower Park

The **Lower Park** (Нижний парк; adult/student R500/250, Nov-Apr free; ⊘9am-8pm) contains most of Peterhof's sights and is where you will arrive if you take the hydrofoil from St Petersburg to get here. Forming the lion's share of the palace grounds, it boasts an incredible symphony of gravity-powered golden fountains, beautiful waterways and interesting historical buildings, making it one of St Petersburg's most dazzling attractions.

DON'T MISS...

→ Grand Palace
→ Water Avenue
→ Monplaisir
→ Hermitage

PRACTICALITIES

→ Большой дворец
→ adult/student R550/300, audioguide R500
→ ⊘10.30am-6pm Tue-Sun, closed last Tue of month

Criss-crossed by bridges and bedecked by smaller sprays, **Water Avenue** (☺May-Sep) is a canal leading from the hydrofoil dock to the palace. It culminates in the magnificent Grand Cascade, a symphony of over 140 fountains engineered in part by Peter himself. The central statue of Samson tearing open a lion's jaws celebrates – as so many things in St Petersburg do – Peter's victory over the Swedes at Poltava. Shooting up 62m, it was unveiled by Rastrelli for the 25th anniversary of the battle in 1735.

Grand Palace

The Grand Palace is an imposing edifice, although with 30-something rooms, it's not as large as many tsarist palaces. From the start of June to the end of September it is open to foreign tourists only between 10.30am and noon, and again from 2.30pm until 4.15pm, due to guided tours being given only in Russian at other times (while you have to enter the palace as part of a guided tour, it's quite possible to slip away).

While Peter's palace was relatively modest, Rastrelli grossly enlarged the building for Empress Elizabeth. Later, Catherine the Great toned things down a little with a redecoration, although that's not really apparent from the glittering halls and art-filled galleries that are here today. All of the paintings, furniture and chandeliers are original, as everything was removed from the premises before the Germans arrived in WWII. The Chesme Hall is full of huge paintings of Russia's destruction of the Turkish fleet at Çesme in 1770. Other highlights include the exquisite East and West Chinese Cabinets, Peter's study and the Picture Hall, which lives up to its name, with hundreds of portraits crowding its walls. The Throne Room is the biggest in the palace, and the centrepiece is Peter's red velvet throne.

After WWII, Peterhof was largely left in ruins. Hitler had intended to throw a party here when his plans to occupy the Astoria Hotel were thwarted. He drew up pompous invitations, which obviously incensed his Soviet foes. Stalin's response was to preempt any such celebration by bombing the estate himself, in the winter of 1941–42, so it is ironic but true that most of the damage at Peterhof occurred at the hands of the Soviets.

Monplaisir

This far more humble, sea-facing villa was always Peter the Great's favourite retreat. It's easy to see why: **Monplaisir** (Монплезир; adult/student R400/200; ☺10.30am-6pm late May-early Oct) is woodpanelled, snug and elegant, peaceful even when

HYDROFOIL

From May to September, the Peterhof Express (adult single/return R650/1100, student R450/800; 30 minutes) departs from the jetty in front of the Admiralty every 30 minutes from 9am. It's a highly enjoyable way to get to Peterhof, and you arrive right in front of the palace. The last hydrofoil leaves Peterhof at 7pm.

Even though the hydrofoil is fast and convenient, it's rather expensive. You can save money by getting here by *marshrutka*. Marshrutky 300, 424 and 424A (R55) leave from outside the Avtovo metro station. All pass through the town of Peterhof, immediately outside the palace. Tell the driver you want to go 'v dvaryéts' ('to the palace') and you'll be let off near the main entrance to the Upper Garden, on Sankt-Peterburgsky pr.

TRAIN

There's a frequent train (R67, 30 minutes) from Baltic Station (Baltiysky vokzal) to Novy Petrodvorets, from where you can walk (20 minutes) or take any bus except 357 to the fifth stop, which takes another 10 minutes.

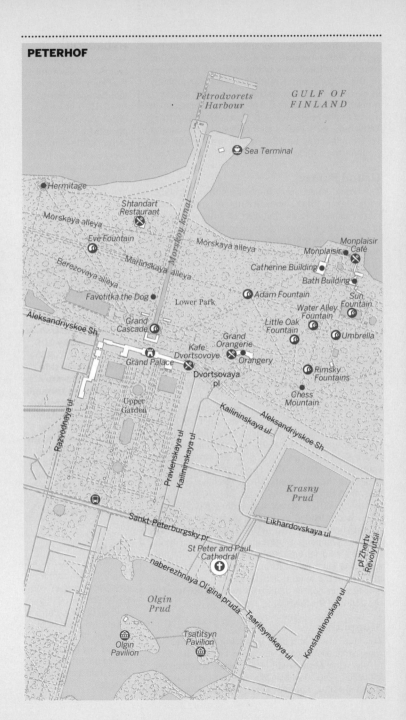

PETERHOF

Petrodvorets Harbour

GULF OF FINLAND

Sea Terminal

Hermitage

Shtandart Restaurant

Morskaya alleya

Eve Fountain

Morskaya alleya

Marlinskaya alleya

Berezovaya alleya

Morskoy kanal

Monplaisir Café

Monplaisir

Catherine Building

Bath Building

Sun Fountain

Favotitka the Dog

Lower Park

Adam Fountain

Water Alley Fountain

Aleksandriyskoe Sh

Grand Cascade

Little Oak Fountain

Umbrella

Grand Orangerie

Kafe Dvortsovoye

Orangery

Rimsky Fountains

Grand Palace

Dvortsovaya pl

Chess Mountain

Upper Garden

Razvodnaya ul

Pravlenskaya ul

Kalininskaya ul

Kalininskaya ul

Aleksandriyskoe Sh

Krasny Prud

Sankt-Peterburgsky pr

Likhardovskaya ul

pl Zhertv Revolyutsii

St Peter and Paul Cathedral

naberezhnaya Ol'gina pruda

Tsaritsynskaya ul

Konstantinovskaya ul

Olgin Prud

Olgin Pavilion

Tsatitsyn Pavilion

...terhof grounds

NEED TO KNOW

....

Peterhof is 29km west of St Petersburg. The area Code ☑812

....

In the Lower Park itself, the best eating options are the **Grand Orangerie** (set menus R450 to R800; open 11am to 8pm), a cafe in the former palace orangery, or the **Shtandart Restaurant** (www.restaurantshtandart.spb.ru; mains R500 to R800; open 11am to 8pm), a bigger place with a terrace and views towards the Gulf of Finland. Outside the palace grounds, try the **Duck & Drake Pub & Restaurant** inside the New Peterhof Hotel (☑812-319 1090; www.new-peterhof.com), where you can eat sandwiches and burgers (mains R600 to R900).

TOP TIP

....

Remember to bring mosquito repellent or to keep your legs and arms covered if you're here during summer; the mosquitoes on the palace grounds are fierce.

there's a crowd – which there used to be all the time, what with Peter's mandatory partying ('misbehaving' guests were required to gulp down huge quantities of wine).

Also in this complex is an annexe called the **Catherine Building** (Екатерининский корпус; adult/student R360/180; ☺10.30am-6pm), which was built by Rastrelli between 1747 and 1755. Its name derives from the fact that Catherine the Great was living in this building when her husband Peter III was overthrown, and it was from here that she set out for the capital to assume the Russian throne. The interior contains the bedroom and study of Alexander I, as well as the huge Yellow Hall. On the right side is the magnificent **Bath Building** (Банный корпус; adult/student R400/200; ☺10.30am-6pm Thu-Tue), built by Quarenghi in 1800, which is nothing special inside. Look out for some more trick fountains in the garden in front of the buildings.

Hermitage

Along the shore to the west, the 1725 **Hermitage** (Эрмитаж; adult/student R250/150; ☺10.30am-6pm Wed-Mon May-Oct) is a two-storey yellow-and-white box featuring the ultimate in private dining: special elevators hoist a fully laid table into the imperial presence on the 2nd floor, thereby eliminating any hindrance by servants. The elevators are circular and directly in front of each diner, whose plate would be lowered, replenished and replaced. The device is demonstrated on Saturdays and Sundays at 1pm, 2pm and 3pm. Further west is yet another palace, **Marly**, inspired by the Versailles hunting lodge of the same name so loved by Louis XIV.

Park Alexandria

Even on summer weekends, the rambling and overgrown **Park Alexandria** (Парк Александрия; adult/student R200/100; ⊙9am-10pm) is peaceful and practically empty. Built for Tsar Nicholas I (and named for his tsarina), these grounds offer a sweet retreat from the crowds. Originally named for Alexander Nevsky, the **gothic chapel** (adult/student R250/150; ⊙10.30am-6pm Tue-Sun) was completed in 1834 as the private chapel of Nicholas I. Nearby is the **cottage** (Коттедж; adult/student R400/200; ⊙10.30am-6pm Tue-Sun) that was built around the same time as his summer residence. Also part of this same ensemble is the beautifully restored **Farmer's Palace** (Фермерский дворец; adult/student R500/250; ⊙10.30am-6pm Tue-Sun), built here in 1831 as a pavilion in the park and designed to reify pastoral fantasies of rural life for the royal family. It became the home of the teenage Tsarevitch Alexander (later Alexander II), who loved it throughout his life.

Peterhof Town

Outside the palace grounds is the handsome **St Peter and Paul Cathedral** (Петропавловский собор; Sankt Petersburgsky pr; ⊙8am-8pm) FREE, and, continuing around the edge of Olgin Prud (Olga's pond), **Tsaritsyn and Olgin Pavilions** (adult/student R500/250; ⊙10.30am-6pm, last entry 4pm), two buildings sitting on islands in the middle of the pond. Nicholas I had these elaborate pavilions built for his wife (Alexandra Fyodorovna) and daughter (Olga Nikolayevna) respectively. Only recently restored and reopened, they boast unique Mediterranean architectural styles reminiscent of Pompeii.

Further down Sankt-Peterburgsky pr is the **Raketa Petrodvorets Watch Factory** (☑8-921-632 0313; www.raketa.com; Sankt-Peterburgsky pr 60; ⊙9am-4pm Mon-Fri) FREE, one of the town's biggest employers, which has an onsite shop selling *very* cool watches.

TICKETS FOR PETERHOF

On arrival, you'll need to pay to enter the grounds of the palace, known as the Lower Park, and then for each additional sight within it. Sadly, however, it's not cheap, as you're paying more than locals and the sights add up, so choose what you want to see carefully. Inexplicably, many museums also have different closing days, although all buildings are open Friday to Sunday. Nearly all tours and posted information are in Russian, so buy an information booklet at the kiosks near the entrances, or in the Grand Palace take an English-language audioguide. Almost all of the buildings require an extra ticket to take photographs or videos, while in the Grand Palace it's not allowed at all. Online tickets can be purchased for the Grand Palace at www.peterhof museum.ru, which can avoid long lines in the summer months.

TOP SIGHT   PUSHKIN & PAVLOVSK
ПУШКИН И ПАВЛОВСК

The sumptuous palaces and sprawling parks at Tsarskoe Selo and Pavlovsk are, thanks to Catherine the Great and Pushkin, entrenched in Russian history and immortalised in literature. These two neighbouring complexes can be combined in a day's visit – although if you're not in the mood to rush, there is plenty at both of them to keep you entertained for an entire day.

DON'T MISS...

➡ Catherine Palace

➡ Catherine Park

➡ Pavlovsk Great Park

➡ Pavlovsk Great Palace

The Parks

Almost adjacent yet very different in style and design, Tsarskoe Selo and Pavlovsk are both huge imperial estates with impressive gardens, palaces and various other embellishments. Both also have towns that have grown up around them over the centuries. (The town surrounding Tsarskoe Selo was originally called Tsarskoe Selo too, but changed its name to Pushkin in 1937.)

Tsarskoe Selo (the 'tsar's village') is understandably the big hitter of the two thanks to the beautiful Catherine Palace and its sumptuous grounds. Pavlovsk, just a short bus ride away, is far less visited and much quieter as a result, but its grounds are wilder and arguably even more lovely and make for a perfect place to get lost in.

Catherine Palace

The centrepiece of Tsarskoe Selo, created under Empresses Elizabeth and Catherine the Great between 1744 and 1796, is the vast baroque **Catherine Palace** (Екатерининский дворец; http://eng.tzar.ru; adult/student R400/200, audioguide R150; ☺10am-6pm Wed-Sun, to 9pm Mon), designed by Rastrelli and named after Peter the Great's second wife. From May to September the palace can only be visited by individuals between noon and 2pm and 4pm and 5pm, otherwise it's reserved for prebooked tour groups, such is its rightful popularity. The audioguide is well worth taking, as it gives detailed explanations of what you'll see in each room.

As at the Winter Palace, Catherine the Great had many of Rastrelli's original interiors remodelled in classical style. Most of the gaudy exterior and 20-odd rooms of the palace

NEED TO KNOW

Pushkin is 25km south of St Petersburg, Pavlovsk 29km. The area code is ☎812.

From Moskovskaya station, take the exit marked 'Buses for the airport', then pick up marshrutky 286, 299, 342 or K545 towards Pushkin (R35). These continue to Pavlovsk (R40). Look for 'Пушкин' or 'Дворец' on buses. Trains go from Vitebsk Station, but are infrequent during the week. For Pushkin, get off at Detskoe Selo (Детское село), and for Pavlovsk at Pavlovsk Station (Павловск).

EATING

In Tsarskoe Selo try 19th Century Restaurant (www.restaurantpushkin.ru; Srednyaya ul 2; mains R400 to R750), popular with tours but it has atmosphere and good food. In town, try cosy White Rabbit (ul Moskovskaya 22; mains R500 to R1000; open 11am to 11pm). In Pavlovsk, try Podvorye (☎812-465 1399; www.podvorye.ru; Filtrovskoye sh 16; mains R600 to R1500; open noon to 11pm), near the train station by Great Park's most eastern entrance.

Painting and panel in the Amber Room

have been beautifully restored – compare them to the photographs of the devastation left by the Germans.

The interiors are superb, with highlights including the Great Hall, the Arabesque Hall, the baroque Cavalier's Dining Room, the White State Dining Room, the Crimson and Green Pilaster Rooms, the Portrait Hall and of course the world-famous Amber Room. The panels used in the Amber Room were a gift given to Peter the Great, but not put to any use until 1743 when Elizabeth decided to use them decoratively, after which they were ingeniously incorporated into the walls here. What you see is a reconstruction of the original that disappeared during WWII and is believed to have been destroyed.

Catherine Park

The lovely **Catherine Park** (Екатерининский парк; adult/student R120/60 May-Sep, Oct-Apr free; ⊙9am-6pm), with its main entrance on Sadovaya ul next to the palace chapel, surrounds the Catherine Palace. It extends around the ornamental Great Pond and contains an array of interesting buildings, follies and pavilions.

Near Catherine Palace, the **Cameron Gallery** has rotating exhibitions. The park's outer section focuses on the Great Pond. In summer you can take a **ferry boat** (adult/child R200/100; ⊙11am-6pm May-Sep) to the little island to visit the **Chesme Column** (adult/child R250/150; ⊙11am-6pm May-Sep), a monument to Russia's victory over the Turkish fleet. Beside the pond, the blue baroque **Grotto Pavilion** (☺10am-5pm Fri-Wed) FREE houses temporary exhibitions in summer. A walk around the Great Pond will reveal other buildings that the royals built over the years, including the very incongruous-looking **Turkish Bath** with its minaret-style tower, the wonderful **Marble Bridge**, the **Chinese Pavilion** and a **Concert Hall** isolated on an island.

Alexander Palace & Park

A short distance north of the Catherine Palace, and surrounded by the overgrown and tranquil **Alexander Park** (Александровский парк; admission free), is the classical **Alexander Palace** (Александровский дворец; Dvortsovaya ul 2; adult/student/under 18 R300/150/free, audioguide R100; ☺10am-5pm Wed-Mon, closed last Wed of month). This palace, built by Quarenghi between 1792 and 1796 for the future Alexander I, was the favourite residence of Nicholas II, the last Russian tsar. Only three rooms are open to visitors, but they're impressive, with a huge tiger-skin carpet and an extremely ropy portrait of a young Queen Victoria to boot. It's a poignant and forgotten place that doesn't get many tourists and is a welcome contrast to the Catherine Palace.

Pavlovsk Great Palace

Between 1781 and 1786, on orders from Catherine the Great, architect Charles Cameron designed the **Pavlovsk Great Palace** (Большой павловский дворец; www.pavlovskmuseum.ru; adult/child R450/250; ☺10am-6pm, closed Fri mid-Sep & mid-May) in Pavlovsk. The palace was designated for Catherine's son Paul (hence the name, Pavlovsk), and it was Paul's second wife, Maria Fyodorovna, who orchestrated the design of the interiors. Tragically, the original palace was burnt down two weeks after the end of WWII when a careless Soviet soldier's cigarette set off German mines (the Soviets blamed the Germans). As at Tsarskoe Selo, the restoration is remarkable.

The finest rooms are on the middle floor of the central block. Cameron designed the round Italian Hall beneath the dome and the Grecian Hall to its west, though the lovely green fluted columns were added by his assistant Vincenzo Brenna. Flanking these are two private suites designed mainly by Brenna: Paul's along the north side of the block and Maria Fyodorovna's on the south. The Hall of War of the insane, military-obsessed Paul contrasts with Maria's Hall of Peace, decorated with musical instruments and flowers. On the middle floor of the south block are Paul's Throne Room and the Hall of the Maltese Knights of St John, of whom he was the Grand Master.

THE MYSTERY OF THE AMBER ROOM

The original Amber Room was created from exquisitely engraved amber panels given to Peter the Great by King Friedrich Wilhelm I of Prussia in 1716. Rastrelli later combined the panels with gilded woodcarvings, mirrors, agate and jasper mosaics to decorate one of the rooms of the Catherine Palace. Plundered by the Nazis during WWII, the room's decorative panels were last exhibited in Königsberg's castle in 1941. Four years later, with the castle in ruins, the Amber Room was presumed destroyed. Or was it?

In 2004, as Putin and then German Chancellor Gerhard Schröder presided over the opening of the new US$18 million Amber Room, restored largely with German funds, rumours about the original panels continued to swirl. There are those who believe that parts, if not all, of the original Amber Room remain hidden away somewhere and have survived (see www.amberroom.org).

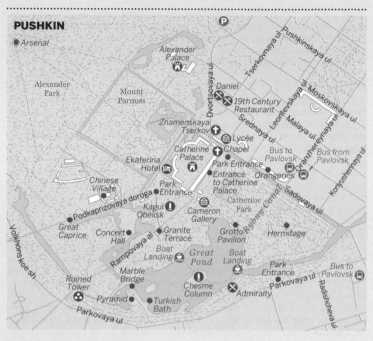

Pavlovsk Great Park

If you decide to skip the palace, you may simply wish to wander around the serene **Pavlovsk Great Park** (Павловский парк; adult/child R150/80; ☺10am-6pm, closed Fri mid-Sep–mid-May) – and as you'll have to pay to enter them just to access the palace, it's worth exploring and seeing what you come across. Filled with rivers and ponds, tree-lined avenues, classical statues and hidden temples, it's a delightful place to get lost. Highlights include the **Rose Pavilion** (Розовый павильон; adult/student R200/100) and the **Private Garden** (Собственный садик; adult/student R150/75), with its beautifully arranged flowerbeds and impressive sculpture of the Three Graces. Bike hire (R250 per hour) is available at several locations around the park and is a great way to explore, as distances are large.

Gatchina
Гатчина

Explore

The furthest flung of the imperial palaces surrounding St Petersburg, Gatchina is rather different from the rest on many counts. First of all, it's in the middle of a busy town, meaning that it doesn't feel grandly isolated like so many tsarist bolt-holes. Secondly, the extensive landscaped grounds are all public, meaning that you're more likely to encounter picnicking locals than tour groups as you walk around. That said, Gatchina's grounds are some of the most beautiful of all the imperial parks, and the restored palace, complete with its dark and dramatic history, is a fascinating place to explore.

The Best...
→**Sight** Gatchina Great Palace
→**Place to Eat** Kafe Piramida
→**Quirky Sight** Birch House (p170)

Top Tip

Avoid the weekends if you'd prefer to enjoy the grounds without crowds of picnicking Russians.

Getting There & Away
→**Bus** This is the quickest way to get here. Buses K18, K18A and 431 (R70, 45 minutes) run from outside Moskovskaya metro station and stop right by the park. Bus 100 (R70, one hour) also runs regularly from Moskovskaya; buses wait outside the House of Soviets and stop just short of Gatchina Park. Tell the driver you want to go to the palace ('v dvaryéts') – the bus turns off before you get to the park.
→**Train** There are trains to Gatchina Baltiysky (R84, one hour) from Baltic Station (Baltiysky vokzal) every one to two hours. The train station is directly in front of the palace.

Need to Know
→**Area Code** ⌨812
→**Location** 45km south of St Petersburg

◉ SIGHTS

GATCHINA GREAT PALACE PALACE
(Большой гатчинский дворец; www.gatchinapalace.ru/en; adult/student R200/100, photos R100, audioguide R200; ⏱10am-6pm Tue-Sun, closed 1st Tue of month) Shaped in a graceful curve around a central turret, the Gatchina Great Palace certainly lives up to its name – its enormous (if surprisingly plain) facade is quite a sight to behold, overlooking a vast parade ground and backing onto the huge landscaped grounds. Built by Rinaldi between 1766 and 1781 in an early classicism style for Catherine the Great's favourite Grigory Orlov, the palace curiously combines motifs of a medieval fortress with elements commonly seen in Russian imperial residences.

It's hard to call it beautiful, but there's no doubt that it's extremely impressive. After Orlov's death in 1783, Catherine the Great bought the palace from his heirs and gifted it to her son Paul, who redesigned the exterior between 1792 and 1798.

Inside, the 10 State Rooms on the 2nd floor are impressive, including Paul I's Throne Room, hung with huge tapestries, and his wife Maria Fyodorovna's Throne Room, the walls of which are covered in

---

EATING AT GATCHINA

There are a few eating options in the palace and grounds, but as the place was made for picnicking your best bet is to bring your own lunch. However, if you haven't done so, head to the town centre; try **Kafe Piramida** (Кафе Пирамида; ul Sobornaya 3a; mains R180-300; ⏱10am-11pm) on the main pedestrian precinct or the **Slavyansky Dvor** (Славянский двор; ul Dostoevskogo 2; mains R200-500; ⏱11am-midnight) restaurant inside a hotel complex of the same name.

paintings. Most impressive of all is the White Hall, a Rinaldi creation dating from the 1770s that was redone by Brenna in the 1790s. On the balcony is an impressive collection of sundials.

GATCHINA PARK PARK

(Гатчинский парк; ⊘dawn-dusk) **FREE**
Gatchina Park is more overgrown and romantic than the other palaces' parklands. The park has many winding paths through birch groves and across bridges to islands in the large White Lake. Look out for the frankly bizarre **Birch House** (Березовый домик; adult/student R50/20; ⊘10am-6pm Tue-Sun May–Sep), which was a present from Maria Fyodorovna to Paul I. With a rough facade made of birch logs, the interior is actually very refined, with a beautiful hardwood floor made from timber from around the world.

Paul I later built a neoclassical 'mask' to hide the Birch House's facade from the view of casual strollers.

Down on the lake, the **Venus Pavilion** (Павильон Венеры; adult/student R50/20; ⊘10am-6pm Tue-Sun May–mid Sep) is a beautiful spot jutting out into the water with an elaborately painted interior. Continue around the lake to find the best picnicking spots – it's even possible to swim in a second lake (see where the locals go) if the weather is good.

It's also possible to visit Paul I's **private garden** (Собственный садик; adult/student R50/20; ⊘10am-6pm Tue-Sun May–mid-Sep), adjacent to the palace, laid out in the late-18th century by Vincenzo Brenna for the private use of the royal family. It's a charming place to stroll, full of sculptures, flowers and neatly trimmed hedges.

GATCHINA TOWN TOWN

In the nearby town there are a couple of interesting churches. The baroque **Pavlovsk Cathedral** (Павловский собор; ul Sobornaya), at the end of the pedestrianised shopping street off the central pr 25 Oktyabrya, has

a grandly restored interior with a soaring central dome. A short walk west is the **Pokrovsky Cathedral** (Покровский собор; Krasnaya ul), a red-brick building with bright blue domes.

Oranienbaum
Ораниенбаум

Explore

Anyone interested in Prince Menshikov, best friend of Peter the Great, and the first governor of St Petersburg, will be fascinated by this testament to his growing vanity. While Peter was building Monplaisir at Peterhof, Menshikov began his own palace at Oranienbaum (Orange Tree), 12km further down the coast. Peter was unfazed by the fact that his subordinate's palace in St Petersburg (Menshikov Palace) was grander than his own, and Menshikov also outdid his master in creating this fabulous retreat. While not particularly opulent compared to the palaces that Elizabeth and Catherine the Great favoured, by Petrine standards Oranienbaum was off the scale. Oranienbaum (which is also known by its Soviet-era name, Lomonosov) recently finished a vast restoration project and is looking better than ever.

The Best...
➡**Sight** Great Palace
➡**Place to Eat** Mimino
➡**Quirky Sight** Chinese Palace

Top Tip

It's very easy to combine Oranienbaum with a visit to Peterhof. From the palace at Peterhof, walk down to the main road and pick up any *marshrutka* with Ломоносов

EATING AT ORANIENBAUM

With kilometres of quiet paths through pine woods and sombre gardens, Oranienbaum is a lovely place for a picnic. Otherwise, try tour-group favourite **Okhota** (Охота; Dvortsovy pr 65a; mains R500-1000; ⊘noon-midnight; 🖟), opposite the main entrance to the palace on the main road, or the cheaper and more local Georgian cafe **Mimino** (Мимино; mains R200-400; ⊘11am-2am), near the train station.

written on it. Tell the driver you want to go '*v dvaryéts*'.

Getting There & Away

➤ **Marshrutky** Take *marshrutka* 300, 424 or 424A (R70, 50 minutes) from outside Avtovo metro station. Once in town, the bus eventually comes down a hill with the Archangel Michael Cathedral at the bottom. Get off here and follow the park perimeter to the left until you reach the entrance.

➤ **Train** Alternatively the train from St Petersburg's Baltic Station to Peterhof continues to Oranienbaum (R62, one hour). Get off at Lomonosov Station and walk diagonally across the little park outside it. Keep going up to the main road, turn right, pass the unmissable Archangel Michael Cathedral and the park entrance is on your left.

Need to Know

➤ **Area Code** ☏812
➤ **Location** 41km west of St Petersburg

⊙ SIGHTS

GREAT PALACE   PALACE

(Большой дворец; adult/student R400/200; ⊙10.30am-6pm Wed-Mon) Menshikov's impressive Great Palace underwent a full restoration and reopened its state rooms in 2014. Most of the interiors are restorations of the 19th-century ones, so reflect the taste of the various Romanovs who used the palace, rather than Menshikov himself, of whom there is no trace.

There are impressive ceiling mouldings in the Concert Hall, while the ground floor is given over to an exhibit about the long restoration project, but overall the palace is more impressive from the outside. Following Peter's death and Menshikov's exile, the palace served briefly as a hospital and then passed to Tsar Peter III. Of course, Peter III didn't much like ruling Russia, so he spent a lot of time here before he was dispatched in a coup led by his wife, the future Catherine the Great.

ORANIENBAUM PARK   PARK

(Музей-заповедник Ораниенбаум; www.peterhofmuseum.ru; adult/student R200/100 May-Oct, Nov-Apr free; ⊙9am-8pm) Spared Nazi occupation, after WWII Oranienbaum was renamed for the scientist-poet Mikhail Lomonosov. Now known as Oranienbaum again, it doubles as a museum and public park, with lots of beautiful pathways, ornamental lakes and other follies and pavilions to enjoy.

Beyond the beautiful lake, the Palace of Peter III, also called Peterstadt, is a boxy toy palace, with rich interiors. It was restored in the late 1950s and early 1960s, but is in dire need of attention again and its salmon pink walls are now flaking and chipped. Approach the 'palace' through the monumental Gate of Honour, all that remains of a small-scale fortress where Peter amused himself drilling his soldiers.

Worth a peek also is Catherine's over-the-top **Chinese Palace** (Китайский дворец; adult/student R400/200; ⊙10.30am-6pm Tue-Sun), designed by Antonio Rinaldi, and recently fully restored, it boasts rococo on the inside and baroque on the outside. The private retreat also features painted ceilings and fine inlaid-wood floors and walls.

Palaces

The Romanovs built and constantly embellished several extraordinary palace complexes around St Petersburg, all of which can be visited on easy day trips from the city. Most extraordinary are Peterhof (Peter the Great's palace with a spectacular ensemble of fountains) on the Gulf of Finland, and Tsarskoe Selo in Pushkin, beloved of Catherine the Great.

KATIE GARROD / GETTY IMAGES ©

MANFRED HOFER / GETTY IMAGES ©

1. Great Palace (p171)
Prince Menshikov's palace in Oranienbaum.

2. Catherine Palace (p165)
Cavalier's Dining Rom in the grand centrepiece palace at Tsarskoe Selo.

3. Catherine Park (p166)
A statue at the Chinese Pavilion in the Catherine Palace grounds.

4. Peterhof (p160)
Gilded fountains outside Peter's summer palace.

5. Gatchina Great Palace (p169)
The imposing curved facade of Rinaldi's palace.

WALTER BIBIKOW / GETTY IMAGES ©

Sleeping

Accommodation in St Petersburg doesn't come cheap, and it pays to book well in advance as places fill up during the White Nights and throughout the summer. The hospitality industry has improved enormously in the past decade, however, with Soviet hotels now largely a thing of the past, replaced instead by a range of youth hostels, mini-hotels and luxury options.

Hotels

There has been a revolution in hotel accommodation in St Petersburg and a large expansion of modern, professionally run establishments. Old Soviet fleapits have been reconstructed as contemporary and appealing hotels, some of the city centre's most desperately derelict buildings have been rebuilt as boutique or luxury properties and the overall standards of service have risen enormously. That said, most hotels are still fairly expensive, with a lack of good midrange places in the city centre. Though they do exist, they tend to get booked up well in advance (particularly during the summer months), so plan ahead if you want to stay in the historic heart.

Mini-Hotels

Mini-hotels are a real St Petersburg phenomenon. While most aspiring hoteliers are not able to pay for the renovation and conversion of entire buildings themselves, lots of small-time entrepreneurs have been able to buy an apartment or two and create a small hotel in otherwise normal residential buildings. Due to their individuality and the care that often goes into their running, mini-hotels are some of the best places to stay in the city. They also tend to be well located in the centre of the city where demand for rooms is highest.

On the downside, they are by their very nature rather small places, so rooms book up quickly.

Hostels

Once a city with just a handful of very average, far-flung and depressing hostels, St Petersburg now positively spoils budget travellers with a wide range of places to sleep for well under R1000 a night. Central, well run, safe, clean and with free wi-fi, this new generation of hostels will be a very welcome surprise to anyone coming to Russia for the first time. Hostels here tend to be run by enthusiastic staff who themselves have travelled widely and are passionate about sharing their knowledge of their hometown with travellers. Again, book ahead to ensure you get a place at the hostel you want.

Apartments

As hotels for individual travellers tend to be fairly expensive even in midrange categories, renting an apartment is a great option and St Petersburg is full of large flats that are regularly rented out to tourists. Security is generally very good, with multiple locks on doors, entry phones and well-lit corridors – a far cry from how renting apartments used to be. Many local travel agencies offer apartments, and the city's profile on rental websites such as Airbnb is growing all the time.

Lonely Planet's Top Choices

Baby Lemonade Hostel (p177) A fun, friendly pop-art hostel with boutique-hotel worthy private rooms.

Soul Kitchen Hostel (p180) This charming place overlooking the Moyka is one of the most charming on the city's hostel scene.

Alexander House (p181) A beautiful privately run hotel overlooking the Kryukov Canal.

Andrey & Sasha's Home-stay (p181) The best possible cultural immersion with passionate and fun hosts.

Rossi Hotel (p179) A gorgeous boutique hotel overlooking the charming Fontanka River.

Rachmaninov Antique Hotel (p177) Sublime location and great value for money behind the Kazan Cathedral.

Best by Budget

€

Soul Kitchen Hostel (p180) This simply gorgeous hostel is fantastically well-located and lots of fun to stay at.

Baby Lemonade Hostel (p177) Psychedelic design and a friendly environment with great views from the roof.

Friends Hostel on Griboe-dov (p177) Our favourite of the many branches of this truly friendly, very colourful hostel chain.

Hostel Life (p182) Great option with unbeatable Nevsky pr location.

Hello Hostel (p180) Arty hostel housed in a decaying mansion right on the banks of the Neva.

€€

Rachmaninov Antique Hotel (p177) A winner on all fronts, this smart place is an insider's top choice.

Hotel Indigo (p182) Breathing new life into an old building, this superb transformation is an excellent choice.

Tradition Hotel (p184) This charming Petrograd Side hotel is a consistent traveller favourite due to its helpful staff.

Casa Leto (p178) Interesting, discreet and stylish boutique hotel with high ceilings and a historic edge.

Pushka Inn (p178) Housed in a historic 18th-century building, this charming hotel has wonderful views over the Moyka.

€€€

Rossi Hotel (p179) This excellent boutique hotel has wonderful views of the Fontanka and pampers its guests thoroughly.

Belmond Grand Hotel Europe (p180) The classic St Petersburg luxury hotel, the Europe is the choice of kings and presidents.

Hotel Astoria (p180) A wonderfully modernised classic luxury hotel full of history.

Kempinski Hotel Moyka 22 (p180) A superb international luxury hotel right on the doorstep of the Hermitage.

Hotel Domina Prestige (p181) This cool place is a worthy new addition to the top end of St Petersburg's hotels.

NEED TO KNOW

Price Ranges
We use the following price indicators to represent the price of the cheapest room available during the high season (usually May to July): Prices include bathroom unless otherwise stated.

€ less than R3000
€€ R3000–8000
€€€ more than R8000

Reservations
➡ It is usually essential to reserve at least a month (and preferably more) in advance for accommodation during the White Nights (late May to early July).

➡ Booking online via a hotel's website is usually the cheapest method, as there are few accommodation websites worth bothering with, and most hotels post their best rates online.

Tipping
Tipping hotel staff and porters will only be expected in the very top hotels in St Petersburg, although for good service it will always be appreciated, of course.

Breakfast
Breakfast is nearly always a *shvetsky stol* (buffet) in St Petersburg, and except in four- and five-star hotels, will usually be fairly unexciting, with limited choice.

Where to Stay

Neighbourhood	For	Against
Historic Heart	Quite frankly, this is where you want to be if you have the chance. Everything is here, right on your doorstep, and it takes a maximum of 20 minutes to get anywhere within this neighbourhood on foot.	Accommodation here can be more expensive.
Sennaya & Kolomna	Far quieter and less busy than the historic heart, while still definitely historic and central itself. Great for access to the Mariinsky Theatre.	Distances on foot can be very long, especially if you're staying in Kolomna, where there's no metro.
Smolny & Vosstaniya	Equally in the thick of things as the historic heart, this happening part of town around the lower half of Nevsky pr is home to much of St Petersburg's youth culture and artistic life.	Smolny, in particular, can feel surprisingly remote from the rest of the city due to bad transport links and its own backwater ambience.
Vasilyevsky Island	A very pleasant residential area. Very well connected to the rest of the city as long as you're within easy walking distance of one of the two metro stations here.	If you're not near the metro, you will feel very isolated out here. If you are looking to party in St Petersburg during the summer months, this is not a good option as the bridges rise at night.
Petrograd & Vyborg Sides	The Petrograd Side is both central and very pleasant, with lots of local sights and easy transport links to the centre of town.	If you are looking to party in St Petersburg during the summer months, this is not a good option as the bridges rise at night.

🛌 Historic Heart

⭐ BABY LEMONADE HOSTEL   HOSTEL €

Map p256 (☎812-570 7943; www.facebook.com/pages/Baby-Lemonade-Hostel; Inzhernernaya ul 7; dm/d without bathroom from R790/2590, d with bathroom from R3250, all incl breakfast; @🛜; MGostiny Dvor) The owner of Baby Lemonade is crazy about the 1960s and it shows in the pop-art, psychedelic design of this friendly, fun hostel with two pleasant, large dorms and a great kitchen and living room. However, it's worth splashing out for the boutique-hotel-worthy private rooms that are in a separate flat with great rooftop views.

⭐ FRIENDS HOSTEL ON GRIBOEDOV   HOSTEL €

Map p256 (☎812-571 0151; www.friendsplace.ru; nab kanala Griboyedova 20; dm/d R500/2500; @🛜; MNevsky Prospekt) In a quiet courtyard near Kazan Cathedral, this is our favourite out of the many branches of this truly friendly, colourful hostel chain. Dorms and rooms are spotless, have lockers and share good bathrooms and a kitchen. Perks include free international calls, English-speaking staff and organised daily events such as pub crawls and historical walks. Other locations: **Friends on Bankovsky** (Map p256; ☎812-310 4950; www.friendsplace.ru/druzya-na-bankovskom; Bankovsky per 3; dm/r without bathroom R800/2500; @🛜; MSennaya Pl); **Friends on Nevsky** (Map p260; ☎812-272 7178; www.friendsplace.ru/druzya-na-nevskom; Nevsky pr 106; dm/r without bathroom R800/2500; @🛜; MMayakovskaya); **Friends on Chekhova** (Map p260; ☎812-272 7178; www.friendsplace.ru/druzya-na-chehova/; ul Chekhova 11; r without bathroom from R2500; @🛜; MMayakovskaya); **Friends on Vosstaniya** (Map p260; ☎812-401 6155; www.en.friendsplace.ru/friends-on-vosstaniya; ul Vosstaniya 11; dm/r without bathroom R800/2700; @🛜; MPloshchad Vosstaniya); **Friends on Kazanskaya** (Map p256; ☎812-331 7799; www.friendsplace.ru/druzya-na-kazanskaya; Kazanskaya ul 11; r without bathroom R2600; @🛜; MNevsky Prospekt); **Friends by the Hermitage** (Map p256; ☎921-429 2640; www.friendsplace.ru/friends-by-the-hermitage; ul Bolshaya Konyushennaya 11; dm/r without bathroom R800/3000; @🛜; MAdmiralteyskaya).

CUBA HOSTEL   HOSTEL €

Map p256 (☎812-921 7115; www.cubahostel.ru; Kazanskaya ul 5; dm/tw from R500/1350; @🛜; MNevsky Prospekt) One of the first contemporary-style hostels in town is still a great place to stay. Rainbow-coloured paint covers the walls in dorm rooms that are equipped with metal bunk beds and private lockers. Bathrooms are cramped, but very clean. Staff members are young, speak English and are eager to please.

ARTWAY HOSTELS SLEEPBOX MALAYA SADOVAYA   HOSTEL €

Map p256 (☎921-943 4084; http://hotelrachmaninov.com/artway-hostels-sleepbox; Malaya Sadovaya ul 3/54; dm R950; @🛜; MGostiny Dvor) The same friendly folks who run the excellent Rachmaninov Hotel are behind this new hostel tucked away in a courtyard (with a kids play area) that couldn't be more central. The decor is colourful and arty and the dorm beds partitioned in spacious wooden boxes with curtains for a bit more privacy. A second branch with private rooms at Nevsky pr 16 should be open by the time you read this.

ARCHITECTOR HOSTEL   HOSTEL €

Map p256 (☎812-959 8310; www.architector-hostel.ru; Millionnaya ul 10; dm/r from R800/2500; @🛜; MNevsky Prospekt) Painted in bold colours with big, pine bunk beds, exposed-brick walls and wood floors, this laid-back hostel will remind you (in a good way) of IKEA. It's also in stumbling distance of the building's multiple hipster tenants, including a vegetarian cafe, bike shop and no less than five bars. Downside is that it's a hike to the metro.

SIMPLE HOSTEL   HOSTEL €

Map p256 (☎812-385 2528; www.simplehostel.com; Gorokhavaya ul 4; dm from R850; ⊜@🛜; MAdmiralteyskaya) The kitchen and common area is tiny, but if all you need is a bed, then this new place works well and lives up to its name in its pared-back yet creative design. At the back of a courtyard on the ground floor, its location is also ace, a short stroll from both the Hermitage and St Isaac's.

⭐ RACHMANINOV ANTIQUE HOTEL   BOUTIQUE HOTEL €€

Map p256 (☎812-327 7466; www.hotelrachmaninov.com; Kazanskaya ul 5; s/d incl breakfast from R6300/7100; @🛜; MNevsky Prospekt) The long-established Rachmaninov still feels like a secret place for those in the know. Perfectly located and run by friendly staff, it's pleasantly old world with hardwood floors and attractive Russian furnishings, particularly in the breakfast salon which has a grand piano.

Each bedroom door has been individually painted by a local artist, turning the hallways into an interesting gallery.

FD HOSTEL — HOSTEL €€

Map p256 (☎931-341 9652; http://fdhostel.ru; Nevsky pr 11; r without bathroom R2300-2400; @🛜; ⓂAdmiralteyskaya) Although it's called a hostel there are no dorms (just plain but pleasant private rooms) that share bathrooms and the rest of the good facilities that come along with the Freestel anti-cafe. The extra bonus is its brilliant location and rooftop terrace with views all along Nevsky.

CASA LETO — BOUTIQUE HOTEL €€

Map p256 (☎812-314 6622; http://casaleto.com; Bolshaya Morskaya ul 34; r incl breakfast from R7900; ✳@🛜; ⓂAdmiralteyskaya) A dramatically lit stone stairwell sets the scene for this discreet and stylish boutique hotel with five guest rooms named after famous St Petersburg architects. With king-size beds, heated floors, soft pastel shades and plenty of antiques, the spacious, high-ceilinged quarters are deserving of such namesakes.

PUSHKA INN — BOUTIQUE HOTEL €€

Map p256 (☎812-312 0913; www.pushkainn. ru; nab reki Moyki 14; s/d incl breakfast from R6000/11,500; ✳🛜🔃; ⓂAdmiralteyskaya) On a particularly picturesque stretch of the Moyka River, this charming inn is housed in a historic 18th-century building. The rooms are decorated in dusky pinks and caramel tones, with wide floorboards and – if you're willing to pay more – lovely views of the Moyka. Multi-bedroom family-style apartments are also available from R17,000.

3MOSTA — BOUTIQUE HOTEL €€

Map p256 (☎812-332 3470; www.3mosta.com; nab reki Moyki 3a; s/d from R4500/8000; ✳🛜; ⓂNevsky Prospekt) Near three bridges over the Moyka River, this 26-room property is surprisingly uncramped given its wonderful location. Even the standard rooms are of a good size with tasteful furniture, minibars and TVs. Some rooms have great views across to the Church on the Spilled Blood, and all guests have access to the roof for the panoramic experience.

ANICHKOV PENSION — HOTEL €€

Map p256 (☎812-314 7059; www.anichkov. com; apt 4, Nevsky pr 64; s/d incl breakfast R5240/6460; ✳✳🛜; ⓂGostiny Dvor) On the 3rd floor of a handsome apartment building with an antique lift, this self-styled pension has just six rooms. The standard rooms are fine, but the suites are well worth paying a little more for. The delightful breakfast room offers balcony views of the bridge from which the pension takes its name. Look for the entrance on Karavannaya ul.

VODOGRAY HOTEL — HOTEL €€

Map p256 (☎812-570 1717; www.vodogray-hotel. ru; Karavannaya ul 2; s/d incl breakfast from R4000/6000; 🛜; ⓂGostiny Dvor) Its Ukranian country-cottage style, all pretty patchwork quilts, pillows and dried flowers, puts this well-located mini-hotel in a grade of its own. Breakfast is served in the even more stylised Ukranian restaurant on the ground floor.

GUEST HOUSE NEVSKY 3 — HOTEL €€

Map p256 (☎812-710 6776; www.nevsky3.ru; Nevsky pr 3; s/d incl breakfast R4700/5300; 🛜; ⓂAdmiralteyskaya) The four individually decorated rooms here sport a fridge, TV, safe and a fan, and overlook a surprisingly quiet courtyard just moments from the Hermitage. Guests are able to use the kitchen, making self-catering a doddle – no wonder it gets rave reviews. Find it by going into the courtyard of Nevsky pr 3, and calling apartment 10 on the intercom next to the bookshop Staraya Kniga.

PETRO PALACE HOTEL — HOTEL €€

Map p256 (☎812-571 2880; www.petropalacehotel.com; Malaya Morskaya ul 14; r incl breakfast from R7000; ✳@🛜✉; ⓂAdmiralteyskaya) This 194-room hotel, superbly located between St Isaac's Cathedral and the Hermitage, has excellent facilities, including a great basement fitness centre with a small pool, Finnish sauna and full gym. Standard rooms are spacious and tastefully designed, but without any real individuality. It's popular with groups, though it rarely feels overrun.

BELVEDERE-NEVSKY — BUSINESS HOTEL €€

Map p256 (☎812-571 8338; www.hotelbn.ru; Bolshaya Konyushennaya ul 29; r incl breakfast from R5500; ✳@🛜; ⓂNevsky Prospekt) Not your standard business hotel, the Belvedere-Nevsky takes things to the next level. Automatic doors open onto corridors covered with golden, diamond-patterned wallpaper, while the decoration of the large rooms also veers towards the opulent with gold-striped wallpaper, flowing window drapes and richly patterned bedspreads.

POLIKOFF HOTEL
HOTEL €€

Map p256 (☑812-314 7809; www.polikoff. net; Nevsky pr 64/11; s/d incl breakfast from R4900/5680; ☎; ⓜGostiny Dvor) For style gurus on a budget, this quiet haven of contemporary cool is just steps away from Nevsky pr, but can be hard to find. Enter through the brown door at Karavannaya ul 11 and dial 26. You will find soothing decor that features subdued lighting, blond-wood veneer and soft brown and cream tones.

TIM CLUB
HOTEL €€

Map p256 (☑812-312 4500; www.timclub.ru; Millionnaya ul 19; r incl breakfast from R4700; ☎; ⓜNevsky Prospekt) Handy for the Hermitage and a slight cut above the average mini-hotel, this eight-room property has exposed-brick walls as a room feature, nice mosaic-tile bathrooms and monochrome linens and furnishings.

PIO ON GRIBOYEDOV
HOTEL €€

Map p256 (☑812-571 9476; www.hotelpio.ru; apt 5, nab kanala Griboyedova 35; s/d/tr/q without bathroom R4200/4930/6420/7250; ☎; ⓜNevsky Prospekt) The six rooms here share bathrooms and toilets, but it is much more like staying in a large apartment than a hostel. The communal areas are very pleasant and the rooms are comfortable and clean. Even better is the friendly service, central location and big windows overlooking the canal, which bathe the whole place in light.

FORTECIA PETER
HOTEL €€

Map p256 (Фортеция Питер; ☑812-315 0828; www.fortecia.ru; ul Millionnaya 29; r incl breakfast from R7000; ✳@☎; ⓜAdmiralteyskaya) Just seconds from the Hermitage, this pleasant eight-room mini-hotel is found in a quiet and unassuming courtyard. Staff are friendly, some English is spoken and the rooms, while on the small side, are comfortable and more than a little charming with their exposed brickwork and beams. Rates are much lower outside of White Nights season.

STONY ISLAND HOTEL
HOTEL €€

Map p256 (☑812-740 1588; www.stonyisland. com; ul Lomonosova 1; r incl breakfast from R4500; ✳✉; ⓜNevsky Prospekt) Right in the thick of the nightlife hot spot of Dumskaya ul, the Stony Island offers 17 minimalist rooms in four different categories, with many of them in interesting shapes thanks to the quirky historic building. Inside, there's a fairly good stab at cool decor as well as flat-screen TVs, mini-bars and good bathrooms. Not one for the noise sensitive, but otherwise it's a great choice.

★ROSSI HOTEL
BOUTIQUE HOTEL €€€

Map p256 (☑812-635 6333; www.rossihotels. com; nab reki Fontanki 55; s/d/ste incl breakfast from R12,000/12,900/18,000; ✳@☎; ⓜGostiny Dvor) Occupying a beautifully restored building on one of St Petersburg's prettiest squares, the Rossi's 53 rooms are all designed differently, but their brightness and moulded ceilings are uniform. Antique beds, super-sleek bathrooms, exposed-brick walls and lots of cool designer touches create a great blend of old and new. The best rooms have superb views over the Fontanka River. A new spa with sauna and plunge pool adds to overall cachet.

★W HOTEL
LUXURY HOTEL €€€

Map p256 (☑812-610 6161; www.wstpetersburg.com; Voznesensky pr 6; r from R18,630; ✳@☎✉; ⓜAdmiralteyskaya) If you're familiar with the W brand, then little at its St Petersburg outpost will disappoint. Rooms in several different categories are spacious and

SLEEPING HISTORIC HEART

ACCOMMODATION AGENCIES

The following recommended agencies can help you with short-term accommodation.
➡ **Airbnb** (airbnb.com)
➡ **Bed & Breakfast** (www.bednbreakfast.sp.ru)
➡ **City Realty** (www.cityrealtyrussia.com)
➡ **HOFA** (www.hofa.ru)
➡ **Travel Russia** (www.travelrussia.su)
➡ **Intro by Irina** (www.introbyirina.com)

luxurious, with contemporary styling. The lobby is also a very inviting space. The rooftop MiXup Bar offers superb views, there's good food at the Alain Ducasse restaurant MiX, and there's a beautiful spa with sauna, Jacuzzi, treatment rooms and plunge pool.

BELMOND GRAND HOTEL
EUROPE   LUXURY HOTEL €€€
Map p256 (☑812-329 6000; www.grandhotel-europe.com; Mikhailovskaya ul 1/7; r/ste from R18,000/41,890; ✳ @ 🛜 🌊; ⓂNevsky Prospekt) Since 1830, when Carlo Rossi united three adjacent buildings with the grandiose facade we see today, little has been allowed to change in this heritage building. No two rooms are the same at this iconic hotel, but most are spacious and elegant in design.

Regular guests quite rightly swear by the terrace rooms that afford spectacular views across the city's rooftops.

ANGLETERRE HOTEL   LUXURY HOTEL €€€
Map p256 (☑812-494 5666; www.angleterre hotel.com; Malaya Morskaya ul 24; r/ste from R12,000/47,000; ✳ @ 🛜 🌊; ⓂAdmiralteyskaya) With supremely comfortable king-sized beds, huge bathrooms and a confidently understated style, the Angleterre's best rooms provide breathtaking views of St Isaac's Cathedral. More pluses are a great fitness centre, a small pool, a cinema showing original-language movies, and an excellent Italian restaurant, Borsalino.

HOTEL ASTORIA   LUXURY HOTEL €€€
Map p256 (☑812-494 5757; www.roccoforteho-tels.com; Bolshaya Morskaya ul 39; r/ste from R26,600/35,990; ✳ @ 🛜 🌊; ⓂAdmiraltey-skaya) What the Hotel Astoria has lost of its original Style Moderne decor, it more than compensates for in contemporary style and top-notch service. Little wonder it's beloved by visiting VIPs, from kings to rock stars. Rooms marry the hotel's heritage character with a more modern design, while the best suites are sprinkled with antiques and have spectacular views onto St Isaac's Cathedral.

The same views – at a slightly lower price – are also available next door at its sister property, the Angleterre Hotel, where guests can use the gym and pool.

KEMPINSKI HOTEL
MOYKA 22   LUXURY HOTEL €€€
Map p256 (☑812-335 9111; www.kempinski. com; nab reki Moyki 22; r/ste incl breakfast from R19,800/27,300; ✳ @ 🛜; ⓂNevsky Prospekt)

Practically on the doorstep of the Hermitage, this superb hotel has all the comforts you'd expect of an international luxury chain. Rooms have a stylish marine theme, with cherry-wood furniture and a handsome navy-blue-and-gold colour scheme. The 360-degree panorama from the rooftop Belle View restaurant and bar is unbeatable.

FOUR SEASONS HOTEL
LION PALACE   LUXURY HOTEL €€€
Map p256 (☑812-339 8000; www.fourseasons. com/stpetersburg; Voznesensky pr 1; r/ste from R22,500/44,286; ✳ @ 🛜 🌊; ⓂAdmiralteyskaya) Housed in a meticulously restored palace, the Four Season's lower-priced rooms fail to match the lavish promise of the lobby and grand staircase, but those fortunate enough to occupy one of the plush suites are unlikely to be disappointed.

Designed by Montferrand, the architect of the next-door St Isaac's Cathedral, and formely the home of Prince Lobanov-Rostovsky, the palace also has two attractively designed restaurants, a great bar, winter garden for afternoon tea and spa with plunge pool.

🛏 Sennaya & Kolomna

★SOUL KITCHEN HOSTEL   HOSTEL €
Map p264 (☑8-965-816 3470; www.soulkitchen-hostel.com; apt 9, nab reki Moyki 62/2, Sennaya; dm/d from R900/3600; 🌐 @ 🛜; ⓂAdmiraltey-skaya) Soul Kitchen blends boho hipness and boutique-hotel comfort, scoring perfect 10s in many key categories: private rooms (chic), dorm beds (double-wide with privacy-protecting curtains), common areas (vast), kitchen (vast *and* beautiful) and bathrooms (downright inviting). There is also bike hire, table football, free Macs to use, free international phone calls and stunning Moyka views from a communal balcony.

★HELLO HOSTEL   HOSTEL €
Map p264 (☑812-643 2556; www.hellohostel.ru; Angliyskaya nab 50, Kolomna; dm R600-1000, d with shared bathroom R2500-3000, all incl breakfast; 🌐 🛜; ⓂAdmiralteyskaya) This eclectic, arty hostel has a party vibe thanks to its popular lobby bar, and nice touches such as film screenings on its impressive central staircase. The big dorm rooms have extra-tall wooden bunk beds, some with curtains for privacy, and incredible (if semi-decayed)

ceiling mouldings. There are also four good-value private doubles.

The hostel occupies a gorgeous historic building on the Neva embankment, and still has the atmosphere of the communal flat it was under the Soviets. Welcome extras include free washing-machine use, bike hire (R600 per 24 hours) and superb Neva views.

GOLDEN AGE RETRO HOTEL HOTEL €

Map p264 (Золотая Середина; ☑812-315 1212; www.retrohotel.ru; Grazhdanskaya ul 16, Sennaya; s/d R3000/3300, without bathroom R2000/2300; ☎; ⓂSadovaya) Tucked into a quiet courtyard in the narrow streets north of Sennaya pl, this friendly little hotel is a great bargain. A few antiques are scattered around to justify its 'retro' claims, but most furniture and all facilities are quite modern, with a kitchen for guest use as well as a washing machine.

To access the hotel (which clearly has something against signage), ring 88 at the Grazhdanskaya ul 16 entry phone (even though the official street address is different) and then go up to flat 14 on the 2nd floor.

★ANDREY & SASHA'S HOMESTAY APARTMENT €€

Map p264 (☑8-921-409 6701, 812-315 3330; asamatuga@mail.ru; nab kanala Griboyedova 51, Sennaya; s/d without bathroom R2600/4000; ⓂSadovaya) Energetic Italophiles Andrey and Sasha extend the warmest of welcomes to travellers lucky enough to rent out one of their three apartments (by the room or in their entirety). All are centrally located and eclectically decorated with lots of designer touches and an eye for beautiful furniture, tilework and mirrors. Bathrooms are shared, as are kitchen facilities.

Socialising is definitely encouraged, and your hosts will likely invite you to join them sipping wine by the fire or drinking coffee on the rooftop. Staying here is a great way to get to know the city through bohemian locals.

HOTEL GOGOL HOTEL €€

Map p264 (☑812-571 1841; www.gogolhotel.com; nab kanala Griboyedova 69, Sennaya; s/d from R3600/4500; ⓂSadovaya) There's great value to be had at this centrally located hotel, a conversion of the house where the great writer Nikolai Gogol himself apparently once lived. The rooms are cosy and enjoy inoffensive decoration, with views of over the canal or a quiet residential courtyard. Reception is on the 2nd floor, and there's a basement restaurant.

NEVSKY BREEZE HOTEL HOTEL €€

Map p264 (☑812-570 1146; www.hon.ru; ul Galernaya 12, Kolomna; s/d R6200/7100; ⓂAdmiralteyskaya) This hotel is in one of the city centre's most charming streets, just one block back from the Neva River. The 33 rooms are comfortable and simple, all with private bathrooms but without fridges. It's thoroughly contemporary inside, and little mileage is made out of the historic building, but despite this it's a popular choice.

DOSTOEVSKY HOUSE HOTEL HOTEL €€

Map p264 (☑812-314 8231; www.ddspb.ru; ul Kaznacheyskaya 61/1, Sennaya; s/d incl breakfast R4000/4500; ☎; ⓂSennaya Ploshchad) While it's hard to imagine Dosters living anywhere so sanitary, he apparently resided in this house next to the Griboyedov Canal between 1861 and 1863. The 10 rooms here are comfortable but plain, and range from spacious to tiny, but the price is right. There's free tea and coffee throughout your stay and a fan in the room to keep you cool.

★ALEXANDER HOUSE BOUTIQUE HOTEL €€€

Map p264 (☑812-334 3540; www.a-house.ru; nab kanala Kryukova 27, Kolomna; s/d incl breakfast from R10,625/11,475; ⓂSadovaya) Owners Alexander and Natalya have converted this historic building opposite the Nikolsky Cathedral, styling each of the 14 spacious rooms after their favourite international cities. While these can vary in success and taste, when they get it right, the effect is great. Lovely common areas include a fireplace-warmed lounge and a vine-laden courtyard containing a guests-only restaurant. Book in advance.

HOTEL DOMINA PRESTIGE HOTEL €€€

Map p264 (☑812-385 9900; www.dominarussia.com; nab Reki Moyki 99, Sennaya; r from R7590; ⓂAdmiralteyskaya) This excellent new property makes an immediate impression as its traditional Moyka embankment exterior gives way to a bright, modern and colourful atrium. Some of the decor is undoubtedly rather Russian in taste, but it's still stylish and fun. Rooms are comfortable and spacious, with extras such as coffee facilities and great bathrooms. There's also a sauna, gym and restaurant.

🛏 Smolny & Vosstaniya

LOCATION HOSTEL
HOSTEL €

Map p260 (📞812-329 1274; www.hostel74.ru; Ligovsky pr 74, Vosstaniya; dm/r from R700/1500, design rooms R6000; 🖥🛜; Ⓜ Ligovsky Prospekt) Come and stay in St Petersburg's coolest art gallery and cultural space – the 3rd floor of Loft Project Etagi is given over to this super-friendly hostel. Some of the dorms here are enormous (one has 20 beds in it!) but the facilities are spotless, and include washing machines and a small kitchen. As well as the dorms there are three 'design rooms' that are boutique-hotel quality at budget price.

ALL YOU NEED HOSTEL
HOSTEL €

Map p260 (📞8-921-950 0574; www.youneedhostel.com; ul Rubinshteyna 6, Vosstaniya; dm from R650; 🖥🛜; Ⓜ Mayakovskaya) With one of the best locations in town, this friendly and stylish hostel is basically one large apartment with three dorm bedrooms sleeping six to 12. Each room has lockers and wooden bunks, while the kitchen and sitting room are spacious, the latter having a balcony overlooking buzzing ul Rubinshteyna. Be prepared for chalk stains from the walls!

HOSTEL LIFE
HOSTEL €

Map p260 (📞812-318 1808; www.hostel-life.ru; Nevsky pr 47, Vosstaniya; dm from R950, tw/tr R3325/3515; 🖥🛜; Ⓜ Mayakovskaya) From the moment you arrive you're made to feel at home – slippers are provided – and the premises are spacious and bright. The 15 rooms range from doubles to dorms sleeping eight and Room 7 has an amazing corner window on Nevsky pr – surely the best view available for this low price!

There's a big kitchen, clean bathrooms, free laundry and professional English-speaking staff – all in all, a great option.

RED HOUSE HOSTEL
HOSTEL €

Map p260 (📞812-380 7527, 8-921-443 8424; www.redhousehostel.com; Liteyny pr 46, Smolny; dm/d incl breakfast from R550/1990; 🖥🛜; Ⓜ Mayakovskaya) With its very desirable central location and unusually interesting building, the Red House Hostel is a great choice. There's a Jimi Hendrix theme, and while the dorms are somewhat cramped, there's a very friendly atmosphere, good communal areas and even a double room available. Other services include a washing machine (R100) and bike hire.

NILS BED & BREAKFAST
HOMESTAY €

Map p260 (📞812-923 0575; www.rentroom.org; 5-ya Sovetskaya ul 21, Smolny; s/d/tr from R2500/3500/4200; 🛜; Ⓜ Ploshchad Vosstaniya) Nils' Bed & Breakfast is an excellent option at a great price. Four spacious rooms share two modern bathrooms, as well as a beautiful light-filled common area and kitchen. Nils renovated this place himself, taking great care to preserve the mouldings, wooden floors and other architectural elements. He now exhibits the same consideration in taking care of his guests.

HOTEL INDIGO
HOTEL €€

Map p260 (📞812-454 5577; www.indigospb.com; ul Chaykovskogo 17, Smolny; r from R6300; 🖥❄🛜; Ⓜ Chernyshevskaya) A total overhaul of the original building, a prerevolutionary hotel in its day, has paved the way for the brand-new Hotel Indigo, a sleek and stylish hotel with an excellent management team. The incredible atrium makes even the interior-facing rooms light-filled, and touches such as rain showers and free minibars in rooms are also welcome. Super city views, a gym, sauna and small pool complete this excellent and much-needed midrange deal.

PIO ON MOKHOVAYA
B&B €€

Map p260 (📞812-273 3585; www.hotelpio.ru; Mokhovaya ul 39, Smolny; s/d/tr/q incl breakfast R4200/5000/6000/6800; 🖥🛜♿; Ⓜ Chernyshevskaya) This lovely lodging is the second Pio property in Petersburg. It's spacious, stylish and comfortable, as well as child friendly, with family groups warmly welcomed and provided for. In a quiet, residential neighbourhood a short walk from the historic heart. There is a Finnish sauna on-site. Call 10 on the interphone to be buzzed in.

HELVETIA HOTEL & SUITES
HOTEL €€

Map p260 (📞812-326 5353; www.helvetiahotel.ru; ul Marata 11, Vosstaniya; r incl breakfast from R6650; 🖥❄🛜; Ⓜ Mayakovskaya) Pass through the wrought-iron gates into a wonderfully private and professionally run oasis of calm and class. The rooms may be a little less atmospheric than the early-19th-century exterior might suggest, but they make up for it in comfort, each having a bath-tub, safe and minibar. The buffet breakfast is excellent and there are two on-site restaurants.

BROTHERS KARAMAZOV
BOUTIQUE HOTEL €€

Map p260 (📞812-335 1185; www.karamazovhotel.ru; Sotsialisticheskaya ul 11a, Vosstaniya; r incl

breakfast from R5865; ⊖✳☎; MVladimirskaya)
Pack a copy of Dostoevsky's final novel to
read while staying at this appealing boutique hotel – the great man penned *The
Brothers K* while living in the neighbourhood. In homage, the hotel's 28 charming
rooms are all named after different female
Dostoevsky characters to help you answer
that age-old question: which 19th-century
fallen woman are you?

ARBAT NORD HOTEL BOUTIQUE HOTEL €€
Map p260 (☑812-703 1899; www.arbat-nord.ru;
Artilleriyskaya ul 4, Smolny; s/d incl breakfast
R3900/4600; ✳@☎; MChernyshevskaya) Facing an unsightly Soviet-era hotel across the
street, the sleek modern Arbat Nord seems
to be showing its neighbour how to run a
good establishment. The modern rooms are
decorated in gold and green hues, and even
though the furniture is fairly cheap, there's
plenty of space. Efficient English-speaking
staff are on hand and the welcome is warm.

ART HOTEL HOTEL €€
Map p260 (☑812-740 7585; www.art-hotel.
ru; Mokhovaya ul 27-29, Smolny; s/d from
R4100/5100; ⊖☎; MChernyshevskaya) This
rather misleadingly named hotel retains a
straightforward elegance in its 14 rooms,
but has nothing particularly arty about it.
Indeed, the mood is bourgeois-on-a-budget,
with heavy pleated drapes framing the windows, crystal chandeliers, ceiling mouldings
and a ceramic-tiled stove in the corridor. On
the plus side, breakfast is served to you each
morning in your room.

GREEN APPLE HOTEL HOTEL €€
Map p260 (☑812-272 1023; www.greenappleho-
tel.ru; ul Korolenko 14, Smolny; s/d/tr incl breakfast from R2700/3200/3700; ⊖✳☎; MChernyshevskaya) This stylish, thoroughly modern
15-room hotel in the backstreets of Liteyny
has the feel of an adult youth hostel. Some
of the best-value rooms are the so-called
ekonom (economy) ones, which sleep up to
three people (the third bed is on a mezza-
nine). They're a great bargain, as the location is good, and there's also a communal
kitchen you can use.

HOTEL AZIMUT HOTEL €€
(☑812-740 2640; www.azimuthotels.com;
Lermontovsky pr 43/1, Vosstaniya; s/d from
R3200/3500; ⊖☎; MBaltiyskaya) The ambitious Azimut hotel chain has done a great
job of making you forget that you're in one
of St Petersburg's ugliest buildings with
their clever renovation of a massive Soviet-
era hotel. While only four floors here have
been given a full refit, even the other floors
have perfectly good (if cramped) rooms.

Prices are low, and the funky lobby and
amazing top-floor Sky Bar sweeten the deal
further.

NEVSKY FORUM BOUTIQUE HOTEL €€€
Map p260 (☑812-333 0222; www.forumhotel.ru;
Nevsky pr 69, Smolny; s/d from R8900/11,000;
design s/d R11,400/12,500, all incl breakfast;
⊖✳@☎; MMayakovskaya) This smart bolt-
hole has the whole range of facilities and
comforts you'd expect, but compared to the
other luxury properties in town, it caters
to a more cost-conscious traveller. All 29
rooms are spacious and comfortable, with
king-size beds, big double-glazed windows
and environmentally friendly cork flooring.
The premium-priced design rooms cater for
the more aesthetically driven.

**OFFICIAL STATE
HERMITAGE HOTEL** LUXURY HOTEL €€€
Map p260 (☑812-777 9810; www.thehermitage-
hotel.ru; ul Pravdy 10, Vosstaniya; r from R9410;
⊖✳☎; MZvenigorodskaya/Vladimirskaya)
Despite its rather odd location, which is
central but rather incongruously rundown
for a hotel with such lofty aspirations, the
126-room Official State Hermitage Hotel
is a dazzling affair with enough Italian
marble and chandeliers to keep even the
fussiest of Romanovs happy. Rooms are
spacious and old-world elegant without being too chintzy, and Hermès goodies stuff
the bathrooms.

The Hermitage connection is fairly weak:
there's a free shuttle bus to the museum every two hours, and guests staying for more
than three nights get free entry as well.

🛏 Vasilyevsky Island

NASHOTEL HOTEL €€
Map p270 (☑812-323 2231; www.nashotel.ru;
11-ya liniya 50; s/d from R5800/6400; ✳☎;
MVasileostrovskaya) Despite being half a decade old, this spotless place still looks like
it has just opened. The very tall, beautifully remodelled building on this quiet side
street has a striking exterior and its rooms
are blazes of colours, complete with modern furnishings and great views from the
higher floors.

Garish touches include some truly dreadful room art and a preponderance of plants throughout, but these gripes aside, this is generally a smart and stylish modern hotel.

SOKOS HOTEL VASILYEVSKY HOTEL €€€
Map p270 (☏812-335 2290; www.sokoshotels.com; 8-ya liniya 11-13; r from R8500; ❄✳☎; ⓂVasileostrovskaya) This surprisingly enormous hotel has more than 200 rooms, although you hardly notice it from the street. It's a sleek, well-designed place aimed at business travellers and the upper end of the holiday market. The rooms are spacious, with nice design touches, while the large Repin Lounge downstairs takes care of all food and drink needs.

TREZZINI PALACE HOTEL LUXURY HOTEL €€€
Map p270 (☏812-313 6622; www.trezzinipalace.com; Universitetskaya nab 21; r incl breakfast from R14,400; ✳☎; ⓂVasileostrovskaya) This elaborately decorated hotel gives you a taste of 18th- and 19th-century imperial grandeur without compromising on modernity or convenience. The 21 rooms are very spacious, with enormous bathrooms and elaborate wooden minibars that overflow with goodies. While the Trezzini teeters on the edge of being totally tasteless, its savvy staff and homogenous style throughout miraculously reprieve it.

🛏 Petrograd & Vyborg Sides

HOTEL AURORA HOTEL €
Map p268 (☏812-233 3641; www.hotel-aurora.ru; Malaya Posadskaya ul 15; s/d R2450/3150, without bathroom R2100/2800, all incl breakfast; ☎; ⓂGorkovskaya) Not far from the Peter & Paul Fortress, this spunky mini-hotel offers affordable, friendly accommodation. The four spacious rooms sport quaintly charming, Soviet-style decor, with parquet floors, rickety beds and monochrome linens. Nonetheless, the sparkling-clean bathrooms and a kitchen make this an excellent deal.

ART-HOTEL KONTRAST HOSTEL €
Map p268 (☏8-981-686 4246; http://hotel-contrast.com; Bolshoy pr 51/9; dm/s/d from R550/1300/1500; @☎; ⓂPetrogradskaya) Young aspiring artists were hired to decorate this quirky hostel hidden away in the corner of a courtyard accessed from ul Lenina. It's all a lot more cramped than the wide-angle-lens photos on its website would lead you to believe. Still, it's about as modern as hostels get over this side of the city.

APART-HOTEL KRONVERK BUSINESS HOTEL €€
Map p268 (☏812-703 3663; www.kronverk.com; ul Blokhina 9; r incl breakfast from R5280, apt from R9790; ✳@☎; ⓂSportivnaya) If you're after something more contemporary for your lodgings, then here's a place for you. Occupying the upper floors of a slick business centre, the Kronverk offers appealing modern rooms with basic self-catering facilities. English-speaking staff are efficient and professional.

TRADITION HOTEL HOTEL €€€
Map p268 (☏812-405 8855; www.tradition-hotel.ru; pr Dobrolyubova 2; s/d incl breakfast R11,220/12,710; ✳@☎; ⓂSportivnaya) This charming small hotel is a consistent traveller favourite due to its smiling, helpful staff who really go out of their way for guests. Its rooms are comfortable and well appointed with good-size bathrooms and a vaguely antique style.

SLEEP LIKE A TSAR

If you've always wanted to sleep in a tsarist palace, here is your chance. Peter the Great built his summer palace at Strelna, a town about 24km from St Petersburg, and now it is Putin's presidential palace, used for international meetings and state visits. Putin houses his guests on the grounds at the **Baltic Star Hotel** (☏812-438 5700; www.balticstar-hotel.ru; Beriozovaya al 3; r from R5800, ste R9000; ❄✳@☎🏊). If it's not otherwise occupied, you could stay here too. Besides the 100 well-appointed rooms in the main hotel, there are 18 VIP cottages on the shore of the Gulf of Finland, each equipped with a private dining room, study, sauna, swimming pool and, of course, staff quarters for your entourage.

Understand
St Petersburg

St Petersburg Today

Not since the paint first dried on Rastrelli's buildings in the late 18th century has St Petersburg looked so good. The 20 years of massive investment after 70 years of neglect under the Soviets has certainly paid off, and the city's facades are bursts of beautifully painted pastels and primes once again. But glimpse inside the buildings and you'll see there's a lot of work yet to be done: overall the city remains poor, despite a burgeoning middle class, and many challenges – economic and political – lie ahead.

Best on Film

Irony of Fate (1975) Perhaps the best-loved Leningrad comedy of all time.
Brother (1997) Sergei Bodrov Jr fights the mafia on the mean streets of post-Soviet St Petersburg.
Russian Ark (2002) Alexander Sokurov's one-shot meditation on Russian history filmed inside the Hermitage.
The Stroll (2003) A delightfully playful film in which three friends wander from situation to situation on the streets of St Petersburg.
Onegin (1999) Pushkin's epic tale of lost love and regret is beautifully retold by Martha Fiennes.

Best in Print

Crime and Punishment (Fyodor Dostoevsky; 1866) The quintessential St Petersburg novel explores the mind of the deluded Rodion Raskolnikov.
Speak, Memory (Vladimir Nabokov; 1951) A wonderfully bittersweet literary memoir of Nabokov's own St Petersburg childhood.
The Nose (Nikolai Gogol; 1836) Follow Major Kovalyov around the city in pursuit of his errant nose.
Ten Days That Shook the World (John Reed; 1919) A remarkable first-hand account of the Russian revolution.

Reconstructing Piter

The past decade has been marked by considerable and much-needed investment in St Petersburg's infrastructure. Neglected and sidelined under the Soviets and then forced for the first two decades after the end of communism to concentrate on urgent conservation rather than development, St Petersburg has finally completed several huge engineering projects in the past few years. These include the construction of a new ring road around the city, a flood barrier, the new M5 metro line, the Bolshoy Obukhovsky Bridge (the only bridge over the Neva big enough not to have to rise at night) and the Marine Facade cruise port on Vasilyevsky Island. All are significant, and herald the city's determination to enter the modern world and be taken seriously as a business and tourism destination.

Another important prestige project for the city was the opening of the Mariinsky II in 2013, a superb state-of-the-art theatre worthy of one of the world's leading ballet and opera troupes. Likewise the Hermitage is in the process of undergoing enormous changes as the museum's modern art collection is being moved from the Winter Palace to the General Staff Building on the other side of Palace Sq. This heralds a transformation for Russia's most famous museum into an institution for the 21st century.

Steps Backwards

Yet while undeniable infrastructural progress has been made in recent years, St Petersburg has also been the origin of a far less progressive wave of homophobia that has spread out in waves across Russia since 2011. Local arch-conservative and pro-Putin deputy Vitaly Milonov, long considered something of a comical character by many Petersburgers, rose to national prominence in Russia when he introduced a law to St Petersburg's

Legislative Assembly in 2011 outlawing 'the promotion of sodomy, lesbianism, bisexuality and transgenderism to minors'. This law was then seized upon by politicians on a national level who introduced it to the Duma in 2013, where it sailed through and became law for the whole of Russia. The irony that such a backwards piece of legislation originated in Peter the Great's 'window on Europe' has been lost on nobody, and Milonov remains a darling of the right and nationalists in St Petersburg today, while gay people in St Petersburg feel increasingly under attack and there's a palpable atmosphere of homophobia.

Cigarettes & Alcohol

Meanwhile the city has made much-needed efforts to combat the perennial problem of alcoholism. It's now illegal to sell alcohol in shops from 10pm until 11am the next morning, although these rules are routinely worked around, and of course it's still perfectly legal to drink in bars. The city government has even gone as far as banning the sale of alcohol totally for 24 hours before big national holidays, to forestall the extraordinary *zapoy* (bender) that many Russians embark upon on during such occasions. More strictly enforced seems to be the nationwide smoking ban introduced in 2014, which has finally made St Petersburg's once smokey bars, cafes and nightclubs into far more user-friendly smoke-free environments.

A Showcase City

With Putin's continued stranglehold on politics seemingly continuing, his hometown rides high in prestige within Russia. As a showcase for the country, it hosts international summits and conferences, and enjoys continued federal budgetary favour, second in influence and cachet only to Moscow.

Not everyone welcomes this, however, as was made clear in 2014 when St Petersburg hosted Manifesta, the European biennial of contemporary art. The event taking place in the city was highly controversial given Russia's simultaneous annexation of Crimea, involvement in Eastern Ukraine and its national law against homosexual propaganda, and indeed several key figures from the Russian art world criticised the decision, as well as many artists abroad.

This dual perception sums up the city's position today very well: a stark mix of positive and negative, St Petersburg has come a long way from post-communist semi-ruin, and is easily one of Europe's most beautiful cities, but everyone from the Kremlin down agrees there's still a huge distance to go.

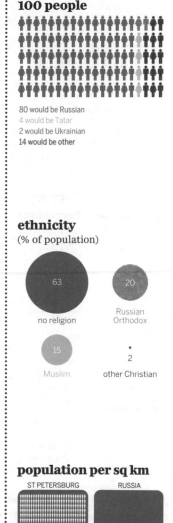

if Russia were 100 people

80 would be Russian
4 would be Tatar
2 would be Ukrainian
14 would be other

ethnicity
(% of population)

63 no religion

20 Russian Orthodox

15 Muslim

2 other Christian

population per sq km

ST PETERSBURG   RUSSIA

= 8 people

History

The history of St Petersburg (make that Petrograd and Leningrad, as well) is one of struggle. First came a struggle of identity – forcing Russia's inward-looking head to look towards Europe and to recast itself in its image, arguably a task that will never truly be complete. This was followed by a struggle of ideas – and whether it be despotism versus reform, communism versus fascism or simply democracy versus autocracy, it's one that is still being fought today. St Petersburg has been deeply marked by each of these struggles, making its three-century history one of the world's most eventful over such a relatively short amount of time.

City by the Sea

Precocious Prince

For a great biography of the man himself, pick up a copy of Lindsey Hughes' *Peter the Great: A Biography*. Never pulling punches in her detailed retelling of his less-than-laudable personal life and his often barbaric childishness, Hughes manages to present both the genius and failings of Peter I.

For three centuries, Moscow was the home of Russia's tsars. The traditional, inward-looking capital was deep in the heart of Russia and terribly conservative. This was the place the future Peter the Great would be born into in 1672. Peter was the son of Tsar Alexey I and his second wife, Natal ya Naryshkina, and was one of 16 siblings. He stood out as exceptional however, both by his enormous height (he reached 2m in adulthood) and by his insatiable curiosity for knowledge about the outside world. He spent long hours in the city quarter for foreign merchants, who regaled the young prince with tales of the modern age.

Once on the throne, Peter became the first tsar to venture beyond Russia's borders. Travelling in disguise, Peter and a raucous Russian entourage criss-crossed the continent, meeting with monarchs, dining with dignitaries and carousing with commoners. He recruited admirals, academics and artisans to apply their skill in his service. Having seen Western Europe in the age of the Enlightenment, Peter was more than ever convinced that Russians were still living in the dark ages and became more determined than ever to replace superstition with science, backwardness with progress and East with West.

Peter abruptly ended his European expedition when news came of a Kremlin coup. The young tsar hurried back to Moscow where

TIMELINE	1703	1712–14	1718
	On 27 May Peter the Great establishes the Peter and Paul Fortress on Zayachy Island, thus founding the new city of Sankt Pieter Burkh, Russia's 'window to the West'.	At the behest of Peter I, government institutions begin to move from Moscow, and St Petersburg assumes the administrative and ceremonial role as the Russian capital.	Peter the Great's son Alexey dies under torture in the Peter and Paul Fortress, where his father has him interrogated about his purported plan to depose him and reverse his reforms.

he vengefully punished the plotters, sending more than 1000 to their deaths and terrorising anyone who questioned his rule. He humiliated and subdued the old elite, forcing aristocrat elders to shave their beards and wear Western clothes, while he subordinated the Orthodox Church to earthly political authority, and sent the Old Believers, who cursed him as the Antichrist, into internal exile in Russia's icy north. Peter upended the established social order, forbidding arranged marriages and promoting the humble to high rank. He even changed the date of New Year's Day – from September to January. By now, the undisputed tsar had grown to despise Moscow, and was ready to start afresh.

The Great Northern War

Peter was anxious to turn Russia westward and he saw the Baltic Sea as the channel for change. The problem was that Sweden already dominated the region and it had been more than 400 years since Russia's medieval hero prince, Alexander Nevsky, had defeated the Swedes near the site of Peter's future city. In 1700 Peter put his new army to the test against the powerful Swedish Empire, and the Great Northern War was on. For the next 20 years northern Europe's modernising autocrats, Charles II and Peter, fought for supremacy over the eastern Baltic.

To Peter's dismay, his troops were badly beaten in their first engagement at the Battle of Narva in Estonia, by a smaller, more adept Swedish force. But Russia found allies in Poland, Saxony and Denmark, who diverted Charles' attention. Peter used the opportunity to revamp his army and launch his navy. He established a small Baltic foothold on tiny Hare Island (Zayachiy Island) at the mouth of the Neva River, and used it as a base to rout a nearby Swedish garrison. This primitive outpost would become the kernel of Peter's northern capital.

By the time Charles tried to retake the territory, Peter commanded a formidable fighting force. Russia's first naval victory came at the Battle of Hanko, where a galley fleet overwhelmed a Swedish squadron and secured Russian control over the Neva and access to the gulf. His military chief and boyhood friend, Alexander Menshikov, led a series of impressive battlefield victories, further extending Russian presence on the Baltic coast and causing his Scandinavian foe to flee and the Swedish Empire to expire. The Great Northern War shifted the balance of power to the advantage of Peter's Russia. Hostilities officially ended with the signing of the Treaty of Nystad (1721), which formally ceded Sweden's extensive eastern possessions to Russia, including its new capital city, St Petersburg.

When he realised there wasn't enough stone available locally to build his city in polished marble and granite, Peter decreed a stone tax, by which all new arrivals had to bring with them a fixed amount of building materials before they'd be allowed to enter the town (not so unusual for a guy who previously issued a tax on beards).

1725	1725	1727	1728
Some 13 years after St Petersburg was declared the new capital, its population is now 40,000 and as much as 90% of all foreign trade passes through its port.	Peter the Great dies of uraemia in St Petersburg, having reigned Russia for 42 years of his 52-year life. He had anointed no successor and his wife becomes Catherine I.	Catherine I, an illiterate former housemaid, dies after ruling Russia for two years in tandem with Peter's best friend, Prince Menshikov. Peter's grandson becomes Tsar Peter II.	After the death of Peter I and two years of rule by his wife, his grandson Peter II returns the Russian capital back to Moscow.

Peter's Paradise

Peter did not wait for the war to end before he started building. The wooden palisade encampment on Hare Island became the red-brick Peter and Paul Fortress. In June 1703 Peter gave the site a name – Sankt Pieter Burkh, in his beloved Dutch tongue and named after his patron saint, who stands guard before the gates to paradise.

Peter's vision for the new capital was grandiose; so was the task ahead. To find enough dry ground for building, swamps were drained and wetlands filled. To protect the land from flooding, seawalls were built and canals dug. A hands-on autocrat, Peter pitched in with the hammering, sawing and joining. Thousands of fortune-seeking foreigners were imported to lend expertise: architects and engineers to design the city's intricate waterways, and craftsmen and masons to chisel its stone foundations. The hard labour of digging ditches and moving muck was performed by nonvoluntary recruits. Peter pressed 30,000 peasant serfs per year into capital construction gangs, plus Russian convict labourers and Swedish prisoners of war. The work regimen was strict and living conditions were stark: more than 100,000 died. But those who survived could earn personal freedom and a small piece of land to call their own.

Russia's new city by the sea began to take shape, inspired by Peter's recollections of canal-lined Amsterdam. The locus of power was the military stronghold, the Peter and Paul Fortress. Next, he ordered the chief accompaniments of tsarist authority – a church and a prison. A more impressive dwelling, the Menshikov Palace, put up by the territory's first governor-general, Alexander Menshikov, soon adorned the Vasilyevsky Island embankment.

In 1712 the tsar officially declared St Petersburg to be the capital. Inspired by the Vatican's crossed keys to paradise, he adopted a city coat of arms that presented crossed anchors topped with an imperial crown. Peter demanded the rest of Russia's ruling elite join him, or else. He said St Petersburg was the place they ought to be, so they packed up their carriages and moved to the Baltic Sea. The tsar's royal court, the imperial senate and foreign embassies were also quickly relocated. Apprehension turned to horror when Moscow's old aristocratic families reluctantly began to arrive; to them Peter's paradise was a peaty hell. They were ordered to bring their own stones to the party, with which to build elegant mansions and in which to start behaving like Westerners, complete with beardless faces and German dress, something that went against their conservative Orthodox beliefs.

When Peter died in 1725, at the age of 52, some thought they might get the chance to abandon his creation, but they were wrong. The wilful

Peter's fascination with 'freaks' is well documented, but his most politically incorrect act remains the dwarf wedding he organised for his servant Iakim Volkov. Peter ordered all the dwarves of Moscow be rounded up and sent to St Petersburg, where a dwarf wedding ceremony and ball was performed for the amusement of Peter and his court.

1732	1740	1741–61	1754–62
Empress Anna reverses the decision of Peter II and moves the capital to St Petersburg, presiding over the recommencement of the city's construction and development.	Empress Anna dies after a 10-year rule that brought much progress. Peter the Great's daughter Elizabeth ascends the throne after a coup against infant tsar Ivan VI.	Empress Elizabeth fulfills her father's goal of a grand European capital, commissioning the construction of countless sumptuous buildings and creating a glittering court.	Bartolomeo Rastrelli constructs the Winter Palace as the primary residence of the royal family. Empress Elizabeth dies three months before the building is completed.

spirit of Peter the Great continued to possess the city and bedevil its inhabitants. Within less than a hundred years of its improbable inception, a new magnificent capital would stand on the edge of Europe.

Imperial Capital

Peter the Great's Heirs

By the end of the 18th century St Petersburg would take its place among Europe's great cities. But in the years immediately following Peter's death, the fate of the Baltic bastion was still uncertain.

While Peter's plans for his imperial capital were clear, those for his personal legacy were murky. His eldest son and heir apparent, Alexey, was estranged from his father early on, suspected of plotting against him later, and eventually tortured to death during interrogation in the Peter and Paul Fortress in 1718. The evidence for treachery was flimsy, though it was clear to Peter that his son would never be fit to rule, and that he would undo many of Peter's reforms, were he ever to ascend the throne. On his death bed in 1725, Peter tried to dictate a last will, but could not name an heir before his demise. His wife Catherine I assumed the throne for the next two years, with Peter's confidant and closest ally Menshikov acting as the power behind the throne. When Catherine died just two years later though, the simmering anti-Peter reaction started.

The St Petersburg–Moscow power struggle was on. The aristocracy's Old Muscovite faction seized the opportunity to influence the succession. Without his protector, the mighty Menshikov was stripped of all titles and property, and sent packing into Siberian exile. Peter's 11-year-old grandson, Peter II, was chosen as heir. Delivering to his enabling patrons, the pliable Peter II returned the capital to Moscow. St Petersburg's population fell by a half and its public works came to rest.

The Romanovs were a delicate dynasty and the teen tsar soon succumbed to smallpox. Moscow's princely power brokers now entrusted the throne to another supposed weakling, Duchess Anna Ioanovna, Peter the Great's niece. But Anna was no pushover and she became the first in a line of tough women rulers. In 1732 Anna declared St Petersburg to be the capital once more, and bade everyone return to the Baltic.

Not until the reign of Peter's second-oldest daughter, the Empress Elizabeth (r 1741–62), did the city's imperial appetite return in full. Elizabeth created one of the most dazzling courts in Europe. She loved the pomp as much as the power and her 20-year reign was a nonstop cabaret. The Empress was a bit eccentric (she was certainly her father's daughter in that respect), and she enjoyed a hedonistic lifestyle that revolved around hunting, drinking and dancing. She most loved hosting

In 1737 Empress Anna celebrated victory in the Russo-Turkish War by having a palace carved in ice for herself, complete with turrets 30m tall. Anna forced Prince Golitsyn, who had incurred her displeasure, to marry a rotund Kalmyk girl inside, before spending the night and consummating the marriage on an ice bed.

1762	1764	1782	1796
Catherine II (later Catherine the Great) is brought to the throne by a coup against her husband Peter III, ushering in the Russian Enlightenment era.	Catherine the Great begins to purchase paintings from European collectors to display in her 'hermitage', the foundation for the State Hermitage Museum collection.	The *Bronze Horseman*, a statue of Peter the Great, is unveiled by Catherine before a huge crowd. Absent is the sculptor, Falconet, who has returned to France after a falling-out with Catherine.	Upon the death of Catherine the Great, her embittered son Paul I ascends the throne. One of his first acts as tsar is to decree that women may never again rule Russia.

elaborate masquerade balls, at which she performed countless costume changes, apparently preferring to end the night in drag. Bawdy though she was, Elizabeth also got the Russian elite hooked on high culture. The court was graced by poets, artists and philosophers. Journalism and theatre gained popularity, and an academy of arts was founded. While her resplendent splurges may have left imperial coffers empty, Elizabeth made her father's majestic dream a reality.

Catherine the Great

In 1745, at the age of 16, Sophie Augusta of Prussia was betrothed to Duke Peter of Holstein: quite a score for her ambitious mother, as he was a Romanov and heir to the imperial Russian throne. Sophie moved to St Petersburg, learned to speak Russian, delighted the court with her coy charm, and took the name Catherine when she converted to Orthodoxy.

More than just a court coquette, Catherine possessed keen political instincts and a strong appetite for power, attributes that had adverse effects on the men in her life. Her husband Tsar Peter III, as it turned out, was not terribly interested in ruling. In a plot hatched by her lover, Prince Orlov, Catherine was complicit in a coup that landed her on the throne, lifted Orlov to general-in-chief, and left her helpless husband under guard at a remote estate where he was assassinated shortly afterwards.

Despite the details of her unsavoury ascension, Catherine reigned for 34 years and presided over a golden age for St Petersburg. Relations between crown and aristocracy were never better. Empress Catherine was a charter member of a club of 18th-century monarchs known as the 'enlightened despots' – dictators who could hum Haydn. On the 'enlightened' side, Catherine corresponded with French philosophers, patronised the arts and sciences, promoted public education and introduced potatoes to the national cuisine. On the 'despotic' side, Catherine connived with fellow enlightened friends to carve up Poland, censored bad news, tightened serfs' bonds of servitude to their lords, and introduced potatoes to the national cuisine.

Great Power St Petersburg

1812 Overture

The downside to becoming a great power in European politics is that you become drawn into European wars. Though, in fairness to the Hanovers and Hapsburgs, the Romanovs were pretty good at picking fights on their own. From the 19th century on, Russia was at war and St Petersburg was transformed.

Contrary to rumour, Catherine the Great categorically did not die underneath a stallion – her death was a far more prosaic affair. She collapsed from a stroke in her bathroom and died tucked up in her bed. No horses are believed to have been present.

Despite her reputed fondness for anything sexual, including the aforementioned horses, there is little evidence that Catherine the Great's lovers even went into double digits. Her long love affair with Grigory Potemkin is fascinatingly described in Simon Sebag Montefiore's *Catherine the Great & Potemkin*.

1799	1800	1801	1812–14
The birth of poet Alexander Pushkin ushers in the era of Russian romanticism and the golden age of Russian literature. Revered as the national bard, Pushkin's legacy endures to this day.	St Petersburg has grown exponentially in its first century, and its population reaches 220,000. By this time, the city has gained all the glory of a cosmopolitan capital.	Tsar Paul is murdered in his bedroom in Mikhailovsky Castle. The coup places his son Alexander on the throne. He vows to continue the reformist policies of his grandmother.	Alexander I oversees victory in the Napoleonic Wars and troops occupy Paris. Monuments are strewn about St Petersburg, including the Alexander Column and Narva Gates.

It was Napoleon who coined the military maxim, 'first we engage, then we will see'. That was probably not the best tactic to take with Russia, as Napoleon himself found out when he suffered his greatest military defeat during the ill-fated campaign of 1812. Tsar Alexander I, Catherine the Great's successor, first clashed with Napoleon after joining an ill-fated anti-French alliance with Austria and Prussia. The Little Corporal targeted Moscow instead of the more heavily armed St Petersburg, however, and his multinational 600,000-strong force got there just in time for winter and had little to show for the effort besides vandalising the Kremlin.

The War of 1812 was a defining event for Russia, stirring national-ist exaltation and orchestral inspiration. Alexander I, having defeat-ed Napoleon and led victorious Russian soldiers into Paris, presided over a period of prosperity and self-assuredness in St Petersburg. His army's exploits were immortalised in triumphal designs that recalled imperial Rome, while the Kazan Cathedral and the Alexander Column were shining symbols for a new Russian empire that stretched halfway across the globe.

God Preserve Thy People

War did more than confer Great Power status on Russia: it was also a stimulus for new ideas on political reform and social change. In the 19th century, the clash of ideas spilled out of salons and into its streets.

On a frosty December morning in 1825, more than 100 soldiers amassed on Senate Sq (now Decembrists' Sq), with the intention of up-setting the royal succession. When Alexander I died unexpectedly with-out a legitimate heir, the throne was supposed to pass to his brother Constantine, Viceroy of Poland, but he declined, preferring not to com-plicate his contented life. Instead, the new tsar would be Alexander's youngest brother, Nicholas I, a cranky conservative with a fastidious obsession for barracks-style discipline. The Decembrist revolt was staged by a small cabal of officers, veterans of the Napoleonic Wars, who saw first-hand how people in other countries enjoyed greater free-dom and prosperity. They demanded Constantine and a constitution, but instead got exile and execution. The 'people', however, were now part of the discussion.

Russia's deeply disappointing performance in another war prompted another reform attempt, this time initiated by the tsar. In the 1850s, better-equipped British and French armies trounced Russia in a fight over the Crimean Peninsula. The new emperor Alexander II concluded from the fiasco that Russia had to catch up with the West, or watch its empire unravel. A slew of reform decrees were issued, promoting public

Catherine the Great adopted the Russian language, and, some suggest, not always entirely success-fully. One story runs that the German princess spelled the word 'ещё' (more) as 'исчто' (sounding phonetically quite similar) – giving rise to the joke at court: 'How can five spelling mistakes occur in a word of three letters?'

1825	1836	1837	1849
Alexander I dies. Reformers assemble on Senate Sq to protest the succession of conservative Nicholas I. The new tsar brutally crushes the Decembrist revolt, killing hundreds.	Construction of Russia's first railway line, from St Petersburg to Tsarskoe Selo, the imperial family's summer residence, begins. Initially trains are horse-drawn.	Poet Alexander Pushkin is shot in a duel with Frenchman Georges d'Anthès and later dies at his Moyka River house in St Petersburg, an unfathomable loss to Russian literature, still mourned today.	Author Fyodor Dostoevsky is exiled to Siberia for four years of hard labour after participating in discussions with a liberal intellectual group, the Petrashevsky Circle.

education, military reorganisation and economic modernisation. Alexander dropped the death penalty, curtailed corporal punishment and abolished serfdom, kind of – his solution that serfs pay their masters redemptive fees in exchange for freedom in fact pleased no one.

By now the 'people' were becoming less abstract. Political movements that claimed to better understand and represent them were sprouting up. On a Sunday morning in March 1881, several young student members of the Peoples' Will radical sect waited nervously by the Griboyedov Canal as the tsar's procession passed. Their homemade bombs hardly dented the royal armoured coach, but badly wounded scores of spectators and fatally shredded the reforming monarch when he insisted on leaving his carriage to investigate. On the hallowed site, the magnificent and melancholy Church on the Spilled Blood was constructed, its twisting onion domes trying to steady St Petersburg's uncertain present with Russia's enduring past.

Competition between Russia and Europe's other great powers compelled a state-directed campaign of economic development. St Petersburg became the centre of a robust military-industrial economy that was established to fight the wars of the modern age. A ring of ugly sooty smokestacks grew up around the still-handsome city centre. Tough times in the rural villages and job opportunities in the new factories hastened a human flood into the capital. By the 1880s, the population climbed past a million, with hundreds of thousands cramped into slummy suburban squalor. The gap between high society and the lower depths had long been manageable, but now they kept running into each other. The people had arrived.

If you're interested in the bizarre circumstances that led to Pushkin's fatal duel with Gerges d'Anthès, read *Pushkin's Buttons*, by Serena Vitale, for the definitive account.

God Save the Tsar

'We, workers and inhabitants of the city of St Petersburg, our wives, children, and helpless old parents, have come to you, Sovereign, to seek justice and protection.' So read the petition that a large group of workers intended to present to Tsar Nicholas II on a Sunday in January 1905.

Nicholas II ascended the throne in 1894, when his iron-fisted autocratic father, Alexander III, died suddenly. Nicholas was of less steely stuff. Most contemporary accounts agree: he was a good guy and a lousy leader, possessive of his power to decide, except that he could never make up his mind. In 1904 Nicholas followed the foolish advice of a cynical minister, who said that what Russia needed most was a 'small victorious war' to get peoples' minds off their troubles. Unfortunately, the Russo-Japanese War ended in humiliating defeat and the people were more agitated than ever.

1851	1861	1866	1870
Upon completion of the construction of Nikolaevsky Station (now Moscow Station), the first trains linking Moscow and St Petersburg begin running, introducing rail travel to Russia.	The emancipation of serfs frees up labour for the Industrial Revolution. The flood of workers into the capital leads to overcrowding, poor sanitation, disease epidemics and societal discontent.	Dostoevsky's classic novel of life and death in St Petersburg's poverty-stricken garrets, *Crime and Punishment*, is published, making him Russia's greatest late-19th-century author.	After breaking from the Academy of Arts, a group of upstart artists known as the Peredvizhniki (Wanderers) starts organising travelling exhibitions to widen their audience.

By January 1905 the capital was a hotbed of political protest. As many as 100,000 workers were on strike, the city had no electricity and all public facilities were closed. Nicholas and the royals departed for their palace retreat at Tsarskoe Selo. In this charged atmosphere, Father Georgy Gapon, an Orthodox priest who apparently lived a double life as holy man and police agent, organised a peaceful demonstration of workers and their families to protest against the difficult conditions. Their petition called for eight-hour work days and better wages, universal suffrage and an end to the war.

Singing 'God Save the Tsar', the crowd solemnly approached the Winter Palace, hoping to present its requests to the tsar personally. Inside, the mood was jittery: panicky guardsmen fired on the demonstrators, at first as a warning and then directly into the crowd. More than 1000 people were killed by the gunshots or the trampling that followed. Although Nicholas was not even in the palace at the time, the events of Bloody Sunday shattered the myth of the Father Tsar. The Last Emperor was finally able to restore order by issuing the October Manifesto, which promised a constitutional monarchy and civil rights; in fact, not much really changed.

At the start of WWI, nationalist fervour led St Petersburg to change its name to the more Slavic, less German-sounding Petrograd. A hundred years earlier, war with France had made the Russian Empire a great power, but now yet another European war threatened its very survival. The empire was fraying at the seams as the old aristocratic order limped onward into battle. Only the strength of the Bronze Horseman could hold it all together. But Peter's legacy rested on the shoulders of an imperial inheritor who was both half-hearted reformer and irresolute reactionary: the combination proved revolutionary.

> **St Petersburg's Top Historic Sites**
>
> *Peter and Paul Fortress (Petrograd & Vyborg Sides)*
>
> *Winter Palace (Hermitage, Historic Heart)*
>
> *Alexander Nevsky Monastery (Smolny & Vosstaniya)*
>
> *Tsarskoe Selo (Pushkin)*

Cradle of Communism

Act One: Down with the Autocracy

In 1917, 23 February began like most days in Petrograd since the outbreak of the war. The men went off to the metalworks and arms factories. The women went out to receive the daily bread ration. And the radical set went out to demonstrate, as it happened to be International Women's Day. Although each left their abode an ordinary individual, by day's end they would meld into the most infamous 'mass' in modern history: the Bronze Horseman's heirs let go of the reigns; the Russian Revolution, a play in three acts, had begun.

After waiting long hours in the winter chill for a little food, the women were told that there would be none. This news coincided with the end of the day shift and a sweaty outpouring from the factory

1881	1883	1890	1896
A bomb kills Alexander II as he travels along the Griboyedova Canal. His reactionary son, Alexander III, undoes many of his reforms, but oversees the building of the Trans-Siberian Railway.	The dazzling Church on the Spilled Blood is inaugurated as a private place of mourning for the imperial family for the dead Alexander II.	*Queen of Spades,* Pyotr Tchaikovsky's opera based on the poem by Alexander Pushkin, premieres at the Mariinsky Theatre, drawing excited crowds and rave reviews.	At the coronation of Nicholas II, a stampede by the massive crowd ends with more than a thousand deaths and almost as many injuries.

gates. Activist provocateurs joined the fray as the streets swelled with the tired, the hungry and now the angry. The crowd assumed a political purpose. They marched to the river, intent on crossing to the palace side and expressing their discontent to somebody. But they were met at the bridge by gendarmes and guns.

Similar meetings had occurred previously, in July and October, on which occasions the crowd retreated. But now it was February and one did not need a bridge to cross the frozen river. First a brave few, then emboldened small groups, and finally a defiant horde of hundreds were traversing the ice-laden Neva toward the Winter Palace.

They congregated in the Palace Sq, demanding bread, peace and an end to autocracy. Inside, contemptuous counts stole glances at the unruly rabble and waited for them to grow tired and disperse. But they did not go home. Instead, they went around the factories and spread the call

THE MAD MONK

Russia's most legendary letch and holy man was Grigory Rasputin, mystic and healer. He was born in 1869 into poverty in a small village east of the Urals. After a dissolute boyhood and a short-lived marriage, he discovered religion. Rasputin preached (and practised) that the way to divine grace was through sin and redemption: binge drinking and engaging in sexual orgies, and then praying for forgiveness.

St Petersburg's high society was receptive to Rasputin's teachings. Despite his heavy drinking and sexual scandals – or perhaps because of them – he earned the adoration of an army of aristocratic ladies. More notable, Rasputin endeared himself to Emperor Nicholas II and his wife Alexandra, largely as he had the power to ease the pain of their son Alexey, who suffered from haemophilia.

The holy man's scandalous behaviour and his influence over the tsarina evoked the ire of the aristocracy. The powerful Prince Felix Yusupov and the tsar's cousin Grand Duke Dmitry decided that the Siberian peasant must be stopped. On a wintry night in 1916, they invited Rasputin to the sumptuous Yusupov Palace overlooking the Moyka. They plied the monk with wine and cakes that were laced with potassium cyanide, which seemed to have no effect. In a panic, the perpetrators then shot the priest at close range. Alarmingly, this didn't seem to get the job done either. Rasputin finally drowned when he was tied up in a sheet and dropped into the icy Neva River. He was buried in secret at Pushkin.

Besides mystical powers and lecherous behaviour, Grigory Rasputin is famous for another exceptional attribute: his enormous penis (30cm, if you must know). Legend has it that Rasputin's foes did not stop at murder. Yusupov's maid supposedly found Rasputin's severed organ when cleaning the apartment after the murder. Which explains the prize artefact at the so-called Museum of Erotica: it is indeed Rasputin's preserved penis. Even in its detached state, the Mad Monk's member is still attracting attention.

1896	1899	1900	1905
Anton Chekhov's classic play *The Seagull* opens to poor reviews at the Alexandrinsky Theatre. The playwright was apparently so unnerved by the audience's hostility that he left the theatre.	Vladimir Nabokov, the future author of *Lolita*, is born at his family's mansion on Bolshaya Morskaya ul in St Petersburg. He immortalises the house in his autobiography *Speak, Memory*.	By the turn of the 20th century, St Petersburg (population 1.44 million) is Russia's cultural centre. It's also a centre of political unrest.	Hundreds of people are killed when troops fire on peaceful protestors presenting a petition to the tsar. Nicholas II is held responsible for the tragedy, dubbed 'Bloody Sunday'.

for a general strike. By the next day a quarter of a million people were rampaging through the city centre. Overwhelmed local police took cover.

When word reached the tsar, he ordered military troops to restore order. But his troops were no longer hardened veterans: they were long dead at the front. Rather, freshly conscripted peasant youths in uniform were sent to put down the uprising. When commanded to fire on the demonstration, they instead broke rank, dropped their guns and joined the mob. At that moment, the 300-year-old Romanov dynasty and 500-year-old tsarist autocracy came to an end.

Act Two: All Power to the Soviets

Perhaps the least likely political successor to the tsar in February 1917 was the radical socialist Bolshevik Party. The Bolsheviks were on the fringe of the fringe of Russia's political left. Party membership numbered a few thousand, at best. Yet, in less than eight months, the Bolsheviks occupied the Winter Palace, proclaiming Petrograd the capital of a worldwide socialist revolution.

In the days that followed Nicholas' abdication, the Russian Provisional Government was established. It mainly comprised political liberals, representing reform-minded nobles, pragmatic civil servants, and professional and business interests. Simultaneously, a rival political force emerged, the Petrograd Soviet. The Soviet (the Russian word for council) was composed of more populist and radical elements, representing the interests of the workers, peasants, soldiers and sailors. Both political bodies were based at the Tauride Palace.

Part love story and part political thriller, Robert K Massie's *Nicholas and Alexandra* gives the nitty-gritty on the royal family, Rasputin and the resulting revolution.

The Provisional Government saw itself as a temporary instrument, whose main task was to create constitutional democracy. It argued over the details of organising an election, rather than dealing with the issues that had caused the revolution – bread and peace. At first, the Soviet deferred to the Provisional Government, but this soon changed.

On 3 April, Bolshevik leader Vladimir Lenin arrived at the Finland Station (Finlyandsky vokzal) from exile in Switzerland. Lenin's passage across enemy lines had been arranged by German generals, who hoped that he would stir things up at home, and thus distract Russia from its participation in the war. As expected, Lenin upset the political status quo as soon as he arrived. His rabid revolutionary rhetoric polarised Petrograd. In the Soviet, the Bolshevik faction went from cooperative to confrontational. But even his radical colleagues dismissed Lenin as a stinging gadfly, rather than a serious foe. By summer's end, Lenin had proved them all wrong.

The Provisional Government not only refused to withdraw from the war but, at the instigation of the allies, launched a new offensive –

1906	1914	1915	1916
The first Duma election is held, a decision that is made, but greatly resented, by Nicholas II on the urging of the prime minister. The Duma meets four times a year in the Tauride Palace until 1917.	Russia enters WWI, simultaneously invading Austrian Galicia and German Prussia with minimal success. St Petersburg changes its name to the less Germanic sounding Petrograd.	The first suprematist art show takes place in Petrograd, showcasing Malevich's infamous *Black Square*, creating a critical storm and putting the Russian avant-garde firmly on the map.	After evoking the ire of aristocrats, Grigory Rasputin is invited to Yusupov Palace for cyanide-laced tea by a group of plotters, who then drown him in the icy Moyka River.

prompting mass desertions at the front. Meanwhile, the economic situation continued to deteriorate. The same anarchic anger that fuelled the February Revolution was felt on the streets again. Lenin's Bolsheviks were the only political party in sync with the public mood. September elections in the Petrograd Soviet gave the Bolsheviks a majority.

Lenin had spent his entire adult life waiting for this moment. For 20 years he did little else than read, write and rant about revolution. He enjoyed Beethoven, but avoided listening to his music from concern that the sentiment it evoked would make him lose his revolutionary edge. A successful revolution, Lenin observed, had two preconditions: first, the oppressed classes were politically mobilised and ready to act; and, second, the ruling class was internally divided and questioned its will to continue. This politically explosive combination now existed. If the Bolsheviks waited any longer, he feared, the Provisional Government would get its act together and impose a new bourgeois political order, ending his dream of socialist revolution in Russia. On 25 October the Bolsheviks staged their coup. According to Lenin's chief accomplice and coup organiser, Leon Trotsky, 'power was lying in the streets, waiting for someone to pick it up'. Bolshevik Red Guards seized a few buildings and strategic points. The Provisional Government was holed up in the tsar's private dining room in the Winter Palace, protected by a few Cossacks, the Petrograd chapter of the Women's Battalion of Death, and the one-legged commander of a bicycle regiment. Before dessert could be served, their dodgy defences cracked. Mutinous mariners fired a window-shattering salvo from the cruiser *Aurora* to signal the start of the assault; and the Red Guards – led by Lenin – moved in on the Winter Palace. Three shells struck the building, bullet holes riddled the square side of the palace and a window was shattered on the 3rd floor before the Provisional Government was arrested in the Small Dining Room behind the Malachite Hall. This largely bloodless battle would be celebrated for 70 years as the most glorious moment in history.

At the Tauride Palace the Soviet remained in emergency session late into the night when Lenin announced that the Provisional Government had been arrested and the Soviet was now the supreme power in Russia. Half the deputies walked out in disgust. Never one to miss an opportunity, Lenin quickly called a vote to make it official. It passed. Incredibly, the Bolsheviks were now in charge.

Act Three: Consolidating Communism

Nobody really believed the Bolsheviks would be around for long. Even Lenin said that if they could hold on for just 100 days, their coup would

1917	1918	1920	1921
The February Revolution results in the abdication of Nicholas II, followed by the Bolshevik coup in October. Vladimir Ilych Lenin seizes power and civil war ensues.	Lenin pulls Russia out of WWI and moves the capital to Moscow. Civil war continues throughout the country, and Petrograd enters a period of political and cultural decline.	The ongoing civil war and the change of capital take their toll in St Petersburg. The population falls to 722,000, one-third of the pre-revolutionary figure.	Kronshtadt sailors and soldiers rebel against the increasingly dictatorial regime. They are brutally suppressed and this is the last uprising against Communist rule until the Soviet collapse.

be a success by providing future inspiration. It was one thing to occupy a few palaces in Petrograd, but across the empire's far-flung regions Bolshevik-brand radicalism was not so popular. From 1918 to 1921 civil war raged in Russia: between monarchists and socialists, imperialists and nationalists, aristocrats and commoners, believers and atheists. When it was over, somehow Soviet power was still standing. In the final act of the Russian Revolution, the scene shifted from the Petrograd stage. The imperial capital would never be the same.

In December 1917, an armistice was arranged and peace talks began with the Germans. The Bolsheviks demanded a return to prewar imperial borders, but Germany insisted on the liberation of Poland, where its army was squatting. Trotsky defiantly walked out of negotiations, declaring 'neither war, nor peace'. The German high command was a bit confused and not at all amused – hostilities immediately resumed. Lenin had vowed never to abandon the capital, but that was before a German battle fleet cruised into the Gulf of Finland. Exit stage left. In 1918 the Bolsheviks vacated their new pastel digs in Petrograd and relocated behind the ancient red bricks of Moscow. It was supposed to be temporary (Lenin personally preferred St Petersburg). But Russia was turning inward, and Peter's window to the West was closing.

Along with the loss of its capital political status, St Petersburg also lost its noble social status. The aristocratic soul gave up the proletarian body. The royal family had always set the standards for high society, but now the royals were on the run. No Romanov stepped forward to claim the once coveted throne. Nicholas II and his family, meanwhile, were placed under house arrest in the Alexander Palace at Tsarskoe Selo, before leaving on a one-way trip to Siberia. The breakdown of the old order made the old elite vulnerable. The tsar's favourite ballerina, Mathilda Kshesinskaya, pleaded in vain as her Style Moderne mansion was commandeered by the Bolsheviks as their party headquarters. The more fortunate families fled with the few valuables they could carry; the less fortunate who stayed were harassed, dispossessed and killed.

The revolution began in Petrograd and ended there in March 1921 when Kronshtadt sailors staged a mutiny. These erstwhile Bolshevik boosters demanded the democracy they had been promised now that the civil war was won. But Lenin, who had since renamed his political party 'the Communists', was reluctant to relinquish political power. The sailors' revolt was brutally suppressed in a full-scale military assault across the frozen bay, confirming the historical adage that revolutions eat their children.

Focusing on the colourful characters of the imperial period and the dramatic events leading up to the revolution, D Bruce Lincoln's *Sunlight at Midnight* is a definitive history of the period as well as being highly readable and academically rigorous.

1924	1930	1934	1937–38
Lenin dies without designating a successor. The city's name is renamed Leningrad in his honour. Power is assumed by a 'triumvirate' but Stalin increasingly takes control.	Dmitry Shostakovich's satirical opera *The Nose* premiers at Maly Operny Theatre. He is accused of 'formalism' by Stalinist critics and the opera is not performed again until the 1970s.	Leningrad party boss Sergei Kirov is murdered as he leaves his office at the Smolny Institute. The assassination kicks off the Great Purge, ushering in Stalin's reign of terror.	The height of Stalin's Great Purge (Yezhovshchina) terrorises the whole of Russia, but particularly Leningrad, liquidating much of its local intelligentsia and party organisation.

Red Piter

Soviet Second City

Moscow finally reclaimed its coveted ancient title with the caveat that it was now the world's first communist capital. Petrograd consoled itself as the Soviet second city.

The redesignation of the capital prompted the departure of the bureaucracies: the government ministries, the military headquarters, the party apparatus, which took with them a host of loyal servants and servile lackeys. The population dropped by two-thirds from its prewar count. Economic exchange was reduced to begging and bartering. To make matters worse, the food shortages that first sparked the revolu-

BONES OF CONTENTION

What happened to the last members of the royal family – even after their execution in 1918 – is a mixture of the macabre, the mysterious and the just plain messy.

The Romanov remains resurfaced in 1976, when a group of local scientists found them near Yekaterinburg. So politically sensitive was this issue that the discovery was kept secret until the remains were finally fully excavated in 1991. The bones of nine people were tentatively identified as Tsar Nicholas II, his wife Alexandra, three of their four daughters, the royal doctor and three servants. Absent were any remains of daughter Maria or the royal couple's only son, the tsarevich Alexey.

According to a 1934 report filed by one of the assassin-soldiers, all five children died with their parents when they were shot by a firing squad in Yekaterinburg. The bodies were dumped in an abandoned mine, followed by several grenades intended to collapse the mine shaft. When the mine did not collapse, two of the children's bodies were set on fire, and the others were doused with acid and buried in a swamp. Even then, most of the acid soaked away into the ground – leaving the bones to be uncovered 73 years later.

In mid-1998 the royal remains were finally given a proper burial in the Romanov crypt at SS Peter and Paul Cathedral, alongside their predecessors dating back to Peter the Great. A 19-gun salute bade them a final farewell. President Boris Yeltsin was present, together with many Romanov family members.

Despite the controversy, it seemed the story had finally come to an end (however unsatisfying for some). But in 2007 amateur archaeologists in Yekaterinburg found the bodies of two more individuals – a male aged between 10 and 13 and a female aged 18 to 23. The location corresponds with the site described in the 1934 report; and the silver fillings in the teeth are similar to those in the other family members. Genetic tests carried out in 2008 confirmed that these were indeed the remains of the tsarevich Alexey and his sister Maria. After almost a century of mystery, the end of the Russian royal family is finally known.

1940	1941	1942	1944
Rapid industrialisation shows results: the population of the city has rebounded, reaching 3.1 million, and Leningrad is now responsible for 11% of Soviet industrial output.	The Nazis invade the Soviet Union and Leningrad is surrounded, blocking residents from all sources of food and fuel, as the city comes under attack.	The Leningrad Radio Orchestra performs the Seventh Symphony by Dmitry Shostakovich. Musicians are given special rations so they can perform, and the music is broadcast throughout the city.	The Germans retreat. Leningrad emerges from its darkest hour, but more than one million are dead from starvation and illness. The city's population has dropped to an estimated 600,000.

tion during the war continued well afterwards. Fuel was also in short supply – homes went unheated, factory gates stayed shut and city services were stopped.

Leningrad was eventually revived with a proletarian transfusion. At the beginning of the 1930s the socialist state launched an intensive campaign of economic development, which reinvigorated the city's industrial sector. New scientific and military research institutes were fitted upon the city's strong higher-education foundations. On the eve of WWII, the population had climbed to over three million. Public works projects for the people were undertaken – polished underground metro stations, colossal sports complexes and streamlined constructivist buildings muscled in next to the peeling pastels and cracked baroque of the misty past.

The Leningrad Purges

Though no longer the capital, Leningrad still figured prominently in Soviet politics. Its party machine, headquartered in the Smolny Institute, was a plum post in the Communist Party. The First Secretary, head of the Leningrad organisation, was always accorded a seat on the Politburo, the executive board of Soviet power. In the early years Leningrad was a crucial battlefront in the bloody intraparty competition to succeed Lenin.

Lenin died from a stroke at the age of 53, without designating a successor. He was first replaced by a troika of veteran Old Bolsheviks, including Leningrad party head, Alexander Zinoviev. But their stay at the top was brief; they were outmanoeuvred by the most unlikely successor to Lenin's mantle, Josef Stalin, a crude, disaffected Georgian bureaucrat.

In 1926 Zinoviev was forced to relinquish his Leningrad seat to Sergei Kirov, a solid Stalin man. In high-profile Leningrad, Kirov soon became one of the most popular party bosses. He was a zealous supporter of Stalin's plans for rapid industrialisation, which meant heavy investment in the city. But the manic-paced economic campaign could not be sustained, causing famine and food shortages. Kirov emerged as a proponent of a more moderate course instead of the radical pace that Stalin still insisted on. The growing rift in the leadership was exposed at a 1934 party congress, where a small cabal of regional governors secretly connived to remove Stalin in a bureaucratic coup and replace him with Kirov. It was an offer that Kirov flatly refused.

But it was hard to keep a secret from Stalin. Wary of Kirov's rising appeal, Stalin ordered that he be transferred to party work in Moscow, where he could be watched more closely. Kirov found reasons to delay

Vsevolod Pudovkin's 1927 silent film *The End of St Petersburg* was produced to commemorate the 10th anniversary of the October Revolution and it remains a landmark for Soviet realist cinema.

1953	1955	1956	1960
Stalin dies in Moscow, marking the end of decades of terror, and the eventual liberalisation of Soviet society.	The first seven stations of the city's metro open 15 years after construction began, hampered initially by war and then by the marshy earth under the city, making the metro a technical marvel.	After the death of Stalin, party leader Nikita Khrushchev makes a 'Secret Speech' denouncing Stalin, thus commencing a period of economic reform and cultural thaw.	A collection of 186 mass graves, the Piskaryovskoe Cemetery opens in northern Leningrad, with almost 500,000 civilian and military casualties from the blockade.

the appointment. He remained in Leningrad – but not for long. On 1 December 1934 as he left a late-afternoon meeting, Kirov was shot from behind and killed in the corridor outside his Smolny office, on orders from Stalin.

Kirov's murder was the first act in a much larger drama. According to Stalin, it proved that the party was infiltrated by saboteurs and spies and the ensuing police campaign to uncover these hidden enemies became known as the Great Purges, which consumed nearly the entire post-revolutionary Soviet elite. Leningrad intellectuals were especially targeted. More than 50 Hermitage curators were imprisoned, including the Asian art specialist, accused of being an agent of Japanese imperialism, and the medieval armour specialist, accused of harbouring weapons. Successive waves of arrest, exile and execution effectively transformed the Leningrad elite, making it much younger, less assertive and more Soviet. When it was finally over, Stalin stood as personal dictator with unrivalled power – even by tsarist standards.

The Siege

Nadezhda Mandelstam, the wife of poet Osip Mandelstam, wrote *Hope Against Hope*, an incredibly moving memoir about their lives as dissidents in Stalinist Russia leading up to Osip Mandelstam's death in a transit camp in 1938. The title is a play on words, as *nadezhda* means 'hope' in Russian.

On 22 June 1941 Leningraders were basking in the summer solstice when Foreign Minister Molotov interrupted state radio to announce an 'unprecedented betrayal in the history of civilised nations'. That day, German Nazi forces launched a full-scale military offensive across the Soviet Union's western borders. Stalin's refusal to believe that Hitler would break their nonaggression pact left Leningrad unprepared and vulnerable.

The German code-name for its assault on Leningrad was Operation Nordlicht (Operation Northern Lights). The Führer ordered his generals to raze the city rather than incur the cost of feeding and heating its residents in winter. By July German troops had reached the suburbs, inflicting a daily barrage of artillery bombardment and aerial attacks. All Leningraders were mobilised around the clock to dig trenches, erect barricades and board up buildings. The city's factories were dismantled, brick by brick, and shipped to the other side of the Urals. Hermitage staff crated up Catherine's collection for a safer interior location; what they did not get out in time was buried on the grounds of the Summer Garden. The spires of the Admiralty and Peter and Paul Fortress were camouflaged in coloured netting, which was changed according to the weather and season. The youngest and oldest residents were evacuated; everybody else braced themselves.

At the end of August the Germans captured the east-bound railway: Leningrad was cut off. Instead of a bloody street fight, the Nazi command vowed to starve the city to death. Food stocks were low to begin with but became almost nonexistent after napalm bombs burned down the warehouse district. Moscow dispatched tireless and resourceful Dmitry Pavlov to act as Chief of Food Supply. Pavlov's teams ransacked cellars, broke into box cars and tore up floorboards in search of leftover cans and crumbs. The city's scientists were pressed to develop something edible out of yeast, glue and soap. As supplies dwindled, pets and pests disappeared. A strict ration system was imposed and violators were shot. Workers received 15 ounces (425g) of bread per day; everyone else got less. It was not enough. The hunger was relentless, causing delirium, disease and death. Hundreds of thousands succumbed to starvation, corpses were strewn atop snow-covered streets, mass graves were dug on the outskirts.

Relief finally arrived in January, when food supplies began to reach the city from across the frozen Lake Ladoga lifeline. Trucks made the perilous night-time trek on ice roads, fearing the Luftwaffe above and chilled water below. Soviet military advances enabled the supply route to stay open in the spring when the lake thawed. Leningrad survived the worst; still the siege continued. The city endured the enemy's pounding guns for two more years. At last, in January 1944, the Red Army arrived in force. They pulverised the German front with more rockets and shells than were used at Stalingrad. Within days, Leningrad was liberated. The 900 days marked history's longest military siege of a modern city. The city was badly battered but not beaten. The St Petersburg spirit was resilient.

Harrison Salisbury's *The 900 Days: The Siege of Leningrad* is a fascinating forensic reconstruction of the Nazi blockade. It's not for those with a passing interest in the blockade, but for those who want to vicariously suffer through the darkest hours of the city.

The Return of Peter

From Dissent to Democracy

Throughout the Soviet period, Moscow kept suspicious eyes trained on Leningrad. After WWII, Stalin launched the 'Leningrad Affair', a sinister purge of the Hero City's youthful political and cultural elite, who were falsely accused of trying to create a rival capital. Several thousand were arrested, several hundred were executed. Kremlin apparatchiks were committed to forcing conformity onto the city's free-thinking intellectuals and keeping closed the window to the West. They ultimately failed.

Leningrad's culture club was irrepressible. Like in tsarist times, it teased, goaded and defied its political masters. Stalin terrorised, Khrushchev cajoled and Brezhnev banished, yet the city still became a centre of dissent. As from Radishchev to Pushkin, so from Akhmatova to Brodsky. By the 1970s the city hosted a thriving independent underground of jazz and rock musicians, poets and painters, reformists and radicals. Like the Neva in spring, these cultural currents overflowed

1991	1997	1998	1998
On Christmas Day, Gorbachev announces the dissolution of the Soviet Union. Leningrad's name reverts to St Petersburg after a referendum on the issue.	Mikhail Manevich, vice-governor of the city, is assassinated by a sniper in the middle of town as he travels to work, marking the height of St Petersburg's lawlessness.	The bodies of the last tsar, Nicholas II, and most of his family are finally buried in the SS Peter and Paul Cathedral after their murders by the Bolsheviks 80 years earlier.	St Petersburg politician and human rights activist Galina Starovoitova is murdered outside her apartment by hitmen, another blow to Russia's reputation as a free and safe society.

when Mikhail Gorbachev finally came to power and declared a new policy of openness and reform. The Leningrad democratic movement was unleashed.

Gorbachev forced long-time Leningrad party boss Grigory Romanov and his communist cronies into retirement. He held elections for local office that brought to power liberal-minded Anatoly Sobchak, the darling of the progressive intelligentsia and the first popularly elected mayor in the city's history. Leningrad was at the forefront of democratic change, as the old regime staggered towards the exit.

Whereas Gorbachev sought to reform Soviet socialism, his rival Boris Yeltsin was intent on killing it off for good. Just two months after Sobchak's historic election, reactionary hardliners staged a coup. While Yeltsin mollified Moscow, a hundred thousand protestors filled Palace Sq in Leningrad. The ambivalent soldiers sent to arrest Sobchak disobeyed orders, and instead escorted him to the local TV station where the mayor denounced the coup and encouraged residents to do the same. Anxiously waiting atop flimsy barricades, anticommunist demonstrators spent the evening in fear of approaching tanks. But the inebriated coup plotters lost their nerve, thanks in large part to the people of Leningrad.

Did people ever laugh under communism? Ben Lewis proves that they did – and how – in his book *Hammer & Tickle: A History of Communism Told Through Communist Jokes*. Brush up on your best NKVD, bread queue and Brezhnev jokes.

Finding the Future in the Past

In 1991, by popular referendum, the citizens of Leningrad voted to change their city's name once more, restoring its original name, St Petersburg.

As reviled as the communist regime may have been, it still provided a sufficient standard of living, a predictable day at the office and a common target for discontent. The familiar ways of life suddenly changed. The communist collapse caused enormous personal hardship; economic security and social status were put in doubt. Mafia gangs and bureaucratic fangs dug into the emerging market economy, creating contemptible crony capitalism. The democratic movement splintered into petty rivalries and political insignificance. One of its shining stars, Galina Starovoitova, social scientist turned human rights advocate, was brazenly shot dead in her St Petersburg apartment stairwell in 1998. Out on the street, meanwhile, prudish reserve gave way to outlandish exhibitionism. Uncertainty and unfairness found expression in an angry and sometimes xenophobic reaction.

With the old order vanquished, the battle to define the new one was on. The symbols of the contending parties were on display throughout the city. The nouveau riche quickly claimed Nevsky pr for their Milano designer get-ups and Bavarian driving machines. The disaf-

2000	2003	2006	2010
St Petersburg native Vladimir Putin is elected president of Russia, beginning a new era of far greater central control and 'managed democracy'.	Putin's favoured candidate, Valentina Matvienko, prevails in gubernatorial elections. Winning 63% of votes, she becomes the governor of St Petersburg.	Putin hosts the G8 Summit in St Petersburg, the most significant international political event ever held in the city, marking its reinvention as a ceremonial showpiece for Putin's Russia.	Governor Matvienko announces that after years of protests and international criticism, the controversial 400m-high Okhta Centre will no longer be built in the city centre.

fected youth used faded pink courtyard walls to spray-paint Zenit football insignias, swastikas and the two English words they all seemed to know. Every major intersection was adorned with gigantic billboard faces of prima ballerinas and pop singers sipping their favourite cups of coffee. And, like all their St Petersburg predecessors, the new ruling elite wanted to leave its own distinctive mark on the city, as witnessed by a slew of ugly new office blocks that have been allowed to be built in the city centre.

Local Spook Makes Good

When St Petersburg native Vladimir Putin was elected president in 2000, speculation was rife that he would transfer the Russian capital back to his home town. When Lenin relocated the capital to Moscow rather hastily in 1918, it was supposed to be a temporary move. Furthermore, the new millennium brought a new regime: what better way to make a significant break with the past? Most importantly, Putin's personal attachment to his home town was significant.

Born in 1952, Putin spent his childhood in the Smolny district. Little Vlad went to school in the neighbourhood and took a law degree at Leningrad State University, before working in Leningrad, Moscow and East Germany for the KGB. In 1990 he returned to his home town, where he was promptly promoted through the ranks of local politics. By 1994 he was deputy to St Petersburg mayor Anatoly Sobchak. In his office in the Smolny Institute, Putin famously replaced the portrait of Lenin with one of Peter the Great. Quite where this apparent reformer went is anyone's guess, but as Putin went from the Smolny to the Kremlin, his newfound reformist instincts clearly became clouded by his atavistic KGB loyalties.

As the city economy slowly recovered from collapse and shock, Sobchak was voted out of office in 1996. Putin was then recruited by fellow Leningrader, Anatoly Chubais, to join him in the capital in the Kremlin administration. After another rapid rise through the ranks, he took over the FSB (the postcommunist KGB). In 1999, after Yeltsin sacked two prime ministers in quick succession, politically unknown Putin was offered the inauspicious post. On New Year's Eve that year Yeltsin finally resigned and Putin was appointed acting president. Putin went on to win two presidential elections, before resigning to become prime minister in 2008, due to constitutionally mandated term limits. Putin returned to the presidency in 2012, and will remain until at least 2016, and very likely until 2020.

If you can't get enough of Dostoevsky, why not tackle *The Idiot*, which takes place both in St Petersburg and in nearby Pavlovsk. The descriptions are not quite as evocative as those in *Crime and Punishment*, but the characters are equally complex and the debates no less esoteric.

2011	2011	2013	2014
Valentina Matvienko is moved sideways out of the governor's seat in St Petersburg to become the speaker of the Federation Council by President Dmitry Medvedev.	Former KGB officer and Putin loyalist Georgy Poltavchenko is appointed governor of St Petersburg.	The Mariinsky II opens after a decade of planning and construction, giving St Petersburg a state-of-the-art ballet and opera theatre.	St Petersburg hosts Manifesta 10, the European Biennial of Contemporary Art, despite critics calling for a boycott due to Russia's annexation of Crimea.

Architecture

Peter the Great intended to build a city that rivalled Paris and Rome for architectural splendour. He envisioned grand avenues, weaving waterways and magnificent palaces. His successors, especially Empresses Anna, Elizabeth and Catherine the Great, carried out their own even more elaborate versions of their forebear's plan. Today, the historic centre of St Petersburg is a veritable museum of 18th- and 19th-century architecture, with enough baroque, neoclassical and Empire style extravagances to keep you ogling indefinitely.

Petrine Baroque

Top Five Architectural Sights

....

Winter Palace
(Historic Heart)

....

Mariinsky II
(Kolomna)

....

Chesme Church
(Smolny &
Vosstaniya)

....

Smolny Cath-
edral (Smolny &
Vosstaniya)

....

House of
Soviets (Smolny &
Vosstaniya)

The first major building in the city was the Peter and Paul Fortress (p144), completed in 1704 and still intact today. Peter recruited Domenico Trezzini from Switzerland to oversee early projects. It was Trezzini, more than any other architect, who created the style known as Petrine baroque, which was heavily influenced by Dutch architecture, of which Peter was enamoured. Trezzini's buildings included the Alexander Nevsky Monastery (p114), the SS Peter and Paul Cathedral (p144) within the fortress and Twelve Colleges (p136) on Vasilyevsky Island.

Initially, most funding was diverted to the war against Sweden, meaning there wasn't enough money to create the European-style city that Peter dreamed of. Once Russia's victory was secured in 1709, the city began to see feverish development. In 1711, the Grand Perspective (later Nevsky pr) was initially built as a road to transport building supplies from Russia's interior. Nevsky pr was supposed to be a perfectly straight avenue heading to Novgorod. The existing kink (at pl Vosstaniya) is attributed to a miscalculation by builders.

Stone construction was banned outside the new capital, in order to ensure that there would be enough masons free to work on the city. Peter ordered Trezzini to create a unified city plan designed around Vasilyevsky Island. He also recruited Frenchman Jean Baptiste Alexander LeBlond from Paris. The two architects focused their efforts on Vasilyevsky Island, even though most people preferred to live across the river on the higher ground of Admiralty Island. The Menshikov Palace (p136), the home of Peter's best friend and St Petersburg's first governor, was the finest in the city, and far grander than Peter's Winter Palace.

The Age of Rastrelli

Empress Anna oversaw the completion of many of Peter's unfinished projects, including the Kunstkamera (p134) and Twelve Colleges (p136). Most significantly, she hired Italian Bartolomeo Rastrelli as chief architect, a decision that more than any other influenced the city's look today. His major projects under Anna's reign were the Manege Central Exhibition Hall (p105) and the Third Summer Palace (since destroyed). Rastrelli's greatest work, however, was yet to come.

Anna left her mark on the face of St Petersburg in many ways. She ordered all nobles to pave the street in front of their properties, thus ensuring the reinforcement of the Neva Embankment and other major thoroughfares. A massive fire in 1737 wiped out the unsightly and run-down wooden housing that surrounded the Winter Palace, thus freeing the historic centre for the centralised city planning that would be implemented under Elizabeth.

Elizabethan St Petersburg was almost entirely the work of Rastrelli, whose Russian baroque style became synonymous with the city. His crowning glory, of course, was the construction and remodelling of the Winter Palace (p79), completed in 1762, shortly after Elizabeth's death.

Rastrelli's second major landmark was Anichkov Palace (p85). After that creation, he became the city's most fashionable architect. Commissions soon followed to build the Stroganov Palace (p79), Vorontsov Palace (p85), Kamennoostrovsky Palace, Catherine Palace (p165) at Tsarskoe Selo and the extension of LeBlond's Grand Palace at Peterhof (p160). The sumptuous Smolny Cathedral (p116) is another Rastrelli landmark. His original design included a massive bell tower that would have been the tallest structure in Russia. The death of Empress Elizabeth in 1761 prevented him from completing it, however.

Rastrelli's baroque style would go out of fashion quickly after Elizabeth's death. But his legacy would endure, as he created some of the most stunning facades in the city, thus contributing to the Italianate appearance of St Petersburg today.

Catherine's Return to Classicism

Despite her fondness for Elizabeth personally, Catherine the Great was not a fan of her predecessor's increasingly elaborate and sumptuous displays of wealth and power. Catherine's major philosophical interest was the Enlightenment, which had brought the neoclassical style to the fore in Western Europe. As a result, she began her long reign by departing from baroque architecture and introducing neoclassicism to Russia.

The first major neoclassical masterpiece in Catherine's St Petersburg was the Academy of Arts (p137) on Vasilyevsky Island, designed by Jean-Baptiste-Michel Vallin de la Mothe. Catherine employed a wide range of architects, including foreigners such as Vallin de la Mothe, Charles Cameron, Antonio Rinaldi and Giacomo Quarenghi, as well as home-grown architects such as Ivan Starov and Vasily Bazhenov.

Catherine's plan was to make the palace embankment the centre-piece of the city. To this end, she commissioned the Little Hermitage by Vallin de la Mothe, followed by the Old Hermitage and the Hermitage Theatre (p94) on the other side of the Winter Canal. These buildings on Dvortsovaya pl were followed by Quarenghi's magnificent Marble Palace (p80). Catherine also developed the embankment west of the Winter Palace, now the English Embankment (Angliyskaya nab), creating a marvellous imperial vista for those arriving in the city by boat.

The single most meaningful addition under Catherine's reign was the *Bronze Horseman* (p81) by Etienne-Maurice Falconet, an eques-trian statue dedicated to Peter the Great. It is perched atop an enormous 1500-tonne boulder, known as the Thunder Stone, which is from the Gulf of Finland and is supposedly the largest stone ever moved.

Other notable additions to the cityscape during Catherine's reign included the new Gostiny Dvor (p96), one of the world's oldest surviving shopping centres. Elizabeth had commissioned Rastrelli to rebuild an arcade that had burned down in 1736; but Catherine removed Rastrelli from the project and had it completed by Vallin de la Mothe, who created a more subtle and understated neoclassical facade. The purest classical construction in St Petersburg was perhaps Vasily Stasov's Tauride Palace (p116), built for Prince Potemkin and surrounded by William Gould's expansive English-style gardens.

While wandering down Nevsky pr, don't miss the beautiful equestrian sculptures on the Anichkov Bridge and check out for yourself a local legend that says the sculptor portrayed a man he didn't like (some say it was Napoleon, others say it was his wife's lover) on the testicles of one of the stallions.

1. Smolny Cathedral (p116) 2. Bolshoy Gostiny Dvor (p96)
3. General Staff Building (p68) 4. Singer Building (p96)

Architectural Styles

St Petersburg will fascinate anyone with even a passing interest in architectural forms of the past three centuries. From baroque to austere Soviet via neoclassicism, Russian Empire style and Style Moderne, here are the more prominent styles you'll encounter.

Baroque

Best epitomised by Bartolomeo Rastrelli's **Smolny Cathedral** (p116), the baroque style in St Petersburg reached its zenith under Empress Elizabeth, and can be seen most prominently in the **Winter Palace** (p79). Other examples are the **Stroganov Palace** (p79) and the **Catherine Palace** (p165).

Neoclassical

The **Academy of Arts** (p137) is the most obvious example of the neoclassical style popular with Catherine the Great. With its references to the colonnaded architecture of ancient Greece and Rome, this is one of the most recognisable styles of the city and can also be seen in **Bolshoy Gostiny Dvor** (p96) and in the **Tauride Palace** (p116).

Russian Empire Style

Having defeated Napoleon, Russia under Alexander I and Nicholas I was ready for an architectural style of its own. Russian Empire style is best represented by the **General Staff Building** (p68), built by Carlo Rossi.

Style Moderne

Perhaps the style most associated with St Petersburg, Style Moderne remains one of its richest architectural legacies. One of its best examples is the **Singer Building** (p96).

Soviet Style

There are many different eras of Soviet architecture in the city, but there's no better example of this bombastic, intimidating and regimented style than the **House of Soviets** (p119).

Russian Empire Style

Alexander I (r 1801–25) ushered in the new century with much hope that he would see through Catherine's reforms, becoming the most progressive tsar yet. His most enduring architectural legacy would be the new Alexandrian Empire style, a Russian counterpart of the style that had become popular in prewar Napoleonic France. This style was pioneered by a new generation of architects, most famously Carlo Rossi.

Before the Napoleonic Wars, the two most significant additions to the cityscape were the Strelka (p136), the 'tongue of land' at the tip of Vasilyevsky Island, and the Kazan Cathedral (p79), prominently placed on Nevsky pr by Andrei Voronikhin. The Strelka had long been the subject of designs and proposals as a centrepiece to St Petersburg. Thomas de Thomon finally rebuilt Quarenghi's Stock Exchange and added the much-loved Rostral Columns to the tip of the island. The result was a stunning sight during summer festivities when the columns lit the sky with fire, a tradition that still continues today. The Kazan Cathedral is a fascinating anomaly in St Petersburg's architectural history. It had been commissioned by Tsar Paul I and reflected his tastes and desire to fuse Catholicism and Orthodoxy. As such it is strikingly un-Russian, borrowing many of its features from the contemporaneous Italian architecture of Rome and Florence.

Following the Napoleonic wars, Carlo Rossi initiated several projects of true genius. This Italian architect defined the historic heart of St Petersburg with his imperial buildings – arguably even more than Rastrelli. On Palace Sq, he created the sumptuous General Staff Building (p68), which managed to complement Rastrelli's Winter Palace without outshining it. The building's vast length, punctuated by white columns, and its magnificent triumphal arch make Palace Sq one of the most awe-inspiring urban environments in the world. The final touch to Palace Sq was added by Auguste Montferrand, who designed the

Arthur George's *St Petersburg* is the first comprehensive popular history of St Petersburg and is a superb read for anyone interested in the city's architectural development. Taking the reader from Petrine baroque to Stalinism, George is an expert guide to the differing styles that so define the city.

ST PETERSBURG GOES STYLE MODERNE

Industrialisation during the latter part of the 19th century brought huge wealth to the city, which resulted in an explosion of commissions for major public buildings and mansions, many in the much-feted style of the time – art nouveau, known in Russia as Style Moderne.

You only have to walk down Nevsky pr to see several of the key results of this daring architectural departure: the Singer Building (p96) and Kupetz Eliseevs (p96), both of which have been restored to their full glory in recent years, are ostentatious in their decorative details. Elsewhere in the historic heart, search out Au Pont Rouge (p85), a revival of the old department store Esders and Scheefhaals, which combines Moderne and Italianate features, and DLT (p97), finished in 1909 as the department store for the elite St Petersburg Guards regiments, and still operating as the city's most luxurious fashion house. The romantic interior of the Vitebsk Station (Vitebsky vokzal), crafted at the turn of the 19th century, offers up stained glass, sweeping staircases and beautiful wall paintings in its spacious waiting halls.

But it is over on the Petrograd Side, the most fashionable district of the era, that the majority of Style Moderne buildings can be found. Highlights include the Troitsky Most (p87), the fabulous mansion of the ballet dancer Mathilda Kshesinskaya (now the Museum of Political History; p147) and much of Kamennoostrovsky pr, which is lined with prime examples. Poke around the district's back streets to discover many gems from the early 20th century, including Chaev Mansion (p149) and Leuchtenberg House (p147).

MARIINSKY II: SUCCESS OR SCANDAL?

After a decade of debate, financial and legal wrangling, political involvement and abandoned plans, the Mariinsky II (p109), the showcase new ballet and opera house for the world-famous Mariinsky, finally opened its doors in May 2013. The second design for the building to have been approved, it's far from an iconic building, and has been compared to a shopping centre by some locals. Inside it's arguably far more interesting, and its sightlines and acoustics are superb. Go along and see a performance here while you're in St Petersburg to make up your own mind.

Alexander Column, a monument to the 1812 trouncing of Napoleon. Rossi also completed the Mikhailovsky Palace (now the Russian Museum; p70) as well as the gardens behind it and pl Iskusstv (Arts Sq; p84) in front of it.

Rossi's genius continued to shine through the reactionary rule of Nicholas I. In fact, Nicholas was the last of the Romanovs to initiate mass municipal architecture, and so Rossi remained in favour, despite Nicholas' personal preference for the Slavic Revival style that was very popular in Moscow at the time.

Rossi's largest projects under Nicholas were the redesign of Senate Sq (now pl Dekabristov) and Alexandrinskaya Sq (now pl Ostrovskogo), including the Alexandrinsky Theatre and Theatre St (now ul Zodchego Rossi). The Theatre St ensemble is a masterpiece of proportions: its width (22m) is the same height as its buildings, and the entire length of the street is exactly 10 times the width (220m).

Imperial St Petersburg

Although Rossi continued to transform the city, the building that would redefine the city's skyline was Montferrand's St Isaac's Cathedral (p78). An Orthodox church built in a classical style, it is the fourth-largest cathedral in Europe. Montferrand's unique masterpiece took over three decades to construct and remains the highest building in central St Petersburg.

The reigns of Alexander II and Alexander III saw few changes to the overall building style in St Petersburg. Industrialisation under Alexander II meant filling in several canals, most significantly the Ligovsky Canal (now Ligovsky pr). A plan to fill in Griboyedov Canal thankfully proved too expensive to execute and the canal remains one of the city's most charming.

The main contribution of Alexander III was the Church of the Resurrection of Christ, better known as the Church on the Spilled Blood (p77), built on the site of his father's 1881 assassination. Alexander III insisted the church be in the Slavic Revival style, which explains its uncanny similarity to St Basil's Cathedral on Red Square in Moscow. Architects Malyshev and Parland designed its spectacular multicoloured tiling, the first hints of Russian Style Moderne, which by the end of the 19th century would take the city by storm. Painters such as Mikhail Nesterov and Mikhail Vrubel contributed to the interior design.

Soviet Leningrad

As in all other spheres of Russian culture, the collapse of the tsarist regime in 1917 led to huge changes in architecture. In the beleaguered city, all major building projects stopped; the palaces of the aristocracy and the mansions of the merchant classes were turned over to the state or split up into communal apartments. As the Germans approached Petrograd in 1918, the title of capital returned to Moscow; the city went into a decline that was to last until the 1990s.

The architectural form that found favour under the Bolsheviks in the 1920s was constructivism. Combining utilitarianism and utopianism, this modern style sought to advance the socialist cause, using technological innovation and slick unembellished design. Pl Stachek is rich with such buildings, such as the Kirov Region Administrative Building on Kirovskaya pl and the incredibly odd Communication Workers' Palace of Culture on the Moyka Canal.

Stalin considered the opulence of the imperial centre of renamed Leningrad to be a potentially corrupting influence on the people. So, from 1927, he began to relocate the centre to the south of the city's historic heart. His traditional neoclassical tastes prevailed. The prime example of Stalinist architecture is the vast House of Soviets (p119), which was meant to be the centrepiece of the new city centre. Noi Trotsky began this magnificent monstrosity in 1936, although it was not finished until after the war (by which time Trotsky had himself been purged). With its columns and bas-reliefs, it is a great example of Stalinist neoclassical design – similar in many ways to the imperial neoclassicism pioneered a century earlier. The House of Soviets was never used as the Leningrad government building, as the plan to relocate the centre was shelved after Stalin's death in 1953.

WWII and Stalin's old age saved many buildings of great importance: the Church on the Spilled Blood, for example, was slated for destruction before the German invasion of the Soviet Union intervened. Many other churches and historical buildings, however, were destroyed.

During the eras of Khrushchev and Brezhnev, St Petersburg's imperial heritage was cautiously respected, as the communist leadership took a step back from Stalin's excesses. Between the 1950s and 1970s, a housing shortage led to the construction of high-rise Soviet apartment buildings, which would cover huge swaths of the city outside the historic centre. For many visitors, this is their first and last view of the city. Examples of archetypal post-Stalinist Soviet architecture include the massive Grand Concert Hall, near pl Vosstaniya, and the nondescript Finland Station (Finlyandsky vokzal; p153), on the Vyborg Side.

The planned total regeneration of New Holland being undertaken at present will probably be one of the most exciting architectural projects of the next decade. As well as art and educational spaces, there are plans to incorporate a hotel, restaurants, shops, a cinema and a park.

Contemporary St Petersburg

Following the end of communism in the early 1990s, efforts were focused on the reconstruction of imperial-era buildings, many of which were derelict and literally falling down due to 70 years of neglect. Between 1991 and St Petersburg's tercentennial celebrations in 2003, much of the historic heart was restored at vast expense, although efforts are still continuing today.

The governorship of Valentina Matvienko (2003–11) was marked by a shift from preservation to construction, and the city saw a large growth in new building projects during this time, not always to the delight of campaigners for the protection of St Petersburg's architectural heritage, or Unesco, who awarded St Petersburg's historic centre World Heritage status in 1990. The most noteworthy of contemporary architecture projects in St Petersburg are the construction of the Mariinsky II next to the Mariinsky Theatre, and, even more controversially, the Okhta Centre. This 400m-tall skyscraper was originally slated to be built next to the Smolny Cathedral but after worldwide condemnation and an unusually strong local protest movement it was relocated far from the city centre. It is currently due to be completed in 2018.

Arts

Despite the evident European influences, St Petersburg's Russian roots are a more essential source of inspiration for its artistic genius. Musicians and writers have long looked to Russian history, folk culture and other national themes. That St Petersburg has produced so many artistic and musical masterpieces is in itself a source of wonder for the city's visitors and inhabitants today, and it's no coincidence that St Petersburg is often referred to as Russia's cultural capital.

Ballet

First introduced in the 17th century, ballet in Russia evolved as an offshoot of French dance combined with Russian folk and peasant dance techniques. In 1738, French dance master Jean Baptiste Lande established the Imperial Ballet School in St Petersburg – a precursor to the famed Vaganova School of Choreography.

The French dancer and choreographer Marius Petipa (1819–1910) is considered the father of Russian ballet, acting as principal dancer and premier ballet master of the Imperial Theatres and Imperial Ballet. All told, he produced more than 60 full ballets, including the classics *Sleeping Beauty* and *Swan Lake*.

In 1907, Petipa wrote in his diary, 'I can state that I created a ballet company of which everyone said: St Petersburg has the greatest ballet in all Europe.' At the turn of the 20th century, the heyday of Russian ballet, St Petersburg's Imperial Ballet School rose to world prominence, producing superstar after superstar. Names such as Vaslav Nijinsky, Anna Pavlova, Mathilda Kshesinskaya, George Balanchine, Michel Fokine and Olga Spessivtzeva turned the Mariinsky Theatre into the world's most dynamic display of the art of dance.

Sergei Diaghilev graduated from the St Petersburg Conservatory in 1892, but he abandoned his dream of becoming a composer when his professor, Nikolai Rimsky-Korsakov, told him he had no talent for music. Instead he turned his attention to dance, and his Ballets Russes took Europe by storm. The Petipa-inspired choreography was daring and dynamic, and the stage decor was painted by artists such as Alexander Benois, Mikhail Larionov, Natalya Goncharova and Leon Bakst. The overall effect was an artistic, awe-inducing display unlike anything taking place elsewhere in Europe.

Under the Soviets, ballet was treated as a natural resource. It enjoyed highly privileged status, which allowed schools such as Vaganova and companies such as the Kirov to maintain a level of lavish production and no-expense-spared star-searches. Still, the story of 20th-century Russian ballet is connected with the West, to where so many of its brightest stars emigrated or defected. Anna Pavlova, Vaslav Nijinsky, Rudolf Nurcyev, Mikhail Baryshnikov, George Balanchine, Natalya Makarova, Mathilda Kshesinskaya, to name a few, all found fame in Western Europe or America, and most of them ended up living there.

The Kirov, now known by its pre-revolutionary name, the Mariinsky, has its home at the Mariinsky Theatre (p109) and has been rejuvenated

Of the huge range of productions it's possible to see at the Mariinsky Theatre, Prokofiev's thoroughly modernist ballet *Romeo and Juliet* is perhaps one of the most enjoyable. It premiered on this very stage in 1940 and has changed little since – a true classic.

under the fervent directorship of artistic director Valery Gergiev. The Mariinsky's calling card has always been its flawless classical ballet, but in recent years names such as William Forsythe and John Neumeier have brought modern choreography to this establishment. The Mariinsky's credibility on the world stage has been bolstered by the 2013 opening of the Mariinsky II (p109), built adjacent to the original theatre on the Kryukov Canal.

Some of the hottest tickets in town are for the new Mariinsky II theatre, which opened in 2013. Book early at www.mariinsky.ru to guarantee your seats for famous operas and ballets, and for anything during the month of June!

Music

St Petersburg has a rich musical legacy, dating back to the days when the Group of Five (Mily Balakirev, Alexander Borodin, César Cui, Modest Mussorgsky and Nikolai Rimsky-Korsakov) and Pyotr Tchaikovsky composed here. Opera and classical music continue to draw crowds, and the three Mariinsky theatres and Philharmonia regularly sell out their performances of home-grown classics. Surprisingly, earlier music, such as baroque and medieval, is not as well known or as well loved, though the citys' Early Music Festival has long campaigned to change that.

Music lovers come in all shapes and sizes, however. Even when rock and roll was illegal it was played in basements and garages. Now, 20 years after the weight of censorship was lifted, St Petersburg is the centre of *russky rok,* a magnet for musicians and music lovers, who are drawn to its atmosphere of innovation and creation.

Classical Music & Opera

As the cultural heart of Russia, St Petersburg was a natural draw for generations of composers, its rich cultural life acting as inspiration for talent from throughout Russia. Mikhail Glinka is often considered the father of Russian classical music. In 1836 his opera *A Life for the Tsar* premiered in St Petersburg. While European musical influences were evident, the story was based on Russian history, recounting the dramatic tale of a peasant, Ivan Susanin, who sacrificed himself to save Mikhail Romanov.

In the second half of the 19th century, several influential schools – based in the capital – formed, from which emerged some of Russia's most famous composers and finest music. The Group of Five looked to folk music for uniquely Russian themes. They tried to develop a distinct sound using unusual tonal and harmonic devices. Their main opponent was Anton Rubinstein's conservatively rooted Russian Musical Society, which became the St Petersburg Conservatory in 1861. The competition between the two schools was fierce. Rimsky-Korsakov wrote in his memoirs: 'Rubinstein had a reputation as a pianist, but was thought to have neither talent nor taste as a composer.'

Tchaikovsky (1840–93) seemed to find the middle ground, embracing Russian folklore and music as well as the disciplines of the Western European composers. In 1890 Tchaikovsky's *Queen of Spades* premiered at the Mariinsky. His adaptation of the famous Pushkin tale surprised and invigorated the artistic community, especially as his deviations from the original text – infusing it with more cynicism and a brooding sense of doom – tied the piece to contemporary St Petersburg.

Tchaikovsky is widely regarded as the doyen of Russian national composers and his compositions, including the magnificent *1812 Overture,* concertos, symphonies, ballets (*Swan Lake, Sleeping Beauty* and *The Nutcracker*) and operas *(Yevgeny Onegin),* are among the world's most popular classical works.

Following in Tchaikovsky's romantic footsteps was the innovative Igor Stravinsky (1882–1971). He fled Russia after the revolution, but his memoirs credit his childhood in St Petersburg as having a major effect on his music. *The Rite of Spring* (which created a furore at its first performance in Paris), *Petrouchka* and *The Firebird* were all influenced by Russian folk music. The official Soviet line was that Stravinsky was a 'political and ideological renegade'; but he was rehabilitated after he visited the USSR and was formally received by Khrushchev himself.

Similarly, the ideological beliefs and experimental style of Dmitry Shostakovich (1906–75) led to him being alternately praised and condemned by the Soviet government. As a student at the Petrograd conservatory, Shostakovich failed his exams in Marxist methodology, but still managed to write his First Symphony before he graduated in 1926. He wrote brooding, bizarrely dissonant works, as well as accessible traditional classical music. After official condemnation by Stalin, his Seventh Symphony (Leningrad Symphony) brought him honour and international standing when it was performed during WWII. The authorities changed their mind and banned his anti-Soviet music in 1948, then 'rehabilitated' him after Stalin's death. These days he is held in high esteem as the namesake of the acclaimed Shostakovich Philharmonia (p93).

Since becoming its artistic director in 1988, Valery Gergiev has revitalised the Mariinsky (p109). The Russian classics still top the list of performances, but Gergiev is also willing to be a little adventurous, taking on operas that had not been performed in half a century or more. Gergiev is also responsible for initiating the Stars of White Nights Festival, an annual event that showcases the best and brightest dancers and musicians.

Rock

Russian music is not all about classical composers. Ever since the 'bourgeois' Beatles filtered through in the 1960s, Russians both young and old have supported the rock revolution. Starved of decent equipment and the chance to record or perform to big audiences, Russian rock groups initially developed underground. By the 1970s – the Soviet hippy era – rock music had developed a huge following among the disaffected, distrustful youth in Leningrad.

Although bands initially imitated their Western counterparts, a real underground sound emerged in Leningrad in the 1980s. Boris Grebenshchikov and his band Akvarium (Aquarium) caused sensations wherever they performed; his folk rock and introspective lyrics became the emotional cry of a generation. Yury Shevchuk and his band DDT emerged as the country's main rock band. The god of Russian rock was Viktor Tsoy and his group Kino. His early death in a 1990 car crash ensured his legend would have a long life. On the anniversary of Tsoy's death (15 August), fans still gather to play his tunes and remember the musician, especially at his grave at the Bogoslovskoe Cemetery, which is located a short distance from the Piskaryovskoe Cemetery (p153). A former boilerhouse bunker where Tsoy and his Kino bandmates once worked as caretakers is now a shrine-cum-concert-venue (Kamchatka; p157) on the Petrograd Side.

Visual Arts

It should come as no surprise that St Petersburg is an artistic place, having been designed by the leading artists of the day. In the early years, aristocrats and emperors filled their palaces with endless collections of paintings and applied arts, guaranteeing a steady stream of

For a truly surreal night at the opera, treat yourself to tickets to see the Mariinsky's production of Shostakovich's opera *The Nose*, based on the hilarious satirical short story by Nikolai Gogol about a socially aspirant bureaucrat who wakes up one morning to find his nose has left him and is gadding around town.

Five Classic St Petersburg Albums

Kino – Gruppa Krovi

Leningrad – Piraty XXI Veka

Akvarium – Peski Peterburga

DDT – Chorny Pyos Peterburg

Dva Samolyota – Ubitsy Sredi Nas

artistic production. These days, hundreds of thousands of visitors come here to see the masterpieces that hang in the Hermitage (p54) and the Russian Museum (p70).

But St Petersburg's artistic tradition is not only historical. The city's winding waterways, crumbling castles and colourful characters continue to inspire creative types and in recent years the city has become a nurturing space for artists to work, with plentiful studios, gallery spaces and new museums interested in modern work. Anyone interested in the state of contemporary art in the city should head to Loft Project ETAGI (p120), the Rizzordi Art Foundation (p120) and the Street Art Museum (p154). St Petersburg has always been a city of artists and poets, and that legacy endures.

Academy of Arts

This state-run artistic institution was founded in 1757 by Count Ivan Shuvalov, a political adviser, education minister and longtime lover of Empress Elizabeth. It was Catherine the Great who moved the Academy out of Shuvalov's home, commissioning the present neoclassical building on Vasilyevsky Island (p137).

The Academy was responsible for the education and training of young artists. It focused heavily on French-influenced academic art, which incorporated neoclassicism and romanticism. Painters such as Fyodor Alexeyev and Grigory Chernetsev came out of the Academy of Arts.

The Wanderers

In the 19th century, artist Ivan Kramskoy led the so-called 'revolt of 14' whereby a group of upstart artists broke away from the powerful but conservative Academy of Arts. The mutineers considered that art should be a force for national awareness and social change, and they depicted common people and real problems in their paintings. The Wanderers (Peredvizhniki), as they called themselves, travelled around the country in an attempt to widen their audience (thus inspiring their moniker).

The Wanderers included Vasily Surikov, who painted vivid Russian historical scenes, and Nicholas Ghe, who favoured both historical and biblical landscapes. Perhaps the best-loved of all Russian artists, Ilya Repin has works that range from social criticism (*Barge Haulers on the Volga*) to history (*Cossacks Writing a Letter to the Turkish Sultan*) to portraits.

By the end of the 19th century, Russian culture was retreating from Western influences and looking instead to nationalistic themes and folk culture for inspiration. Artists at this time invented the *matryoshka,* the quintessential Russian nesting doll. One of the world's largest collections of *matryoshki* is on display at the Toy Museum (p149).

Mikhail Vrubel was inspired by Byzantine mosaics and Russian fairy tales. Painters such as Nikolai Roerich and Mikhail Nesterov incorporated mystical themes, influenced by folklore and religious traditions. All of these masters are prominently featured at the Russian Museum (p70).

Avant-Garde

From about 1905 Russian art became a maelstrom of groups, styles and 'isms', as it absorbed decades of European change in a few years. It finally gave birth to its own avant-garde futurist movements.

Mikhail Larionov and Natalya Goncharova were the centre of a Cézanne-influenced group known as the Knave of Diamonds. This husband-and-wife team went on to develop neo-primitivism, based

---

Best Artist House-Museums

....

Rimsky-Korsakov Flat-Museum (Smolny & Vosstaniya)

....

Chaliapin House Museum (Petrograd & Vyborg Sides)

....

Anna Akhmatova Museum at the Fountain House (Smolny & Vosstaniya)

....

Brodsky-House Museum (Historic Heart)

on popular arts and primitive icons. They worked closely with Sergei Diaghilev, the founder of Ballets Russes, designing costumes and sets for the ballet company that brought together some of the era's greatest dancers, composers and artists.

The most radical members of the Knave of Diamonds formed a group known as Donkey's Tail, which exhibited the influences of cubism and futurism. Larionov and Goncharova were key members of this group, as well as Marc Chagall and Kazimir Malevich.

In 1915 Malevich announced the arrival of suprematism. His abstract geometrical shapes (with the black square representing the ultimate 'zero form') freed artists from having to depict the material world and made art a doorway to higher realities. See one of his four *Black Square* paintings, and other examples of Russian avant-garde, at the General Staff Building (p68).

Soviet Art

Futurists turned to the needs of the revolution – education, posters, banners – with enthusiasm. They had a chance to act on their theories of how art shapes society. But at the end of the 1920s abstract art fell out of favour. The Communist Party wanted socialist realism. Images abounded of striving workers, heroic soldiers and healthy toiling peasants, some of which are on display at the Russian Museum (p70). Two million sculptures of Lenin and Stalin dotted the country; Malevich ended up painting portraits and doing designs for Red Square parades.

After Stalin, an avant-garde 'Conceptualist' underground group was allowed to form. Ilya Kabakov painted, or sometimes just arranged, the debris of everyday life to show the gap between the promises and realities of Soviet existence. Erik Bulatov's 'Sotsart' pointed to the devaluation of language by ironically reproducing Soviet slogans or depicting words disappearing over the horizon. In 1962 artists set up a show of 'unofficial' art in Moscow: Khrushchev called it 'dog shit' and sent it back underground. Soviet underground art is particularly well represented in the collection of the excellent Erarta Museum of Contemporary Art (p135) on Vasilyevsky Island.

For an engaging account of how culture and politics became intertwined during the early Soviet period, read Solomon Volkov's *Shostakovich and Stalin*, which examines the fascinating relationship between two of the main representatives of each field.

Neo-Academism & Non-Conformist Art

As the centre of the avant-garde movement in Russia at the turn of the last century, St Petersburg never gave up its ties to barrier-breaking, gut-wrenching, head-scratching art. After the end of communism the city rediscovered its seething artistic underbelly.

SERGEI KURYOKHIN

A key figure in the Leningrad undergound and a national star of the avant-garde in post-Soviet Russia, Sergei Kuryokhin (1954–96) is little known outside his homeland, but he casts a long shadow over St Petersburg's music and art scene. As an accomplished musician, activist, actor, artist and writer Kuryokhin became a big star during the years of *glasnost* (openness), even collaborating with local supergroup Akvarium on several albums, and starring in several popular countercultural films. He remains perhaps best known for scandalising Soviet society during the last days of the USSR by claiming on a TV show to have evidence that Lenin had been a mushroom. He died suddenly in 1996 from a heart condition, but his legacy of non-conformism and artistic originality is continued at the Sergei Kuryokhin Contemporary Art Centre (p141), on Vasilyevsky Island, where annual events include the excellent Sergei Kuryokhin International Festival of avant-garde music and the Electro-Mechanica electronic music and audiovisual festival.

Much of St Petersburg's post-Soviet contemporary art revolved around the artistic collective at Pushkinskaya 10 (p119), where artists and musicians continue to congregate and create. This place was 'founded' in the late 1980s, when a bunch of artists and musicians moved into an abandoned building near Pl Vosstaniya. The centre has since developed into an artistic and cultural institution that is unique in Russia, if not the world, even if its heyday has long now passed.

In the early 1990s Timur Novikov founded the Neo-Academic movement as an antidote to 'the barbarism of modernism'. This return to classicism (albeit with a street-level, junk-shop feel) culminated in his foundation of the Museum of the New Academy of Fine Arts, which is housed at Pushkinskaya 10. Although he died in 2002, he continues to cast a long shadow on the city's artistic scene.

More commercial ventures currently dominate the St Petersburg art scene, however, with such so-called 'creative spaces' as Loft Project ETAGI (p120) and Tkachi (p129) blurring the lines between commerce and art. Smaller, private galleries in the centre of town also showcase contemporary art, while the commerical galleries at the Erarta Museum remain the best place to look at Petersburg's current artistic output.

Cinema

The Lenfilm studio on the Petrograd Side was a centre of the Soviet film industry, producing many much-loved Russian comedies and dramas – most famously, Sergei Eisenstein's *October* (1928). Lenfilm has continued in the post-communist era to work with some success as a commercial film studio. However, the removal of Soviet-era state funding for film-making has inevitably led to torpor in the local industry.

A charming and whimsical film, Alexey Uchitel's *The Stroll* (Progulka, 2003), follows three young Petersburgers as they wander around the city getting into all sorts of situations, from a soccer riot to an argument between friends and a rainstorm. Great for St Petersburg local colour.

There are, of course, exceptions. Ever since *Russian Ark* (2002), St Petersburg native Alexander Sokurov has been recognised as one of Russia's most talented contemporary directors. The world's first unedited feature film, *Russian Ark* was shot in one unbroken 90-minute frame. Sokurov's films have tackled a wide range of subjects, most significantly the corrupting influence of power, which was explored in a tetralogy of films observing individual cases, including Hitler *(Molokh)*, Lenin *(Taurus)*, Japanese Emperor Hirohito *(The Sun)* and Faust *(Faust)*. Another Sokurov production that was critically acclaimed is *Alexandra* (2007), the moving tale of an elderly woman who visits her grandson at an army base in Chechnya. The title role is played by Galina Vishnevskaya, opera doyenne and wife of composer-conductor Mstislav Rostropovich.

Another star of the St Petersburg film industry was Alexey German, who gained attention with his 1998 film *Khrustalyov, My Car!* Based on a story by Joseph Brodsky, the film tells the tale of a well-loved military doctor who was arrested during Stalin's 'Doctor's Plot'. German died in 2013, leaving his final film, *Hard to Be a God*, almost finished. It was completed with the help of his son and wife, and garnered excellent reviews from critics. The film, which *Variety* called 'utterly incomprehensible', took a decade to make and tells the story of a planet trapped in the dark ages.

Other Lenfilm successes include Alexey Balabanov's *Of Freaks and Men*, the joint project of Boris Frumin and Yury Lebedev, *Undercover*, and Andrei Kravchuk's *The Italian*, all of which enjoyed some critical acclaim in the West.

Theatre

While it may not be completely accessible to most travellers due to language barriers, theatre plays a major role in St Petersburg performing arts. At least a dozen drama and comedy theatres dot the city streets, not to mention puppet theatres and musical theatres. As in all areas of the performing arts, contemporary playwrights do not receive as much attention as well-known greats and adaptations of famous literature. Nonetheless, drama has a long history in Russia and St Petersburg, as the cultural capital, has always been at the forefront.

In the early days, theatre was an almost exclusive vehicle of the Orthodox Church, used to spread its message and convert believers. In the 19th century, however, vaudeville found its way to Russia. More often than not, these biting, satirical one-act comedies poked fun at the rich and powerful. Playwrights such as Alexander Pushkin and Mikhail Lermontov decried the use of their art as a tool of propaganda or evangelism. Other writers – Nikolai Gogol, Alexander Griboyedov and Alexander Ostrovsky – took it a step further, writing plays that attacked not just the aristocracy but the bourgeoisie as well. Anton Chekhov wrote for St Petersburg newspapers before writing one-act, vaudevillian works. Yet it is his full-length plays that are his legacy.

Towards the end of the 19th century Maxim Gorky represented an expansion of this trend in anti-establishment theatre. His play *The Song of the Stormy Petrel* raised workers to a level superior to that of the intellectual. This production was the first of what would be many socialist realist performances, thus earning its author the esteem of the Soviet authorities.

The futurists had their day on the stage, mainly in the productions of the energetic and tirelessly inventive director Vsevolod Meyerhold, who was one of the most influential figures of modern theatre. His productions of Alexander Blok's *The Fair Show Booth* (1906) and Vladimir Mayakovsky's *Mystery-Bouffe* (1918) both caused a sensation at the time. Both Anna Akhmatova and Dmitry Shostakovich cited Meyerhold's 1935 production of *Queen of Spades* by Tchaikovsky as one of the era's most influential works.

During the Soviet period, drama was used primarily as a propaganda tool. When foreign plays were performed, it was for a reason – hence the popularity in Russia of *Death of a Salesman,* which showed the inevitable result of Western greed and decadence. However, just after the revolution, theatre artists were given great, if short-lived, freedom to experiment – anything to make theatre accessible to the masses. Avantgarde productions flourished for a while, notably under the mastery of poet and director Igor Terentyev. Artists such as Pavel Filonov and Kazimir Malevich participated in production and stage design.

Even socialist theatre was strikingly experimental: the Theatre of Worker Youth, under the guidance of Mikhail Sokolovsky, used only amateur actors and encouraged improvisation, sudden plot alterations and interaction with audience members, striving to redefine the theatregoing experience. Free theatre tickets were given out at factories; halls that once echoed with the jangle of upper-class audience's jewellery were now filled with sailors and workers. The tradition of sending army regiments and schoolchildren to the theatre continues to this day.

Today theatre remains important to the city's intellectuals, but it isn't at the forefront of the arts, receiving little state support and, unlike the ballet or opera, unable to earn revenues from touring abroad. If you're interested in the state of contemporary Russian theatre, the Maly Drama Theatre (p128), Baltic House (p157) and the Priyut Komedianta Theatre (p94) are particularly worth checking out.

For a comprehensive rundown of the history of drama from classical staging to the revolutionary works of Meyerhold and Mayakovsky, see Konstantin Rudnitsky's excellent *Russian & Soviet Theatre: Tradition & the Avant-Garde.*

ARTS THEATRE

Literature

St Petersburg's very existence, a brand-new city for a brand-new Russia, seems sometimes to be the stuff of fiction. Indeed, its early history is woven into the fabric of one of Russia's most famous epic poems, Pushkin's *The Bronze Horseman*, which muses on the fate of the city through the eyes of Falconet's famous equestrian statue of Peter the Great. In just three centuries the city has produced more great writers than many cities do over a millennium.

Romanticism in the Golden Age

Among the many ways that Peter and Catherine the Great brought Westernisation and modernisation to Russia was the introduction of a modern alphabet. Prior to this time, written Russian was used almost exclusively in the Orthodox church, which employed an archaic and incomprehensible Church Slavonic. During the Petrine era, it became increasingly acceptable to use popular language in literature and this development paved the way for two centuries of Russian literary prolificacy, with St Petersburg at its centre.

Romanticism was a reaction against the strict social rules and scientific rationalisation of previous periods, exalting emotion and aesthetics. Nobody embraced Russian romanticism more than the national bard, Alexander Pushkin, who lived and died in St Petersburg. Most famously, his last address on the Moyka River is now a suitably hagiographic museum, its interior preserved exactly as it was at the moment of his death in 1837 (p83). The duel that killed him is also remembered with a monument on the site (p153).

Pushkin's epic poem *Yevgeny Onegin* (often *Eugene Onegin* in English) is partly set in the imperial capital. Pushkin savagely ridicules its foppish aristocratic society, despite being a fairly consistent fixture of it himself for most of his adult life. The wonderful short story *The Queen of Spades* is set in the house of a countess on Nevsky pr and is the weird supernatural tale of a man who uncovers her Mephistophelean gambling trick. Published posthumously, *The Bronze Horseman* is named for the statue of Peter the Great that stands on pl Dekabristov (p81). The story takes place during the great flood of 1824. The main character is the lowly clerk Yevgeny, who has lost his beloved in the flood. Representing the hopes of the common people, he takes on the empire-building spirit of Peter the Great, represented by the animation of the *Bronze Horseman*.

No other figure in world literature is more closely connected with St Petersburg than Fyodor Dostoevsky (1821–81). He was among the first writers to navigate the murky waters of the human subconscious, blending powerful prose with psychology, philosophy and spirituality. Born in Moscow, Dostoevsky moved to Petersburg to study in 1838, aged 16, and he began his literary and journalistic career there, living at dozens of addresses in the seedy and poverty-stricken area around Sennaya pl, where many of his novels are set.

Four Statues of Pushkin in St Petersburg

Ploshchad Iskusstv (Historic Heart)

Pushkin House (Vasilyevsky Island)

Pushkinskaya ul (Smolny & Vosstaniya)

Site of Pushkin's Duel (Petrograd & Vyborg Sides)

Pushkin statue outside the Russian Museum (p70)

His career was halted – but ultimately shaped – by his casual involvement with a group of young free thinkers called the Petrashevsky Circle, some of whom planned to overthrow the tsar. Nicholas I decided to make an example of some of these liberals by having them arrested and sentencing them to death. After a few months in the Peter and Paul Fortress prison, Dostoevsky and his cohorts were assembled for execution. As the guns were aimed and ready to fire, the death sentence was suddenly called off and the group was committed instead to a sentence of hard labour in Siberia. After Dostoevsky was pardoned by Alexander II and returned to St Petersburg, he wrote *Notes from the House of the Dead* (1861), a vivid recounting of his prison sojourn.

The ultimate St Petersburg novel and literary classic is Dostoevsky's *Crime and Punishment* (1866). It is a tale of redemption, but also acknowledges the 'other side' of the regal capital: the gritty, dirty city that spawned unsavoury characters and unabashed poverty. It's a great novel to read before visiting St Petersburg, as the Sennaya district in which it's largely set retains its dark and sordid atmosphere a century and a half later.

In his later works, *The Idiot, The Possessed* and *The Brothers Karamazov,* Dostoevsky was explicit in his criticism of the revolutionary movement as being morally bankrupt. A true believer, he asserted that only by following Christ's ideal could humanity be saved. An incorrigible Russophile, Dostoevsky eventually turned against St Petersburg and its European tendencies. His final home near Vladimirskaya pl now houses the Dostoevsky Museum (p120), and he is buried at Tikhvin Cemetery within the walls of the Alexander Nevsky Monastery (p114), a suitably Orthodox setting for such a devout believer.

Crime and Punishment may be on everyone's reading list before they head to the northern capital, but another (far shorter) St Petersburg work from Dostoevsky is *White Nights,* a wonderful short story that has been adapted for cinema by no less than nine different directors.

Dostoevsky portrait in a Nevsky Prospekt cafe

Amid the epic works of Pushkin and Dostoevsky, the absurdist short-story writer Nikolai Gogol (1809–52) sometimes gets lost. But his troubled genius created some of Russian literature's most memorable characters, including Akaki Akakievich, tragicomic hero of *The Overcoat,* and the brilliant social-climber Major Kovalyov, who chases his errant nose around St Petersburg in the absurdist masterpiece *The Nose.* Gogol came to St Petersburg from his native Ukraine in 1829, and wrote and lived here for a decade before spending his final years abroad. He was not impressed by the legendary capital: in a letter to his mother he described it as a place where 'people seem more dead than alive' and complained endlessly about the air pressure, which he believed caused illness. He was nevertheless inspired to write a number of absurdist stories, collectively known as *The Petersburg Tales,* which are generally recognised as the zenith of his creativity.

If you want to get inside the mind of St Petersburg's most surreal writer, try Simon Karlinsky's explosive *The Sexual Labyrinth of Nikolai Gogol,* which argues that the key to understanding the writer was that he was a self-hating homo-sexual. Supported very strongly by textual analysis, the book is convincing, if rather polemical.

Symbolism in the Silver Age

The late 19th century saw the rise of the symbolist movement, which emphasised individualism and creativity, purporting that artistic endeavours were exempt from the rules that bound other parts of society. The Stray Dog Café, an underground bar on pl Iskusstv (Arts Sq), was a popular meeting place where symbolist writers, musicians and artists exchanged ideas and shared their work.

Alexander Blok and Andrei Bely, who both lived in St Petersburg, were the most renowned writers of the symbolist movement. While Bely was well known and respected for his essays and philosophical discourses, it is his mysterious novel *Petersburg* for which he is remembered. The plot, however difficult to follow, revolves around a revolutionary who is hounded by the Bronze Horseman (the same statue that harasses Pushkin's Yevgeny) and is ordered to carry out the assassination of his own father, a high-ranking tsarist official, by his revolutionary cell. Many critics see Bely's masterpiece as a forerunner of Joyce's far later modernist experiments in *Ulysses,* even though *Petersburg* wasn't even translated into English until the 1950s.

Blok took over where Dostoevsky left off, writing of prostitutes, drunks and other characters marginalised by society. Blok sympathised with the revolutions and he was praised by the Bolsheviks once they came to power in 1917. His poem *The Twelve,* published in 1918, is pretty much a love letter to Lenin. However, he later became disenchanted with the revolution and consequently fell out of favour; he died a sad, lonely poet in 1921, before his fall out with the communists could have more serious consequences.

Revolutionary Literature

The immediate aftermath of 1917 saw a creative upswing in Russia. Inspired by social change, writers carried over these principles into their work, pushing revolutionary ideas and ground-breaking styles.

The trend was temporary, of course. The Bolsheviks were no connoisseurs of culture, and the new leadership did not appreciate literature unless it directly supported the goals of communism. Some writers managed to write within the system, penning some excellent poetry and plays in the 1920s; however, most found little inspiration in the prevailing climate of art 'serving the people'. Stalin later announced that writers were 'engineers of the human soul' and as such had a responsibility to write in a partisan direction.

The clampdown on diverse literary styles culminated in the early 1930s with the creation of socialist realism, a literary form created to promote the needs of the state, praise industrialisation and demonise social misfits. While Stalin's propaganda machine was churning out novels with titles such as *How the Steel Was Tempered* and *Cement,* St Petersburg's literary community was secretly writing about life under tyranny. The tradition of underground writing, which had been long established under the Romanovs, once again flourished.

Literature of Dissent & Emigration

Throughout the 20th century, many talented writers were faced with silence, exile or death as a result of the Soviet system. Many accounts of Soviet life were *samizdat* (literally 'self-publishing') publications, secretly circulated among the literary community. The Soviet Union's most celebrated writers – the likes of Boris Pasternak, Alexander Solzhenitsyn, Mikhail Bulgakov and Andrei Bitov – were silenced in their own country, while their works received international acclaim. Others left Russia in the turmoil of the revolution and its bloody aftermath, including perhaps St Petersburg's greatest 20th-century writer, Vladimir Nabokov.

Born to a supremely wealthy and well-connected St Petersburg family in 1899, the 18-year-old Nabokov was forced to leave St Petersburg in 1917 due to his father's previous role in the Provisional Government. Leaving Russia altogether in 1919, Nabokov was never to return to his homeland and died in Switzerland in 1977. His fascinating autobiography, *Speak, Memory,* is a wonderful recollection of his idyllic Russian childhood amid the gathering clouds of revolution, and the house he grew up in now houses the small, but very worthwhile, Nabokov Museum (p104).

No literary figure is as inextricably linked to the fate of St Petersburg-Petrograd-Leningrad as Anna Akhmatova (1889–1966), the long-suffering poet whose work contains bittersweet depictions of the city

Another very original interpretation of Gogol can be found in Vladimir Nabokov's wonderful biography, *Nikolai Gogol.* Written in English by the polyglot Nabokov, it discusses in English the impact of much of Gogol's Russian language – something quite inaccessible to most readers!

she loved. Akhmatova's family was imprisoned and killed, her friends were exiled, tortured and arrested, and her colleagues were constantly hounded – but she refused to leave her beloved city and died there in 1966. Her former residence in the Fountain House now contains the Anna Akhmatova Museum (p118), a fascinating and humbling place.

Akhmatova was the dazzling Petrograd poet of the so-called Silver Age of Russian poetry. She was well travelled, internationally feted and an incorrigible free spirit who, despite having the chance after the revolution, decided not to leave Russia and go abroad. This decision sealed her fate, and within a few years her ex-husband would be shot by the Bolsheviks, and decades of harassment and proscription would follow as Akhmatova's work was denounced by Communist Party officials as 'the poetry of a crazed lady, chasing back and forth between boudoir and chapel'.

However, as a reward for her cooperation with the authorities in the war effort, Akhmatova was allowed to publish again after WWII. Nonetheless, she was cautious, and she worked in secret on masterpieces such as *Requiem,* her epic poem about the terror. Through all this, her love for her city was unconditional and unblinking. As she wrote in *Poem Without a Hero:* 'The capital on the Neva/Having forgotten its greatness/Like a drunken whore/Did not know who was taking her'. Despite unending official harassment, Akhmatova refused to leave her beloved Leningrad and died there in 1966, having outlived Stalin by over a decade. Her sad life, marked by the arrest and murder of so many friends and even her own son, is also given a very poignant memorial (p117) opposite the Kresty Holding Prison, where the poet queued up for days on end to get news of her son following one of his many arrests.

When Nikita Khrushchev came to power following Stalin's death in 1953, he relaxed the most oppressive restrictions on artists and writers. As this so-called 'thaw' slowly set in, a group of young poets known as 'Akhmatova's Orphans' started to meet at her apartment to read and discuss their work. The star of the group was the fiercely talented Joseph Brodsky, who seemed to have no fear of the consequences of writing about what was on his mind. In 1964 he was tried for 'social parasitism' (ie being unemployed) and was exiled to the north of Russia. His sentence was shortened after concerted international protests led by French philosopher Jean-Paul Sartre. He returned to Leningrad in 1965, only to immediately resume his thorn-in-the-side activities.

Postcommunist St Petersburg Writing

The post-*glasnost* era of the 1980s and 1990s uncovered a huge library of work that had been suppressed during the Soviet period. Authors such as Yevgeny Zamyatin, Daniil Kharms, Anatoly Rybakov, Venedict Erofeev and Andrei Bitov – banned in the Soviet Union – are now recognised for their cutting-edge commentary and significant contributions to world literature.

Surprisingly, however, St Petersburg is not a magnet for Russian writers in the 21st century (unlike artists and musicians). The contemporary literary scene is largely based in Moscow, and, to some degree, abroad, as émigré writers continue to be inspired and disheartened by their motherland.

Action-packed thrillers and detective stories have become wildly popular in the 21st century, with Darya Dontsova, Alexandra Marinina and Boris Akunin ranking among the best-selling and most widely translated authors. Realist writers such as Tatyana Tolstaya and Ludmilla Petrushevskaya engage readers with their moving portraits of everyday people living their everyday lives.

Survival Guide

Transport

ARRIVING IN ST PETERSBURG

St Petersburg is well connected to the rest of Europe by plane, train, ferry and bus links. The vast majority of travellers arrive in St Petersburg by air at Pulkovo Airport. Flight time from London and Paris to St Petersburg is three hours, from Berlin it's a two-hour flight, and from Moscow it's under an hour.

Train is also a popular way to get here – from Moscow there are pleasantly slow overnight sleeper trains as well as six to eight fast four-hour daytime Sapsan trains. See www.rzd.ru for details. From Helsinki there are four daily Allegro express trains that take you from the Finnish capital to St Petersburg in an impressive 3½ hours. See www.vr.fi for prices and timetables.

An increasing number of travellers arrive at one of St Petersburg's five cruise and ferry terminals. There are regular connections between St Petersburg and Stockholm (22 to 24 hours), Tallinn (14 hours) and Helsinki (10 hours). Those who arrive this way also have the option of 72-hour visa-free travel. See www.stpeterline.com for prices and timetables.

Flights, cars and tours can be booked online at lonelyplanet.com.

Pulkovo Airport

Most travellers arrive in St Petersburg at **Pulkovo International Airport** (LED; www.pulkovoairport.ru), 23km south of the city. Following the closure of the two old terminals and opening of a brand-new, state-of-the-art one in early 2014, the airport is now a joy to fly in to. The new terminal building, confusingly still referred to as Terminal 1, handles all domestic and international flights and is St Petersburg's only airport.

Taxi

From Pulkovo Airport, taking a taxi to the city centre has never been easier or safer. Leave the terminal building and outside you'll find an official taxi dispatcher who will ask you for your destination's address, indicate which taxi to go to and write you a price on a slip of official paper that you can then give to your driver. Prices vary, but expect between R800 to R1000 to the centre, depending on where exactly you're headed. Drivers usually won't speak much English, but just hand over the money on arrival – you don't need to tip.

Marshrutka & Bus

For those on a budget, *marshrutka* (minibus) K39 shuttles you from outside the terminal building to the nearest metro station, Moskovskaya (R30, every five minutes, from 7am to 11.30pm). The bus terminates at Moskovskaya, so

CLIMATE CHANGE & TRAVEL

Every form of transport that relies on carbon-based fuel generates CO_2, the main cause of human-induced climate change. Modern travel is dependent on aeroplanes, which might use less fuel per kilometre per person than most cars but travel much greater distances. The altitude at which aircraft emit gases (including CO_2) and particles also contributes to their climate change impact. Many websites offer 'carbon calculators' that allow people to estimate the carbon emissions generated by their journey and, for those who wish to do so, to offset the impact of the greenhouse gases emitted with contributions to portfolios of climate-friendly initiatives throughout the world. Lonely Planet offsets the carbon footprint of all staff and author travel.

BUYING TICKETS IN ST PETERSBURG

You'll most likely have your onward travel tickets when you arrive in St Petersburg, but if not it's easy to purchase tickets for boat, bus, train and plane travel. First of all, try online – you can buy train tickets (www.rzd.ru), bus tickets (www.luxexpress.eu) and, of course, airline tickets via websites.

Buying train tickets in person can be done at any train station (even at a different terminus from where your train departs), although waiting time can be long if you buy them at a counter. Far quicker are the new ticket machines, which all work in English and usually accept both cash and credit card. Another option is the centrally located **Train Tickets Centre** (Кассы ЖД; Map p256; nab kanala Griboyedova 24; ⊗8am-8pm Mon-Sat, until 4pm Sun; ⓂGostiny Dvor), where there are also ticket machines, which makes waiting in line unnecessary.

You can buy ferry tickets for nearly all boats at the **Ferry Centre** (Паромный центр; Map p260; ☑812-327 3377; www.paromy.ru; ul Vosstaniya 19; ⓂPloshchad Vosstaniya), a short walk from the Moscow Station. Alternatively, it's possible to buy ferry tickets in the **Sea Port** (Морской вокзал; ☑812-337 2060; www.mvokzal.ru; pl Morskoy Slavy 1) at the far-flung end of Vasilyevsky Island, as well as online through the ferry companies themselves.

If time is tight, then nearly all travel agencies can organise onward travel tickets for you, although of course there's usually a mark-up on the cost and a delivery fee.

you don't need to worry about where to get off, and you can connect to the rest of the city from there.

There's also bus 39 (R25, every 15 minutes, from 5.30am to 1.30am) that runs the same route over longer hours, but trundles along somewhat more slowly.

Moscow Station

If you're arriving from Moscow, you'll come to the **Moscow Station** (Moskovsky vozkal; Московский вокзал; Map p260; www.moskovsky-vokzal. ru; Nevsky pr 85; ⓂPloshchad Vosstaniya), in the centre of the city. There are two metro stations close by: Pl Vosstaniya (Line 1) and Mayakovskaya (Line 3). To get here (you can enter both stations through one building) turn left outside the main entrance to the Moscow Station, and the exit is in one side of the building on Ligovsky pr.

Finland Station

Trains from Helsinki arrive at the **Finland Station** (Finlyandsky vozkal; Финляндский вокзал; www.finlyandsky.dzvr. ru; pl Lenina 6; ⓂPloshchad Lenina). From here you can connect to anywhere in the city by metro from the Ploshchad Lenina station (Line 1) on the square outside the station.

Ladozhsky Station

Some trains from the Leningradskaya Oblast and those from Helsinki to Moscow stop en route in St Petersburg at the **Ladozhsky Station** (Ладожский вокзал; www.lvspb.ru; Zanevsky pr 73; ⓂLadozshskaya). It's served by the Ladozhskaya metro station (Line 4).

Bus Station

St Petersburg's main bus station, or **Avtovokzal** (Автобусный вокзал; ☑812-766 5777; www.avokzal.ru; nab Obvodnogo kanala 36; ⓂObvodny Kanal), has bus connections to cities all over western Russia, including Veliky Novgorod, but most travellers won't use it. If you do arrive here, it's a short walk along the canal to the metro station Obvodny Kanal (Line 5).

Bus Services

Lux Express (☑812-441 3757; www.luxexpress.eu; Mitrofanievskoye sh 2, Admiral Business Centre; ⊗9am-9pm; ⓂBaltiyskaya) runs buses from both Avtovokzal and from outside the **Baltic Station** (Baltiysky vozkal; Балтийский вокзал; Obvodny Kanal 120; ⓂBaltiyskaya). Its buses run very regularly to Tallinn (from R1850, 10 daily) and Riga (from R1095, six daily).

Ecolines (☑325 2152; www.ecolines.ru; Podezdny per 3; ⓂPushkinskaya) runs daily buses from the **Vitebsk Station** (Viteebsky vozkal; Витебский вокзал; Zagorodny pr 52; ⓂPushkinskaya) to Tallinn (R1000 four daily), Riga (R1320, five daily), Vilnius (R1900, daily) and Minsk (R1920, daily).

There are several other places where various bus services from Helsinki arrive. These include marshrutky from Helsinki, which stop on pl Vosstaniya, right opposite the Pl Vosstaniya metro station.

Sea Ports

There are a number of places where cruise ships arrive in St Petersburg, while all ferries from elsewhere in the Baltic arrive at the Sea Port on Vasilyevksy Island. Anyone on a river cruise from Moscow will arrive at the **River Port** (Речной вокзал; www.mvokzal.

ru; pr Obukhovskoy Oborony 195) in the south of the city, which is a short walk away from the Proletarskaya metro station (Line 3). Upon leaving the metro turn right onto pr Obukhovskoy Oborony and it's five minutes up the road.

Infoflot (☎812-600 1455; www.infoflot.com) Cruises range from near-direct St Petersburg–Moscow tours via Yaroslavl, Uglich, Valaam and other towns.

Mosturflot (☎812-600 7020; www.mosturflot.ru) Ships take between three and 12 days to cruise between the two capitals, depending on the number of stops and the route being taken.

Orthodox Cruise Company (www.cruise.ru) Various cruise ships make the seven-day journey between the capitals, stopping in Mandroga, Kizhi, Goritsy, Yaroslavl and Uglich.

Rechturflot (www.rtflot.ru) Offers three- to 13-day cruise options to Moscow via a number of other towns in central Russia.

Vodohod (www.bestrussian cruises.com) Cruises ranging from 10 to 13 days make stops in Svirstroy, Mandroga, Kizhi, Goritsy, Yaroslavl, Kostroma and Uglich along the way.

GETTING AROUND ST PETERSBURG

The metro is the fastest way to cover long distances: it has around 70 stations, costs a flat fare of R28 and runs from approximately 5.45am to 12.45am each day.

Buses are better for shorter distances in areas without good metro coverage. They can be slow going, but views are good. Trolleybuses are the slowest of the lot, but are cheap and plentiful. *Marshrutky* are the private sector's contribution – fast fixed-route minibuses which you can get on or off anywhere along their routes.

Trams are largely obsolete and little used, but are still useful in areas such as Kolomna and Vasilyevsky Island where there is little else available.

Metro

The St Petersburg **Metro** (www.metro.spb.ru; ⏰5.45am-12.45am) is a very efficient five-lined system. The network of some 70 stations is most usefully employed for travelling long distances, especially connecting the suburbs to the city centre.

Look for signs with a big blue 'M' signifying the entrance to the metro. The flat fare for a trip is R28; you will have to buy an additional ticket if you are carrying a significant amount of baggage. If you wish to buy a single journey, ask for '*adin proyezd*' and you will be given a *zheton* (token) to put in the machine.

If you are staying more than a day or two, however, it's worth buying a smart card (R55), which is good for multiple journeys to be used over the course of a fixed time period. Their main advantage is that you won't have to line up to buy tickets – the ticket counters can have very long lines during peak hours.

The metro is fully signed in English throughout the system, so it's quite easy to use even for first-timers in Russia.

Bus, Trolleybus & Marshrutka

Buses and particularly *marshrutky* (minibuses) are a very handy way to get around the city and they tend to cover routes that the metro doesn't, making them essential for certain parts of town. Most travellers

---

CATCHING A CAR

Stand on practically any street and stick out your arm: you can be assured that sooner rather than later a car will stop for you. The drivers may be on their way somewhere, or they may just be trying to supplement their income. These unofficial taxis are the cheapest way to cover distances in the city centre.

So, you've stuck your arm out and a car has stopped. This is where the fun starts. You state your destination, say, '*ulitsa Marata!*' The driver looks away for a second and shouts back '*skolko?*' (how much?) You bark back a price. If they're happy with that amount, they'll say, '*sadites*' (sit down), at which point you get in and drive off. If the driver is not happy with that price, a period of negotiation will ensue.

At any time, during the negotiation you are welcome to give a gruff '*nyet*' and simply shut the door. Stick your arm out again and there'll be another car stopping in a minute. You should definitely do this if you feel that the driver is trying to rip you off, or if there's more than one person in the car.

If your ride is less than five minutes long, R200 to R300 is acceptable. For a greater distance reckon on paying R400. This method is only for the very self assured, though, as of course the driver could demand more money if a price wasn't agreed upon.

find taking them a bit daunting, however, as there's no signage in English. On buses and trolleybuses, you get on and then pay a conductor who comes through the bus. Fares are usually R22 to R30. *Marshrutky* work rather differently: you flag them down anywhere along the route (there are no bus stops for *marshrutky*), open the door yourself and jump in, then once you've taken your seat you pay the driver (pass the money via your fellow passengers if you're not sitting within reaching distance). You'll need to request the stop you want – usually telling the driver the name of the street or the place you're going to shortly before you get there. Alternatively, when you want to get off, simply say (or shout!): *'AstanavEEtye pazhalsta!'* (Stop please!) and the driver will pull over as soon as possible.

Taxi

The best way to get a taxi is to order one through a company as prices will be a lot lower than those charged if you flag a driver down on the street. Operators will usually not speak English, so unless you speak Russian you might want your hotel reception to call one of the following numbers for you:

Peterburgskoye Taxi (068, 812-324 7777; www. taxi068.spb.ru)

Taxi-4 (812-633 3333; www.taxi-4.ru)

Taxi Blues (812-321 8888; www.taxiblues.ru)

Taxi Million (812-600 0000; www.6-000-000.ru) Has operators and drivers who speak English.

Bicycle

Bicycles are becoming more common on the streets of St Petersburg, but cycling is

BRIDGE TIMETABLE

From mid-April until late November all bridges across the Neva rise at the following times nightly to allow ships to pass through the city, meaning you cannot cross the river during these times. Therefore, if you're staying on Vasilyevsky Island, the Petrograd Side or the Vyborg Side and go out late in the city centre, you'll need to time your trip home well, or wait until dawn. All times are am. Note that the Grenadersky, Kantemirovsky and Sampsonievsky Bridges over the Bolshaya Nevka River (connecting the Vyborg and Petrograd Sides) only go up rarely, and two days' notice is given beforehand. You can check the full, up-to-date timetable at www.razvodka-mostov.ru (in Russian only). Note also that that the M5 metro line shuttles back and forth between Admiralteyskaya and Sportivnaya stations between 1am and 3am, creating an easy way to get between the islands and the historic heart.

BRIDGE	UP	DOWN	UP	DOWN
Alexandra Nevskogo	2.20	5.10		
Birzhevoy	2.00	4.55		
Blagoveshchensky	1.25	2.45	3.10	5.00
Bolsheokhtinsky	2.00	5.00		
Dvortsovy (Palace)	1.25	2.50	3.10	4.55
Finlyandsky	2.20	5.30		
Grenadersky	2.45	3.45	4.20	4.50
Kantemirovsky	2.45	3.45	4.20	4.50
Liteyny	1.40	4.45		
Sampsonievsky	2.10	2.45	3.20	4.25
Troitsky	1.35	4.50		
Tuchkov	2.00	2.55	3.35	4.55
Volodarsky	2.00	3.45	4.15	5.45

still difficult: pothole-riddled roads and lunatic drivers unaccustomed to cyclists make it a dangerous proposition. You'll notice many cyclists stay entirely on the pavement when they ride, such is the level of danger on the road. Indeed, many drivers seem to consider cyclists to be in the wrong if they're on the road at all, regarding them as a form of pedestrian. Helmets are highly recommended.

That said, the city centre's relatively compact size means that it is easy to get around by bike – and often much quicker than public transport. Many adventurers

swear by their bikes as the ideal form of transport in St Petersburg (at least from May to October). You can hire bikes from **Skatprokat** (Map p260; 812-717 6838; www.skatprokat.ru; Goncharnaya ul 7; per day from R400; ⏰11am-8pm; MPloshchad Vosstaniya), **Rentbike** (Map p264; 812-981 0155; www. rentbike.org; ul Yefimova 4A; per day from R400; ⏰24hr; MSennaya Ploshchad) and many hostels.

In 2014 a new bike-sharing scheme was launched in St Petersburg, which makes for a great alternative to hiring a bike. Check it out at www. velobike-spb.ru.

Directory A–Z

Customs Regulations

Customs controls in Russia are relatively relaxed these days. Searches beyond the perfunctory are quite rare. Apart from the usual restrictions, you are limited by the amount of cash you can bring in. If you are carrying more than US$3000 – or valuables worth that much – you must declare it and proceed through the red channel.

Otherwise, on entering Russia, you can pick up your luggage and go through the green channel, meaning 'nothing to declare'.

If you intend to take home anything vaguely 'arty' (manuscripts, instruments, coins, jewellery) it must be assessed by the **Cultural Security Department** (Map p256; ☎812-311 5196; Malaya Morskaya ul 17; ☺11am-5pm Mon-Fri; Ⓜ Admiralteyskaya). Take along your passport, a sales receipt and the item in question. The experts will issue a receipt for tax paid and a certificate stating that the item is not an antique. It is illegal to export anything over 100 years old.

Discount Cards

If you're a student then bring an International Student Indentity Card (ISIC) to get discounts – cards issued by non-Russian universities will not always be accepted. The Hermitage is the blissful exception where anyone with a student card from any country gets in for free. Senior citizens (usually anyone over the age of 60) are often also eligible for discounts, so bring your passport with you as proof of age.

The City Tour Pass, sold by the St Petersburg Tourist Centre (p234) for R350, gives a range of discounts to places such as the Hermitage, Peterhof and Tsarskoe Selo, but the savings aren't huge.

Electricity

Electricity in Russia is supplied at 220v/50hz, and European-style plugs are used.

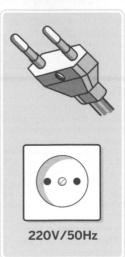

220V/50Hz

PRACTICALITIES

➡ **Newspapers & Magazines** Check out the St Petersburg Times (www.sptimes.ru) and In Your Pocket (www.inyourpocket.com).

➡ **TV & Radio** As well as the main state TV channels, St Petersburg has several local channels. Satellite TV is available at most top-end hotels.

➡ **Weights & Measures** Russia uses the metric system.

➡ **Smoking** Russia introduced a comprehensive smoking ban in 2014. It is no longer legal to smoke inside except in your own home.

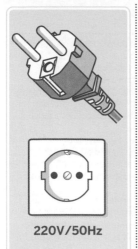

220V/50Hz

Embassies & Consulates

Despite not being a capital city, St Petersburg has a good level of consular representation. If your country is not represented here, contact your embassy in Moscow in an emergency.

Australian Consulate (Map p268; ☎812-325 7334; www.russia.embassy.gov.au; 14 Petrovsky pr; ⓂSportivnaya)

Finnish Consulate (Map p260; ☎812-331 7600; www.finland.org.ru; Preobrazhenskaya pl 4; ⓂChernyshevskaya)

French Consulate (Map p256; ☎812-332 2270; www.ambafrance-ru.org/-Consulat-Saint-Petersbourg; 5th fl, Nevsky pr 12; ⓂAdmiralteyskaya)

German Consulate (Map p260; ☎812-320 2400; www.germania.diplo.de; Furshtatskaya ul 39; ⓂChernyshevskaya)

Netherlands Consulate (Map p256; ☎812-334 0200; stpetersburg.nlconsulate.org; nab reki Moyki 11; ⓂAdmiralteyskaya)

UK Consulate (☎812-320 3200; pl Proletarskoy Diktatury 5; ⓂChernyshevskaya)

US Consulate (Map p260; ☎812-331 2600; stpetersburg.usconsulate.gov; Furshtatskaya ul 15; ⓂChernyshevskaya)

Emergency

Ambulance (☎03)
Fire Department (☎01)
Police (☎02)

Gay & Lesbian Travellers

When it comes to tolerance towards gay travellers, St Petersburg is liberal by Russian standards, but still far behind the rest of Europe. It should be no problem at all to book a double room for same-sex couples, although outside top-end hotels you can expect some curiosity from staff. Same-sex public displays of affection are never a good idea in St Petersburg, however: always err on the side of caution.

Sadly homophobia has been steadily growing, stoked by first a local, then a national law prohibiting 'gay propaganda', which, while having few legal ramifications for most people, unleashed some latent homophobia in a country where so-called 'non-traditional orientations' were previously little discussed and thus largely ignored.

There is a busy and growing gay scene, but it remains fairly discreet. Gay pride marches are routinely attacked by far right groups and the police often harass protesters.

Here are a few useful links:

www.english.gay.ru The English version of this site includes club listings and tour guides, plus information on gay history and culture in Russia.

www.lesbi.ru An active site for lesbian issues; Russian only.

www.qguys.ru The most popular gay dating website.

www.xs.gay.ru The local gay and lesbian portal; Russian only.

Health

Health insurance for any trip to St Petersburg is necessary (and often a pre-condition of getting your visa). Note that, officially at least, most Russian embassies issuing visas require you to purchase travel insurance from a list of companies given on the embassy website. This doesn't appear to be strictly implemented, however; by all means try sending them a copy of a non-approved policy if you already have one.

Health care in the city is very good if you're going private. Using public hospitals is not something you should consider, so even if your local Russian embassy doesn't require valid health insurance, you should definitely purchase it.

St Petersburg does not pose any particular threats to your health, although you should be aware of the risks associated with drinking the tap water (see p232); you're strongly advised to only drink bottled water, or at least to boil local water thoroughly.

Also be aware that the city was built on a swamp, which means the mosquitoes are nasty in the summer months. Be sure to bring plenty of insect repellent. You may also want to bring some painkillers with you – those post-vodka mornings can be hard work without them.

TO DRINK OR NOT TO DRINK

Reports about the harmful effects of drinking tap water in St Petersburg have been widely publicised and greatly exaggerated. The city's water supplier, Vodokanal, insists that the water is safe to drink, as many local residents do. Nonetheless, the pipes are antiquated, so the water may contain some metal pollutants. Furthermore, traces of *Giardia lamblia* have been found on a very small scale. This is a nasty parasite that causes unpleasant stomach cramps, nausea, bloated stomach, diarrhoea and frequent gas. There is no preventative drug, and it is worth taking precautions against contracting it.

To be absolutely safe, only drink water that has been boiled for 10 minutes or filtered through an antimicrobial water filter (PUR brand makes a good portable one). It's probably safe to accept tea or coffee at someone's house, and all restaurants and hotels will have filtration systems. Bathing, showering and brushing your teeth cause no problems at all.

If you develop diarrhoea, be sure to drink plenty of fluids, preferably including an oral rehydration solution. Imodium is to be taken only in an emergency; otherwise it's best to let the diarrhoea run its course and eliminate the parasite from the body. Metronidazole (brand name Flagyl) or Tinidazole (known as Fasigyn) are the recommended treatments for *Giardia lamblia*.

Internet Access

Internet access is now very good in St Petersburg. Nearly all hotels have free wireless internet. Many restaurants, cafes, bars and clubs also have wi-fi – often there won't even be a password, but when there is, simply ask the staff.

If you are travelling without a laptop or smartphone, there are a few good old-fashioned internet cafes in the city centre:

Cafe Max (Map p260; www. cafemax.ru; Nevsky pr 90/92; per hr R120; ⊗24hr; MMayakovskaya) A big fancy place with 150 computers, a game zone and a comfy cafe and beer bar. It's located on the 2nd floor.

Internet Centre (Map p264; Kazanskaya ul 26/27; per hr R100; ⊗24hr; MNevsky Prospekt) A rather dark and down-at-heel internet centre full of teenage gamers, but it gets the job done.

Legal Matters

It's not unusual to see police officers randomly stopping people on the street to check their documents. This checking tends to be directed at those with darker skin colour, but the police have the right to stop anyone. In the past readers have complained about police pocketing their passports and demanding bribes, but reports of this nature have decreased of late as the Russian police slowly become more professional and accountable. The best way to avoid such unpleasantness is to carry a photocopy of your passport, visa and registration, and present that when a police officer demands to see your *dokumenty*. A photocopy is sufficient for such inquiries, despite what the officer may argue. Threatening to phone your consulate usually clears up any such misunderstandings.

Medical Services

Clinics

These private clinics have facilities of an international standard and are pricey, but generally accept major international insurance policies, including direct billing.

American Medical Clinic (Map p264; ☑812-740 2090; www.amclinic.ru; nab reki Moyki 78; ⊗24hr; MAdmiralteyskaya)

Euromed (Map p260; ☑812-327 0301; www.euromed.ru; Suvorovsky pr 60; ⊗24hr; MChernyshevskaya)

Medem International Clinic & Hospital (Map p260; ☑812-336 3333; www.medem.ru; ul Marata 6; ⊗24hr; MMayakovskaya)

Pharmacies

Look for the sign АПТЕКА (*apteka*) or the usual green cross to find a pharmacy. **36.6 Pharmacy** (www.366.ru) is a chain of 24-hour pharmacies with many branches around the city, including the following:

36.6 (Historic Centre) (Map p256; Gorokhovaya ul 16; ⊗24hr; MSadovaya)

36.6 (Petrograd Side) (Map p268; Bolshoy pr 62; ⊗24hr; MPetrogradskaya)

36.6 (Smolny) (Map p260; Nevsky pr 98; ⊗24hr; MMayakovskaya)

Money

Russian currency is the rouble, written as рубль or abbreviated as руб. There are 100 kopeks (копеек or коп) in the rouble, and these come in small coins that are worth one, five, 10 and 50 kopeks. Roubles are issued in coins in amounts of one, two, five and 10 roubles. Banknotes come in values of 10, 50, 100, 500, 1000 and 5000 roubles. Small stores, kiosks and many other vendors have difficulty changing large notes, so prize your 50s and 100s! The rouble has been relatively stable since it was revalued in 1998.

ATMs

ATMs linked to international networks such as Amex, Maestro, Eurocard, MasterCard and Visa can be found everywhere in St Petersburg. Look for the sign БАНКОМАТ (bankomat). Using a credit or debit card, you can always obtain roubles, although US dollars and euros are sometimes available, too.

Changing Money

US dollars and euros are easy to change around St Petersburg, but other currencies will undoubtedly cause more hassle than they are worth. Whatever currency you bring should be in good condition, as banks and exchange bureaus do not accept old, tatty bills with rips or tears. When you visit the exchange office, be prepared to show your passport.

Credit & Debit Cards

Credit cards, especially Visa and MasterCard, and various debit cards are widely accepted in hotels, restaurants and shops. You can also use your credit card to get a cash advance at most major banks in St Petersburg. You may be asked for photo ID when you use a credit card in a shop or restaurant, but this is increasingly rare as their use becomes more and more normal locally.

Opening Hours

We only supply opening hours for establishments when they differ from the following norms:

Banks 9am-6pm Mon-Fri

Businesses & Shops 10am-9pm Mon-Fri, 10am-7pm Sat & Sun

Bars & Clubs 6pm-6am

Information 9am-6pm

Restaurants 11am or noon-11pm

Museum hours vary widely, as do their weekly days off. Nearly all museums shut their ticket offices an hour before closing time. Many close for a sanitarny den (cleaning day), during the last week of every month, so it's worth checking for these. There's a new trend in St Petersburg for some museums to operate unusually late hours once a week (usually Wednesday). See individual museum listings for details.

Post

Although service has improved dramatically in recent years, the usual warnings about delays and disappearances of incoming and outgoing mail apply to St Petersburg. Airmail letters and postcards take up to two or three weeks to Europe, and up to three to four weeks to the USA or Australasia.

To send parcels home, head to the elegant **main post office** (Map p264; Pochtamtskaya ul 9; ☺24hr; ⓂAdmiralteyskaya). Smaller post offices may refuse to send parcels internationally; most importantly, your package is more likely to reach its destination if you send it from the main post office. You will need to provide a return address in St Petersburg – your hotel name will be fine.

Public Holidays

During the major holiday periods – the first week in January (between New Year's Day and Orthodox Christmas) and the first week or two of May (around May Day and Victory Day) – St Petersburg empties out as many residents retreat from the city. Transport can be difficult to book around these periods, but accommodation is usually not a problem. Although many residents leave, the city is a festive place over New Year's and during the May holidays, usually hosting parades, concerts and other events. The downside is that many museums and other institutions have shortened hours or are closed altogether on some days during these periods.

By contrast, the Stars of White Nights Festival was designed with tourists in mind: theatres, museums and other institutions often host special events between late May and early July to appeal to the massive influx of visitors during this period. If you are visiting St Petersburg at this time, book your travel and accommodation in advance and expect to pay top rates.

The following covers St Petersburg's public holidays.

New Year's Day 1 January

Russian Orthodox Christmas Day 7 January

Defenders of the Motherland Day 23 February

International Women's Day 8 March

Easter Monday April/May (varies)

International Labour Day/ Spring Festival 1 & 2 May

Victory Day 9 May

Russian Independence Day 12 June

234

DIRECTORY A–Z SAFE TRAVEL

Day of Reconciliation and Accord (the rebranded Revolution Day) 7 November

Constitution Day 12 December

Safe Travel

You can disregard the dated horror stories you may have heard about the mafia in Russia. A far bigger threat is petty theft, especially pickpocketing in the city centre. Take care among the crowds on Nevsky pr and in the metro. Be cautious about taking taxis late at night, especially near bars and clubs that are in isolated areas. It's always best to call a taxi rather than get one on the street if you're alone and don't speak Russian. Never get into a car that already has two or more people in it.

One far grimmer problem is the rise of the skinhead and neo-Nazi movement in St Petersburg. You are unlikely to encounter these thugs, but you will undoubtedly read about some acts of violence that have been committed against people from the Caucasus and Central Asia and other darker-skinned or foreign-looking residents of the city. Non-white travellers should therefore exercise caution when wandering around the city after dark and at any time of day in the suburbs. While this violence peaked around 2005 and has since declined, it's still a very real, if unlikely, threat.

Telephone

Russia's international code is ✆7. The international access code from landline phones in Russia is ✆8 followed by 10 after the second tone, then the country code and number. From mobile phones, however, just dial +[country code] to place an international call.

Mobile Phones

Mobile phone numbers start interchangeably with either the country code (✆7) or the internal mobile code (✆8), plus three digits that change according to the service provider, followed by a seven-digit number. Nearly all Russians will give you their mobile number with an initial 8, but if you're dialing from a non-Russian number, replace this 8 with a 7.

To call a mobile phone from a landline, the line must be enabled to make paid calls (all local numbers are free from a landline anywhere in Russia). To find out if this is the case, dial 8, and then if you hear a second tone you can dial the mobile number in full. If you hear nothing, hang up – you can't call anywhere but local landlines from here.

Main mobile providers include Beeline, Megafon, MTS and Sky Link. You can buy a local SIM card at any mobile phone shop, which you can slot into your home handset during your stay. SIM cards cost as little as R200, and usually include free internet data, meaning you only pay to make calls. You'll need to bring your passport to buy one.

Time

St Petersburg is GMT +3 hours, the same as Moscow time.

Toilets

Around nearly all metro stations and tourist attractions there's at least one blue Portakabin-type toilet staffed by an attendant who will charge around R25 for the honour of using it. There are also pay toilets in all main-line train stations and free ones in museums. As a general rule, it's far better to stop for a drink in a cafe or

duck into a fancy hotel and use their cleaner facilities.

Tourist Information

Tourist information has finally got halfway decent in St Petersburg, and the **St Petersburg Tourist Information Centre** (Map p256; ✆812-310 2822; http://eng.ispb.info; Sadovaya ul 14/52; ⏰10am-7pm Mon-Fri, noon-6pm Sat; MGostiny Dvor) has its main office just off Nevsky pr, as well as several kiosks around the city and desks at Pulkovo International Airport and the Marine Facade Terminal on Vasilyevsky Island.

Travellers with Disabilities

Inaccessible transport, lack of ramps and lifts, and no centralised policy for people with physical limitations make Russia a challenging destination for travellers with restricted mobility.

Toilets are frequently accessed from stairs in restaurants and museums; distances are great; public transport can be extremely crowded; and many footpaths are in a poor condition and are hazardous even for the fully mobile.

This situation is changing (albeit very slowly), as buildings undergo renovations and become more accessible. Most upmarket hotels (especially Western chains) offer accessible rooms and have lifts, and the Hermitage is also now fully accessible.

Visas

Russia's visa regime is the single biggest turnoff for potential visitors to St Petersburg. Nearly all visitors require a visa to enter Russia, and while it's certainly an annoyance that needs to be dealt with, it's not nearly as painful a procedure as many people imagine. The following agencies can issue the invitations (also called visa support) needed to apply for a Russian visa:

City Realty (Map p256; ☑812-570 6342; www.cityrealty russia.com; Muchnoy per 2; ⊙9am-7pm Mon-Fri, 9am-5pm Sat; Ⓜ Nevsky Prospekt)

Ost-West Kontaktservice (Map p260; www.ostwest.com; Ligovsky pr 10; ⊙9am-6pm Mon-Sat; Ⓜ Ploshchad Vosstaniya)

Travel Russia (Map p260; www.travelrussia.su; Office 408, 4th fl, Senator Business Centre, 2-ya Sovetskaya ul 7; ⊙9am-8pm Mon-Fri, 9am-5pm Sat; Ⓜ Ploshchad Vosstaniya)

Way to Russia (www.wayto-russia.net)

Application

Apply as soon as you have all the documents you need (but not more than two months ahead). Processing time ranges from 24 hours to two weeks, depending on how much you are willing to pay.

It's possible to apply at your local Russian consulate by dropping off all the necessary documents with the appropriate payment or by mailing it all (along with a self-addressed, postage-paid envelope for the return). When you receive the visa, check it carefully – especially the expiry, entry and exit

dates and any restrictions on entry or exit points.

A third option is to use a visa agency. While more expensive than doing it all yourself it's a great way to delegate the hassles to someone else. Some agencies charge very reasonable fees to submit, track and collect your visa. The following are some recommended ones:

Action-visas.com (www.action-visas.com)

CIBT (www.uk.cibt.com)

Comet Consular Services (www.cometconsular.com)

Real Russia (www.realrussia.co.uk)

VisaHQ.com (www.russia.visahq.com)

Visalink.com.au (www.visalink.com.au)

Registration

On arrival you will be issued with an immigration card, which is normally filled out for you by the immigration officer's printer. This will be stamped along with your visa, and one half of the card will be given to you, while the immigration officer will retain the other half. When you are checking in at a hotel, you'll have to surrender your passport and immigration card so the hotel can register you with the OVIR (Office of Visas and Registrations). Usually they are given back the next morning, if not the same day.

If you're not staying at a hotel, you will need to have

your visa registered if you are staying for more than a week. The easiest way to do this is to take it to a travel agency where staff will usually offer registration for between R500 and R1000. If you are staying in Russia for fewer than seven working days, there is no need to register your visa.

Registration is very rarely checked these days, but can theoretically be demanded at any time, including at immigration on your way out of the country. While it's a pain, registering your visa remains wise.

Women Travellers

Foreign women are likely to receive some attention, mostly in the form of genuine, friendly interest. An interested stranger may approach you and ask: *'Mozhno poznakomitsa?'* (May we become acquainted?) Answer with a gentle, but firm, *'Nyet'* (No) and it usually goes no further, although drunken men may persist. The best way to lose an unwelcome suitor is to enter an upmarket hotel or restaurant, where ample security will come to your aid. Women should avoid taking non-official taxis alone at night.

Russian women dress up and wear lots of make-up on nights out. If you are wearing casual gear, you might feel uncomfortable in a restaurant, club or theatre.

Language

Russian belongs to the Slavonic language family and is closely related to Belarusian and Ukrainian. It has more than 150 million speakers within the Russian Federation and is used as a second language in the former republics of the USSR, with a total number of speakers of more than 270 million people.

Russian is written in the Cyrillic alphabet (see the next page), and it's well worth the effort familiarising yourself with it so that you can read maps, timetables, menus and street signs. Otherwise, just read the coloured pronunciation guides given next to each Russian phrase in this chapter as if they were English, and you'll be understood. Most sounds are the same as in English, and the few differences in pronunciation are explained in the alphabet table. The stressed syllables are indicated with italics.

BASICS

Hello.	Здравствуйте.	zdrast·vuy·tye
Goodbye.	До свидания.	da svi·da·nya
Excuse me.	Простите.	pras·ti·tye
Sorry.	Извините.	iz·vi·ni·tye
Please.	Пожалуйста.	pa·zhal·sta
Thank you.	Спасибо.	spa·si·ba
You're welcome.	Пожалуйста.	pa·zhal·sta
Yes.	Да.	da
No.	Нет.	nyet

WANT MORE?

For in-depth language information and handy phrases, check out Lonely Planet's *Russian phrasebook*. You'll find it at **shop.lonelyplanet.com**, or you can buy Lonely Planet's iPhone phrasebooks at the Apple App Store.

How are you?

Как дела?		kak di·la

Fine, thank you. And you?

Хорошо, спасибо.		kha·ra·sho spa·si·ba
А у вас?		a u vas

What's your name?

Как вас зовут?		kak vas za·vut

My name is ...

Меня зовут ...		mi·nya za·vut ...

Do you speak English?

Вы говорите по-английски?		vi ga·va·ri·tye pa·an·gli·ski

I don't understand.

Я не понимаю.		ya nye pa·ni·ma·yu

ACCOMMODATION

Where's a ...?	Где ...?	gdye ...
boarding house	пансионат	pan·si·a·nat
campsite	кемпинг	kyem·ping
hotel	гостиница	ga·sti·ni·tsa
youth hostel	общежитие	ap·shi·zhih·ti·ye

Do you have a ... room?	У вас есть ...?	u vas yest' ...
single	одно-местный номер	ad·na·myest·nih no·mir
double	номер с двуспальней кроватью	no·mir z dvu·spal'·nyey kra·va·tyu

How much is it for ...?	Сколько стоит за ...?	skol'·ka sto·it za ...
a night	ночь	noch'
two people	двоих	dva·ikh

The ... isn't working.	... не работает.	... ne ra·bo·ta·yit
heating	Отопление	a·ta·plye·ni·ye
hot water	Горячая вода	ga·rya·cha·ya va·da
light	Свет	svyet

DIRECTIONS

Where is ...?
Где ...? — gdye ...

What's the address?
Какой адрес? — ka·koy a·dris

Could you write it down, please?
Запишите, пожалуйста. — za·pi·shih·tye pa·zhal·sta

Can you show me (on the map)?
Покажите мне, пожалуйста (на карте). — pa·ka·zhih·tye mnye pa·zhal·sta (na kar·tye)

Turn ...	Поверните ...	pa·vir·ni·tye ...
at the corner	за угол	za u·gal
at the traffic lights	на светофоре	na svi·ta·fo·rye
left	налево	na·lye·va
right	направо	na·pra·va

behind ...	за ...	za ...
far	далеко	da·li·ko
in front of ...	перед ...	pye·rit ...
near	близко	blis·ka
next to ...	рядом с ...	rya·dam s ...
opposite ...	напротив ...	na·pro·tif ...
straight ahead	прямо	prya·ma

EATING & DRINKING

I'd like to reserve a table for ...	Я бы хотел/ хотела заказать столик на ... (m/f)	ya bih khat·yel/ khat·ye·la za·ka·zat' sto·lik na ...
two people	двоих	dva·ikh
eight o'clock	восемь часов	vo·sim' chi·sof

What would you recommend?
Что вы рекомендуете? — shto vih ri·ka·min·du·it·ye

What's in that dish?
Что входит в это блюдо? — shto fkho·dit v e·ta blyu·da

That was delicious!
Было очень вкусно! — bih·la o·chin' fkus·na

Please bring the bill.
Принесите, пожалуйста счёт. — pri·ni·sit·ye pa·zhal·sta shot

I don't eat ...	Я не ем ...	ya nye yem ...
eggs	яиц	ya·its
fish	рыбы	rih·bih
poultry	птицы	ptit·sih
red meat	мяса	mya·sa

CYRILLIC ALPHABET

Cyrillic	Sound	
А, а	a	as in 'father' (in a stressed syllable); as in 'ago' (in an unstressed syllable)
Б, б	b	as in 'but'
В, в	v	as in 'van'
Г, г	g	as in 'god'
Д, д	d	as in 'dog'
Е, е	ye	as in 'yet' (in a stressed syllable and at the end of a word);
	i	as in 'tin' (in an unstressed syllable)
Ё, ё	yo	as in 'yore' (often printed without dots)
Ж, ж	zh	as the 's' in 'measure'
З, з	z	as in 'zoo'
И, и	i	as the 'ee' in 'meet'
Й, й	y	as in 'boy' (not transliterated after ы or и)
К, к	k	as in 'kind'
Л, л	l	as in 'lamp'
М, м	m	as in 'mad'
Н, н	n	as in 'not'
О, о	o	as in 'more' (in a stressed syllable);
	a	as in 'hard' (in an unstressed syllable)
П, п	p	as in 'pig'
Р, р	r	as in 'rub' (rolled)
С, с	s	as in 'sing'
Т, т	t	as in 'ten'
У, у	u	as the 'oo' in 'fool'
Ф, ф	f	as in 'fan'
Х, х	kh	as the 'ch' in 'Bach'
Ц, ц	ts	as in 'bits'
Ч, ч	ch	as in 'chin'
Ш, ш	sh	as in 'shop'
Щ, щ	shch	as 'sh-ch' in 'fresh chips'
Ъ, ъ	–	'hard sign' meaning the preceding consonant is pronounced as it's written
Ы, ы	ih	as the 'y' in 'any'
Ь, ь	'	'soft sign' meaning the preceding consonant is pronounced like a faint y
Э, э	e	as in 'end'
Ю, ю	yu	as the 'u' in 'use'
Я, я	ya	as in 'yard' (in a stressed syllable);
	ye	as in 'yearn' (in an unstressed syllable)

Signs	
Вход	Entrance
Выход	Exit
Открыт	Open
Закрыт	Closed
Справки	Information
Запрещено	Prohibited
Туалет	Toilets
Мужской (М)	Men
Женский (Ж)	Women

Key Words

bottle	бутылка	bu·tihl·ka
bowl	миска	mis·ka
breakfast	завтрак	zaf·trak
cold	холодный	kha·lod·nih
dinner	ужин	u·zhihn
dish	блюдо	blyu·da
fork	вилка	vil·ka
glass	стакан	sta·kan
hot (warm)	жаркий	zhar·ki
knife	нож	nosh
lunch	обед	ab·yet
menu	меню	min·yu
plate	тарелка	tar·yel·ka
restaurant	ресторан	ris·ta·ran
spoon	ложка	losh·ka
with/without	с/без	s/byez

Meat & Fish

beef	говядина	gav·ya·di·na
caviar	икра	i·kra
chicken	курица	ku·rit·sa
duck	утка	ut·ka
fish	рыба	rih·ba
herring	сельдь	syelt'
lamb	баранина	ba·ra·ni·na
meat	мясо	mya·sa
oyster	устрица	ust·rit·sa
pork	свинина	svi·ni·na
prawn	креветка	kriv·yet·ka
salmon	лососина	la·sa·si·na
turkey	индейка	ind·yey·ka
veal	телятина	til·ya·ti·na

Fruit & Vegetables

apple	яблоко	yab·la·ka
bean	фасоль	fa·sol'
cabbage	капуста	ka·pu·sta
capsicum	перец	pye·rits
carrot	морковь	mar·kof'
cauliflower	цветная капуста	tsvit·na·ya ka·pu·sta
cucumber	огурец	a·gur·yets
fruit	фрукты	fruk·tih
mushroom	гриб	grip
nut	орех	ar·yekh
onion	лук	luk
orange	апельсин	a·pil'·sin
peach	персик	pyer·sik
pear	груша	gru·sha
plum	слива	sli·va
potato	картошка	kar·tosh·ka
spinach	шпинат	shpi·nat
tomato	помидор	pa·mi·dor
vegetable	овощ	o·vash

Other

bread	хлеб	khlyep
cheese	сыр	sihr
egg	яйцо	yeyt·so
honey	мёд	myot
oil	масло	mas·la
pasta	паста	pa·sta
pepper	перец	pye·rits
rice	рис	ris
salt	соль	sol'
sugar	сахар	sa·khar
vinegar	уксус	uk·sus

Drinks

beer	пиво	pi·va
coffee	кофе	kof·ye
(orange) juice	(апельсиновый) сок	(a·pil'·si·na·vih) sok
milk	молоко	ma·la·ko
tea	чай	chey
(mineral) water	(минеральная) вода	(mi·ni·ral'·na·ya) va·da
wine	вино	vi·no

EMERGENCIES

Help!	Помогите!	pa·ma·gi·tye

Call ...!	Вызовите ...!	vih·za·vi·tye ...
a doctor	врача	vra·cha
the police	милицию	mi·li·tsih·yu

Leave me alone!
Приваливай! — pri·va·li·vai

There's been an accident.
Произошёл — pra·i·za·shol
несчастный случай. — ne·shas·nih slu·chai

I'm lost.
Я заблудился/ — ya za·blu·dil·sa/
заблудилась. (m/f) — za·blu·di·las'

Where are the toilets?
Где здесь туалет? — gdye zdyes' tu·al·yet

I'm ill.
Я болен/больна. (m/f) — ya bo·lin/bal'·na

It hurts here.
Здесь болит. — zdyes' ba·lit

I'm allergic to (antibiotics).
У меня алергия — u min·ya a·lir·gi·ya
на (антибиотики). — na (an·ti·bi·o·ti·ki)

SHOPPING & SERVICES

I need ...
Мне нужно ... — mnye nuzh·na ...

I'm just looking.
Я просто смотрю. — ya pros·ta smat·ryu

Can I look at it?
Покажите, — pa·ka·zhih·tye
пожалуйста? — pa·zhal·sta

How much is it?
Сколько стоит? — skol'·ka sto·it

That's too expensive.
Это очень дорого. — e·ta o·chen' do·ra·ga

There's a mistake in the bill.
Меня обсчитали. — min·ya ap·shi·ta·li

bank	банк	bank
market	рынок	rih·nak
post office	почта	poch·ta
telephone office	телефонный пункт	ti·li·fo·nih punkt

TIME, DATES & NUMBERS

What time is it?
Который час? — ka·to·rih chas

It's (10) o'clock.
(Десять) часов. — (dyc·sit') chi·sof

morning	утро	ut·ra
afternoon	после обеда	pos·lye ab·ye·da
evening	вечер	vye·chir

yesterday	вчера	vchi·ra
today	сегодня	si·vod·nya
tomorrow	завтра	zaft·ra

Monday	понедельник	pa·ni·dyel'·nik
Tuesday	вторник	ftor·nik
Wednesday	среда	sri·da
Thursday	четверг	chit·vyerk
Friday	пятница	pyat·ni·tsa
Saturday	суббота	su·bo·ta
Sunday	воскресенье	vas·kri·syen·ye

January	январь	yan·var'
February	февраль	fiv·ral'
March	март	mart
April	апрель	ap·ryel'
May	май	mai
June	июнь	i·yun'
July	июль	i·yul'
August	август	av·gust
September	сентябрь	sin·tyabr'
October	октябрь	ak·tyabr'
November	ноябрь	na·yabr'
December	декабрь	di·kabr'

1	один	a·din
2	два	dva
3	три	tri
4	четыре	chi·tih·ri
5	пять	pyat'
6	шесть	shest'
7	семь	syem'
8	восемь	vo·sim'
9	девять	dye·vyat'
10	десять	dye·syat'
20	двадцать	dva·tsat'
30	тридцать	tri·tsat'
40	сорок	so·rak
50	пятьдесят	pi·dis·yat
60	шестдесят	shihs·dis·yat
70	семьдесят	syem'·dis·yat

Question Words		
What?	Что?	shto
When?	Когда?	kag·da
Where?	Где?	gdye
Which?	Какой?	ka·koy
Who?	Кто?	kto
Why?	Почему?	pa·chi·mu

KEY PATTERNS

To get by in Russian, mix and match these simple patterns with words of your choice:

When's (the next bus)?
Когда (будет следующий автобус)? — kag·da (bu·dit slye·du·yu·shi af·to·bus)

Where's (the station)?
Где (станция)? — gdye (stant·sih·ya)

Where can I (buy a padlock)?
Где можно (купить нависной замок)? — gdye mozh·na (ku·pit' na·vis·noy za·mok)

Do you have (a map)?
Здесь есть (карте)? — zdyes' yest' (kart·ye)

I'd like (the menu).
Я бы хотел/хотела (меню). (m/f) — ya bih khat·yel/khat·ye·la (min·yu)

I'd like to (hire a car).
Я бы хотел/хотела (взять машину). (m/f) — ya bih khat·yel/khat·ye·la (vzyat ma·shih·nu)

Can I (come in)?
Можно (войти)? — mozh·na (vey·ti)

Could you please (write it down)?
(Запишите), пожалуйста? — (za·pi·shiht·ye) pa·zhal·sta

Do I need (a visa)?
Нужна ли (виза)? — nuzh·na li (vi·za)

I need (assistance).
Мне нужна (помощь). — mnye nuzh·na (po·mash)

80	восемьдесят	vo·sim'·di·sit
90	девяносто	di·vi·no·sta
100	сто	sto
1000	тысяча	tih·si·cha

TRANSPORT

Public Transport

A ... ticket (to Novgorod).	Билет ... (на Новгород).	bil·yet ... (na nov·ga·rat)
one-way	в один конец	v a·din kan·yets
return	в оба конца	v o·ba kan·tsa
bus	автобус	af·to·bus
train	поезд	po·ist
tram	трамвай	tram·vai
trolleybus	троллейбус	tra·lyey·bus
first	первый	pyer·vih
last	последний	pas·lyed·ni

metro token	жетон	zhi·ton
platform	платформа	plat·for·ma
(bus) stop	остановка	a·sta·nof·ka
ticket	билет	bil·yet
ticket office	билетная касса	bil·yet·na·ya ka·sa
timetable	расписание	ras·pi·sa·ni·ye

When does it leave?
Когда отправляется? — kag·da at·prav·lya·it·sa

How long does it take to get to ...?
Сколько времени нужно ехать до ...? — skol'·ka vrye·mi·ni nuzh·na ye·khat' da ...

Does it stop at ...?
Поезд останавливается в ...? — po·yist a·sta·nav·li·va·yit·sa v ...

Please stop here.
Остановитесь здесь, пожалуйста. — a·sta·na·vit·yes' zdyes' pa·zhal·sta

Driving & Cycling

I'd like to hire a ...	Я бы хотел/хотела взять ... на прокат. (m/f)	ya bih kha·tyel/kha·tye·la vzyat ... na pra·kat
4WD	машину с полным приводом	ma·shih·nu s pol·nihm pri·vo·dam
bicycle	велосипед	vi·la·si·pyet
car	машину	ma·shih·nu
motorbike	мотоцикл	ma·ta·tsikl
diesel	дизельное топливо	di·zil'·na·ye to·pli·va
regular	бензин номер 93	ben·zin no·mir di·vi·no·sta tri
unleaded	очищенный бензин	a·chi·shi·nih bin·zin

Is this the road to ...?
Эта дорога ведёт в ...? — e·ta da·ro·ga vid·yot f ...

Where's a petrol station?
Где заправка? — gdye za·praf·ka

Can I park here?
Здесь можно стоять? — zdyes' mozh·na sta·yat'

I need a mechanic.
Мне нужен автомеханик. — mnye nu·zhin af·ta·mi·kha·nik

The car has broken down.
Машина сломалась. — ma·shih·na sla·ma·las'

I have a flat tyre.
У меня лопнула шина. — u min·ya lop·nu·la shih·na

I've run out of petrol.
У меня кончился бензин. — u min·ya kon·chil·sa bin·zin

GLOSSARY

(m) indicates masculine gender, (f) feminine gender and (n) neuter gender

aeroport – airport
alleya – alley
apteka – pharmacy
avtobus – bus
avtomaticheskie kamery khranenia – left-luggage lockers
avtovokzal – bus station

babushka – grandmother
bankomat – ATM
banya – bathhouse
bolshoy/bolshaya/bolshoye (m/f/n) – big, great, grand
bulvar – boulevard
bylina – epic song

dacha – country cottage
datsan – temple
deklaratsiya – customs declaration
dom – house
duma – parliament
dvorets – palace

elektrichka – suburban train; also *prigorodnye poezd*

galereya – gallery
glasnost – openness; policy of public accountability developed under the leadership of Mikhail Gorbachev
gorod – city, town
kafe – cafe
kamera khranenia – left-luggage office or counter
kanal – canal
kladbische – cemetery
kolonnada – colonnade
kon – horse
korpus – building within a building
koryushki – freshwater smelt
kruglosutochno – open 24 hours

lavra – most senior grade of Russian Orthodox monastery
letny sad – summer garden
liteyny – foundry

maly/malaya/maloye (m/f/n) – small, little
marshrutka – minibus that runs along a fixed route; diminutive form of *marshrutnoye taxi*
Maslenitsa – akin to Mardi Gras; fete that celebrates the end of winter and kicks off Lent
matryoshka – nesting doll; set of painted wooden dolls within dolls
mekh – fur
mesto – seat
militsioner – police officer
militsiya – police
morskoy vokzal – sea port
morzh – literally walrus, but the name commonly given to ice swimmers in the Neva
most – bridge
muzey – museum

naberezhnaya – embankment
novy/novaya (m/f) – new
Novy God – New Year

ostrov – island

parilka – steam room (at a *banya*)
Paskha – Easter
passazhirskiy poezd – passenger train
perekhod – transfer
pereryv – break, recess
perestroika – reconstruction; policy of reconstructing the economy developed under the leadership of Mikhail Gorbachev
pereulok – lane, side street
pivnaya – beer bar
ploshchad – square
prigorodnye poezd – suburban train; also *elektrichka*

proezd – passage
prospekt – avenue

rechnoy vokzal – river port
reka – river
restoran – restaurant
Rozhdestvo – Christmas
rynok – market
ryumochnaya – equivalent of the local pub

samizdat – underground literary manuscript during the Soviet era
sanitarny den – literally 'sanitary day'; a day during the last week of every month on which establishments such as museums shut down for cleaning
shosse – highway
skory poezd – fast train; regular long-distance service
sobor – cathedral
stary/staraya/staroye (m/f/n) – old
stolovaya – cafeteria

tapochki – slippers
teatralnaya kassa – theatre kiosk; general theatre box office scattered about the city
troika – sleigh drawn by three horses
tserkov – church

ulitsa – street

vagon – carriage (on a train)
veniki – bundle of birch branches used at a *banya* to beat bathers to eliminate toxins and improve circulation
vokzal – station
vyshaya liga – Russia's premier football league

zal – hall
zamok – castle

MENU DECODER

bliny – pancakes блины
borsch – beetroot soup борщ
buterbrod – open-faced sandwich бутерброд

garnir – garnish, or side dish гарнир

ikra (chyornaya, krasnaya) – caviar (black, red) икра (чёрная, красная)

kartoshki – potatoes картошки
kasha – porridge каша
kefir – sour yoghurt drink кефир
khleb – bread хлеб
kvas – mildly alcoholic fermented-rye-bread drink квас

lapsha – noodle soup лапша
losos – salmon лосось

mineralnaya voda (gazirovannaya, negazirovannaya) – water (sparkling, still) минеральная вода (газированная, негазированная)

moloko – milk молоко
morozhenoye – ice cream мороженое
myaso – meat мясо

obed – lunch обед
okroshka – cold cucumber soup with a *kvas* base окрошка
ovoshchi – vegetables овощи
ovoshnoy salat – tomato and cucumber salad, literally 'vegetable salad' овошной салат

pelmeni – dumplings filled with meat or vegetables пельмени
pirog/pirogi (s/pl) – pie пирог/пироги
pivo (svetloe, tyomnoe) – beer (light, dark) пиво (светлое, тёмное)
ptitsa – poultry птица

ris – rice рис
ryba – fish рыба

salat olivier – see *stolichny salat* салат Оливье

seld pod shuboy – salad with herring, potatoes, beets and carrots, literally 'herring in a fur coat' сельдь под шубой
shashlyk (myasnoy, kuriny, rybnoy) – kebab (meat, chicken, fish) шашлык (мясной, куриный, рыбной)
shchi – cabbage soup щи
sok – juice сок
solyanka – a tasty meat soup with salty vegetables and hint of lemon солянка
stolichny salat – 'capital salad', which contains beef, potatoes and eggs in mayonnaise; also called *salat olivier* столичный салат
svekolnik – cold beet soup свекольник

tvorog – soft sweet cheese similar to ricotta творог

uzhin – dinner ужин

zakuski – appetisers закуски
zavtrak – breakfast завтрак

Behind the Scenes

SEND US YOUR FEEDBACK

We love to hear from travellers – your comments keep us on our toes and help make our books better. Our well-travelled team reads every word on what you loved or loathed about this book. Although we cannot reply individually to your submissions, we always guarantee that your feedback goes straight to the appropriate authors, in time for the next edition. Each person who sends us information is thanked in the next edition – and the most useful submissions are rewarded with a selection of digital PDF chapters.

Visit **lonelyplanet.com/contact** to submit your updates and suggestions or to ask for help. Our award-winning website also features inspirational travel stories, news and discussions.

Note: We may edit, reproduce and incorporate your comments in Lonely Planet products such as guidebooks, websites and digital products, so let us know if you don't want your comments reproduced or your name acknowledged. For a copy of our privacy policy visit lonelyplanet.com/privacy.

OUR READERS

Many thanks to the travellers who used the last edition and wrote to us with helpful hints, useful advice and interesting anecdotes: Jane Charlotte, Dave Coenen, Sonia Conly, Maria Cooper, Jean-Robert Franco, Philip Glover, Greta Grishanova, Andras Havas, Nina Hoor, Alan Hu, Tadek Huskowski, Nikolai Iakovlev, Daniel Just, Peter Kozyrev, David Lewis, Chiara Manenti, Baudouin de Marsac, Atindra Mazumder, Matt McAllister, Ana Mendes, Bill Miller, Peter Miller, Serhat Narsap, Thomas Sarosy, Annie Schulz Begle, Raymond Shamash

AUTHOR THANKS

Tom Masters

Huge thanks to my many friends in St Petersburg, but especially Anatoliy Buzinskiy at Dozhd, Biblioteka Gogolya and Letovpitere for making such huge efforts to help me with contacts and introductions. Thanks to my old friend and tireless Petersburger Simon Patterson, his wife Olga Dmitrieva and their amazing children for making me feel at home during my stay, and also for organising my accommodation. Thanks also to such reliable comrades as Nikita Yumanov, Gena Bogolepov, Alexei Dmitriev, Alexei Chernov, Nikita Slavich, Dima Dzhafarov, Sasha and Andrey, Peter Kozyrev and Nastya Makarova. At Lonely Planet big thanks to Simon Richmond, Anna Tyler, Brana Vladisavljevic and all the in-house eds and cartos for their hard work on this title.

Simon Richmond

Many thanks to Sasha and Andrey for a lovely place to stay, the ever knowledgeable Peter Kozyrev, Chris Hamilton, Adelya Dayanova, Polina Adrianova, Dimitri Ozerkov, Vladimir Stolyarov, Yegor Churakov, Oksana, Maxim Pinigin, Alexander Kim, Maria Isserlis, Yevgenia Semenoff and Polina at the Street Art Museum.

ACKNOWLEDGMENTS

Cover photograph: Church on the Spilled Blood (p77), Walter Bibikow/AWL.
Illustration p567 by Javier Zarracina

THIS BOOK

This 7th edition of Lonely Planet's *St Petersburg* guidebook was researched and written by Tom Masters and Simon Richmond, who also wrote the previous edition. This guidebook was commissioned in Lonely Planet's London office, and produced by the following:

Destination Editor Branislava Vladisavljevic

Coordinating Editor Nigel Chin

Product Editor Kate James

Senior Cartographer Valentina Kremenchutskaya

Book Designer Jessica Rose

Assisting Editors Charlotte Orr, Gabrielle Stefanos, Jeanette Wall

Cover Researcher Naomi Parker

Assisting Book Designer Virginia Moreno

Thanks to Sasha Baskett, Anna Harris, Claire Naylor, Karyn Noble, Angela Tinson, Anna Tyler

See also separate subindexes for:

✕ **EATING P249**

🍷 **DRINKING & NIGHTLIFE P312**

☆ **ENTERTAINMENT P250**

🔒 **SHOPPING P251**

🏃 **SPORTS & ACTIVITIES P251**

🛏 **SLEEPING P251**

Index

St Petersburg Maps

Sights
- Beach
- Bird Sanctuary
- Buddhist
- Castle/Palace
- Christian
- Confucian
- Hindu
- Islamic
- Jain
- Jewish
- Monument
- Museum/Gallery/Historic Building
- Ruin
- Shinto
- Sikh
- Taoist
- Winery/Vineyard
- Zoo/Wildlife Sanctuary
- Other Sight

Activities, Courses & Tours
- Bodysurfing
- Diving
- Canoeing/Kayaking
- Course/Tour
- Sento Hot Baths/Onsen
- Skiing
- Snorkelling
- Surfing
- Swimming/Pool
- Walking
- Windsurfing
- Other Activity

Sleeping
- Sleeping
- Camping

Eating
- Eating

Drinking & Nightlife
- Drinking & Nightlife
- Cafe

Entertainment
- Entertainment

Shopping
- Shopping

Information
- Bank
- Embassy/Consulate
- Hospital/Medical
- Internet
- Police
- Post Office
- Telephone
- Toilet
- Tourist Information
- Other Information

Geographic
- Beach
- Hut/Shelter
- Lighthouse
- Lookout
- Mountain/Volcano
- Oasis
- Park
- Pass
- Picnic Area
- Waterfall

Population
- Capital (National)
- Capital (State/Province)
- City/Large Town
- Town/Village

Transport
- Airport
- Border crossing
- Bus
- Cable car/Funicular
- Cycling
- Ferry
- Metro station
- Monorail
- Parking
- Petrol station
- S-Bahn/Subway station
- Taxi
- T-bane/Tunnelbana station
- Train station/Railway
- Tram
- Tube station
- U-Bahn/Underground station
- Other Transport

Note: Not all symbols displayed above appear on the maps in this book

Routes
- Tollway
- Freeway
- Primary
- Secondary
- Tertiary
- Lane
- Unsealed road
- Road under construction
- Plaza/Mall
- Steps
- Tunnel
- Pedestrian overpass
- Walking Tour
- Walking Tour detour
- Path/Walking Trail

Boundaries
- International
- State/Province
- Disputed
- Regional/Suburb
- Marine Park
- Cliff
- Wall

Hydrography
- River, Creek
- Intermittent River
- Canal
- Water
- Dry/Salt/Intermittent Lake
- Reef

Areas
- Airport/Runway
- Beach/Desert
- Cemetery (Christian)
- Cemetery (Other)
- Glacier
- Mudflat
- Park/Forest
- Sight (Building)
- Sportsground
- Swamp/Mangrove

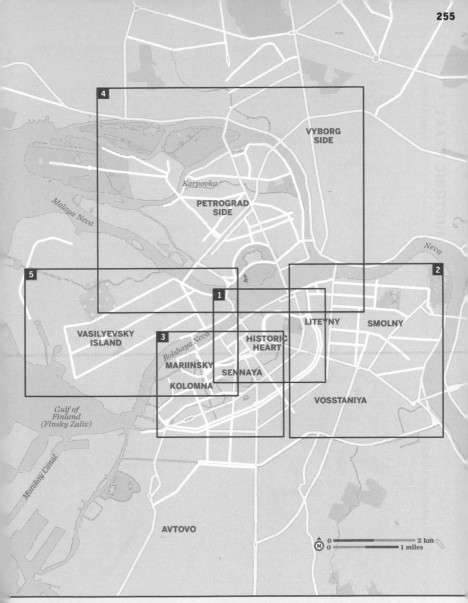

VYBORG
SIDE

Karpovka

PETROGRAD
SIDE

Malaya Neva

Neva

VASILYEVSKY
ISLAND

LITEYNY

SMOLNY

HISTORIC
HEART

Bolshaya Neva

MARIINSKY

SENNAYA

KOLOMNA

VOSSTANIYA

*Gulf of
Finland
(Finsky Zaliv)*

Morskoy Canal

AVTOVO

0 — 2 km
0 — 1 miles

MAP INDEX

Key on p258

See map p268

Malaya Neva

nab Makarova

Tiflisskaya ul

Birzhevoy most

Birzhevaya pl

Birzhevoy proezd

Birzhevoy proezd

Neva

108
98

Moshkov per

Ermitazhny most

39 91

Entrance to Hermitage Theatre

123

Hermitage 4

Large Hermitage

Little Hermitage

Atlantes

Pervy Zimny most 135

65

Vtoroy Zimny most 131

37 Winter Palace

Pevchesky most 90

Dvortsovy most

Bolshaya Neva

Universitetskaya nab

Tamozhenny pr

Dvortsovy

Chernomorsky per

Alexander Column 26

General Staff Building 3

Dvortsovaya pl (Palace Square)

63 Volynsky per

Triumphal Arch

Admiralteyskaya nab

Senatskaya pl (pl Dekabristov) 14

7

129

146

25

138 46

54

Admiralteyskaya M 122

104

Zelyony most 119

42

35

See map p270

Galernaya ul

Alexander Garden

8

Admiralteysky proezd

Admiralteysky pr

124 61

142

58

145

Malaya Morskaya ul

132

56

Kirpichny per

43

Konnogvardeysky bul

19

St Isaac's Cathedral 6

51

113

31

130

Voznesensky pr

Bol Morskaya ul

45

120

110

143

11

Krasny most

Moyka

nab reki Moyki

HISTORIC HEART 121

136

Pochtamtskaya ul

Bol Morskaya ul

111

Siny most

Grivtsova pr

Gorokhovaya ul

81 57

128

67

59

Muchnoy most 133

144

Prachechny per

Fonarny per

per Pirogova

per Antonenko

Kazanskaya ul

Kamenny most

48

Muchnoy per

Stolyarny per

Grazhdanskaya ul

Demidov most

Griboyedov Canal

SENNAYA

Spassky per

Lviny most

See map p264

Voznesensky pr

Sadovaya M

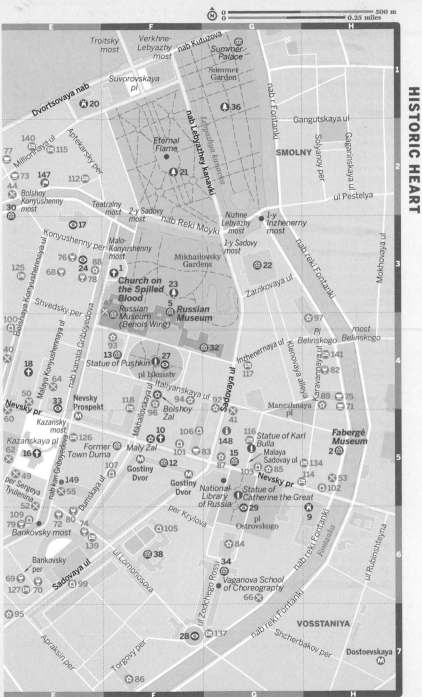

HISTORIC HEART *Map on p256*

SMOLNY & VOSSTANIYA

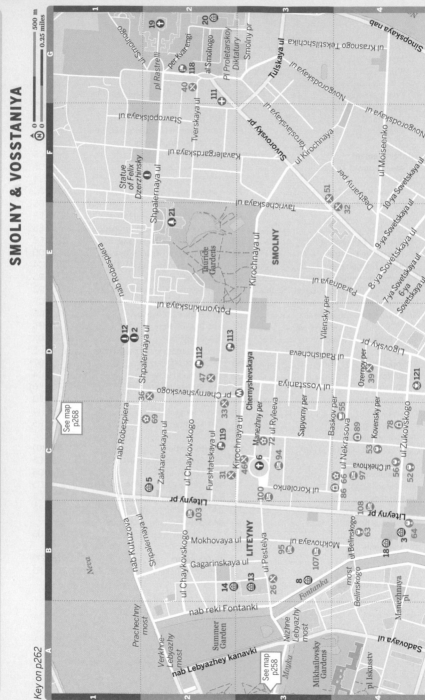

Key on p262

See map p268

See map p258

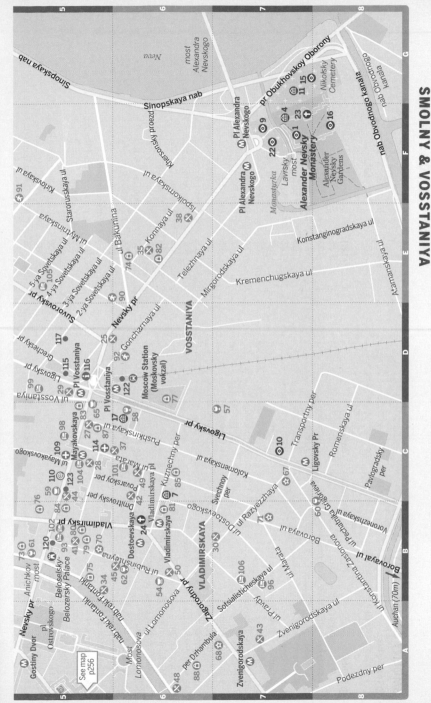

SMOLNY & VOSSTANIYA Map on p260

SMOLNY & VOSSTANIYA

SENNAYA & KOLOMNA

VASILYEVSKY ISLAND

See map p270

Blagoveshchensky most

Bolshaya Neva

Angliyskaya nab

Galernaya ul

22 63

35

52
48
44

67

Angliyskaya nab

60

16

Konnogvardeysky bulvar

33
26
17

66

ul Yakubovicha

Galernaya ul

nab Admiralteyskogo kanala

pl Truda

4 MARIINSKY

Novoadmiratelsky

Novo-Admiralteyskiy Canal

41

11

nab Krukova kanala

ul Truda

Pochtamtskaya ul

Bolshaya Morskaya ul

Khrapovitsky most

Moika

Novaya Gollandiya

nab reki Moyki

Prachechny per

8

Angliyskaya nab

Matveevsky most

Potseluev most

2 Yusupov Palace

Matisov most

Angliysky pr

most Dekabristov

34

Lviny most (Bridge of Four Lions)

Matisov

nab reki Pryazhki

46

50

1

47

ul Glinki

Teatralnaya pl

45

ul Dekabristov

7

Small Synagogue

Minsky per

Mariinsky Theatre

ul A Bloka

3 KOLOMNA

Masterskaya ul

ul Soyuza Pechatnikov

nab Krukova kanala

Nikolskaya pl

Nikolsky Gardens

32

Torgovy most

12

Pryazhka

nab reki Pryazhki

Angliysky pr

31

Drovyanoy per

ul V Ermaka

Myasnaya ul

pr Rimskogo-Korsakova

Mogilyovsky most

Griboyedov Canal

Staro-Nikolsky most

nab kanala Griboyedova

Alarchin most

Kanonerskaya ul

per Makarenko

Krukov Canal

56

Pskovskaya ul

Pokrovsky

pl Turgeneva

Smezhny most

pl Repina

Sadovaya ul

ul Labutina

Klimov per

Pryadilny per

Angliysky most

Egyptetsky most

Staro-Kalinkin most

Malo-Kalinkin most

Fontanka

nab reki Fontanki

nab reki Fontanki

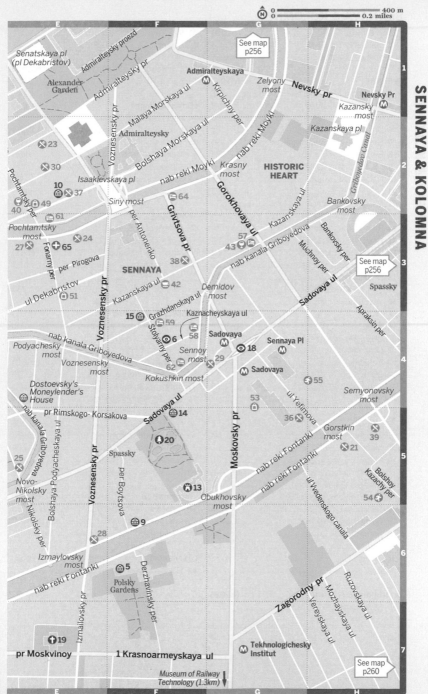

N
0 — 400 m
0 — 0.2 miles

See map p256

Senatskaya pl (pl Dekabristov)

Admiralteysky proezd

Admiralteysky pr

Alexander Garden

Admiralteyskaya

Zelyony most

Nevsky pr

Nevsky Pr

Kazansky most

Kazanskaya pl

Voznesensky pr

Malaya Morskaya ul

Kirpichny per

nab reki Moyki

Admiralteysky

Bolshaya Morskaya ul

Krasny most

23

30

Isaakievskaya pl

nab reki Moyki

HISTORIC HEART

10

37

Pochtamtsky per

49

40

61

per Antonenko

Siny most

64

Grivtsova pr

Gorokhovaya ul

Kazanskaya ul

Bankovsky most

Grib.oedov Canal

Pochtamtsky most

24

27

65

Fonarny per

per Pirogova

57

43

nab kanala Griboyedova

Bankovsky per

Muchnoy per

See map p256

ul Dekabristov

38

nab kanala Griboyedova

Sadovaya ul

Spassky

SENNAYA

42

Demidov most

Apraksin per

Kazanskaya ul

Grazhdanskaya ul

Voznesensky pr

15

59

Kaznacheyskaya ul

nab kanala Griboyedova

Stolyarny per

6

58

Sadovaya

18

Sennaya Pl

Podyachesky most

62

Sennoy most

29

Sadovaya

55

Voznesensky most

Kokushkin most

Semyonovsky most

Dostoevsky's Moneylender's House

pr Rimskogo- Korsakova

Sadovaya ul

14

Moskovsky pr

53

ul Yefimova

36

Gorstkin most

39

nab kanala Griboyedova

Spassky

20

21

25

Novo-Nikolsky most

per Boytsova

13

Obukhovsky most

nab reki Fontanki

nab reki Fontanki

ul Vvedenskogo canala

Bolshoy Kazachy per

54

Bolshaya Podyacheskaya ul

Nikolsky per

28

9

Izmaylovsky most

nab reki Fontanki

5

Polsky Gardens

Derzhavinsky per

Zagorodny pr

Ruzovskaya ul

Mozhayskaya ul

Vereyskaya ul

Izmaylovsky pr

19

pr Moskvinoy

1 Krasnoarmeyskaya ul

Tekhnologichesky Institut

See map p260

Museum of Railway Technology (1.3km)

SENNAYA & KOLOMNA *Map on p264*

PETROGRAD & VYBORG SIDES *Map on p268*

PETROGRAD & VYBORG SIDES

Staraya Derevnya

1 Hermitage Storage Facility

Dibunovskaya ul

ul Savushkina

7

3-y Elagin most

Bolshaya Nevka

Serebryakov per

ul Oskalenko

57

Primorsky pr

Shkolnaya ul

Chyornaya Rechka

Site of Pushkin's Duel (250m)

Chyornaya Rechka

Ushakovsky most

nab reki Bolshoy Nevki

Lipovaya al

PETROGRAD SIDE

70

37 Glavnaya al
Kirov Park

38

Yelagin Island

Seaside Park of Victory (Primorsky Park Pobedy)

Sredniyaya Nevka

2-y Elagin most

nab Martynova

Deputatskaya ul

Teatralnaya al

Polevaya al

2-ya Beryozovaya al

Kamenny Island

1-ya Beryozovaya al

17

11

nab reki Maloy Nevki

Kamenno-ostrovsky most

Vyazemsky per

ul Ryukhina

Konstantinovsky pr

nab Krestovki

27

Sibur Arena (1km)

19

14

Krestovsky Ostrov

Morskoy pr

Krestovsky Island

Krestovsky pr

22

Maly Krestovsky most

pl Dinamo

Petrogradskaya ul

Pesochnaya nab

Vyazemsky Gardens

ul Daly

ul Professora Popova

35

Dinamo Stadium

pl Dinamo

Vyazovaya ul

Malaya Nevka

Lazersky most

Bolshoy Petrovsky most

Bolshoy Krestovsky most

Bolshaya Zelenina ul

PETROGRAD SIDE

Levashovsky pr

39

Karpovka

Bolshaya Zelenina ul

21

Polozova ul

ul Lenina

71

Petrovskaya pl

Petrovsky pr

Novoladozhskaya ul

Korpusnaya ul

Chkalovsky pr

Chkalovskaya

77

Kolpinskaya ul

Maly pr

46

30

41

Pionerskaya ul

ul Krasnogo Kursanta

Rybatskaya ul

Baltika Stadium

78

Petrovsky Park

Zhdanovskaya ul

Zhdanovskaya nab

10

Petrogradsky Island

Bolshoy pr

Uralskaya ul

Dekabristov Island

ul Odoevskogo

Petrovsky Pond

Petrovsky Stadium

Maly pr

33

Sportivnaya

66

ul Lizy Chaykinoy

Zverinskaya ul

ul Blokina

65

72

Smolenskoe Cemetery

Uralsky most

nab reki Smolenki

Malaya Neva

nab Makarova

Sportivnaya

pr Dobrolyubova

ul Yablochkova

50

12-13 linii

Maly pr

10-11 linii

4-ya i 5-ya linii

2-ya i 3-ya linii

Sredny pr

1-ya liniya i Kadetskaya liniya

Tuchkov most

Birzhevoy most

nab Makarova

VASILYEVSKY ISLAND

See map p270

See map p270

Vasileostrovskaya

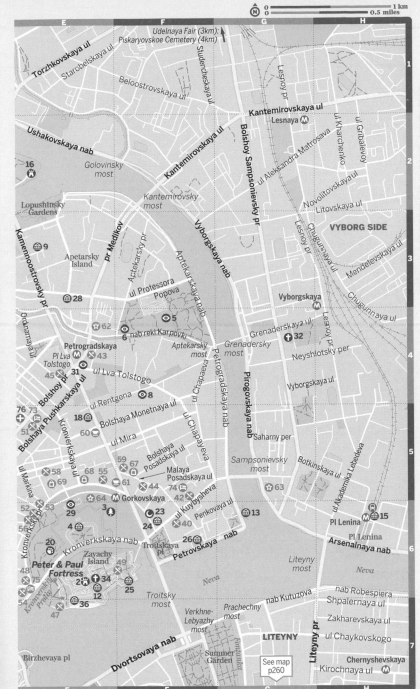

0   0   1 km
0   0   0.5 miles

Udelnaya Fair (3km);
Piskaryovskoe Cemetery (4km)

Torzhkovskaya ul
Starobelskaya ul
Beloostrovskaya ul
Studencheskaya ul
Kantemirovskaya ul
Bolshoy Sampsonievsksy pr

Kantemirovskaya ul
Lesnaya M
Lesnoy pr
ul Kharchenko
ul Gribalevoy

Ushakovskaya nab

VYBORG SIDE

16

Golovinsky
most

Kantemirovsky
most

ul Aleksandra Matrosava
Novolitovskaya ul
Litovskaya ul

Lopushinsky
Gardens

Kamennoostrovsky pr

9

Apetarsky
Island

pr Medikov
Aptekarsky pr
Vyborgskaya nab

Chugunnaya ul
Lesnoy pr
Mendelevskaya ul
Chugunnaya ul

28

Ordnarnaya ul

ul Professora
Popova

Aptekarskaya nab

62

5

6 nab reki Karpovki

Aptekarsky
most

Grenaderskaya ul
Grenadersky
most

Vyborgskaya
32

Petrogradskaya
Pl Lva
Tolstogo
43

Aptekarsky
most

Petrogradskaya nab

Neyshlotsky per

45 31
ul Lva Tolstogo

Bolshoy pr
Kronverkskaya ul
Bolshaya Pushkarskaya ul

ul Rentgena

8

Pirogovskaya nab

Vyborgskaya ul

76 73
51

18
60

Bolshaya Monetnaya ul
ul Mira

ul Chapayeva

Saharny per

Sampsonievsky
most

59 67
Bolshaya
Posadskaya ul

Botkinskaya ul

ul Markina

58
69

68 55
61
Malaya
Posadskaya ul

44
74

ul Akademika Lebedeva

52 53
64
Gorkovskaya

42

63

29 3
4

23
24

ul Kuybysheva
Penkovaya ul

40

13

Pl Lenina
15

20
Kronverksky pr
Kronverkskaya nab

Troitskaya
Pl

26

Petrovskaya nab

Pl Lenina
Arsenalnaya nab

Peter & Paul
Fortress

Zayachy
Island

49

Liteyny
most

Neva

48 75
2 34

25

Neva

54
47

12
36

Kronverkskiy Proliv

Troitsky
most

Verkhne-
Lebyazhy
most

Prachechny
most

nab Kutuzova

nab Robespiera
Shpalernaya ul

Zakharevskaya ul
ul Chaykovskogo

Birzhevaya pl

Dvortsovaya nab

Summer
Garden

LITEYNY

Liteyny pr

See map
p260

Chernyshevskaya
Kirochnaya ul

VASILYEVSKY ISLAND

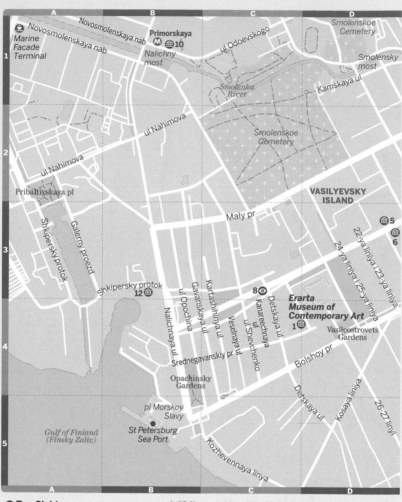

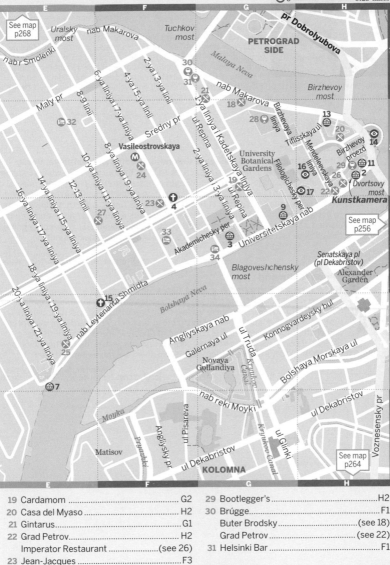

Our Story

A beat-up old car, a few dollars in the pocket and a sense of adventure. In 1972 that's all Tony and Maureen Wheeler needed for the trip of a lifetime – across Europe and Asia overland to Australia. It took several months, and at the end – broke but inspired – they sat at their kitchen table writing and stapling together their first travel guide, *Across Asia on the Cheap*. Within a week they'd sold 1500 copies. Lonely Planet was born.

Today, Lonely Planet has offices in Franklin, London, Melbourne, Oakland, Beijing and Delhi, with more than 600 staff and writers. We share Tony's belief that 'a great guidebook should do three things: inform, educate and amuse'.

Our Writers

Tom Masters

Coordinating author, Sennaya & Kolomna, Smolny & Vosstaniya, Vasily-evsky Island, Day Trips Tom first came to St Petersburg in 1996 while studying Russian at the School of Slavonic & East European Studies, part of the University of London. He loved the city so much that he came back after graduating and worked as a writer and editor at the *St Petersburg Times*, a job that allowed him to get to know the city in intimate detail. While since living in London and Berlin, Tom has always retained a strong link with the city, authoring Lonely Planet's *St Petersburg* guide for the third time this edition. You can see more of Tom's work at www.tommasters.net.

Read more about Tom at:
lonelyplanet.com/members/tommasters

Simon Richmond

Historic Heart, Petrograd & Vyborg Sides Simon first visited Russia in 1994 when he was amazed by the treasures of the Hermitage and Lenin's mummified corpse in Red Square. He's since travelled the breadth of this vast nation from Kamchatka to Kaliningrad and many points in between. An award-winning writer and photographer, Simon is the co-author of Lonely Planet's *Russia* and *Trans-Siberian Railway* guides over the last four editions as well as many other titles for the company, from *Cape Town* to *Korea*. Read more about him at www.simonrichmond.com.

Read more about Simon at:
lonelyplanet.com/members/simonrichmond

Published by Lonely Planet Publications Pty Ltd
ABN 36 005 607 983
7th edition – Mar 2015
ISBN 978 1 74220 994 4
© Lonely Planet 2015 Photographs © as indicated 2015
10 9 8 7 6 5 4 3 2 1
Printed in China